PERSPECTIVES ON WRITING
Series Editor, Susan H. McLeod

PERSPECTIVES ON WRITING
Series Editor, Susan H. McLeod

The Perspectives on Writing series addresses writing studies in a broad sense. Consistent with the wide ranging approaches characteristic of teaching and scholarship in writing across the curriculum, the series presents works that take divergent perspectives on working as a writer, teaching writing, administering writing programs, and studying writing in its various forms.

The WAC Clearinghouse and Parlor Press are collaborating so that these books will be widely available through free digital distribution and low-cost print editions. The publishers and the Series editor are teachers and researchers of writing, committed to the principle that knowledge should freely circulate. We see the opportunities that new technologies have for further democratizing knowledge. And we see that to share the power of writing is to share the means for all to articulate their needs, interest, and learning into the great experiment of literacy.

Other Books in the Series

Charles Bazerman, Adair Bonini, and Débora Figueiredo (Eds.), *Genre in a Changing World* (2009)

David Franke, Alex Reid, and Anthony Di Renzo (Eds.), *Design Discourse: Composing and Revising Programs in Professional and Technical Writing* (2010)

Martine Courant Rife, Shaun Slattery, and Dànielle Nicole DeVoss (Eds.), *Copy(write): Intellectual Property in the Writing Classroom* (2011)

Doreen Starke-Meyerring, Anthony Paré, Natasha Artemeva, Miriam Horne, and Larissa Yousoubova, *Writing in Knowledge Societies* (2011)

Andy Kirkpatrick and Zhichang Xu, *Chinese Rhetoric and Writing: An Introduction for Language Teachers* (2012)

Chris Thaiss, Gerd Bräuer, Paula Carlino, Lisa Ganobcsik-Williams, and Aparna Sinha (Eds.), *Writing Programs Worldwide: Profiles of Academic Writing in Many Places* (2012)

Charles Bazerman, Chris Dean, Jessica Early, Karen Lunsford, Suzie Null, Paul Rogers, and Amanda Stansell (Eds.), *International Advances in Writing Research: Cultures, Places, Measures* (2012)

THE CENTRALITY OF STYLE

Edited by Mike Duncan and Star Medzerian Vanguri

The WAC Clearinghouse
wac.colostate.edu
Fort Collins, Colorado

Parlor Press
www.parlorpress.com
Anderson, South Carolina

The WAC Clearinghouse, Fort Collins, Colorado 80523-1052
Parlor Press, 3015 Brackenberry Drive, Anderson, South Carolina 29621

© 2013 by Mike Duncan and Star Medzerian Vanguri. This work is licensed under a Creative Commons Attribution-Noncommercial-No Derivative Works 3.0 United States License.

Printed in the United States of America.

Library of Congress Cataloging-in-Publication Data

The centrality of style / edited by Mike Duncan and Star Medzerian Vanguri.
    pages cm. -- (Perspectives on writing)
  Includes bibliographical references.
  ISBN 978-1-60235-422-7 (pbk. : alk. paper) -- ISBN 978-1-60235-423-4 (hardcover : alk. paper)
  1. English language--Style. I. Duncan, Mike, 1975- editor of compilation. II. Vanguri, Star Medzerian, 1980- editor of compilation.
  PE1421.C46 2013
  808'.042'0711--dc23
                        2013011457

Copyeditor: Don Donahue
Designers: Mike Palmquist
Series Editor: Susan H. McLeod

This book is printed on acid-free paper.

The WAC Clearinghouse supports teachers of writing across the disciplines. Hosted by Colorado State University, it brings together scholarly journals and book series as well as resources for teachers who use writing in their courses. This book is available in digital format for free download at http://wac.colostate.edu.

Parlor Press, LLC is an independent publisher of scholarly and trade titles in print and multimedia formats. This book is available in paperback, cloth, and Adobe eBook formats from Parlor Press at http://www.parlorpress.com. For submission information or to find out about Parlor Press publications, write to Parlor Press, 3015 Brackenberry Drive, Anderson, South Carolina 29621, or e-mail editor@parlorpress.com.

CONTENTS

Foreword . . . . *vii*
        Paul Butler

Introduction to the Centrality of Style . . . . *xi*
        Mike Duncan and Star Medzerian Vanguri

Part One: Conceptualizing Style *1*

Introduction to Part One: Conceptualizing Style *5*
        Mike Duncan and Star Medzerian Vanguri

An Ethics of Attentions: Three Continuums of Classical and
    Contemporary Stylistic Manipulation for the 21st Century
    Composition Classroom *9*
        William C. Kurlinkus

Stylistic Sandcastles: Rhetorical Figures as Composition's
    Bucket and Spade *37*
        William FitzGerald

Using Stylistic Imitation in Freshman Writing Classes: The
    Rhetorical and Meta-Rhetorical Potential of Transitions in
    Geoffrey of Vinsauf's Medieval Treatises *57*
        Denise Stodola

Architectonics and Style *71*
        Russell Greer

Making Style Practically Cool and Theoretically Hip *81*
        Keith Rhodes

Jim Corder's Generative Ethos as Alternative to Traditional
    Argument, or Style's Revivification of the Writer-Reader
    Relationship. *97*
        Rosanne Carlo

Teaching Style as Cultural Performance *119*
        Chris Holcomb and M. Jimmie Killingsworth

Contents

Inventio and *Elocutio*: Language Instruction at St. Paul's
    Grammar School and Today's Stylistic Classroom *135*
    Tom Pace

The Research Paper As Stylistic Exercise *153*
    Mike Duncan

Part Two: Applying Style *167*

Introduction to Part Two: Applying Style *169*
    Mike Duncan and Star Medzerian Vanguri

Style in Academic Writing *173*
    Nora Bacon

Tracking Interpersonal Style: The Use of Functional
    Language Analysis in College Writing Instruction *191*
    Zak Lancaster

Multimodal Style and the Evolution of Digital Writing Pedagogy *213*
    Moe Folk

Voice, Transformed: The Potentialities of Style Pedagogy
    in the Teaching of Creative Nonfiction *239*
    Crystal Fodrey

Fighting Styles: The Pedagogical Implications of Applying
    Contemporary Rhetorical Theory to the Persuasive Prose
    of Mary Wollstonecraft and Mary Hays *259*
    Luke Redington

Style and the Professional Writing Curriculum: Teaching
    Stylistic Fluency through Science Writing *279*
    Jonathan Buehl

Toward a Pedagogy of Psychic Distance *309*
    Erik Ellis

What Scoring Rubrics Teach Students (and Teachers) about Style *341*
    Star Medzerian Vanguri

FOREWORD

Paul Butler
University of Houston

The Centrality of Style presents readers with a paradox. The editors begin with the convincing argument that style must be regarded as central to the discipline of composition studies. Indeed, the collection's rich diversity of chapters reasserts the prominent place of style in the field from different perspectives, historical moments, and theoretical and pedagogical approaches.

Yet despite the book's claim of style's centrality, it makes an equally forceful case—which may appear contradictory at first—that some of the most exciting new ideas in stylistic study have emerged not from the center but the *margins* of the field—and the margins' intersections with other disciplines, ideas, cultures, and sites of inquiry.

The paradox inherent in the tension of seeing style as both central and marginal is not new to those in rhetoric and composition. Mikhail Bakhtin (1981) has described a similar phenomenon in discussing the clash of language's unifying, or *centripetal* forces, and their counterpart—the dispersing, or *centrifugal* forces that often disrupt prevailing norms. In public sphere theory, critical theorist Michael Warner (2005), borrowing from Jurgen Habermas (1989) and others, depicts an identical discordance in the tension between *publics* that dominate social discourse and their counterpart, a culturally less powerful, oppositional group, called a *counterpublic*, which constantly works against that dominance even as it maintains, says Warner, "at some level, conscious or not, an awareness of its subordinate status" (p. 119). With respect to counterpublics, Warner says it is the oppositional aspect of their style that "performs membership" (p. 142).

There is no question that *The Centrality of Style* navigates the push and pull of these kinds of oppositions in compelling new ways. The real question is, How does the volume manage to position style in the field as what Frank Farmer (2008), borrowing from anthropologist Victor Turner, calls a *liminal counterpublic*, emanating from the break or rupture of the public-counterpublic relationship that somehow exists "betwixt and between" the two? How, in other words, does style's very centrality depend on its marginalization, lack of power, and sometimes "renegade" status (Johnson, 2003) both inside, and outside, the field?

Some answers to that question, and paradox, can be found in this volume. While there are many examples throughout the collection, here are some of the representative concepts that suggest even larger ideas in *The Centrality of Style* and show the current push and pull of style's liminal status in the field.

STYLE AS *LINGUA FRANCA*

In his article in this volume, William FitzGerald argues that "[s]tyle has become a contemporary *lingua franca*," and he gives evidence of the centrality of style historically, in popular culture, and in what he calls "the return of the figurative." Yet even as he restores style to a pivotal location in composition and rhetoric, FitzGerald makes a parallel move of relocating style at the periphery—marginalized, he says, by the continuing struggle of the figures of speech for disciplinary legitimacy and for circulation among a broader writing public. Thus, in a move widely used by the writers in this volume, FitzGerald shows the value of style as a common language while maintaining its status as marginal in working toward broader recognition. FitzGerald intimates that both moves are necessary in forging a unique place for style in the field, betwixt and between other disciplinary forces and interests.

A similar move in situating style as liminal is made by Keith Rhodes, who argues, on the one hand, for an "aesthetics of style" that he sees as "persuasively influential" but also recognizes, on the other hand, as "problematized by the conserving and regressive power of monologic forms of art." Thus Rhodes suggests that having an "*art* of writing," with style at the center, remains elusive, on the margins of the field, as we hesitate to embrace an aesthetics that includes nonlinear or affective influences. Rhodes thus demonstrates the complicated aspect of style as a *lingua franca* for composition studies.

STYLE AS RESEARCH

In his essay for the collection, Mike Duncan shows how the traditional research paper reflects the centrality of style, especially in the way research "leads to increased control over many styles" and serves as "a door to a multitude of other demanding styles." Yet Duncan sees competing aspects of the genre as well, connecting some parts of research to the destabilized aspects of style that have historically rendered it powerless, ineffectual: "The generic research paper simultaneously displays all the weaknesses of a rhetoric reduced to ornament." In his focus on research, however, Duncan not only relegates style to the margins it has traditionally occupied but resurrects it as a vital part of research, showing how the research paper genre can function as "a mastery of style, a way of arguing." How does this "stylistic dance," to use Duncan's words, happen? He intimates, much like Warner (2005) does, that research is located in many sites of inquiry, what Warner calls a "multicontextual space of circulation, organized not by a place or institution but by the circulation of discourse" among publics and counterpublics (p. 119). It is significant, then, that Duncan locates the very centrality of research in a contested space where style is part of a freely circulating discourse within a traditionally constrained genre.

In her look at style as research, Nora Bacon argues for a similar move in academic writing, showing the way it reflects variation between normalized styles and those that deviate from the norm and thereby demand our attention. In analyzing academic writing whose "style is sometimes ugly, sometimes lovely, sometimes almost invisible," she includes excerpts that "serve as counterexamples to the idea that academic writing is dry, dull, objective, passionless, or merely utilitarian." Bacon illustrates the way style draws us in, demanding our attention, by quoting from philosopher Elaine Scarry: "The boy copies the face, then copies the face again. Then again and again. He does the same thing when a beautiful living plant—a violet, a wild rose—glides into his field of vision, or a living face: he makes a first copy, a second copy, a third, a fourth, a fifth." Bacon uses Scarry as an example of style that calls attention to itself, a move Warner acknowledges: "Public discourse craves attention like a child. Texts clamor at us. Images solicit our gaze. Look here! Listen! Hey!" (p. 89). Bacon shows how academic styles that we might consider most central are, paradoxically, often those most on the margins, centrifugal, dispersing, and as such, capturing our attention by deviating from the norm.

STYLE AS SCIENCE

Jonathan Buehl begins his piece in the collection with some assumptions about the centrality of style in science when he writes that "specific stylistic foci are often required by programmatic mandates or pedagogical objectives." In terms of science, we normally think of style as normalizing, yet Buehl, much like Warner's counterpublic discourse, moves the intersection of science with style to the margins: "Scientific discourse is difficult and 'strange' for many students—even students in scientific fields." Contrary to conventional wisdom, Buehl says this movement is positive because "by reading, writing, and writing about scientific prose, students engage unfamiliar discourse, which encourages them to apply newly learned strategies." Buehl's call for "defamiliarization" is the opposite of the impulse toward transparency or clarity usually associated with scientific discourse. Buehl thus works against a notion mentioned by Warner— that "a clear style results in a popular audience" (p. 138)—and instead embraces the kind of defamiliarizing language Warner sees as central to counterpublics and a nonnormative style.

STYLE AS ASSESSMENT

Star Medzerian Vanguri exemplifies the paradox of style in her chapter on scoring rubrics in composition classrooms. Vanguri's study reflects the way style remains at the margins, sometimes undergoing a reversal of sorts: "We are more specific about those aspects we value least ... while we are less specific about the qualities we value most." Vanguri goes on to explain the paradox she outlines: "Qualities like eloquence, rhetorical appropriateness, and tone are less quantifiable when placed into the context of a rubric than are the qualities we value least about style—mechanics, sentence structure, documentation, and word choice." Style is thus centralized—and marginalized—at the same time. Style as assessment becomes a lens through which we see a reversal of ideology at work. In the end, we need to see the juxtaposition of the center *and* the margin to understand what we value most.

The examples here offer just a few of the many ways in which the paradox of style plays out in the pages of *The Centrality of Style*. The collection places style at the center of the field. Many of the chapters work within the liminal space in which style serves as both a centralizing and decentralizing force in rhetoric and composition. Clearly, the authors and editors have made an invaluable contribution in their collection by exposing the paradoxical nature of a canon that continues to play a vital role in our disciplinary history.

REFERENCES

Bakhtin, Mikhail. (1981). *The dialogic imagination: Four essays by M. M. Bakhtin*. (Michael Holquist, Ed. Caryl Emerson and Michael Holquist, Trans.). Austin: University of Texas Press.

Farmer, Frank. (2008). Composition studies as liminal counterpublic. *JAC* 28(3-4), 620-34.

Habermas, Jurgen. (1989). *The structural transformation of the public sphere: An inquiry into a category of bourgeois society*. (Thomas Burger, Trans.). Cambridge, MA: MIT Press.

Johnson, T. R. (2003). *A rhetoric of pleasure: Prose Style and Today's Composition Classroom*. Portsmouth, NH: Heinemann-Boynton/Cook.

Warner, Michael. (2005). *Publics and counterpublics*. New York: Zone.

INTRODUCTION TO THE CENTRALITY OF STYLE

Mike Duncan and Star Medzerian Vanguri
University of Houston-Downtown and Nova Southeastern University

In the classical era, Aristotle's *Rhetoric* places style in Book III, almost as an addendum, despite the *Rhetoric*'s recognition of the centrality and power of metaphor to the persuasive enterprise. Cicero realized the inexorable link between form and content, particularly in his *Orator* to Brutus, but in the later Roman empire, his idea of style was simplified into imperial ornamentation, having had already settled into one of the five rhetorical canons. Style remained an auxiliary to rhetoric and persuasion for over a millennium, save occasional questionable revivals, such as the Ciceronian movement in the Renaissance that stressed only using the Latin words present in Cicero's work to achieve an imitative mastery of his style, and the later Ramist reduction of style to tropes and figures only.

In the last hundred years, however, the nuances of *lexis* have enjoyed a different sort of theoretical attention. In particular, studies on sentence structure, paragraph structure, diction, rhythm, tone, genre, visual rhetoric, and document design have grown exponentially in the last fifty years, paralleling the increased specialization of the academy and theoretical study of instruction in rhetoric and composition. These studies, in total, have greatly expanded our understanding of how language works rhetorically and demonstrated the value of attention to stylistic matters.

Style now stands at an interesting crossroads. Considerable work has been done recently to establish style's significance within composition, with the recent authoritative 2010 Bedford St. Martin's collection *Style in Rhetoric in Composition*, edited by Paul Butler, placing it in a long theoretical tradition that offers a stylistic way of understanding compositional pedagogy, parallel and complimentary to other histories. It is only on this formidable bulwark that this collection can stand.

As such, the editors of this volume feel that it is no longer necessary to argue for style. That has been done, and done convincingly and well, by T. R. Johnson, Richard Lanham, Butler, Joseph Williams, and many others. The question, then, is what to do next, now that a growing number of composition scholars and teachers recognize style's relevance and usefulness to composition.

The answer to that question is presented in this collection: to imagine style as central to the act of composition and to the discipline of composition studies and consider what that might involve when enacted.

To explain that claim a bit further, we should reveal its origination. The germinal idea for this collection began shortly after a large workshop on style on the first day of the March 2010 Conference on College Composition and Communication in Louisville, KY. Many of the participants—some of which are represented in this volume—spoke of a need to keep building attention to style in composition studies, and further opined that style was so central to composition that the terms were almost synonymous. It seemed odd to us, the editors of this volume, to be content with style as a specialty subject within the conference if we truly held that style was central to composition studies. As such, we felt that it would be prudent to build a book-length collection that represented this viewpoint far better than one or two authors could.

This collection is the result of that observation and theoretical commitment. Its title reflects a belief by its editors and authors that style is what makes composition an art, that style is composition enacted, and that style is an ideal means by which teachers and theorists of composition can explain what occurs in writing. Furthermore, as Paul Butler has noted, style "offers a way for composition to embrace the cacophony of differences that defines our field" (2010, p. 2).

Style is epistemic, both creating and reflecting knowledge, and as such, style allows us to access the ideology and cultural values of a text. In "Prolegomena to the Analysis of Prose Style," Richard Ohmann presents the notion of style as epistemic choice, wherein he asks us to increase our understanding of our students, whose worldviews are embedded in their prose, as a means of better understanding their written word. Furthermore, as Min-Zhan Lu has acknowledged, style helps us to appreciate difference. Because style is a reflection of a writer, and thus the writer's life experiences and background, it moves us from the conception of non-standard English as error to an appreciation of stylistic difference.

Style also stretches across disciplinary boundaries. Because style has homes in literature, linguistics, rhetoric, technical communication, and other fields, teachers and scholars in composition have multiple traditions from which to draw, reinforcing composition's existing propensity to reference other fields. Style also allows for more productive cross-disciplinary efforts, because style is a term that is already familiar, if not ubiquitous, in these other realms. As such, style can act as a language that guides our discipline by defining our mutual priorities and differences. Even if we do not subscribe to the same theoretical approach to composition, style allows us to talk about what we value and to name those differences. Style also enables us to extend those conversations outside the discipline. We can more easily to share our work with the public when we employ its commonly stylistic definition of composition.

Most particularly, in the classroom, stylistic terminology allows us to discuss writing with our students in detail. We can move beyond impressionistic language that is rooted in value judgments and toward specific language that names those features of writing we value. Perhaps most importantly, the language of style allows students to talk to each other about their writing in meaningful and productive ways. In other words, style keeps composition classes focused on student writing and keeps learning reflexive. In classrooms where style is treated as central to composition, student writing can be the content students study to learn how to write effectively. When students work off an established and shared stylistic vocabulary and deliberately employ stylistic devices, the class can treat these features as intentional. Furthermore, once students understand the nuts and bolts of how writing "works," they can analyze their own texts and choices. A stylistic approach to composition, then, builds reflection into the curriculum. Students must be able to identify what they are doing in their own writing before they can comment on its effectiveness.

Through an emphasis on style, writing is given a methodology. Disrupting the myth of the "artistic genius," stylistic methods of analysis can remove the mystery from writing for students and make it something that can be learned and improved. The methods that Edward P. J. Corbett and Robert Connors offer in *Classical Rhetoric for the Modern Student* ask students to calculate statistics such as word count, sentence types, and average sentence and paragraph lengths so as to recognize the effects these features have on an overall text and to help define an author's style. Style also allows for genre-based approaches in composition; technical communication in particular has long established genre as a paramount concern, but this is not always reflected in rhetoric and composition. Fairly recently, the work of Anis Bawarshi, Amy Devitt, Carolyn Miller, and others has ignited interest in genre studies in rhetoric and composition, arguing that a goal of composition courses should be genre awareness. Style is a necessary consideration within genre-based approaches to composing, as all genre conventions are, at their core, stylistic.

Finally, the term "style" itself, particularly as represented in Part One of this text, is able to simultaneously hold a variety of definitions quite comfortably, with each of those definitions able to dialogue with each other and promote a multifaceted view of the importance of the canon and how it suffuses the act of composition. Further, stylistic principles (namely, rhetorical tropes and schemes) are uniquely able to describe phenomena ranging across mediums and modalities in recognition of composition's many forms. We believe this multifaceted aspect of the canon allows for a position that has not yet been reached in other attempts to align an ancient rhetorical concept with the practices of theorizing and teaching composition. We acknowledge the value of the extensive work arguing for the centrality of other rhetorical canons, namely—and perhaps most notably—invention (Crowley; Lauer & Atwill; Young & Becker); however, in this collection, we focus on style.

This collection is organized into two sections. Each section is prefaced by an introduction that discusses how each chapter builds upon the claim of style's centrality. As such, this collection has some of the qualities of a monograph: the connection between the essays is not merely topical or thematic, but rather is built upon a common claim.

Part One, "Conceptualizing Style," contains essays that offer different—sometimes complementary, and sometimes conflicting—ways of conceptualizing what style is. Style is presented as deception, as figures, as imitation, as Bakhtinian architecture, as style itself, as ethos, as cultural performance, and as invention. Many of these essays also explore pedagogy, but we have placed these nine essays together primarily for their unique theoretical viewpoints on style, which we believe advance the field's understanding of the concept by collectively demonstrating its presence in so many aspects of language.

Part Two, "Applying Style," as its name suggests, explores ways by which style can be incorporated into the teaching of composition. These proposed ways are diverse, including writing across the curriculum (WAC), linguistics, multimodal rhetoric, creative nonfiction, rhetorical/literary criticism, "stylistic sensitivity," the rhetoric of science, and the rhetoric of fiction. Teachers of composition will find much to mull over and consider in this second half of the collection, given that, like in Part One, style again appears in multiple locales as a critical concept, demanding attention due to style's centrality. These essays offer strategies for teachers that allow students to address and grasp style in the classroom.

We see this collection as a step forward for the study of style in composition studies. We hope, in particular, that it will lead to further work in the discipline on stylistic issues in a contemporary environment where the centrality of style to composition can be treated as a given.

THE CENTRALITY OF STYLE

THE CERTAINTY OF JUSTICE

PART ONE: CONCEPTUALIZING STYLE

INTRODUCTION TO PART ONE: CONCEPTUALIZING STYLE

Mike Duncan and Star Medzerian Vanguri

As stated in the introduction, this collection establishes and advances the assumption that style is central to the whole enterprise of composition, from how we theorize and conceptualize the work we do as a discipline, to how that understanding is communicated among us and to our students via our pedagogy. Treating the centrality of style as a given, however, requires that we subscribe to a definition or definitions of style that align(s) with our values as scholars and teachers. As T. R. Johnson and Tom Pace rightfully point out in the introduction to their 2005 collection *Refiguring Prose Style: Possibilities for Writing Pedagogy*, "style means different things to different people," and as a result, style can have so many meanings that it ceases to have meaning at all. We do not have a problem with this plurality, as the following summaries will demonstrate that these essays have far more in common than not. A plurality of definitions, rather, speaks to the pervasive and qualitative centrality of style in rhetoric and composition, as well as in other language-oriented disciplines, much like the vast array of available definitions of "rhetoric" speaks to the term's universality within language use.

Taking a cue from Johnson and Pace's collection, and from other recent scholarship that has sought to revive style, we begin this collection by presenting a variety of conceptions of style that are both theoretically and pedagogically informed. The definitions of style presented by the following essays in Part One are markedly different from one another, but are joined fundamentally by their objective to increase style's visibility in composition and explore the value of scholarship that assumes the centrality of style to composition. Further, the chapters in this section offer relevant ways of understanding style that intersect with the current interests and values of our discipline, so as to not simply revive style from the past.

In "An Ethics of Attentions: Three Continuums of Classical and Contemporary Stylistic Manipulation for the 21st Century Composition Classroom," William Kurlinkus draws upon theories from classical rhetoric to new media to argue that style is a form of deception. He offers a series of three continuums along which he plots the degrees of control that style has on an audience's attention. These three continuums—point of attention, apparent mediation, and felt agency—reveal the manipulation inherent in every stylistic choice that a writer makes. This chapter also brings to light the ethical element of style that, despite its power, has been too often ignored. As rhetorical language is commonly recognized as inherently deceptive due to its selection of focus, Kurlinkus's link between style and deception clarifies the central nature of style to the compositional enterprise.

While Kurlinkus's work draws attention to the responsibility style requires, William FitzGerald's "Stylistic Sandcastles: Rhetorical Figures as Composition's Bucket and Spade" calls, rather, for stylistic play. He argues for a return to "the figurative," including rhetorical tropes and schemes and figures of speech and thought in composition, suggesting that while students may not think of themselves as embodying style, they have surely encountered figurative devices. After presenting a brief historical account of the treatment of figures in composition scholarship, FitzGerald offers a curriculum for an upper-division rhetoric elective titled "Go Figure." He provides this curriculum as an example of how figures can be taught and of the further possibilities that they offer the teaching of composition. Further, FitzGerald suggests that the figures are more easily transferable to visual modes of composition than the sentence level pedagogies with which style has been more traditionally associated. This essay's emphasis on the explanatory power of figures demonstrates the unifying value of style's exhaustive terminology.

Denise Stodola's "Using Stylistic Imitation in Freshman Writing Classes: The Rhetorical and Meta-Rhetorical Potential of Tropes and Transitions in Geoffrey of Vinsauf's Medieval Treatises," like the previous chapter, presents a new application for a traditional form of style instruction. Stodola proposes a meta-rhetorical method of style pedagogy that follows imitation exercises with rhetorical analysis assignments that ask students to reflect on their stylistic choices. A necessary component of Stodola's pedagogy is transitions, not at the text level, but at the curricular level. Situating her approach historically within Geoffrey of Vinsauf's *Documentum de modo et arte dictandi et versificandi*, she suggests that how assignments are sequenced, and the transitions that lie between them, affects their pedagogical value. Her chapter concludes with a sample assignment on figures of thought from a Business Communication course she teaches, demonstrating the pedagogy set forth in the chapter. Like FitzGerald, Stodola's conception of composition pedagogy as an exploration of stylistic choices on the part of the instructor reflects our central claim, though she metacritically reverses the emphasis from student to teacher.

In "Architectonics and Style," Russell Greer draws upon Mikhail Bakhtin's concept of "surplus of vision"—the ability of an outsider to perceive an individual more fully than that person can see him or herself—to argue that it can further our understanding of stylistic clarity. Greer builds on the established relationship between style and clarity by suggesting we must also consider how surplus of vision factors into this relationship. He further suggests that it gives us a way to define good style, in that the most effective style is that which has the most surplus of vision. In using this Bakhtinian lens, Greer speaks to the importance of stylistic awareness, not just stylistic savvy. This concept is illustrated through an analysis of a paragraph of a student essay in David Bartholomae's "Inventing the University." Like Cicero, Greer's emphasis on knowledge of the possible options as well as the implementations (like all writers, even if unconsciously) points again toward how style is key to the rhetorical act.

While the other authors in this section relate style to another concept to define it (style as deception, figures, imitation, and vision, respectively), Keith Rhodes find value in style as style. His "Styling: Making Style Practically Cool and Theoretically Hip" draws from linguistic frame theory and argues that we must abandon the current "stodgy" frame for style and invent a new way to frame it, one that is more accepted in our discipline and relevant for students. Rhodes argues for a progressive pedagogy of style that values stylistic variety and is informed by art, philosophy, and technology. The perception of style, then, can be said to determine its control and use, and vice versa.

In "Jim Corder's Reflective Ethos as Alternative to Traditional Argument, or Style's Revivification of the Writer-Reader Relationship," Rosanne Carlo explores how style and ethos are connected, referencing T. R. Johnson's work on style and audience pleasure. She then analyzes Jim Corder's "Notes on a Rhetoric of Regret" to demonstrate how he simultaneously argues for a particular stylistic theory, that of "enfolding," and enacts that theory to establish ethos as he composes. Carlo suggests that it is Corder's personal, performative style that draws an audience into participation with the text, and that this is what should be the desired effect of stylistic prose. While Carlo makes this point, she enacts, as Corder does, the very style she encourages readers to consider. This performative aspect to style, connected to ethos, is particularly important as it examines not just stylistic effect, but how stylistic effect is accomplished.

Chris Holcomb and M. Jimmie Killingsworth, like Carlo, offer a performative approach to style pedagogy in "Teaching Style as Cultural Performance." They encourage us to reconsider the dichotomy in how style is typically defined (broadly as a way of knowing, or narrowly as an author's choices at the text level) and see these two definitions as interrelated. To elucidate the relationship between these definitions of style, they offer two frameworks for the teaching of style that are based on the interaction between verbal forms and culture. One framework uses what the authors define as the "arenas" of interaction (the textual, social, and cultural) to move students from the textual features of style to its cultural implications, while the other reverses this sequence and begins with style in its cultural context, a realm that is arguably more familiar to students. The chapter outlines in detail, and builds upon, their methodologies for style as performance. We place this essay with that of Carlo's to reflect the growing perception of style as performance, though they have added an important cultural aspect to style.

In "*Inventio* and *elocutio*: Language Instruction at St. Paul's Grammar School and Today's Stylistic Classroom," Tom Pace establishes the curriculum at St. Paul's grammar school in London as a historical precedence to the centrality of style to rhetorical education. Pace situates his argument within recent style scholarship that has highlighted style's inventive potential and public function. This brief overview lays the groundwork for his more thorough historical discussion of the relationship between style and invention in the Renaissance grammar schools. Finally, Pace outlines a first-year composition course he teaches that draws on the historical stylistic pedagogies he presents, by using Gerald Graff and Cathy Birkenstein's *They Say/I Say* as a modern-day equivalent. Pace demonstrates the universality of a style-centric model of composition by borrowing techniques from this historical text as well as Graff and Birkenstein's imitative exercises.

Lastly, Mike Duncan's "The Research Paper As Stylistic Exercise" continues the exploration of the value of past stylistic emphasis. Duncan describes three versions of the genesis of the research paper assignment, and teases apart the assumption that the research paper is both content-driven in form and purpose, placing it firmly within style as a generic stylistic exercise that enables mastery of other, yet-to-be-encountered genres. Furthermore, this piece provides a transition to the discussion of academic style by Nora Bacon that opens Part Two of this collection.

AN ETHICS OF ATTENTIONS: THREE CONTINUUMS OF CLASSICAL AND CONTEMPORARY STYLISTIC MANIPULATION FOR THE 21ST CENTURY COMPOSITION CLASSROOM

William C. Kurlinkus
Ohio State University

I. INTRODUCTION

Throughout the Western rhetorical tradition, rhetors and stylisticians have consistently claimed that some styles are more ethical than others: "Let the virtue of style be defined as 'to be clear;'" "It is good prose when it allows the writer's meaning to come through ... as a landscape is seen through a clear window;" "We owe readers an ethical duty to write precise and nuanced prose;" "Write in a way that draws attention to the sense and substance of writing, rather than to the mood and temper of the author" (Aristotle, trans. 1991, 1404b; Sutherland, 1957, p. 77; Strunk and White, 1979, p. 70; Williams, 2007, p. 221). Thus, popularly, the best style has been the one that *styles the least*; transparency is next to godliness; see the meaning not the writer—clarity is ethical. But clarity, as the existence of every style manual and every writer struggling to be clear exemplify, is also constructed and controlling. "Simplicity," as novelist William Gass reminds us, "is not a given. It is a human achievement, a human invention ..." (305). It is hard work to be clear, and clear authors ask/direct/coerce/manipulate the reader into looking at the meaning behind their words often hiding the act of writing, the medium of construction, and the author.

Yet, if the ethics of alphabetic writing style are often founded on clarity and transparency of language, the stylistic ethics of new media composition appear to be based on an entirely opposing standard. In new media composition, theorists since Marshall McLuhan have argued that "the medium is the message" and, thus, honest new media compositions make readers aware of materiality and how it affects an audience's reception of a text. As Anne Wysocki explains:

> I think we should call "new media texts" those that have been made by composers who are aware of the range of materialities of texts and who then highlight the materiality: such composers design texts that help readers/consumers/viewers stay alert to how any text—like its composers and readers—doesn't function independently of how it is made and in what contexts. Such composers design texts that make as overtly visible as possible the values they embody. (2004, p. 15)

Consequently, the best style becomes the one that *styles the most*. But as Kenneth Burke reminds us, "Even if any given terminology is a reflection of reality, by its very nature as a terminology it must be a selection of reality; and to this extent it must function also as a deflection of reality" (1968, p. 45). "Every way of seeing is a way of not seeing," so when new media authors ask/direct/coerce/manipulate the reader into focusing on specific points of constructedness, author, and medium, what is the audience distracted from (Burke, *1984, p.* 70)?

Through comparing classical and new media stylistic theory, this chapter explores what stylistic venues become available when one acknowledges that every choice of style and every act of rhetoric is one of manipulation; when one understands that concealing in rhetoric is neither immoral nor escapable; when one gets beyond a singular "styles the least" or "styles the most" mindset and comes to understand that the best style is the one that *serves the best*. Thus, this chapter asks: If composition is style, and style is the manipulation of attention, what are the ethics and options for controlling an audience's attention? Upon what values is the current system of stylistic ethics constructed? When is it appropriate and inappropriate to reveal one's stylistic operations to an audience? And to what effect?

Though, as the rest of this collection illustrates, definitions of prose style are wonderfully multifarious, here I discuss style as the aesthetic control of an audience's attention along three different "ethical" continuums—point of attention (where do the author's stylistic devices direct the audience's attention?); apparent mediation (does the rhetor's style appear deceptive or just?); and felt agency (does the audience feel silenced or encouraged to analyze and critique the text's construction, reasoning, etc.?).

In order to elucidate composition's current anomalous notion of stylistic ethics I explore these continuums using a trio of classical and new media pairings—progressing from traditionally[1] unethical to ethical styles. I begin with the Greek rhetorician Longinus's "unethical" notion of the sublime, a stylistic concept that attempts to move listeners to action through an aesthetic arrest that "enslaves the hearer," conceals stylistic device and orator, and makes the topic of oration appear to be present and in need of an immediate response (1972, p. 161). I compare this "unethical" sublime to new media theories of immediacy and erasure, which discuss how many technologies (virtual reality simulators, for instance) are designed to, or simply have the effect of, disappearing when the rhetor and audience use them, making the experience all the more real. Next, I move to Renaissance rhetorician Baldesar Castiglione's slightly more "ethical" concept of sprezzatura or "the art of artlessness." Sprezzatura focuses on disguising the preparation of art so that the orator can appear all the more natural, kairotic, nonchalant, and amazing in delivery: "He who does well so easily, knows much more than he does" (Castiglione, 2000, p. 38). As sprezzatura's new media counterpart I discuss the web, magazine, and advertising design trend of mimicking analog technological markers by using digital technology, a simulacral style I term "leaked constructedness." Finally, I move to an "ethical" conception of style in St. Augustine of Hippo's concepts of confession and Christian oratory, which I argue seek to put the power of authorial and biblical interpretation into the hands of the audience rather than the orator. Similarly, exemplified in the reference to Anne Wysocki above, I compare such confession to several notions of new media construction (Wysocki's new media, Bolter and Grusin's hypermediacy, etc.) that seek to empower the audience by giving them the ability to see, interpret, and construct multiple personal readings of a text.

I pair these classical and new media notions of style to highlight that ethical evaluations of style do not disappear as writers move from paper to screen and to ward off the notion that either a styles-the-least or a styles-the-most approach is always the best option in textual or new media construction.[2] I hope such a pairing elucidates the contradictory nature of a fixed system of stylistic ethics, where "ethical" can mean both the revealing and concealing of textual construction, author, and medium. If notions of ethics change with audiences and mediums, style must also constantly adapt. Thus, multiple notions of style must always be taught seriously, escaping what might be seen as the binary—formal or creative[3]—stylistic system of many contemporary composition classrooms. On a more comprehensive note, I also pair these stylistic options in hopes of offering style as a bridge between classical and new media rhetoric, two fields that (as I hope this chapter illustrates) have much to learn from one another and that must necessarily come together to make a contemporary composition classroom whole.

DEFINITIONS

Before examining these stylistic pairings and continuums, however, I must establish a few definitions—attention, style, manipulation, and ethics. In his *Economics of Attention* Richard Lanham argues, "Information is not in short supply in the new information economy ... What we lack is the human attention to make sense of it all ..." (2006, p. xi). In such an economy, then, neither material possessions nor raw information are the capital; the human attention that interprets, focuses on, and deconstructs that data is. Whoever can get an audience to pay *attention* (and the right kind of attention) to his or her idea, product, or celebrity rules such an economy. Lanham posits that *style* (and this is the definition I build from here) is what directs such attention. Therefore, the best definition of rhetoric might be the stylistically focused "economics of attention." The crux of Lanham's argument is "oscillatio," a rhetorical figure that illustrates how "we alternately participate in the world and step back and reflect on how we attend to it" (2006, p. xiii). We switch between looking at content and the stylistic devices that organize that content, but we have a hard time looking at both sides of the oscillation simultaneously. *Manipulation*, then, is the way in which writers attempt to focus their readers' attentions on either the content of the argument or the style.[4] Like all terministic screens, stylistic manipulation is inescapable because readers will always focus on something and good rhetors aid in that focusing. Something Lanham does not give much attention to, however, is the system of ethics that often gets applied to his concept of oscillatio.[5]

In this chapter I use the framework of manipulation and *ethics* in hopes of challenging the common misconception in rhetoric, composition, and the general public that style is attached in fixed ways to morality. The three continuums I examine are the unsteady formulas upon which these fixed notions are calculated. For too long because style and rhetoric (and specific styles and rhetorics in particular) have been misconstrued as unethical slights of hand in popular thought, compositionists and stylisticians have responded by studying and teaching style as neutral and ethically transparent. Such a fearful reaction to accusations of rhetoric as trickery (and these have been present since Plato[6] at least) has perpetuated the notion of "plain style" and severely limited stylistic options, especially in student writing. In this chapter I offer three diverging but equally "ethical" ways of performing style to disrupt the notion that clarity, or any other style claiming universality, is always the best option. I thus define ethics, like style, as an always local and contextualized process by which one negotiates an "appropriate" relationship between rhetor and audience. I do not endeavor to argue that style is never used unethically or that stylistic devices are neutral. In fact, style is never neutral. Because all style and language hides and reveals, all style is politically charged, but that doesn't mean we shouldn't use it. Style, like language, is unavoidable, and all its manifestations should be embraced as rhetorical possibilities.

II. SUBLIMITY, IMMEDIACY, AND THE CONTINUUM OF ATTENTION

SUBLIMITY

The Greek rhetorician Longinus (fl. ca. 50 C.E.) is the devil of stylistics.[7] He illustrates what every lay audience finds wrong with rhetoric and what every rhetorician finds wrong with the study of style. His willingness to throw off any guises of dialogic persuasion, embracing, rather, an oratorical force that "tears everything up like a whirlwind" and "get[s] the better of every hearer" perpetuates an ideology that a brilliant rhetor should not allow his audience any sort of agency, ability to resist, or even a chance to respond to an argument (1972, p. 144). Such an "unethical" treatment of style is, in part, what has lead to Longinus's relative excommunication from the rhetorical tradition in favor of viewing him as a literary critic. Yet, Longinus discusses rhetoric and designs his sublime to serve rhetorical purposes: "addressing a judge … tyrants, kings, governors …", "hitting the jury in the mind"—"[sublimity] enslaves the reader as well as persuading him" (1972, pp. 164, 166, 161). And if one looks closely at Longinus's *On Sublimity*, one begins to discover not unethical madness but, rather, a serious mode of rhetorical style designed around engaging an audience.

Early in *On Sublimity*, Longinus defines the sublime:

> A kind of eminence or excellence of discourse. It is the source of the distinction of the very greatest poets and prose writers and the means by which they have given eternal life to their own fame. For grandeur produces ecstasy rather than persuasion in the hearer; and the combination of wonder and astonishment always proves superior to the merely persuasive and pleasant. This is because persuasion is on the whole something we can control, whereas amazement and wonder exert invincible power and force and get the better of every hearer. (1972, p. 143)

Sublimity trumps persuasion because persuasion is controllable and permits an audience response, whereas sublime rhetoric is uncritiqueable because it overwhelms the listener. But what is most interesting about the machinations of Longinus's style is where sublimity seeks to keep the audience's attention. Although Longinus says the goal of the sublime is the goal of any great piece of literature, "eternal life" for the author, the sublime act doesn't focus the reader on the greatness of the author: "The speaker vanishes into the text" (Guerlac, 1985, p. 275). Rather, it is the greatness of the oratory that captures the reader—the attention of the listener is so fully transfixed on the world created by words that when the listener snaps out of this sublime ecstasy they are "elevated and exalted.... Filled with joy and pride ... [and] come to believe we have created what we have only heard" (Longinus, 1972, p. 148). Within the Longinian system, the audience doesn't know from where ideas originate. As Suzanne Guerlac explains, "The transport of the sublime ... includes a slippage among positions of enunciation ... the destinateur gets 'transported' into the message and the destinataire achieves a fictive identification with the speaker" (1985, p. 275). The aesthetic arrest created by the sublime is so great that the actual moment of hearing and the author appear to have disappeared: "The artifice of the trick is lost to sight in the surrounding brilliance of beauty and grandeur, and it scapes all suspicion" (Longinus, 1972, p. 164). Longinus seeks to eliminate the constructedness of language by erasing the reader's memory, "hitting the jury in the mind blow after blow" with majesty (1972, p. 166). The sublime is a stylistic concussion. The listener remembers solely the ideas as if they experienced the subject of the speech for themselves. Longinus creates this immediacy and reader absorption through the numerous stylistic devices he lists in *On Sublimity*—complexity of emotion, asyndeton, anaphora, hyperbation, and hyperbole to name a few.

Visualization (phantasia) is the first sublime device Longinus explores at length. He describes how image production through "Enthusiasm and emotion make the speaker *see* what he is saying and bring it *visually* before his audience.... There is much it can do to bring urgency and passion to our words..." (1972, pp. 159, 161).

Mark Antony's "Friends, Romans, countrymen" speech in Shakespeare's *Julius Caesar* is an example of such visual urgency. Antony is attempting to gain control of the Roman crowd in order to help him avenge Caesar's death. The first part of Antony's oration relies on rhetorical persuasion and logic, resulting in analytical responses from the crowd: "Me *thinks* there is much *reason* in his sayings.... Mark Ye his words" (3.2.108, emphasis mine). But once Antony begins his sublime phantasia, reenacting the scene of Caesar's murder using Caesar's corpse ("Through this the well-beloved Brutus stabb'd"), there is a mass identification (3.2.176). The crowd becomes a mob, is elevated through a Longinian communal sublime, and seeks a somewhat mindless revenge,[8] marked by the murder of the wrong Cinna. Antony uses the Longinian sublime to make Caesar's death and the danger of Caesar's murderers immediate to the audience.

Immediacy

In new media composition, such a proximity and a transparency of style is apparent in Jay Bolter and Richard Grusin's discussion of immediacy: "The ultimate mediating technology ... Is designed[9] to efface itself, to disappear from the user's consciousness" (2000, p. 3). Marshall McLuhan expands upon this effect with his concept of technologies as "extensions of man," illustrating how mechanisms (for better or worse) become our body parts through immediacy (2003, p. 67). Video game designers, for instance, create controllers that fade away, becoming actual extensions of players' hands as they are absorbed into the game and the virtual environment becomes more immediate. Only when the technology fails, we drop the controller or a button sticks, does the player again become conscious of the mechanism.

The connection between Bolter's immediacy and the Longinian sublime is, perhaps, best seen in virtual reality environments: "In order to create a sense of presence, virtual reality should come as close as possible to our daily visual experience. Its graphic space should be continuous and full of objects and should fill the viewer's field of vision without rupture" (Bolter & Grusin, 2000, p. 22). The best virtual reality (like the best sublime oration) occupies all the participant's senses so that the device is forgotten, and the virtual experience approaches the real, as if the gamer's own senses, not the machine, are creating the sensorial world. Like the Longinian sublime disguises its own artifice, most websites are designed so that the surfer can easily navigate through beautiful content, unaware of the code or the designer behind the art. Operating systems are designed around metaphors of windows and desktops that make the content easily navigable and more apparently "there," but that also disguise the code that perpetuates them. Immediate technologies, just like sublime stylistics, are designed to make stylistic mediation (alphabetic, oral, or technological) disappear.

Continuum of Attention

In Longinus's sublimity and digital immediacy, we discover our first continuum upon which ethical evaluations of style and manipulation are judged—the object of attention. The Longinian sublime, and to a lesser extent technological immediacy, are sometimes seen as unethical because the orator/programmer seeks to focus the reader's attention on content and message rather than how knowledge of media or rhetor affect and shape that content. Under the aegis of narrative theory, Erik Ellis labels this rhetorical move a closeness of "psychic distance" in his chapter in this collection. A familiar ethical critique of these tactics might be: If something is being revealed, then something is being concealed; if something is being concealed, then something unethical must be going on. Critics may liken such a focus to the sleight of hand of a magician—look at the shiny kerchief, not the rabbit coming out of the magician's sleeve. In alphabetic writing Lanham calls this effect "an aesthetics of subtraction": "Print wants us to concentrate on the content, to enhance and protect conceptual thought. It does this by filtering out all the signals that might interfere with such thinking ... By choosing a single font and a single size, it filters out visual distraction as well. Typographical design aims not to be seen or more accurately, since true invisibility is hard to read, to seem not to be seen ..." (Lanham, 2006, p., 46).

But is such an aesthetic unethical? We like to lose ourselves in books. We often get annoyed when speakers are too self-critical in speeches. When typing in a word processor we don't want the programmer constantly diverting us from our writing.[10] When we go to the movies we don't like to see boom mics hanging in the shot, fake props and settings, or other such signifiers of constructedness that call attention to artificiality. DVDs are designed with the ability to turn director's commentary on and off. One of the biggest questions for a stylistician regarding the continuum of attention, then, is when do audiences enjoy immersion in artificial environments and when do they feel such an immediacy is unethical? Alternatively, when do audiences enjoy viewing the constructedness of writing, and when is such a focus distracting?

The problem with point of attention, as Lanham, Burke, and McLuhan all argue, is that it is difficult to pay attention to more than one thing at a time. It's hard to become absorbed in a book's plot, proofread its grammar, analyze its binding quality, and apply theoretical interpretations simultaneously. This may be the origin of the literature student's common complaint of "you ruined my favorite book!" Once an instructor teaches a student to read in an analytical manner, the point of attention shifts from plot to construction and theory, and the level of absorption changes. This is the "economics of attention." This is why sleight of hand magicians can perform their tricks. We have examined the Longinian sublime as focusing the audience's attention on content and as being "unethical," but the "clear" and ethical style discussed in the opening of this chapter does a shockingly similar thing.[11] Each seeks immediacy of content, but in opposite ways. As Strunk and White direct, "Write in a way that draws attention to the sense and substance of writing, rather than to the mood and temper of the author" (1979, p. 70). If a style of transparent immediacy is offered in so many style manuals, a sublimely immediate style could easily be offered as an "ethical" option as well.

The two other styles this chapter explores, which seem to get more and more traditionally "ethical," similarly direct the audience's attention to two other places. Sprezzatura places the audience's attention on the rhetor and the act of writing, whereas confession places the audience's attention on the medium and the audience's relationship to the text. Each is an act of concealing and an act of manipulation yet, to their champions, each one appears more ethical than the sublime, perhaps because what each conceals, especially in confession, is less apparent than in the sublime. Though Longinus uses some ethically troubling phrasing, "get[s] the better of every hearer," "enslaves the reader," "hitting the jury in the mind," proponents of the more "ethical" styles should investigate whether their style of choice does the same thing. If "Art [and rhetoric] is whatever the artist wishes to call our attention to," every rhetor needs to ask what is and is not being focused on in their composition (Lanham, 2006, p. 43).

Thus, before writing, rhetors should consider what they want their audience to pay attention to at each point of their text and choose a style accordingly. At points where writers want their audience to participate emotionally, a sublime and immediate style is the strongest; where writers want their audience to examine the author and their ethos, a sprezzatura style can be invoked; where writers want their audience to participate in logical and critical analysis of production, a confessional style might be more appropriate.[12]

III. SPREZZATURA, LEAKED CONSTRUCTEDNESS, AND THE CONTINUUM OF APPARENT MEDIATION

Sprezzatura

Renaissance stylistician Baldesar Castiglione (1478-1529) wrote his *Book of the Courtier* to educate courtiers on how to speak, perform, and impress in the presence of royalty. Much of Renaissance rhetoric, especially that of Castiglione's Italy, which underwent massive court restructuring with the invasion of Louis XII in 1499, was built on a system of kairos. A true courtier needed to know how to identify the opinions of the shifting center of power and to adapt not only his speech but also his entire identity to the delight of that authority in order to gain its patronage. Founded upon this intense kairos is Castiglione's primary stylistic point of counsel, sprezzatura:

> To use possibly a new word, to practice in everything a certain spezzatura that shall conceal design and show that what is done and said is done without effort and almost without thought. From this I believe grace is in large measure derived, because everyone knows the difficulty of those things that are rare and well done, and therefore facility in them excites the highest admiration; while on the other hand, to strive … is extremely ungraceful, and makes us esteem everything slightly, however great it be. (2000, pp. 35-36)

Sprezzatura, often defined as "the art of artlessness," requires a rhetor to be well-prepared to argue but also well-prepared to disguise the effort it took to gain and organize that argument. It is key that one's identity not appear constructed to please the court but instead give the impression of being naturally in alliance with the seat of power. Like Longinus's sublime, Castiglione's sprezzatura disguises style. But rather than obscuring artifice through a mesmerizing focus on image and immediacy, sprezzatura controls perceived artifice by focusing on the acting of the casually unprepared orator. In *The Book of the Courtier* such performances usually begin with the courtier feigning ignorance on a topic then slowly unfold into a display of wit and wordplay on a theme the orator has secretly prepared in advance. Part of sprezzatura, therefore, involves steering the course of conversation into an area in which one can thrive. Thus, unlike sublimity, sprezzatura still retains some perceivable styling and the semblance of a creationary act but only enough to illustrate that the act was easily constructed. All hint of the artifice is filtered by the careful hand of the rhetor.

For instance, an orator might plan a digression into his speech that at first appears to be completely detached from the course of conversation but then skillfully connects back to the topic, evoking new thoughts on the subject. Such a digression highlights the orator's quick wit as nonchalant, natural, and kairotic, hinting that "He who does well so easily, knows much more than he does" (Castiglione, 2000, p. 38). Of course, Castiglione is only one champion[13] of natural style and "flow," but, with sophistic echoes, he seems the most honest in holding that the idea of naturalness (as well as the identity of the perfect orator) is subjective and constructed; to survive an orator needs to be deceptive in constructing the strongest "natural" ethos possible.

Beyond casting Longinian shadows in the disguising of art, sprezzatura has a similar effect on the mind of the listener, "[W]hoever hears and sees us may from our words and gestures imagine far more than what he sees and hears, and so be moved to laughter" (Castiglione, 2000, p. 120). Where the concussion of the sublime leaves the audience thinking it was they who came up with the idea they experienced, the manipulation of sprezzatura urges the audience to look carefully into everything they hear; deeper meaning, produced communally by author and interpreter, is always just below wit and style. Thus, casual construction and stylistic devices that encourage interpretation like juxtaposition, subtle extended metaphors, and digressions perpetuate a sprezzatura style.

Castiglione also discusses the fate of rhetors who fail to conceal their art, or worse, fail to conceal the concealing of art: "If it is discovered, it quite destroys our credit and brings us into small esteem" (2000, p. 36). Further, he reminds readers that such failure has consequences, both for creating more wary audiences ("men who are ever fearful of being deceived by art") as well as for compromising an author's ethos ("If it had been detected it would have made men wary of being duped") (2000, p. 36). Audiences are suspicious of the art of concealing because style might cloak bad ideas, intentions, and people. And in the case of the court, a constructed style might reveal that the courtier does not truly agree with the sovereign. At times, though, Castiglione seems less concerned about breaking an audience's trust and more worried about destroying the orator's beauty. The ultimate goal of sprezzatura is grace. An ice skater who performs a nonchalant triple lutz is more graceful than one who performs it while showing great effort.[14] Or, as Castiglione explains, "Do you not see how much more grace a lady who paints (if at all) so sparingly and so little, that whoever sees her is in doubt whether she be painted or not; than another lady so plastered that she seems to have put a mask upon her face" (2000, p. 54).

Leaked Constructedness

A nonchalance similar to that which Castiglione instructs appears in numerous modern publications, advertisements, and websites in the form of what I dub "leaked constructedness." To create leaked constructedness, graphic designers and artists employ bibliographic signifiers that appear to be casual and handmade but which are probably digitally created, such as seemingly hand-scripted fonts, crayon and marker drawings, collage aesthetics, photocopier mimicry, and smudged inks. Highly complex digital design programs are carefully employed to replicate the smear of a fountain pen or a hapless collage in order to cater to an audience that is nostalgic for signs of less mediated personal connections in an impersonal digital world. Thus, leaked constructedness plays to its audience through sprezzaturic styling that has the look of art that was created with ease or through accident. Such a Do-It-Yourself (rather than digitally) aesthetic plays a key role in what is often dubbed "hipster culture" with its postmodern code of radical nonchalance and can be viewed in such magazines and websites as *Adbusters*, *Found* magazine, and the websites of most "indie" music labels and "zines." Though it seems inaccurate to claim that digitally created texts aren't DIY or handmade, analog art often holds a more "authentic" appeal, possibly because it is less mediated and somehow represents the artist more immediately.

But sprezzaturic nostalgia has also been harnessed since computers went personal as seen, again, in the metaphors that govern it—the desktop; the dashboard; the trashcan; the folder and file; copying, cutting, and pasting; space on a hard drive; etc. Just as the metaphor on the computer seeks to focus the reader on content rather than construction, it seeks to revive the physicality of those metaphors through familiar images like the trashcan and the folder. Such a nostalgic immediacy[15] keeps the user's attention away from the fact (and fear) that he or she has no idea how the device is actually operating and focused on the idea that it might be functioning as easily as the metaphor that represents it. Thus, the connection to sprezzatura—the technology seems to be working at a much simpler level than it really is.[16]

CONTINUUM OF APPARENT MEDIATION

Through Castiglione's sprezzatura and the concept of leaked constructedness we begin to explore another continuum upon which ideas of stylistic ethics are formed: apparent mediation and manipulation. Since the time of Sir Francis Bacon, Petrus Ramus, and empiricism, scientists have sought to purge rhetoric and style from language because they felt it obscured truth; it deceived; it mediated too much. Thus, plain style was born because people don't like being, or more precisely *feeling*, deceived. But in examining the U.S. population's hatred of "The Media" we can complicate this continuum as well.

We often don't like too much mediation in our media because we want to create our own views of the news from objective evidence. We want to get as close to pure objective data as we can—we want language to be immediate. Thus, newspapers usually seek to keep the opinion of the writer, and many times any reference to the author, out of journalism.[17] As veteran journalist and pop culture guru Chuck Klosterman explains, "Being a news reporter forces you to adopt a peculiar personality: You spend every moment of your life trying to eradicate emotion. Reporters overcompensate for every nonobjective feeling they've ever experienced" (2003, p. 205). Reporters and editors purge opinion in order to avoid libel and media bias, but, as Klosterman further discusses, such a quest for objectivity, "really just makes them [news stories] longer and less clear. The motivation for doing this is to foster objectivity, but it actually does the complete opposite. It makes finding an objective nearly impossible, because you're always getting facts *plus* requisite equalizing fiction" (2003, p. 209). Rather than producing objective facts for the reader to interpret, equalizing fiction (like transparent language) functions as sprezzatura, creating the appearance of easy objectivity and disguising another layer of mediation. Such an artificial objectivity smacks of deception and the spin that Americans hate and has a somewhat contradictory effect: "Skeptical news consumers often find themselves suspecting that deeper truth can be found on the newspaper opinion pages, or through talk radio.... The assumption is that—since these pundits openly admit their biases—you can trust their insights more" (Klosterman, 2003, p. 209). Thus, an audience trusts confession as a rhetorical style because it makes its deception and spin readily available where sprezzatura, although based on similar selectivity and styling, hides its bias.

But at some point as we begin to trust such confession and the focus of attention switches from spin back to content, do we forget the spin? When bias is confessed, sometimes an audience no longer feels the need to criticize that bias, and when people aren't critical of bias, it fades to the background. This is true, for instance, of both conservative and liberal news programs—at some point, to liberals *The Daily Show* seems less and less biased because it admits its bias; to conservatives, the *O'Reilly Factor* has a similar effect.[18] Sometimes it seems that an audience is more aware of bias and willing to pick it apart when it isn't confessed. Thus, the second continuum of stylistical ethics is related to the first and is labeled *apparent* mediation because audiences react to mediation differently when it is or is not made evident.

Klosterman's discussion of removing the author from the news and the idea of trusting confessors makes ready another important reality of stylistic ethics. In the first continuum I discussed how sublimity is viewed as unethical because it focuses the reader only on content; yet, shouldn't a style that focuses a reader on the author be somehow more ethical? Of course, sprezzatura (and confession, as we will see below) demonstrates that what an author reveals about him or herself is not always the full truth and opens debates about whether the self is socially constructed or not. But shouldn't we want more of the author so that we can decide for ourselves whether we trust their bias or not? Such a complication opens up numerous stylistic moves that are often excluded from "serious writing" because they reveal too much of the author and obviate such advice as "don't use 'I' in a formal paper." The balance between revealing and concealing mediation is a tricky and often contradictory proposition.

Writers, therefore, should consider when it is appropriate to reveal their subjectivity and mediating power and when they should be elided in a sprezzatura-like style. When will readers respond well to confession of bias and when does such a style become a distracting repetition of "seems to me," "I think," and "might"?

IV. CONFESSION, HYPERMEDIATION, AND THE CONTINUUM OF FELT AGENCY

CONFESSION

Progressing to a more typically "ethical" stylistic presence, Saint Augustine of Hippo's (345-430 C.E.) *De Doctrina Christiana* and *Confessions* offer models of style (Christian oratory and confession) that do something few teachers of style had done before him; they give power to the audience through instruction on analysis as well as open the orator to critique and discussions on the subjective nature of confession.

Before his conversion to Christianity, Augustine was trained in, instructed on, and won declamation competitions through classical "pagan" oratory (*Confessions*). After he converted, he sought to take what he saw as a powerful rhetorical model (classical Greek and Roman oratory) and apply it to the radically differently styled Christian rhetorical tradition in order to convert pagans who often disdained the comparatively muted Christian style.

Although Augustine seems to take up Cicero's divisions on the purposes of rhetoric (to teach, delight, and persuade) in his three divisions of style (subdued, moderate, and grand), Augustine's discussion of ethos in Book Four of *De Doctrina Christiana* is somewhat more complex and radical than his classical predecessors. For Augustine the ethos of God, not necessarily the Christian orator himself, is what certifies the reliability and efficacy of the message:

Now Christ is truth and still, truth can be preached, even though not with truth.... . Thus, indeed, Jesus Christ is preached by those who seek their own ends, not those of Jesus Christ.... . And so they do good to many by preaching. (2008, 4.59-60).

Though Christian orators should strive to do justice to the word of God, corrupt people can still preach effectively because the power of Christian rhetoric is housed in God and the listener, not necessarily in the orator.

Indeed the idea of audience in Augustine's works (and in the Hebraic rhetorical tradition more generally) differs from classical models because of the relationship between faith and persuasion. Faith cannot be induced in an audience through persuasion; the Christian rhetor must give his audience information and let God (and the mind of the would-be convert) do the rest, otherwise it wouldn't be faith. As Christine Mason Sutherland explains, "For Hebrew rhetoric, persuasion is vested in the audience, not the speaker.... The object is to enlighten the audience, not to persuade, to empower by knowledge the individuals" (2004, p. 4, 10). Thus, Books Two and Three of *De Doctrina Christiana* contain instructions on "analyzing and resolving the ambiguities of the scriptures" with rules that may be distilled down to four basic concepts that leave room for multiple correct interpretations of the text:

1. The Bible cannot contradict itself;
2. The Bible always promotes love of God and neighbor;
3. Consider the sentence you are interpreting within the context of the sentences around it;
4. In order to interpret correctly, similar to what Cicero outlines in *De Oratore,* you need a broad background of knowledge (about snakes, metals, animals, astronomy, history, law, etc.) (Augustine, 2008, 3.2).

In his *Confessions* Augustine further elaborates on this concept of interpretation and readerly agency in Book Ten when he discusses his relationship with his audience and their belief: "Although I cannot prove that my confessions are true, at least I shall be believed by those whose ears are opened to me by charity.... Charity which makes them good tells them that I do not lie about myself when I confess what I am, and it is this charity in them which believes me" (2010, 10.3.4). Augustine cannot persuade his audience to believe his story but can only give them information to interpret in hopes that they take something from it. Thus, Augustine's favoring of the subdued style and its purpose of teaching over the other two styles (though he ultimately concludes, as does this chapter, that one should mix and match styles): "This, of course, is elegance in teaching, whereby the result is attained in speaking, not that what was distasteful becomes pleasing, nor that what one was unwilling to do is done, but that what was obscure becomes clear" (2008, 4.26).

Augustine continues to explain that the content the confessor and Christian orator provide are flawed (similar to the content of the sprezzaturic orator) because of the impossibility of inclusivity in language: "For I pass over many things, hastening on to those things which more strongly impel me to confess to thee—and many things I have simply forgotten" (Augustine, 2010, 3.12). Like any autobiographer knows, recalling every detail of the past is impossible, and even if it were not, such a retelling would make for a tedious and unpurposeful text. Thus, every act of confession is necessarily selective and manipulative of an audience's attention, despite whether confessional rhetoric makes an audience feel deceived or not. Augustine further elaborates on the subjectivity of memory in Book Ten of *Confessions* saying that "There, in the memory, is likewise stored what we cogitate, either enlarging or reducing our perceptions, or by altering one way or another those things which the senses made contact with ..." (2010, 10.8).

Hypermediation[19]

New media theorists Jay Bolter and Richard Grusin describe their concept of hypermediation as media that "ask us to take pleasure in the act of mediation" and foster a "fascination with media" (2000, p. 14). Or, as Wysocki states with a slightly more ethical connotation, "What is important is that whoever produces the text and whoever consumes it understand—because the text asks them to, in one way or another—that the various materialities of a text contribute to how it ... is read and understood" (Wysocki, 2004, p. 15). Thus true new media confess their materiality by calling the reader's attention to themselves.

Such a style of media confession is fairly young in the rhetorical tradition and truly comes into power, as Bolter and Grusin, and Lanham discuss, with late-modernist art: "It was not until modernism that the cultural dominance of the paradigm of transparency was challenged," (Bolter & Grusin, 2000, p. 38). For instance, in composer John Cage's "4'33," which consists of four minutes and thirty-three seconds of silence, Cage seeks to remind the listener that music is just sound, labeled differently: "I'm talking about sound that doesn't mean anything, that is not inner, just outer ... I don't want sound to pretend it is a bucket or that it's president ... I just want it to be a sound." His work makes music confess itself. Marcel Duchamp's "readymades," objects that become art simply by the fact that they are displayed as art, have a similar effect. Such pieces place the burden of the art not on the composer but on the audience, asking whether art can simply be enjoyed as style.

Moving to new media, Susan Delagrange's hypertext, "Wunderkammer, Cornell, and the Visual Cannon of Arrangement,[20]" exemplifies hypermediation through the interplay of its construction and content by creating a digital wunderkammer on wunderkammer. Through a rich collage-like interaction of text and image that calls attention to its own construction, the reader of Delagrange's "associative knowledge-building" space is encouraged to explore and wander through a history of curiosity cabinets, new media composition, and visual arrangement—propelled on by a design aesthetic that promotes "'critical wonder': a process through which digital media designers can thoughtfully and imaginatively arrange evidence and articulate links in a critical practice of embodied discovery" (2010). Analogy, comparison, and juxtaposition are the stylistic tropes that perpetuate such exploration. Like Augustine's Christian oratory, such tropes are created collaboratively between the author's arrangement and the reader's interpretation. Where digital metaphors designed with a sublime and sprezzatura stylistic aesthetic seek to focus the reader on content rather than construction, reviving a nostalgic physicality, those designed with a confessional aesthetic (such as Delagrange's wunderkammer metaphor) seek to aid readers in deconstructing them through a freedom of interpretation and analysis.

Continuum of Felt Agency

Augustine's Christian and confessional oratory, Delagrange's "Wunderkammer" and similarly, Geoffrey Sirc's "box logic," all seek to empower the reader by, as Sirc explains, imagining "text as box=author as collector," and, I would add, reader as collaborator (2004, p. 117). Rosanne Carlo's discussion of the generative ethos and "enfolding" rhetoric of Jim Corder in this collection is another example of such an argument towards the power of a confessional style. In all these models readers seem more empowered to explore and create and less likely to be manipulated, hypnotized, coerced, and abused. True literacy becomes, as Wysocki and Johndan Johnson-Eilola explain, "the ability to make the instantaneous connections between informational objects that allow us to see them all at once" (1999, p. 363). This notion introduces our third continuum of stylistic ethics—felt or apparent agency.

On this continuum, sublime rhetoric and immediacy become unethical because readers "Lose themselves in reading (and so to come back with different selves that better fit a dominant culture)" (Wysocki & Johnson-Eilola, 1999, p. 366). Such a styling gives us no agency to resist, and we are brainwashed. Yet, such a totalizing view seems to give too much power to the writer and conversely, a viewing of confessional rhetoric as totally empowering might give too much power to the reader. When we delve into a text, we "suspend our belief"; we enter into a contract with the rhetor; and, conversely, we have the choice to refuse: we don't need to fall in; we don't have to enjoy and agree; if we have any sort of analytical training (formal or informal), we can resist.

In *On The Sublime* Longinus analyzes examples of sublimity (Homer, Euripides, etc.), to illustrate how the style functions. Thus, Longinus is able to be critical of the sublime. He can be "sublime on the sublime" (Lamb, 1993, p. 553). As Jonathan Lamb explains, "Being sublime upon the sublime is, according to [John] Dennis, the reader's way of seizing the initiative, just as Longinus himself seizes it from Homer ... converting the servitude of reading into the mastery of writing" (1993, p. 553). The sublime may function as an emollient during the rhetorical act (and even this may be a totalizing fiction), but its existence is largely kairotic; its true power is fleeting. Once the orator stops, the reader begins interpreting (I liked that movie; I hated that movie; etc.) and has agency.

We also must remember that there will always be situations where the rhetorical audience begins with more power than the rhetor, for example, when the writer is part of a minority and the reader is part of a majority. This is what Michel Foucault warns against in his discussions of the transformative nature of confession in his *History of Sexuality: Volume 1: An Introduction*:

> One does not confess without the presence (or virtual presence) of a partner who is not simply the interlocutor but the authority who requires the confession, prescribes and appreciates it, and intervenes in order to judge, punish, forgive, console, and reconcile ... a ritual in which the expression alone ... produces intrinsic modifications in the person who articulates it. (Foucault, 1990, p. 61-62)

As Carlo, in this volume, reminds in her analysis of Corder, "Enfolding is about vulnerability of self," "a vulnerability which is not appropriate to expose in all rhetorical situations." Is it necessary to give even more power to an audience and open oneself up to a critical reading by the majority? Must the writer always play according to the rules set by the audience?[21] Offering any one fixed set of stylistic rules limits authorial moves of resistance as well as those of power. Such thought complicates Joseph Williams's[22] advice that, "We write ethically when as a matter of principle, we would trade places with our intended readers and experience the consequences they do after they read our writing" (2007, p. 215).

In addition, just because a writer uses a confessional style doesn't mean that the audience is empowered through, or will want to accept, the power of analysis. Being constantly analytical and explorative is exhausting. Though it may or may not be the best thing for one to do, readers can choose to ignore, choose to participate, choose to lie back, choose to be active, choose to be lazy—it is true that the rhetor can create an openness to participate or can try to encourage the audience to plunge into the sublime or can seek praise through nonchalance, but the audience doesn't have to respond. As Williams reminds us, "We ought not assume that they [our audience] owe us an indefinite amount of their time to unpack it" (2007, p. 221). Andrew Feenberg espouses a similar view in his *Critical Theory of Technology* surrounding how the democratization of labor "presupposes the desire for increased responsibility and power," and requires "a *culture of responsibility*," that we can see developing in techno-rhetorical culture through the call for multiliteracies[23] (1991, p. 17). Such a breakdown of power and a reminder that, as Foucault states, "in order to be a movement [of power] from above to below there has to be a capillarity from below to above at the same time" make my definition of style transform from "the manipulation of attention" into the *attempted* manipulation of attention (1980, p. 201).

Confessional rhetorics, because they are rhetoric and contain a guiding author or editor, no matter how hard they try, can never entirely cede power to the reader. Hypertext fiction, similar to Delagrange's wunderkammer, are groupings of links and nodes through which authors allow readers to explore and often "choose their own adventure," roving through seemingly random collections of media, creating their own interpretations as they proceed. Such freedom seems to turn readers into authors, but most times the numerous circuits readers roam through are planned in advance. Readers can't navigate outside of the hypertext. New media theorist Lev Manovich calls the inability for an author to ever fully give up control of their text, "the myth of interactivity"; he argues, "interactive media ask us to identify with someone else's mental structure ... to click on a highlighted sentence to go to another sentence ... we are asked to follow pre-formed, objectively existing associations" (2001, p. 61). Again, similar to the transport of the Longinian sublime, "we are asked to mistake the structure of somebody else's mind for our own" (Manovich, 2001, p. 61).

This final breakdown of the traditional continuums of stylistic ethics confirms the argument that there is no fixed relationship between style and morality, no most ethical style, thus, welcoming a plurality of styles. As Wysocki states, "I do not want the instructions on my kitchen fire extinguisher to ask me to stop to think about how the instructions compose me as a rational, modern, gendered, raced, classed, fire-fearing, early twenty-first century individual ... I hope that the fire extinguisher is transparently useful without them ..." (2004, p. 22). Writers must ask, then, when space for interpretation and attention needs to be purposefully constructed and when it is to be brought by the audience. When should texts be immediate and when should they confess and complicate themselves? Which audiences will automatically be critical of which texts? Which audiences need to be urged to pay attention to which points? And when does a critical eye destroy an immersive experience? Certain conditions call for certain styles, and we will only discover those most effective through experimentation with as many styles as possible.

V. BRINGING PLURALISTIC STYLE AND MANIPULATION TO THE COMPOSITION CLASSROOM

This chapter has asked you to consider what commonly eschewed avenues of style become available when one acknowledges that each choice of style and each act of rhetoric is one of manipulation and thus equally valid for ethical use. In conclusion, then, I offer three pluralistic and manipulative stylistic classroom activities that attempt to reintroduce composition students to a more complex notion of style, purpose, and exigence. In doing so I also, admittedly, argue for my own personal composition classroom exigencies: to teach students to be critical of their style and communication methods, to purposefully adapt to and control numerous audiences (whether that means to intrigue, disgust, incense, or hypnotize), and to enjoy experimentation in language.

Basic questions in a classroom of pluralistic styles:
- How do you want the audience to participate in the text?
- How does your audience want to participate in the text?
- What stylistic choices will mediate between these two desires?

1. THE FOUND OBJECT: ABSORBED IN MATERIALITY

Style: Sublimity, Immediacy, and the Continuum of Attention

Goals: Learn to capture and focus an audience's attention, create identification between author and reader, and present issues as in need of immediate action.

Activity: Many writing assignments ask students to make the assumption that the audience will have some knowledge of the writer and his or her exigence: a memo written for a boss, a speech delivered to the city council, an opinion column composed for the local newspaper. The found object assignment, however, asks students to design a message that must engage an unsuspecting audience with no assumed familiarity of the students or their exigences.

For instance, students might create a "shopdropped" item, a consumer good that is redesigned to subvert its original materiality.[24] A shopdropper might buy a sugary children's cereal, take it home, and use a computer program (or simply markers and paste) to redesign the packaging to highlight the cereal's unhealthy content by the addition of images of rotting teeth and obese children. The shopdropper then places the box back on the shelf for the unsuspecting audience to encounter. Through visual interest and interactivity the object is designed to engross the audience in a type of participation similar to that of a confessional object, but rather than directing the audience's critical eye at the construction of the item or the rhetor, it directs attention to the negative elements of the original product.

Thus, the goal of the found object assignment is to create a materially and stylistically engaging object (a dvd, sign, pop-up-book, comic, sticker, game) which will be found by a rhetorical audience, somehow gain their attention, and immediately absorb them in an understandable argument through interactivity.

Beyond wise object design, I ask students to come up with a hypothetical plan of distribution that explains where their object will be placed, how they will get the object there, what legal considerations might affect the placement of their object, and how the location of the object relates to the immediacy of the argument (arguments about nutrition are placed in the grocery store, arguments about fashion are attached to clothing racks, etc.).

Finally, I ask my students to explain the rhetorical choices they made in their object and placement designs: how ethos, pathos, and logos work in this object, how the context in which they place their object will affect their audience's reception, how they designed their object to avoid misreadings, how they think their audience will respond and why.

The purpose of this activity is to prompt students to think critically about audience interaction and immersion in composition. It also asks them to consider how medium affects such immersion. Students must consider the benefits of one medium over another in terms of the exigence of the author, the point of attention, and the continuums of felt deception and agency. Finally, this assignment asks students to consider the ethical implications of surprising an unsuspecting audience, using public/private space, and redesigning/subverting someone else's composition.

Further Question to Consider: When do audiences enjoy immersion in an artificial environment and when do they feel such immediacy is unethical? How does a sublime style occur outside of "creative" venues? How can a sublime author overcome a naturally critical audience?

2. Manipulate Your Teacher through Constructing Yourself

Style: Sprezzatura, Leaked Constructedness, and Apparent Mediation

Goals: Learn to control presentation of self, the subtle use of style, how to adapt to the opinions of an audience, and how materiality affects image of the author.

Activity: Many times in the composition classroom (including in my first activity) students are asked to suspend their belief and imagine that they are writing to a "real" rhetorical audience other than their teacher. This activity asks for just the opposite. In this activity I want my students to manipulate *me* and to do it without my knowledge.

In order to encourage a pluralistic notion of style, students must experiment with simultaneous rhetorical purposes and numerous selves surrounding those purposes. One of the biggest questions I want my students to ask in a style-as-manipulation environment is, "How do I want my audience to react to me?" An easy response like, "I want my audience to be convinced," is not enough. Thus, in this activity, in addition to their original argument/purpose, I ask my students to choose from a list of (or come up with their own) odd sprezzaturic goals such as: make me think you're cool; make me disgusted by your composition process; make me pity you; make me want to be a member of your family; make me think you're pompous but lovable.

The more weirdly complex the achievement of the secondary ethos goal, the more fun my students have and the higher the grade they will receive. But, the *subtle* manipulation of attention towards the author is key here; if I realize where the student is trying to lead me, the effect won't work as well. Thus, a student attempting the "disgusted by your composition process" prompt (and this is an extreme example), wouldn't overtly describe the composition process but might spread just enough peanut butter on the edges of his or her pages for me to notice and be disgusted on the third page turn. A student attempting the "member of your family" prompt might include several subtle and specific familial metaphors or anecdotes, creating familial subtext.

I ask my students to write their sprezzaturic goal at the bottom of the last page so I can't read it until I've finished the paper. If they've succeeded at manipulating my view of them, they generally will get a few extra points though I don't punish them if they fail.

The purpose of this activity is the ambition that encircles sprezzatura, the manipulation of the audience through the presentation of self. It also imparts the idea that every stylistic choice (whether linguistic or material) affects an audience's reception of message and perception of author. Ultimately, this activity attempts to push students beyond the idea that the best style hides the author.

Further Questions to Consider: How does a writer (especially a student writer) encourage an audience to analyze and take seriously the subtle use of language? When does authorial adaptation begin to alter an author's original goals? When is it appropriate to reveal subjectivity and authorial presence (through sprezzatura or confession), and when is such a revealing distracting?

3. Making an Essay Confess Itself

Style: Confession, Hypermediation, and the Continuum of Felt Agency

Goals: Learn to encourage active participation and analysis by an audience, highlight the constructedness of a text, enlighten an audience rather than persuade, help an audience to "take pleasure in the act of mediation" (Bolter & Grusin, 2000, p. 14).

Activity: By the end of a composition course most students have become somewhat experienced in directing audience attention to the flaws of an opposing side's argument. Confessional rhetoric, however, asks writers to do something much more frightening: direct the audience's attention at the constructedness, mediation, and limitations of the writer's own argument and guide the reader in a participatory experience that allows them to understand and rewrite the rules and goals of that experience.

This final activity, then, asks students to take an essay they've already composed and somehow make it confess its own constructedness. To prompt my students' imaginations, we think of messages that are designed to do this in the real world: a director's commentary on a film, a musician's blog kept while recording an album, Joseph Williams's infamous meta-stylistic "The Phenomenology or Error." Together, we examine how each of these confessionally-styled pieces draws readers' attentions to some points of constructedness while eliding others. How each confession paints a picture of the author, process, and materiality that supports a certain view and argument.

Students then begin to make their own previously written papers confess their materialities through a variety of methods. Some choose to play on the footnote by equipping their essays with "making of flaps" which can be lifted to reveal authorial commentary on how their own piece subverts or conforms to their argument. Others use a different font to indicate a running self-critiquing commentary. And some students make their papers interactive through elaborate fill-in-the-blank participation that asks the audience to consider how the student constructs and directs them.

Whatever the method, the key point is that students choose confessional techniques that develop their original argument and make the reader aware of how the student's writing process impacts them. Such confessional writing teaches the student that self-awareness and analysis don't have to occur only in the student's head, they can be invaluable on the page as well.

Further Questions to Consider: How does an audience's awareness of construction and mediation affect their reception of texts? Which audiences will automatically be critical of which texts? What limitations do you want to place on your audience's exploration and analysis?

NOTES

1. This paper assumes a current-traditional baseline of concise and transparent style when referring to "traditional" notions of style in order to engage with popular notions of style outside of the academy.

2. Though no theorist of new media I mention in this chapter makes such clear-cut ethical claims.

3. For further information on this false dichotomy see Winston Weathers's discussion of "Grammar B" in his Grammars of Style: New Options in Composition (2010).

4. I hope, however, that this chapter and collection illustrate "style" and "content" are indivisible.

5. To see how Lanham does address the ethics of style see chapter eight of his Revising Prose (2007).

6. See Plato's Gorgias and Phaedrus.

7. For a more negative view on Longinus and sublimity see Paul de Man's "Hegel on the Sublime" (1982).

8. Indeed, Julius Caesar and many other Shakespearean tragedies might be investigated as models of Longinian ecstatic tragedy rather than Aristotelian cathartic ones.

9. One should note that the idea of agency in immediacy is infinitely complex. Are technologies designed to erase themselves? Do they simply have that effect without purposeful design? Or are users implicit in the act, causing technologies to erase themselves by not paying attention? All three answers are most likely simultaneously true and help bring insight to discussions of agency and style.

10. We all know how distracting it can be when automatic features like the red and green spelling- and grammar-check lines or "Clippy," the talking paperclip, pop up when we are trying to compose in Microsoft Word. For more on hatred for Clippy, see Luke Swartz's electronically available bachelor's thesis, Why People Hate the Paperclip: Labels, Appearance, Behavior, and Social Responses to User Interface Agents (1998).

11. In fact, if one looks closely at popular nineteenth century American rhetoric handbooks (of authors like Day, Hill, and Genung) one sees sublime language (especially references to force, energy, and transport) being applied to the proto current-traditional pedagogy of perspicuity.

12. Though each of these points of attention, like each rhetorical appeal, is almost impossible to separate from one another and should be viewed more as a network of effects.

13. Indeed such an artificial natural style is deeply connected to the history of kairos in the rhetorical tradition and can be viewed in Gorgias's "The Defense of Palamedes;" Aristotle's claim that "A writer must disguise his art and give the impression of speaking naturally and not artificially," in On Rhetoric (1991, 3.2); and in Cicero's statement, "The main object of the orator was that he should both appear himself, to those before whom he was pleading, to be such a man as he would desire to seem ... and that the hearts of his hearers should be touched in such a fashion as the orator would have them touched" (De Oratore, 1.19).

14. Similarly, we might recall how Samuel Taylor Coleridge's claim to have written "Kubla Khan" while dreaming makes the mind of the poet seem all the greater.

15. Regarding the convergence of selectivity, manipulation, nostalgia, and digital metaphor, one might question: Where do these metaphors come from? On whose nostalgias are they based? If every act of collective memory and nostalgia is also an act of selective memory and amelioration of the past, whose oppressed and suppressed experiences are being recalled or elided in these metaphors?

16. For further reading on the sprezzaturic design of digital interfaces see Cynthia and Richard Selfe's Politics of the Interface: Power and Its Exercise in Electronic Contact Zones, 2010).

17. Though, a history of yellow and stunt journalism might disrupt this narrative.

18. Such confessions, however, do not seem to mollify opposing critics, as liberals will still critique O'Reilly and conservatives will still critique Stewart. In addition, Stewart has an even stronger confessional defense in his constant claims that The Daily Show is "the fake news" despite the fact that perhaps a large number of viewers get their only "news" from the show.

19. Though labeling new media conceptions of hypermediacy as "confessional" may be somewhat troubling because few, if any, of the authors I discuss conceive of their ideologies along an ethical continuum, I think the benefits of drawing a comparison between confessional rhetoric and hypermediation outweigh the risk of misinterpretation.

20. Accessed for free online at: http://www.technorhetoric.net/13.2/topoi/delagrange/index.html.

21. See John Schilb's Rhetorical Refusals as well as Schroeder, Fox, and Bizzell's collection Alt Dis: Alternative Discourses in the Academy (2007) for examples of scholars who agree that writers need the ability to resist the style of the majority.

22. Though Williams's other work on style is richly theoretical, his style manual, Style: Ten Lessons in Clarity and Grace, like those of other stylistic mavericks (I'm thinking of Lanham's "paramedic method," here) falls slightly short of the plurality he suggests in his more academic pieces. Indeed, the "grace" of the subtitle refers more to concision than anything else. But maybe such condensing is simply necessary to create a pragmatic manual. For a more complex analysis of the pros and cons of Wiliams's (and Lanham's) stylistic oeuvre, see Lester Faigley's Fragments of Rationality: Postmodernity and the Subject of Composition.

23. See Warschauer's and Banks's multiple accesses; Mossberger, Tolbert, and Stansbury's multiple digital divides; and Selber's muliliteracies.

24. For further information on shopdropping and other culture jamming examples see: www.woostercollective.com.

REFERENCES

Aristotle (1991). *On rhetoric.* (Kennedy, G. A., Trans.). Oxford: Oxford University Press.

Augustine. *Confessions and Enchiridion.* (Outler, A. C. Trans.). Retrieved from http://www.ccel.org/ccel/augustine/confessions.toc.html

Augustine (2008). Book IV: De doctrina christiana. In Enos, R. L. & Thompson, R. et al. (Eds.), *The Rhetoric of St. Augustine of Hippo: De Doctrina Christiana and the Search for a Distinctly Christian Rhetoric* (pp. 33-183). Waco: Baylor University Press.

Banks, A. J. (2006). *Race, rhetoric, and technology: Searching for higher ground.* Mahwah: Lawrence Erlbaum Associates.

Bolter, J. D. & Grusin, R. (2000). *Remediation: Understanding new media.* Cambridge: MIT Press

Burke, K. (1968). *Language as symbolic action: Essays of life, literature, and method.* Berkley: University of California Press.

Burke, K. (1984). *Permanence and change* (3rd ed.). Berkley: University of California Press.

Cage, J. (1992). *Listen* [DVD].

Carlo, R. (2013). Jim Corder's reflective ethos as alternative to traditional argument: Style's revivification of the writer-reader relationship. In M. Duncan & S. Vanguri (Eds.), *The centrality of style.* Fort Collins, CO/ Anderson, SC: The WAC Clearinghouse/Parlor Press.

Castiglione, B. (2000). *The book of the courtier* (Opdycke, L. E., Trans.). Herfordshire: Wordsworth.

Delagrange, S. H. (2009). Wunderkammer, Cornell, and the visual canon of arrangement. *Kairos: A Journal of Rhetoric, Technology, and Pedagogy. 13*(2). Retrieved from http://kairos.technorhetoric.net/13.2/topoi/delagrange/index.html

De Man, P. (1982). Hegel on the sublime. In M. Krupnick (Ed.), *Displacement: Derrida and after* (pp. 139-153). Bloomington: Indiana University Press.

Erasmus, D. *De copia.*

Feenberg, A. (1991). *Critical theory of technology.* Oxford: Oxford University Press.

Foucault, M. (1980). The confessions of the flesh. In Colin Gordon (Ed.), *Power/knowledge: Selected interviews & other writings 1972-1977.* New York: Random House.

Foucault, M. (1990) *The history of sexuality: Volume 1: An introduction.* New York: Vintage Books.

Gass, W. H. (1997). *Finding a form: Essays by William H. Gass*. Ithaca: Cornell University Press.

Guerlac, S. (1985). Longinus and the subject of the sublime. *New Literary History 16*(2), 275-289. *JSTOR*. Retrieved from http://www.jstor.org/stable/468747

Klosterman, C. (2003). *Sex, drugs, and cocoa puffs: A low culture manifesto*. New York: Scribner.

Lamb, J. (1993). Longinus, the dialectic, and the practice of mastery. *English Literary History 60*(3), 545-567. *JSTOR*. Retrieved from http://www.jstor.org/stable/2873404

Lanham, R. (2006). *The economics of attention: Style and substance in the age of information*. Chicago: University of Chicago Press.

Lanham, R. (2007). *Revising prose* (5th ed.). New York: Pearson Education.

Manovich, L. (2001). *The language of new media*. Cambridge: MITP.

McLuhan, M. (2003). *Understanding media: The extensions of man*. Critical Edition. (W. Terrence Gordon, Ed.). Corte Madera: Gingko P, 2003.

Mossberger, K., Tolbert, C., & Stansbury, M. (2003). *Virtual inequality beyond the digital divide*. Georgetown: Georgetown University Press.

Russell, D. A. & Winterbottom, M. (Eds.) (1972). *Classical literary criticism*. Oxford: Oxford University Press.

Schilb, J. (2007). *Rhetorical refusals: Defying audience's expectations*. Carbondale: Southern Illinois University Press.

Schroeder, C., Fox, H., & Bizzell, P. (Eds.). (2002). *Alt dis: Alternative discourses and the academy*. Portsmouth, NH: Boynton/Cook.

Selber, S. (2004). *Multiliteracies for a digital age*. Carbondale: Southern Illinois University Press.

Selfe, C L., & Selfe, R. J., Jr. (1994). The politics of the interface: Power and its exercise in electronic contact zones. *College Composition and Communication 45*(4), 480-504.

Shakespeare, W. (1997). The tragedy of Julius Caesar. *The Riverside Shakespeare: The complete works* (2nd ed.). New York: Houghton Mifflin.

Sirc, G. (2004). Box-Logic. *Writing new media: Theory and applications for expanding the teaching of composition*. Logan: Utah State University Press.

Strunk, W, & White, E. B. (1979). *The elements of style* (3rd ed.). New York: Macmillan Publishing Co.

Sutherland, C. M. (2004). Augustine, ethos, and the integrative nature of Christian rhetoric. *Rhetor 1*, 1-18.

Sutherland, J. (1957). *On English prose*. Toronto: University of Toronto Press.

Swartz, L. (1998). *Why people hate the paperclip: Labels, appearance, behavior, and social responses to user interface agents.* Stanford University. Retrieved from http://xenon.stanford.edu/~lswartz/paperclip/

Warshauer, M. (2003). *Technology and social inclusion: Rethinking the digital divide.* Cambridge: MIT Press.

Weathers, W. (2010). Grammars of style: New options in composition. In P. Butler (Ed.), *Style in rhetoric and composition: A critical sourcebook* (pp. 219-238). New York: Bedford/St. Martins.

Williams, J. (2007). *Style: Lessons in clarity and grace* (9th ed.). New York: Pearson.

Williams, J. (1981). The phenomenology of error. *College Composition and Communication 32*(2), 152-68.

Wysocki, A. F. (2004). Opening new media to writing: Openings & justifications. *Writing new media: Theory and applications for expanding the teaching of composition* (pp. 1-41). Logan: Utah State University Press.

Wysocki, A. F & Johnson-Eilola, J. (1999). Blinded by the Letter: Why are we using literacy as a metaphor for everything else? In G. E. Hawisher & C. Selfe (Eds.), *Passions, pedagogies, and 21st Century technologies* (pp. 349-368). Logan: Utah State University Press.

STYLISTIC SANDCASTLES: RHETORICAL FIGURES AS COMPOSITION'S BUCKET AND SPADE

William FitzGerald
Rutgers

> For all a rhetorician's rules teach nothing but to name his tools.
>
> — Samuel Butler, *Hudibras*

Aposiopesis? Metalepsis? Zeugma? What did my students think when first introduced to these and other terms? I know because they told me. "How do you expect us to remember them? They're all *Greek*!" I replied that I did not expect they would remember them, not all of them, at least not for very long. I confessed that I didn't remember all of them either. "But do we really use them?" All the time—far more than you realize—was my early and repeated assurance until it became clear that, just like the discovery delighting Moliere's bourgeois gentilhomme—that he had been speaking prose his whole life—my students acknowledged they have been performing rhetorical figures by the dozens for much of their life. I emphasized that I was simply providing names, albeit unfamiliar names, for verbal effects abundant in everyday language as well as in literary and academic prose. I hoped to convince them that there is much to be gained from being on formal terms with antonomasia or synecdoche and recognizing them as useful tools for their own acts of composing.

For my students in "Go Figure," an elective course in style centered in rhetorical figures, meeting *litotes* and *polyptoton* was akin to being transported by time machine (or "magic treehouse") to scenes of classical rhetorical education. Such scenes are strikingly different from the modern composition classroom, where terms such as *enallage* or *homeoteleuton* are at best a footnote. What I did was not so very strange, I think. Efforts in time travel are in keeping with pedagogical initiatives such as Sharon Crowley and Debra Hawhee's *Ancient Rhetorics for Contemporary Students*, a textbook inspired by the pioneering work by Edward P. J. Corbett in *Classical Rhetoric for the Modern Student*. If any difference is to be noted in my approach from these, it is in the realization that the figures—the tropes and schemes of classical rhetoric—need not be reclaimed, exactly. To the contrary, the figures are alive and well, as they have always been, if also occluded by current models of writing instruction. More than a subject of antiquarian interest, I argue, rhetorical figures remain a vital, but undervalued, resource for composition pedagogy. Their utility is particularly evident in a multimodal era, when textual, oral and visual performance have become open to new understanding.

This chapter expands on this reasoning to imagine a place for rhetorical figures in contemporary composition. It does so, first, through a reading of style in rhetorical tradition focused on the role of *ornament* (the broadest term for figurative elements of language) and, second, through an account of a recent course on figures for what light it sheds on possibilities for a figure-rich pedagogy. In brief, I propose that approaches to composition through style will be most fruitful if ornament is brought into conjunction with other stylistic virtues of clarity, correctness and propriety.

THE RISE AND FALL OF THE FIGURES

In her magisterial account of the figures in *Rhetorical Figures in Science*, Jeanne Fahnestock observes that what would later come to be understood as ornament in a merely decorative sense was first appreciated in more forceful terms, when rhetoric was a phenomenon of speech more than of writing. As Fahnestock explains, the earliest notions of *ornamentum* are not reducible to present-day notions of embellishment. Rather, ornament was closer in meaning to "armament," akin to the "gear" a foot soldier carries into combat (1999, p. 18). In military terms, a well-prepared rhetor is not only appropriately dressed for the occasion but fully equipped for a mission. One meaning of ornament that bridges decorative and functional notions is the insignia that mark one's military rank and station. If the canon of invention can be likened to an arsenal from which arguments are drawn and the canon of arrangement (in Greek, *taxis*) likewise imagined as a tactical deployment of those arguments in the field, the various figurative devices may be analogized to the thrusts and parries by which one engages an enemy in close quarters.

I appreciate these martial conceits for rhetoric in their emphasis on effective use of force. This chapter, however, offers a more playful image for style in its pairing of bucket and spade—tools for building stylistic sandcastles. Although couched in symbols of child's play, my concerns are equally serious as those animating Fahnestock's investigation of figurative devices in science. Despite the gradual eclipsing of a once lively figurative tradition, the figures offer a vibrant pedagogy of ornament. Powerful tools for constructing arguments, the disappearance of figures from the composition classroom at all levels of the curriculum comes at a significant loss to fluency, and with that loss a corresponding loss of agency. Fortunately, their reappearance—through a return to a pedagogy of ornament—is not something difficult to achieve.

I read this loss of a "feel" for figures in composition as symptomatic of style's ongoing marginalization. It has much to do with anxiety about the status of "literary" language in relation to scientific and technological discourse. It likewise has to do with the perceived status of composition studies in relation to other academic disciplines. For the figures can be seen as rhetoric at its most trivial or cosmetic. Or old fashioned—so many Latin and Greek terms! As Keith Rhodes observes in this volume, style-centered pedagogy risks being labeled uncool or "stodgy" ("Styling"). Rhodes is correct that the contemporary dismissal of style, conceived as a focus on writing at the sentence-level, has typically been expressed as critiques on *clarity* or *correctness*—virtues turned to vice through excess. Similar critiques can be leveled at belletristic notions of *grace* or writing "with style." My approach to ornament moves in a different direction entirely.

For on close inspection, the figures represent opportunities to connect students to a felt sense of writing (and speaking and designing) as rhetorical performance. By way of *hypophora*, the figure of reasoning by question and answer: Why bother teaching the figures when students cannot write clearly and correctly? Because the figures are crucial to a fully developed rhetoric of style. Without them, effective writing remains elusive. By some combination of imitation, instruction, and instinct, successful communicators acquire a robust repertoire of figures appropriate to the contexts in which they compose.

I am by no means the first to call for a reinvigorated canon of style in the teaching of composition. One need only turn to recent accounts of style's manifold practices and shifting fortunes in the rich collection of essays in T. R. Johnson and Tom Pace's *Refiguring Prose Style* (2005) or in Paul Butler's masterful *Out of Style: Reanimating Stylistic Study in Composition and Rhetoric* (2008) and T. R. Johnson's provocative *A Rhetoric of Pleasure* (2003) to confirm that over the past decade scholars in composition have approached rhetoric's central canon afresh. On a parallel track, Barry Brummett claims that style is now "the basis for a rhetoric that undergirds today's *global* culture" (Brummett, 2008, p. xiii, emphasis in original). Style has become a contemporary *lingua franca*—a semiotic code or performative grammar of display in various modes, e.g., speech, dress, and habits of consumption. Brummett identifies in style a figural logic of performance. Thus are emerging paradigms of style heralded, in composition and in cultural studies, even as consensus has yet been reached about specific pedagogies to enact a stylistic vision. Still, prophesies may be self-fulfilling when, the *zeitgeist* read accurately, incipient stirrings leveraged into concrete outcomes.

This is the situation with respect to composition as a stylistic art. The present moment is open to curricular revisions in ways that resonate with Brummett's cultural insight that style has acquired renewed rhetorical agency. This moment is not unlike previous moments, notably in the English Renaissance, when style assumes a character marked by energy and experimentation. Indeed, contemporary discussion of style's wax and wane seeks to make sense of the sources from which, in the subtitle of Paul Butler's *Out of Style,* this "reanimating" occur. Similarly, Johnson and Pace announce a "refiguring" of prose style. Both texts find warrant in notions of restoration, a "once and future" paradigm in which style again plays a vital role in rhetorical education.

I concur with these sentiments, even as I admit that such calls may be overly sanguine in their estimation of style's prospects for reanimation in the near term. Yet on the whole, I believe such calls to be warranted. Marginalized during a "process" era of composition studies, style may emerge "post-process" as equal partner with canons of invention and arrangement and, significantly, memory and delivery. In other words, renewed attention to matters of form and performance signal that style has something to contribute to composition beyond nostrums on clarity and correctness. My efforts in reanimating style or, in the words of Keith Rhodes, in "making style practically cool and theoretically hip" take this "refiguring" announced by Johnson and Pace literally, even though none of the essays in *Refiguring Prose Style* address figurative dimensions of language in a sustained way (this volume). Refiguring the figures addresses the contrast between their prominent role in classical rhetoric and their conspicuous absence today.

The most obvious and crucial difference between classical and contemporary contexts is performative mode—speech vs. writing. As Jay David Bolter and David Grusin observe, later media "remediate" prior media by "representation of one medium in another" (Bolter & Grusin, 2000, p. 45). Classical rhetoric largely imagines performance as speech even as the technology of writing transforms speech. Indeed, "style" (from the Latin *stylus,* a pointed tool for inscription) complicates neat distinctions in a remediated landscape as the English translation of Greek *lexis* and Latin *elocutio*—both terms for speech. The term "figure of speech" links the verbal and the visual in a dynamic pairing in which words perform acrobatic turns (tropes) and other visible patterns (schemes). The account of the figures presented here bridges speech and text, but also recognizes fluidity of mode.

STROLLING THROUGH THE GARDEN OF ELOQUENCE

Amid calls for a stylistic renaissance, not all reanimated pedagogies are commensurate. If past is prologue, various rebirths of style will differ in their aesthetic, philosophical and political commitments, in their streams of inspiration, and in their agendas. What is most valued in prose and its encoding in specific curricula varies from context to context. Obvious though this may be, it bears mentioning when imagining room for figures in an expanded style curriculum.

Consider the focus on clarity in Joseph Williams' *Style: Lessons and Clarity and Grace*. This popular text is one response to a crisis in literacy exacerbated, Williams notes, by an unproductive emphasis on grammatical correctness and arbitrary conventions. Yet Williams' approach to style is not identical with that of Richard Lanham, whose *Revising Prose* resembles *Style* in its advice against nominalizations and for strong agent-action pairs in subject-verb relations. Despite similarities, the differing motivations of Williams and Lanham are evident. *Style* reflects Williams' background as a linguist—his PhD is from the University of Wisconsin—and its substantial debt to cognitive psychology. Indeed, Williams' stylistic precepts have an empirical basis in research on the efficient communication and retention of information.

By contrast, Lanham's *Revising Prose* (famous for its "paramedic method") offers a decidedly political critique of language practices it would seek to remedy. In this respect, Lanham works in a tradition epitomized by George Orwell's celebrated essay, "Politics and the English Language." But Lanham's concerns with style are broadly humanistic rather than narrowly political. Lanham goes after bureaucratic prose not for its inefficiency only, but for its vulgarity and dehumanizing character. He is far more explicit in articulating ethical concerns in drawing connections between our prose and our character. "The moral ingredient in writing, then," Lanham writes, "works first not on the morality of the message but on the nature of the sender, on the complexity of the self" (Lanham, 1974, p. 106). Joseph William is likewise concerned with ethics. Recent editions of *Style* feature a final chapter on the "Ethics of Style." Here, however, ethics refers to a writer's relations with an audience, rather than to a diffuse, if no less important, linkage between the activity of writing and character development. While these differences are not inconsequential, Williams' and Lanham's remedial projects are kindred spirits in many respects. For one, they represent style as a stage of composing that follows upon activities of invention and arrangement. Both *Style* and *Revising Prose* approach style an act of revision and of adapting to the needs of an audience.

While yet more radical differences in understanding and teaching style could be juxtaposed, my purpose is not to delineate motives and means in contemporary approaches to style. Rather, it is to note that surface similarities in style or in style pedagogy can conceal greater variability in the objectives of style, i.e., to what ends style or the teaching of style is directed. Indeed, variability across contexts and change over time are arguably style's most distinctive attribute. Certain things are *in style* and go *out of style,* only to come *back in style* again. We can speak of idiosyncratic styles as well as of style being a reflection of particular historical periods, social movements and cultural traditions. In lay terms, style is recognized as precisely those elements that vary from performer to performer, age to age, or situation to situation.

But what dimensions of style persist across multiple contexts and conditions? Notwithstanding variations in style, conceptions of style, and approaches to teaching style, a spine of tradition extends back more than two millennia. Largely Aristotelian, this stylistic tradition is still relevant, even dominant, in the present era. As noted at this essay's beginning, this tradition is centered in precepts of clarity, correctness and appropriateness. Style's traditional virtues (each with an attendant vice), continue to be represented as desiderata in countless textbooks. Yet to these a fourth may be added in the virtue of ornament (or force)—the domain of the figurative. Writing in Aristotelian tradition, Theophrastus (c. 370-c. 285 BCE) is credited with codifying these virtues in *On Style,* a lost treatise known to Cicero and thus a vital link between Greek and Latin accounts of style. In important respects, my approach is Theophrastean in seeking to square style's triangle by returning ornament to the stable of virtues.

From earliest days, ornament (in Latin, *ornatus*) has had a complicated relationship with style's other virtues. As the force produced through figuration, ornament links style with other dimensions of discourse, other canons of rhetoric. Leaning left, toward invention, ornament discovers appropriate form for arguments. Leaning right, toward delivery, ornament gives speech liveliness of expression and emotive force. As Jeanne Fahnestock observes in *Rhetorical Figures in Science*, the use of figures was especially associated in Ciceronian tradition with the grand style, the highest of style's three levels; by contrast, the plain style, the lowest level, was notable for a lack of verbal embellishment (1999, p. 19). Such associations suggest that the figures function *primarily* as vehicles for, or triggers of, emotion. However, Fahnestock points out, thinking about figuration this way, though widespread, obscures a more complex relationship between figures as tools for argument and figures as carriers of emotional affect. By way of example Fahnestock considers *aposiopesis,* the figure by which a speaker, overcome with emotion (e.g., anger or sadness), breaks off speech in mid-sentence. In this instance, Fahnestock contends, dimension of *pathos* and *logos* of this performative gesture cannot really be separated (1999, p. 19).

Thinking about figures as the embellished expression of thought otherwise plainly expressed—what Fahnestock terms "value added theories" of figuration—papers over a productive tension between two ways of understanding the structural properties of figurative language: "artful" deviation from a norm such that figures stand out from a neutral ground and the characteristic way to express something (1999, p. 22). Surveying the range of theoretical perspectives on the figures, Fahnestock observes that "expressions available for a particular function [exist] on a continuum" rather than being distinct categories of "the literal and the figurative" (1999, p. 22). At the far end of this continuum are "iconic" expressions characterized by Fahnestock as "epitomes" (1999, p. 22). In other words, figures are "formal embodiments of certain ideational and persuasive functions" (1999, p. 22). As epitomes, figures are idealized forms representing some "line of reasoning" or a "condensed or even diagram-like rendering of a relationship among a set of terms" (1999, p. 24).

This notion that figures are inventional *topoi* made visible and hence forceful does much to re-establish their centrality and to explain their ubiquity in discourse of all types. Indeed, Fahnestock's epitomizes *her* argument through the figure of oxymoron in the title of her book, *Rhetorical Figures in Science*, insofar as science is typically regarded as unadorned, even figure-free, discourse. If rhetorical figures such as *antithesis* (paired contrasts in balanced phrases), *gradatio* (stepwise amplification or progression) and *polyptoton* (repetition of words with shared roots) function as arguments in scientific discourse, *a fortiori* they do so in many other discursive domains.

Fahnestock emphasizes the argumentative dimension of figures—style in relation to invention. Chris Holcomb underscores their performative character as style in relation to delivery. In "Anyone Can Be President," Holcomb argues that figures "do more than simply organize or cue other performative elements. They also constitute the performance as such. Working in oral discourse in concert with changes in pitch, volume, pacing, and gesture, the figures help define and manage relationships among speaker, listeners, and subject matter" (Holcomb, 2007, p. 74) Here, Holcomb draws attention to figures as sites of oral and bodily performance. As writing, the figures retain their association with embodied performance. Holcomb's central observation is that the figures must be understood in their capacity to mediate social relations between speakers and audiences, between writers and readers. In this respect, the virtue of ornament is closely tied to the virtue of decorum, or appropriateness. For

Holcomb, then, the figures function as an amalgam of cultural form and social practice. This notion of style as "cultural performance" is the focus of Holcomb and Killingsworth's essay in this volume ("Teaching Style").

Having identified the ornamental dimension of style as simultaneously a matter of argument and performance, I have yet to address the vexed efforts to categorize the profusion of figures within rhetorical tradition in formal and functional terms. Efforts to do so begin with Aristotle's account of style in Book III of the *Rhetoric*, the foundational text for stylistic analysis. Here, Aristotle presents the first definition of metaphor in semantic terms as a word-level substitution involving some deviation from ordinary or accepted meaning (1991, 3.2.6). From this proto-category of analogical reasoning and expression will develop the tropes involving some turn of phrase, including metonymy, synecdoche, simile and personification. Three hundred years later, the influential *Rhetorica ad Herennium* (c. 90 BCE)—for centuries erroneously attributed to Cicero—provides the first comprehensive catalogue of the figures, sixty four in all. Here is the first effort to divide the figures between those that involve a departure in meaning at the word level, the tropes, and those whose effects depend on a deviation from expected or natural word order, the schemes (Greek *schemata* translates into Latin *figura*.).

The *ad Herennium* is also the first effort to distinguish figures of diction (*figurae dictionis*) from figures of thought (*figurae sententiae*). The latter depends not on particular choice of expression but on performative functions, including description, comparison, *commemoratio* (dwelling on a point at length) and *dimunitio* (understatement). Placing understatement with figures of thought, as the *ad Herennium* does, rather than with the tropes, where figures of distortion such as *hyperbole* or *litotes* have traditionally been placed, indicates how overlapping are these categories. Complicating matters further, the author of *ad Herennium* imagines the tropes to be a subset of figures of speech. Two centuries later, Quintilian, in his *Institutio Oratio* (c. 90 CE), places tropes into a category distinct from either the figures of diction or of thought.

Throughout rhetorical tradition, taxonomic relations continue to be contested and further categorizations proposed. Renaissance scholar Philip Melanchthon, in *Institutiones Rhetorices* (1519), divides tropes into those based in words (e.g., metaphor, various forms of pun) and in larger units of discourse (e.g., irony, allegory) and also rearranges the schemes to include a major heading of *amplification* for figures that elaborate, qualify or digress to rhetorical effect. These multiple and conflicting efforts in categorization reveal the figures to be far more than a matter of embellishment to lend distinction to one's speech.

In her essay "Aristotle and Theories of Figuration," Jeanne Fahnestock reads Book III of Aristotle's *Rhetoric* in light of subsequent treatments of the figures within rhetorical tradition. Although Aristotle appears to say very little about the figures, apart from discussing metaphor, Fahnestock observes that Aristotle identifies three figures in metaphor, antithesis, and *energeia,* or bringing something before the eyes. She recognizes these figures as epitomes for what will later develop into categories of tropes, figures of diction, and figures of thought. In other words, Aristotle anticipates the broader bins of a rich catalogue of formal devices and performative moves. These bins correspond to "semantic, syntactic, and pragmatic components of discourse" identified, respectively in tropes, figures of diction, and figures of thought (Fahnestock, 2000, p. 127). Aristotle thus anticipates subsequent theorizing of figurative in recognizing early on that verbal effects are more than optional decoration.

Against this backdrop, a gradual dissipation of a once vibrant figurative tradition in the modern era, following a high water mark in the Renaissance, is all the more striking. Holcomb singles out as arguably the richest account of the figures Henry Peacham's *Garden of Eloquence* (1590), which identifies over two hundred figures, insightfully analyzes their formal and functional properties, and considers the social dimensions of their use. After such careful tending to these "flowers" of rhetoric, the subsequent waning of the figures as a stylistic resource becomes symptomatic of rhetoric's slow decline until more recent stirrings in the latter half of the twentieth century. What happened?

Isolating one factor among many in this development, Fahnestock points to the separation of invention from style in the de-coupling of topical patterns of reasoning and rhetorically expressive figures. Noting that the topics and the figures were once cross-fertilizing contributors to rhetorical aptitude, Fahnestock cites the disparate fortunes of metaphor, the prototypical *semantic* figure, and antithesis, the prototypical *syntactic* figure. In the modern era, metaphor emerges as *the* master trope to the near exclusion of other figurative devices. By comparison, the scheme of antithesis, an epitomizing form for contrastive reasoning, has lost much of its status over time as a valued figure. As a result, antithesis functions as a fine barometer for the eventual association of "the figurative" with poetic modes of discourse; for absent a scene of argumentation, antithesis seems merely a device for heightening contrast.

This separation of the structures of reasoning from the structures of expression reflects a broader historical development in which written language, especially in the medium of print, displace oratory as the paradigmatic mode of communication. Under the influence of Peter Ramus (1515-1572), rhetoric's scope was to become much more limited with the reassignment of the canons of invention and arrangement to dialectical methods of reasoning. With print the canons of memory and delivery also atrophy, so that only style remains as a canon. Rhetoric becomes virtually synonymous with style, conceived in a superficial sense as the dress of thought—artful spin. In this development, the figures, the most performative aspect of style, fare especially poorly and attain their status as a catalog of verbal embellishment.

It is possible to locate an historical and conceptual divide between rhetoric and composition by the perceived value of the figures. In the movement from rhetoric, conceived as training in the performance art of public speaking, to composition, understood as practice in conventions of written prose, the figures are slowly drained of their compelling force. As exemplified in the highly influential *Rhetoric and Belles Lettres* of Hugh Blair (1718-1800), prose style becomes associated with matters of taste, an elevation of the virtue of decorum, or appropriateness, as the divide between speech and text ever more widened. In the polite contexts of written discourse, the vast catalog of figures increasingly comes to be seen as irrelevant or, worse, indecorous. Shaking off an oral residue, written composition leaves the figures behind as an antiquated corpus (with a fearsome, foreign vocabulary) of stylistic devices. Once colorful flowers, the garden of eloquence turned to weeds.

In many respects, the figures are the last elements of classical rhetoric to fade away, not unlike that eerie smile of the Cheshire cat. The catalog of *vital* figures gradually contracted in response to changed circumstances in the production and reception of texts. In this shift from the production to the critical reception of texts, especially literary texts, the tropes, recognized as departures from literal meaning, became privileged over the schemes. Style became stylistics. This narrowing of the canon of style finds its apex in the notion of four master tropes (metaphor, metonymy, synecdoche and irony) with priority assigned to metaphor as the paradigm of figural as distinct from literal expression. Relatedly, the cleavage of poetic from persuasive discourse profoundly influences how the scope of composition is defined and, consequently, how style comes to be understood.

In many respects, recovery of a figurative pedagogy involves running this reel in reverse to reclaim the figures as dynamic elements of discourse for a multimedia age. In an era of montage and "remix," rhetorical practices of ornamentation regain currency. The question, then, is what role can figurative pedagogy play when the print culture that has for so long defined stylistic conventions begins to yield to something new?

THE RETURN OF THE FIGURATIVE: "GO FIGURE"

It may seem peevish to identify rhetorical tradition with the figures when much broader identifications are possible. In the wake of rhetoric's reclamation in the last century, the figures are a narrow slice of rhetorical pie. Indeed, rhetoric's recent rise to respectability and relevance comes about not by association with the figures but largely by moving beyond them (and beyond style, too) to reclaim invention, above all, as the heart of rhetorical inquiry. Even if one grounds composition in a rhetoric of style, there are many other ways to do so besides explicit, intensive instruction on the figures.

In this volume, William Kurlinkus emphasizes stylistic performance at the macro level through strategies of *ethos* writers use to engage readers ("An Ethics of Attentions"). Russell Greer similarly sets sights on the whole composition in dynamic relation to its parts ("Architectonics and Style"). And Denise Stodola reinforces the wisdom received from rhetorical tradition that practices of imitation at the sentence and passage level are indispensable aids to stylistic competence ("Using Stylistic Imitation"). To be clear, this essay, in concert with these other voices, imagines a place for figures in a *comprehensive* rhetorical pedagogy. It does so in the belief that the goals attendant to rhetorical education through style-focused pedagogies are most fully achievable when the figures are returned to a place of prominence.

Despite the availability of multiple frames for rhetorical pedagogy, the impulse to teach rhetoric through style, and style through figures, was one I embraced in "Go Figure: Style and Thought in Word and Image," offered as an advanced elective. Now having occasion to teach this course several times, I would do so again, as a course in its own right and as a laboratory for exploring the pedagogy of style. My experience suggests that a figure-based pedagogy may be productively integrated into a range of pedagogical contexts from first-year composition and beyond. As previously noted, imagining a (re)turn to the figures requires that one understand their absence in the first place. This absence persists. Despite rhetoric's return, even a perfunctory account of the figures is impossible to find in contemporary composition textbooks. One searches in vain for a treatment of *litotes* as an effective form of understatement, of *ploce* as strategic reinforcement through repetition, or of persuasive strategies of impersonation through *prosopopoeia*. Exposure to the figures, if it comes, comes in encounters with a small number of critical terms for the close reading of literature. Students typically have heard of *metaphor*, but not *synecdoche*, *alliteration* but not *anaphora*.

Even so, the remediation of text and image in emerging forms of digital media and across multiple modalities will continue to trouble written discourse as a paradigm of literacy. As we engage composition in various performative domains, the resources of figuration (if not necessarily their classical terms) will regain currency. This will occur because a robust visual and digital rhetoric, like their oral and written counterparts, depends on employing figurative resources in their semantic, syntactic, and pragmatic character as these resources are manifested in any performative domains. This presumption of relevance not only to a discursive past or present but, especially, to our discursive future served as warrant to this course on the figures.

Having taught courses in both prose style and in professional and technical communication with a strong emphasis in style—see Jonathan Buehl's "Style and the Professional Writing Curriculum" in this volume—I discover that the figures are teachable in conjunction with other approaches, including the pedagogies centered on stylistic revision offered by Richard Lanham and Joseph Williams. In the case of "Go Figure," I desired to put into practice a case eloquently made some time ago by Richard Lanham in *Style: An Anti-Textbook* (1974) and later in *Analyzing Prose* (2003). In these texts, Lanham calls for a return to the ludic, or playful, dimensions of language in writing instruction. I had my reasons for not calling the course "Fun With Figures," but I took notions of play quite seriously in my goals for the course. It was necessary to do so given the daunting motivational hurdle: what to do about the arcane nomenclature? Indeed, only a sense of play can transport students to a time when the figures were alive and apply the insights gained from this experience to contemporary contexts.

I taught "Go Figure" twice, in 2007 and in 2010. In both iterations, I was amazed by how well students took to the challenge to learn new and confusing terms only to use them with increasing authority and insight. Their enthusiasm for the value of their new tools was eye-opening. Learning ten or twelve terms per week for the first half of the course along with their classification schemes proved less difficult than I initially imagined. Of course, this was possible because it is not the figures themselves that students had to learn, just their names. My students discovered have been meeting and using the figures all of their lives; they were only lacking a vocabulary.

Prior to the course, few had ever heard more than a smattering of terms they would encounter. As the course progressed, they routinely expressed surprise that they had not learned to assign useful names, whether in Greek, Latin or English, to seemingly ubiquitous phenomena. Indeed, my students were quite open to learning these terms, to puzzling through at times subtle distinctions between related terms, and to discovering new figures not found on venerable lists. They were eager to identify current instances of classical forms and to convince themselves that these rhetorical devices transcended language and era. They learned, for example, that *syllepsis*—a form of *zeugma* in which one word governs several others in unrelated senses (e.g., Alexander Pope's "she stained her honor and her new brocade")—was Greek in name only. They confirmed their ability to invent novel instances of a figure once its form and function were understood. They could identify contexts in which a particular figure might be effective and also those contexts when it was not.

Beyond learning individual figures, my students came to realize that the figures constituted an open-ended, yet not arbitrary, set of linguistic moves. It was not long before class discussion gravitated quite naturally to questions of form and meaning. What, exactly, *is* a figure? When is something *not* a figure? How do figures *work?* Are certain figures unique to one language or culture? How many figures are there? Often, then, our efforts to categorize figures and describe their effects would lead to questions that required more than a simple *yes* or *no*. Often, we would discover that language is complex enough that several figures might be interacting in a given expression.

To achieve these insights on my part and theirs, a range of learning activities beyond introducing, memorizing, and recalling of terms was required. After all, what fun is that? And what transfer value? Among such practices were exercises in imitation along lines outlined by Denise Stodola in "Using Stylistic Imitation" and in *copia* as described in Tom Pace's *"Inventio and Elocution"* as well as an engagement with compilation through use of a commonplace book (see Zak Lancaster's "Tracking Interpersonal Style"). Beyond these activities, the course afforded opportunities for analytic inquiry by writing academic essays on figurative topics. To present a finer-grained account of the course's multiple working parts, I will outline its major features.

TEXTS

Both iterations of "Go Figure" opened with an introduction based on Arthur Quinn's accessible, idiosyncratic *Figures of Speech: Sixty Ways to Turn a Phrase* (1995). An excellent text in many ways, *Figures of Speech* proved useful in the early weeks of the course. Clever thematic arrangements and witty commentary put students at ease and for the most part Quinn does not introduce too many terms at once. However, the examples Quinn draws upon to illustrate the figures, from the Bible, Shakespeare, and other literary sources, are rather limited in appeal. In the absence of a wealth of authoritative and accessible materials from which to choose, Quinn proved to be a reasonable point of entry.

Much of the material one might share with students can be found on a handful of websites, most notably Gideon Burton's "Silva Rhetoricae: The Forest of Rhetoric" (http://rhetoric.byu.edu).("Silva") hosted by Brigham Young University. This comprehensive overview of classical rhetoric includes a deep catalog of rhetorical figures and helpful classification schemes. Non-academic sites include Robert Harris' annotated catalog of figures at "Virtual Salt" and Jay Heinrich's "It Figures," a playful examination of contemporary uses of the figures through sardonic blog entries.

In both iterations of "Go Figure," we turned to primary texts from rhetorical tradition with short excerpts from Aristotle's *Rhetoric*, the *Rhetorica ad Herennium*, Quintilian's *Institutes* and Peacham's *Garden of Eloquence* as historical interludes. In addition, we read Jeanne Fahnestock's magisterial overview, "The Figures as Epitomes," the introduction to *Rhetorical Figures in Science* (1999). All of these texts are appropriately challenging, but in the context of upper-division language study, they provided a necessary intellectual framework.

In each iteration, we turned in later weeks to a deeper engagement of tropes. In 2007, we read George Lakoff and Mark Turner's *More Than Cool Reason: A Field Guide to Poetic Metaphor*(1989). In 2010, we read George Lakoff and Mark Johnson's *Metaphors We Live By* (2003). Each of these texts offered something distinct and valuable. *Metaphors We Live By* demonstrates how profoundly metaphor, and by extension all figurative thought, structures ordinary experience. My students appreciated its scope and intellectual heft and regarded it as an important book. *Metaphors We Live By* generated some of our richest discussions. Yet, on the whole, *More Than Cool Reason*, with its pronounced tilt to literary and stylistic concerns, holds greater promise for integrating stylistic theory and practice. It offers strategies for reading poetic texts structured by figurative devices such as simile or allegory. In general, English majors found *More Than Cool Reason* most valuable. Finally, in both iterations, we read Kenneth Burke's profound "Four Master Tropes." More than any other text, this essay communicated the indispensability of figuration to our ways of seeing things.

In 2010, "Go Figure" featured two additional texts to broaden coverage of style in composition beyond the figures. Chris Holcomb and Jimmie Killingsworth's *Performing Prose: The Study and Practice of Style in Composition* (2010) is among the most promising pedagogical treatments of style to date. A thorough, yet accessible, guide to stylistic analysis, *Performing Prose* proved a useful spine, especially with its exercises in style. Its treatment of the figures in separate chapters devoted to tropes and schemes among other topics allowed it to serve as a broad overview of prose style. Finally, Richard Lanham's *Style: An Anti-textbook* (1974) offered a philosophical perspective on our goals, particularly in its emphasis on going beyond precepts of clarity and efficiency in thinking about the virtues of style.

ACTIVITIES

Daily activities of "Go Figure" were responsive to the range of stylistic exercises provided by *Performing Prose*, even before this text's use in a second iteration. Such exercises draw on a classical tradition of style pedagogy reintroduced to modern audiences through Edward P. J. Corbett's *Classical Rhetoric and the Modern Student*. (This book's unit on style is published by Corbett and Robert Connors as *Style and Statement*.) Central to this pedagogy are practices of imitation and amplification. Following in this tradition, we would on a weekly basis get inside various figurative devices through word-for-word and looser imitations and by efforts to generate figures on demand or impose figures on existing texts.

With a nod to Renaissance pedagogy, we turned to exercises in *copia*, or abundance, in the tradition of Erasmus, specifically his influential textbook, *De Duplici Copia Verborum et Rerum* (1512). As Tom Pace details in "*Inventio and Elocutio*," Erasmus offers in *De Copia* practical means for achieving fluency in thought and expression. "Exercise in expressing oneself in different ways will be of considerable importance in general for the acquisition of style" (Erasmus, 1978, p. 302). As a culminating activity, "Go Figure" adopted Erasmus' celebrated exercise in sentence variation, based on his own 200 variations (in Latin) of the sentence "Your letter pleased me very much." Students in "Go Figure" were asked to compose 50, 100, or even 200 variations on a sentence of their choosing and, in doing so, demonstrate as many figurative elements as possible.

Beyond producing more varied sentences, we embraced opportunities to practice figurative techniques of balance, repetition, omission and contrast, among other moves. The object of these activities in "Go Figure" was to link style with invention and thereby internalize a stylistic repertoire upon which to draw in novel contexts in the belief that verbal fluency contributes to rhetorical dexterity. Students in "Go Figure" discovered that exercises performed independently of assigned papers help them employ stylistic elements more effectively in those papers. Indeed, most students wished they had been exposed to the figures and related exercises much earlier, when it might have better prepared them for the writing they did in college.

The most enjoyable activity was a Figure Journal featuring the figures as found objects. In each iteration of "Go Figure," students compiled 25 to 30 entries illustrative of the range of figurative elements encountered in various media. In the tradition of commonplace books, students prepared individual entries for specific figures by providing an example, a definition, and a brief analysis of how this figure worked in a given context. Twice each term, I collected these journals to read and grade, offering commentary or corrections to any misunderstandings. They were a joy to read because the examples were fresh and reflected increasing understanding of the figures as vehicles for creative and persuasive expression. Many students put great effort into compiling and designing this journal as a window onto popular media, literary texts, oral conversations, text messages and tweets, advertising rhetoric, religious discourse, etc. They drew from verbal and visual domains. In fact, in the final weeks of the course we turned specifically to figures in visual rhetoric, looking at tropes and schemes in political cartoons, print ads, websites and other visual texts. But for time, we could have explored visual figuration more extensively. Even so, this modest effort helped us to understand how figures perform across media and modes.

In the final activity of the course students completed individual projects with a six to eight page essay analyzing figurative language in a particular context. Among the more notable outcome of the course for me was the realization that the figures are productive sites of rhetorical analysis. Writing *about* the figures presents students opportunities for academic writing. Most recently, students wrote about strategies of *copia* in motivational speaking, centered on Vince Lombardi; on the use of color as metonymy in Irish rebel ballads; on the figure of paradox in Bram Stoker's *Dracula*. In the first iteration of "Go Fgure," students addressed such topics as the satiric uses of antithesis in opinion pieces by Maureen Dowd; the use of anaphora in religious language; and the function of isocolon and homeoptaton, or rhyme, in Dr. Seuss. The point to be emphasized is that study of the figures generates intellectual curiosity and *practice* with the figures generates compositional fluency.

GOING FORWARD

"Go Figure" was imagined as a deceptively easy way into rhetoric under the premise that overt attention to argumentation and invention was more difficult. Beyond the use of ornamentation as hook, "Go Figure" was premised on a belief that style is a legitimate and productive portal into rhetorical theory and practice. It posits that attention to formal and functional dimensions of style effectively engage latent interest in rhetoric among a generation of multimodal multitaskers.

Even so, I confess anxiety. Looking over my shoulder, I fear that representing rhetoric as the study of tropes and schemes implicitly endorses rhetoric's reduction to *mere* figuration. This anxiety extends to the place of style in composition more generally, because one reason for style's marginalizatin is that style-centered approaches to composition are suspected of being reductive, overly focused on surface features of texts, too pedantic—in other words, not cool. (See Keith Rhodes' essay "Styling.") "Go Figure" was conceived as a "gut check" to see if there is sufficient heft in the figures to call for deeper engagement with them in other courses. I conclude from my efforts that there is more than enough substance—perhaps too much.

Bringing this account to a close, several points remain open to speculation. First, given that "Go Figure" is an upper-division elective and not a composition course *per se*, what possibilities exist for integrating its approach into composition courses, including in the first year of college ? On the whole, I believe this approach to the figures travels well. A seminar model for composition might well choose style, including the figures, as a focus and employ many of the practices of analysis and writing outlined here. This is especially the case if the figures are brought into dialogue with other elements of style, including the virtues of clarity, correctness and appropriateness or the various levels of style. When offering the course a second time, I was conscious of the recent turn in composition to writing *about* writing as addressed in Doug Downs and Elizabeth Wardle's "Teaching about Writing, Righting Misconceptions: (Re) envisioning 'First-Year Composition' as 'Introduction to Writing Studies'" (2007). Much as other efforts to make writing itself the topic of exploration in a composition course, writing *with* and *about* the figures fosters crucial meta-cognition and rhetorical sensibility. It also provides concrete benchmarks for students to measure their own development as practitioners of the craft of composition.

An entire semester in rhetorical figures is not really necessary, of course. The figures can be productively integrated into writing courses through judicious selection of, say, a half-dozen key figures to be introduced and practiced with each major unit or writing assignment. Building off exercises in copia and imitation, students can practice employing figures of substitution, omission, balance and repetition in their texts as they develop and revise drafts. One assignment might encourage *anaphora,* another *zeugma*. One unit of a composition course might feature the use of *gradatio* to reinforce chained reasoning across clauses or sentences or the use of *antonomasia* to refer to things by other than a proper name. Another might ask students to experiment with one or more figures of thought such as *adynaton,* the expression of inexpressibility, or *correction,* a strategic correcting of oneself. Indeed, students can be invited to highlight, interrogate, even celebrate, their use of specific figures when submitting or revising drafts.

Alternatively, students can embellish texts produced by peers and justify their choice of ornamentation. By such means of systematic exposure to, and practice with, the figures students may come to see speech and writing as performance in ways that other approaches to style do not allow. As the classical treatment of the figures long ago emphasized, rhetorical style pedagogy must foreground the performative dimension of discourse through hands-on experience with ornamentation as rhetorical force.

Finally, a figurative approach to composition that foreground performance opens onto different modes of communication and their interaction. As others in this volume observe, including Moe Folk ("Multimodal Style"), writing is but one mode of performance in a digital age. While figures are located in texts at the level of word, sentence and passage, as performative moves they structure information as well as shape interaction between rhetors and audiences. They are not restricted to verbal modes of speech or text. In addition, there are visual tropes and schemes that parallel their verbal counterparts to manage effects of balance, contrast, progression, etc. A figure is not *in the words* (or image), but the words (or image) *in the figure* (to use an *antimetabole*).

A figure-rich pedagogy for today must span performative modes and prepare students to communicate ornamentally across those modes. In this respect, the figures are an untapped resource—a working vocabulary (not an antiquarian catalog) for twenty-first century communication. To be clear: there remains great value in attaching names to the tools we use. That is the point of learning the names, not to *remember* them, but to *use* them. My experience teaching the figures is that they bring a level of energy and a sense of agency to the composition classroom like few other elements of style.

This is not to say that sentence-based pedagogies focused on matters other than the figures should cease to be a focus of the composition course. Far from it. Renewed attention to the sentence in response to the risk of its "erasure" (Connors) and the possibilities for its "remembering" (Myers) is consistent with my call for a return of the figures. A figure-rich pedagogy serves as an excellent and necessary complement to rhetorically-attuned sentence-level pedagogies, such as those represented in Nora Bacon's *The Well-Crafted Sentence: A Writer's Guide to Style* (2009). This, finally, is the point. The classical tradition developed a fully articulated theory of style, one that recognized an assemblage of virtues at work—or at play—in any rhetorical performance. To the extent that the figures remain marginalized, stylistic pedagogy will never be as robust as it could, and should, be. A modest investment in figuration—composition's bucket and spade—has the potential for equipping our students to build some impressive sandcastles. Go figure.

REFERENCES

Aristotle. (1992). *On rhetoric: A theory of civic discourse.* (Kennedy, G., Trans.). Oxford: Oxford University Press.

Bacon, N. (2009). *The well-crafted sentence.* New York: Bedford/St. Martins.

Brummett, B. (2008). *A rhetoric of style.* Carbondale IL: Southern Illinois University Press.

Burton, G. O. (n.d.) Silva rhetoricae: The forest of rhetoric. Retrieved from http://rhetoric.byu.edu

Butler, P. (Ed.) (2010). *Style in rhetoric and composition: A critical sourcebook.* Boston, MA: Bedford/St. Martin's.

Butler, P. (2008). *Out of style: Reanimating stylistics in composition and rhetoric.* Logan: Utah State University Press.

Burke, K. (1941). Four master tropes. *The Kenyon Review 3*(4), 421-38.

Cicero. (1954). *Rhetorica ad Herennium.* (Caplan, H., Trans.). Harvard: Loeb Classical Library. Retrieved from http://penelope.uchicago.edu/Thayer/E/Roman/Texts/Rhetorica_ad_Herennium/home.html

Connors, R. J. (2000). The erasure of the sentence. *College Composition and Communication 52*(1), 96-128. Retrieved from http://www.jstor.org/stable/358546

Crowley, S. & Hawhee, D. (2008). *Ancient rhetorics for contemporary students* (4th ed.). New York: Longman.

Downs, D. & Wardle, E. (2007). Teaching about writing, righting misconceptions: (Re)Envisioning "first-year composition" as "introduction to writing studies." *College of Composition and Communication 58*(4), 552-584.

Erasmus, D. (1978). Copia: Foundations of the abundant style: De duplici copia verborum ac rerum Commentarii duo (Knott, B. I., Trans. and Ed.). In C. R. Thompson (Ed.), *Collected works of Erasmus: Literary and educational writings* (2nd ed., vol. 28) (pp. 279-660). Toronto: University of Toronto Press.

Fahnestock, J. (1999). *Rhetorical figures in science.* New York: Oxford University Press.

Fahnestock, J. (2000). Aristotle and theories of figuration. In Gross, A. G. & Walzer, A. (Eds.), *Rereading Aristotle's Rhetoric* (pp. 166-184). Carbondale IL: Southern Illinois University Press.

Harris, R. A. (2011). Virtual salt. Retrieved from http://www.virtualsalt.com/rhetoric.htm

Heinrich, J. (2005). It figures. Retrieved from. http://www.figarospeech.com/

Holcomb, C. (2007). "Anyone can be president": Figures of speech, cultural forms, and performance. *Rhetoric Society Quarterly 37*(4), 71-96. doi:10.1080/02773940600865305.

Holcomb, C. & Killingsworth, M. J. (2010). *Performing Prose: The study and practice of style in composition.* Carbondale, IL: Southern Illinois University Press.

Johnson, T. R. (2003). *A rhetoric of pleasure: Prose style in today's composition classroom.* Portsmouth, NH: Boynton/Cook, 2003.

Johnson, T. R. & Pace, T. (Eds.) (2005). *Refiguring prose style: Possibilities for writing studies.* Logan: Utah State University Press.

Lakoff, G. & Johnson, M. (2003). *Metaphors we live by* (2nd ed.). Chicago: University of Chicago Press.

Lakoff, G. & Turner, M. (1989). *More than Cool Reason: A field guide to poetic metaphor.* Chicago: University of Chicago Press.

Lanham, R. A. (1974). *Style: An anti-textbook.* New Haven, CT: Yale University Press.

Lanham, R. A. (1999). *Revising prose* (4th ed.). New York: Longman.

Lanham, R. A. (2003). *Analyzing prose* (2nd ed.). New York: Continuum.

Myers, S. A. (2003). Remembering the sentence. *College Composition and Communication 54*(4), 610-28.

Peacham, H. (1593/1954). *The garden of eloquence.* Gainesville, FL: Scholars' Facsimiles and Reprints.

Quinn, A. (1995). *Figures of speech: Sixty ways to turn a phrase.* Mahwah, NJ: Erlbaum.

Quintilian (2006). *Institutes of oratory.* (Honeycutt, L., Ed., Watson, J. S., Trans.). Iowa State University. Retrieved from http://honeyl.public.iastate.edu/quintilian/

Williams, J. M. (2007). *Style: Lessons in clarity and grace* (9th ed.). New York: Pearson Longman.

USING STYLISTIC IMITATION IN FRESHMAN WRITING CLASSES: THE RHETORICAL AND META-RHETORICAL POTENTIAL OF TRANSITIONS IN GEOFFREY OF VINSAUF'S MEDIEVAL TREATISES

Denise Stodola
Kettering University

Within the last decade or so, the debate over the relationship between form and content in writing pedagogy has been gathering momentum once again. In a *New York Times* article from May 31, 2005, Stanley Fish asserts that form must take precedence over content, suggesting that "[s]tudents can't write clean English sentences because they are not being taught what sentences are." Fish thus has his students create their own languages with parts that operate as English does, so that they can get a sense of how language works. Of course, although Fish rightly observes that grammar has been subordinate to content in much writing pedagogy over the last fifteen years or more, I think that many of us would take a more moderate view of the issue and agree that form and content shape each other. Along these lines, Laura Micciche's article, "Making a Case for Rhetorical Grammar" asserts that grammar overlaps with style, and that both categories shape and are shaped by the rhetorical context in which they operate (2004). Despite the problematic conceptual relationship between form and content as illustrated by the current incarnation of this perennial debate, however, I contend that style actually serves to bridge the two. In fact, much like rhetoric is the discipline without a subject and therefore cuts through all subjects, style has no clear and specific definition, allowing it to transect the rhetorical canons.

More specifically, I assert that the medieval focus on stylistic imitation, as well as the concept of transitions, can help us to bridge the form-content dichotomy actively and construct a pedagogy and course that more effectively enact the writing process for students of prose composition. In other words, while process theory as presented in composition textbooks tends to present the first three rhetorical canons—invention, organization, and style—in that order (providing the potential for a type of imitation that is chronological and task-centered), implying that students should likewise follow that order in their own composing processes, I wish to suggest that focusing on style, essentially disrupting the implied chronology, helps students gain insights about language and their own ideas that can then help them move into invention, adopting a more advanced, recursive form of revision. Transitions play a key role in this dynamic: in fact, Geoffrey of Vinsauf's *Documentum de modo et arte dictandi et versificandi* provides a precedent for a pedagogical emphasis on transitions in prose composition, while simultaneously implying, through its structure, a way of implementing these pedagogical methods (1968). Moreover, an emphasis on transitions is consistent with a lot of work being done in cognitive psychology, which makes it, at least potentially, a valuable tool in the writing classroom.

First, though, we must examine the notion of style more closely, as the various definitions of style can illuminate both how and why the form-content dichotomy has developed, as well as the importance of the role that style can potentially play in the writing process. Several definitions from the *O.E.D.* are significant in this context. The form-content dichotomy is apparent, of course, when one considers the emphasis in the following definition on the "form" end of the dichotomy. This definition states that style includes the "[f]eatures of literary composition which belong to form and expression rather than to the substance of the thought or matter expressed" (2004, p. 14), which is further reinforced by another definition that states that style is "[a] kind, sort, or type, as determined by manner of composition or construction, or by outward appearances" (2004, p. 22.a.)

Style is more broadly defined in other *O.E.D.* entries, however. One states that style is "[t]he manner of expression characteristic of a particular writer (hence of an orator) ... a writer's mode of expression considered in regard to cleanness, effectiveness, beauty, and the like" (2004, p. 13.a.), a definition that, upon close examination, reveals how broadly and varied the concept of style can be: in fact, the concept of "effectiveness" indicates the notion of "content" to some extent, as the author must consider how to gear her message for the audience in order for it to be effective. Indeed, these "features" are intended to culminate in an effect on the audience, as style is further defined as "[a] manner of discourse, or tone of speaking, adopted in addressing others or in ordinary conversation" (2004, p. 15), as well as the "[m]anner of executing a task or performing an action or operation ..." (2004, p. 23.c.) These more nebulous qualities are apparent in "Limits of Grammar in Writing Improvement," when author Rei Noguchi says that style

> ... covers such aspects of "mechanics" as verb tense, sentence fragments, run-ons, comma splices, and subject-verb agreement. But it also covers more than mechanics insofar as it also deals with options that lead to effective communication of content (e.g., the sequencing of linguistic elements, parallelism, subordination, transitions, and pronoun reference. (Noguchi, 1991, p. 11)

All of these various definitions, interestingly, are included in the glossary of the *Harbrace College Handbook*, 13th edition, which says that style is "[a]n author's choice and arrangement of words, sentence structures, and ideas as well as less definable characteristics such as rhythm and euphony"(Hodges, Horner, Webb, & Miller, p. G-44). Of course, from all of these definitions, it would seem that style itself is not particularly definable. Still, it is clear that style operates from the level of small mechanical units, like diction and punctuation, through the broadest conceptual levels, like content, making it a much more important facet of writing and the writing process than many of us acknowledge.
Likewise, imitation has played a role in writing pedagogy, but has also appeared in myriad forms, much like style has done. Like the notion of "style," "imitation" can take place at various levels, and can play a key role in learning and creativity. According to Piaget,

> [I]mitating ... means trying to do something which seems to be useful in reality, but which one's own schemata are not yet prepared for. But to be able to imitate, one must be aware of what is to be imitated and how it can be imitated. Thus, imitation is closely connected with observation and analysis (Geist, 2005, p. 172).

Significantly, the most recent usage note for "imitation" in the O.E.D. points to its pedagogical potential, stating that imitation is "[t]he adoption, whether conscious or not, during a learning process, of the behavior or attitudes of some specific person or model" (2004, 1.c.)

Moreover, the broadness of the definition is illustrated in the ways in which imitation has been applied historically in writing pedagogy. These applications can be subdivided into various categories: imitation at the overall organizational level, and at the sentence level—both in terms of diction and grammatical structure. At the broadest level of overall paper organization, of course, "teaching the modes," more widely popular in writing pedagogy twenty or more years ago, encouraged a kind of fundamental imitation at the essay level. Students would write, for example, comparison-contrast papers following one of two general organizational patterns: block or point-by-point. In the former, students would give all the information about one concept in the comparison, and then the second large chunk would address the other component of the comparison. The point-by-point comparison would take comparable facets of each component and develop the discussion accordingly. Of course, many students find out, very early, that these patterns are not absolute: in other words, one could write a compare-contrast paper with sections of definition and process, two other types of modes.

Imitation has also been used at the sentence level, which may be more useable in the freshman classroom, although it does not seem to have been as widely used, disregarded at times, perhaps, due to the research done by those composition scholars who suggest that students do not transfer the lessons from grammar exercises into their own writing, but must instead be taught by having their grammar issues addressed within the context of their own essays. Still, some have argued for a comeback of sentence imitation, perhaps most notably in Corbett's and Connors' *Classical Rhetoric for the Modern Student*, which first came out in 1965 and which was reprinted in 1971, 1990, and 1999. In this text the authors suggest that students copy, word-for-word, passages written by famous authors. The next step is for students to imitate a variety of sentence patterns. They also include testimonials on the value of imitation by such famous persons as Winston Churchill, Malcolm X, and Ben Franklin.

Although sentence imitation may have benefit in and of itself, the Medieval emphasis on small units of composition and the imitation of figures, just like the modern-day use of sentence-level imitation, are consistent with some of our more modern notions about writing pedagogy and potentially quite useful in the classroom. This is particularly clear in the case of Geoffrey of Vinsauf's *Poetria nova*, a handbook that was extremely popular in the thirteenth century, having survived in more than 200 manuscripts. In this rhetorical handbook for verse composition, Vinsauf included specific exercises that students could use, and which medievalist Marjorie Curry Woods has used in her rhetoric classes at the University of Texas at Austin. In fact, she has adopted, directly, some of the *Poetria nova*'s exercises. According to Woods, one of the most rigid and unexpectedly popular writing assignments requires students to produce a piece of connected discourse using all of the 35 Figures of Words in their traditional order, beginning with *repetitio*, *conversio*, and *complexio*. This type of exercise may be so popular with her students because it

> ... focus[es] on small units of composition (set pieces illustrating a particular technique or approach) compiled by

aggregation from even smaller units (lines or images separable from the work at hand and suitable for re-use in other compositions). (Woods, 2001, p. 13)

While this is not direct imitation of grammatical structure, it does fit in with the types of imitation I have already outlined, in that students are imitating linguistic patterns—in this case, in the figures discussed in the *Poetria*.

Significantly, Vinsauf's other treatise, the *Documentum de modo et arte dictandi et versificandi,* focuses specifically on prose composition. The insights it offers into the nature of prose are clearly more pertinent to any discussion of freshman-level writing courses, where the focus is on prose composition. In fact, most manuscripts of the *Documentum* include sections on *prosecutio* (how to transition from the beginning of the work to the body), as well as on the methods of ending a work, neither of which appears in such extended discussions in the *Poetria*. This emphasis on transitions suggests that, for Vinsauf, at least, transitions were particularly important in prose composition.

Transitions, of course, are forged in a many ways in order to signal a variety of different conceptual connections between two ideas, whether those ideas occur at the sentence level, the paragraph level, or beyond. These connections can be spatial or chronological; they can signal similarity or opposition; they can signal causality, aggregation, exemplification and intensification. Moreover, they can occur through repetition of words or phrases, through brief summary, or through the insertion of transitional phrases.

Interestingly, though, while transitions hold an important place in a piece of writing as well as in the writing process itself, many people, students especially, seem to think of transitions as "only" a matter of style, relegated to surface appearances, which, as we've seen from the various definitions, is faulty: transitions involve diction, grammar, organization and content; style, as such, is really **not** mere ornamentation, but an important part of the organic whole message conveyed in any piece of writing. Indeed, any transition involves juxtaposition of concepts: in order to determine which transition to use in one's writing, one must decide what the relationship between the two concepts actually is.

As such, cognitive psychology can shed some light on the significance of transitions; in fact, this notion of juxtaposition is at the heart of the research done by Gilles Fauconnier in his books *Mappings in Thought and Language,* and *The Way We Think: Conceptual Blending and the Mind's Hidden Complexities,* which he co-authored with Mark Turner. In his books, Fauconnier discusses analogy—more specifically, "analogical counterfactuals"—which involves juxtaposition of concepts, the "projection of structure from one domain to another" (1997, p. 101). An example of an analogical counterfactual would be the sentence "If I were you, I would listen to me." Clearly there are two categories, or domains, at play here: "I" and "you." These are set up as analogous and therefore separate entities. The relationship is counterfactual, though, in that "I" is not the same being as "you"; in other words, this subjunctive construction indicates something that does not exist in fact. This kind of thinking, though, entails a very sophisticated cognitive move, as it creates a relationship between two separate categories—a relationship that does not exist in empirical reality.

At the same time, though, grammatical constructions like this, which create connections between conceptual categories, have additional potential for meaning: in *Mappings in Thought and Language*, Fauconnier cites Langacker to explain that "grammatical constructions and vocabulary items 'call up' meaning schemas" (1997, p. 11). In other words, concepts and relationships bring with them attached sets of other concepts and relationships. If this is true, then transitions may be of particular importance, as they not only call up specific schemas within sentences but also serve as the explicit linguistic **link** to conceptual frames, thereby contributing to the creative process. Furthermore, grammar and creativity, so important in the invention portion of the composing process, are linked: Fauconnier suggests that "[t]he mental operations that allow us to construct meanings for ... simple-looking words and sentences ... are the same ones at work in what we recognize more consciously as creative thought and expression" (1997, p. 99). Juxtaposition of concepts can clearly provide the potential for creative thought.

Juxtaposition also operates in the notion of concept maps, the use of which may provide clarity on the cognitive dynamic under discussion. Concept maps are graphical representations of the relationships between concepts. In other words, they illustrate knowledge. Writing about these tools for understanding conceptual relationships, Novak and Cañas define the word "concept" as a "perceived regularity in events or objects, or records of events or objects, designated by a label" (2008, p. 1). A concept map of this definition is shown in Figure 1.

The boxes contain concepts, while the lines and arrows indicate the conceptual links between those concepts. These units of boxes and arrows constitute propositions, which are "statements about some object or event in the universe, either naturally occurring or constructed ... containing two or more concepts connected using linking words or phrases to form a meaningful statement" (Novak & Cañas, 2008, p. 1). The concept map, like Fauconnier's notion of "analogical counterfactuals," illustrates how important a place comparison holds in the learning process of the human mind, as the act of placing one idea or concept next to another invites the mind to establish relationships between

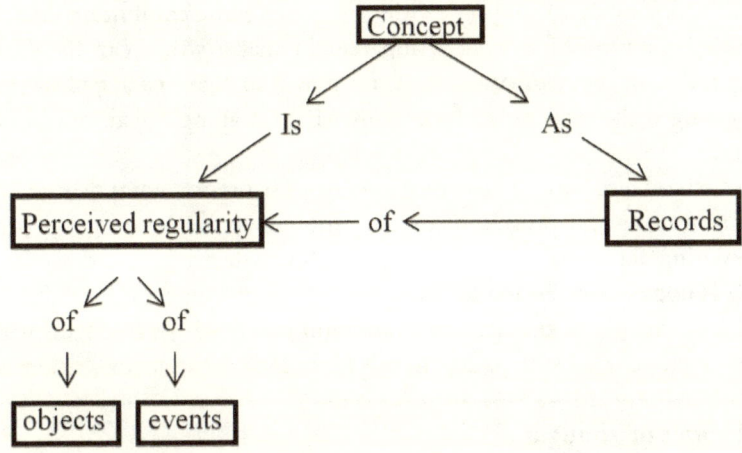

Figure 1. Concept Map of "Concept"

those two things. This is precisely how transitions work: two phrases, sentences, or paragraphs are placed in sequence, and the reader's first thought is "How do these two things connect to each other?"

Indeed, from the audience's perspective, transitions provide coherence for the message of any given piece of writing, providing for us, in effect, the steps comprising the conceptual journey on which the writer wishes us to accompany her. For the reader, in fact, transitions constitute a window into the mind of the writer; for the writer, they function not only as a manner of indicating purpose to the audience, but they also appear at the moments at which she is cognitively able to see her own reasoning in a reflexive manner. The fact that this is the point at which her line of reasoning becomes clearest to her—and that awareness intersects with her awareness of the cues required by her projected audience—possibly explains why so many of the students I have spoken to have such a difficult time with transitions. This difficulty is also explainable in terms of creativity in both the reader's and writer's minds. As Fauconnier states, "To communicate is to trigger dynamic creative processes in other minds and in our own ... mappings can be entrenched (as in conventional metaphor and established grammatical constructions), but ... also operate on-line to yield novel meanings, construals and interpretations" (1997, p. 182).

It is this potential for "novel meaning" that connects the medieval emphasis on prose composition to modern pedagogy—in the form of process theory and post-process theory—and further reinforces the pedagogical potential of style. Much of process theory revolves around the notion of "writing process," which, in composition textbooks, moves through the first three rhetorical canons—invention, organization, and style. Still, it is much more complicated than that: the recursive nature of writing is apparent in that a writer can have an idea (invention) and begin to organize it, only to find that the act of organizing it has changed the underlying focus somewhat—leading the author back into revision.

Recursivity also has a place within with post-process composition theory, which moves beyond process theory by emphasizing how context-dependent every writing act actually is. As George Pullman suggests, "… the process of writing is not context invariant. The genre, the circumstances, the subject, and the whole dynamic of the rhetorical situation influence what process will lead to what document" (1999, p. 26). In this formulation, the act of writing cannot

---

Figures of Thought

"Figures of thought" are kinds of "building blocks"—strategies for conveying your ideas as effectively as possible. Although there are more figures of thought than the ones I've included here, and there are other kinds of figures catalogued in writing handbooks throughout the various historical periods, I've selected the following as those that would possibly be more useful to you in technical and business writing situations.

On your rough draft of paper 2, please select three consecutive sentences or paragraphs, and use two or three of the following figures of thought as you recast and revise those passages. Be sure to include transitions between the figures you use in your text. Once you have accomplished this task, we will discuss your experiences in class.

1) Distribution. Assigns specific roles to various things, people, or ideas: *In this letter I provide information about the JAVA class, the project assignments for the class, and the format of the final exam.*

2) Description. Presents possible consequences for a given situation (while describing both in specific detail): *This example of a memo's format, including the headings and paragraph layout, may help you as you undertake the assignment for COMM class.*

3) Division. Distinguishes between and among alternatives, accompanying each with a reason and/or possible consequence: *My boss is not very good at dealing with people: he either doesn't communicate at all, or he communicates poorly. Both situations prevent the employees from doing their jobs well, and the employees eventually become frustrated.*

Figure 2. Assignment Handout

be distilled into steps, which is precisely what process theory does. In a sense, post-process theory recognizes how changeable a piece of writing can be when one considers the various forces that come into play to initiate and carry out any writing act, forces that change substantively over time. In fact, for the post-process theoretician, revision is something that, when necessary, is just as likely initiated by forces external to the writer as by the writer's own impulse to do so. Indeed, revision may ultimately be even more important for the post-process theoretician because, if the context is ever-changing, that situation would require revision as the context changes—even if revision means revising one's needs in terms of genre and message.

When any type of revision occurs, however, recursivity plays a significant role, especially for more experienced writers. As Nancy Sommers suggests,

---

4) Accumulation. Gathers up details that had been discussed previously: *Clearly, poor communication at work can lead to these additional problems: misunderstandings between co-workers, frustration with the job, and even the production of faulty—or even dangerous—products.*

5) Antithesis. Sets ideas in opposition to each other: *You may not have enough experience to understand the problems caused by poor communication, but my twenty years on the job has shown me the vast array of difficult work situations that are only made even worse with poor communication.*

6) Comparison. Draws out similarities between two dissimilar things or concepts (an analogy):
Just as music requires attention to the notes used and the order in which they are played, writing well in a professional setting requires attention to the words used and the order in which they are presented.

7) Exemplum. Cites a quote or an action of an authority figure: *John Smith, expert in business management, asserted during employee orientation that "a clear, well organized procedural manual contributes to an efficient work environment."*

8) Portrayal. Provides a depiction or portrayal of relevant physical and/or visual characteristics: *While Mr. Smith spoke, his voiced wavered and he couldn't stop shaking: his glasses bounced around on his nose and his unruly white hair stood up in all directions.*

9) Conciseness. Compresses a point into the least number of words necessary (can be a brief summary of what you've already stated): *Thus, while Mr. Smith's presentation was informative, his demeanor and appearance made him less credible to his listeners.*

Figure 2. Assignment Handout, continued

novice writers tend to revise by focusing on change at the lexical level, while experienced writers revise in a way that "confuses the beginning and end, the agent and vehicle; it confuses, in order to find, the line of argument" (Sommers, 1988, p. 125). To put it more directly, more experienced writers revise **as they compose.** Cognitively, of course, when this happens, the writer is forging links between existing material in her mind while creating new links—conceptual transitions at the cognitive level, as it were, many of which will appear in the written text in the form of linguistic transitions.

Vinsauf's treatises illuminate the potential pedagogical and psychological importance of these linguistic transitions not only as a topical focus for composition teaching, but also as a method. In fact, both the *Documentum* and the *Poetria* discuss the figures while they embody the very precepts they describe, making them function both as instructional tools and illustrative meta-rhetorics. Thus, while the *Documentum* includes a discussion of transitions, it also uses transitions within the description itself. If we consider the fact that Vinsauf's treatises are intended for teaching purposes, we can extrapolate another lesson from them—one which can be incorporated into a pedagogical approach: the classroom experience as a meta-rhetorical construct.

Indeed, this notion of meta-rhetoric can inform classroom pedagogy on many levels, bringing together stylistic imitation, transitions, and the writing process. In order to do so, it is clearly necessary to combine the imitation of figures, which may involve a variety of levels—phrases, sentences, brief passages—with transitions, and do so **within** the student's rhetorical purpose (e.g., on specific class assignments). Instead of the instructor making corrective comments in the margin to indicate where improvement is needed, this kind of pedagogy would enable students to strengthen the building blocks of discourse—and to do so in a way that emphasizes invention. In other words, this type of approach would allow the student to build a repertoire of cognitive structures and rhetorical strategies while simultaneously requiring her to build and articulate conceptual linkages between juxtaposed linguistic units—between phrases, sentences, paragraphs, and larger passages. At the level of assignments and class activities, the emphasis would be on imitation of small discursive units—figures as outlined in Vinsauf's *Documentum*.

In order to determine a strategy for building such a pedagogy, I gave a brief informal assignment to my Business Communication class, asking my students to take three consecutive sentences from their drafts and recast them using three different figures of thought. (See Fig. 1.) In providing the examples of the various "figures of thought," I selected those that seemed most pertinent to the assignment at hand, which I explained to them. For example, because "character development" is not used in business writing, I have omitted it on the handout. Indeed, business writing has its own set of stylistic expectations. The same is true of science writing, as Jonathan Buell points out in his article (in this volume) entitled "Style and the Professional Writing Curriculum: Teaching Stylistic Fluency through Science Writing." Once I selected the figures that would work best for professional writing, I then asked the students to be sure to include transitions between the newly revised sentences. Of course, we had been discussing transitions in various contexts throughout the term, but mostly during the individual conferences I hold with students at least twice during our 11-week term (between the first and final drafts of writing assignments 1 and 2).

My goals for this assignment, in terms of seeing how successful stylistic imitation would be for my students' writing, were very basic: essentially, I wanted to know if they could do it, and what sort of changes it would make to their drafts. My rationale for having them use this assignment on an initial draft was to open up the possibility that it would help move them back into "invention" as they revised, helping them revise more substantially. As a follow-up, I wanted to get their opinions on how the assignment worked for them, so I included a couple of questions on it in the teaching evaluation form I give my students at the end of the term. Surprisingly, the students thought that this was a difficult assignment, and, even more surprising, they thought that having this information at the beginning of the paper cycle—during the early stages of drafting—would be most helpful. More than half went on to say that they could see this being useful if it were integrated into the course from the first day of class, as it would help them organize their thoughts more effectively.

In future courses, I plan to take my students' suggestions, but I also want to more fully implement the meta-rhetorical potential suggested by Vinsauf's treatises within the course structure itself. For example, I not only plan to have students work on stylistic imitation and figures of thought from the beginning, as I've already said, but I also want the assignments themselves to "build off of" each other. By this, I mean that the students will select broad topics for which they can write perhaps a business letter and a formal report, thus enacting a kind of conceptual transition that will require them to link mental spaces in what Fauconnier would call "blends." Their writing assignments will thus "transition" from one to the other in much the same way as their sentences and paragraphs will.

Perhaps even more importantly, I plan on having them engage in a self-reflexive move, requiring them to become more aware of their own rhetorical, stylistic choices—by having them perform a rhetorical analysis of their own work—including an analysis of how and the degree to which their use of figures and of various factors associated with style effectively convey the content of the message. By doing this, of course, they will enact the same dynamic they engage in when they must become aware of their own conceptual links in their construction of transitions between sentences and paragraphs. By performing this self-reflexive assignment and then having them re-write the paper they have analyzed, they will also be moving from style to invention.

Interestingly, in outlining some of my ideas here, I too have moved from style to invention. Of course, teaching itself is a rhetorical activity—even an argument, perhaps—one that we make to our students about what sorts of things are important about writing and how they execute different pieces of writing in different rhetorical contexts. It is also an ongoing argument we engage in with ourselves, as we revise and re-think our positions on what and how we should teach—an argument I've entered meta-rhetorically in this chapter that suggests the value of stylistic imitation, the significance of transitions, the lessons we can take and shape from the Middle Ages, the ways in which an emphasis on transitions is consistent with cognitive psychology, and how we undertake the act of writing, both in the papers our students write and in the classrooms we work so hard to compose and revise.

REFERENCES

Corbett, E. P. J. & Connors, R. J. (1999). *Classical rhetoric for the modern student.* New York: Oxford University Press.

Fauconnier, G. (1997). *Mappings in thought and language.* Cambridge: Cambridge.

Fauconnier, G., & Turner, M. (2002). *The way we think: Conceptual blending and the mind's hidden complexities.* New York, NY: Basic Books.

Fish, S. (2005, May 31). Devoid of content. *New York Times.* Retrieved from http://www.nytimes.com/2005/05/31/opinion/31fish.html

Geist, U. (1996). Imitation as a tool in writing pedagogy. In Rijlaarsdam, G., van den Bergh, H., & Couzjin, M. (Eds.), *Effective teaching and learning of writing: Current Trends in research* (pp. 51-60). Amsterdam: Amsterdam University Press.

Geist, U. (2005). Stylistic imitation as a tool in writing pedagogy. In Riklaarsdam, G., Bergh, H., Couzjin, M. (Eds.) *Effective Learning and Teaching of Writing: A handbook of writing education* (pp. 169-180). Boston: Kluwer Academic Publishers.

Geoffrey of Vinsauf. (1967). *Poetria nova.* (Nims, M. F., Trans.). Toronto: Pontifical Institute of Mediaeval Studies.

Geoffrey of Vinsauf (1968). *Documentum de modo et arte dictandi et versificandi* (Parr, R. P., Ed.). Marquette, WI: Marquette University Press.

Hodges, J. C., Horner, W. B., Strobeck Webb, S., & Miller, R. K. (1998). *Harbrace college handbook* (13th ed.). Ft. Worth, TX: Harcourt Brace.

Micciche, L. R. (2004). Making a case for rhetorical grammar. *College Composition and Communication 55*(4), 716-737.

Noguchi, R. R. (1991). *Grammar and the teaching of writing: Limits and possibilities.* Urbana, IL: NCTE.

Novak, J. D. & Cañas, A. J. (2008). *The theory underlying concept maps and how to construct and use them.* Pensacola, FL: Florida Institute for Human and Machine Cognition.

Pullman, G. (1999). Stepping yet again into the same current. In Kent, T. (Ed.), *Post-process theory: Beyond the writing process paradigm* (pp. 16-29). Carbondale: Southern Illinois.

The Oxford English Dictionary. (2004). (V3.1 CD-ROM). Oxford: Oxford University Press.

Sommers, N. (1988). Revision strategies of student writers and experienced adult writers. In G. Tate & E. P. J. Corbett (Eds.), *The writing teacher's sourcebook* (2nd ed.) (pp. 119-27). New York: Oxford University Press.

Woods, M. C. (2001). The teaching of poetic composition in the later middle ages. In J. J. Murphy (Ed.), *A short history of writing instruction: From ancient Greece to modern America* (2nd ed.) (pp. 123-143). Mahwah, NJ: Hermagoras Press.

ARCHITECTONICS AND STYLE

Russell Greer
Texas Woman's University

DEFINING ARCHITECTONICS

Originally, the word "architectonic" pertained to architecture, specifically the construction of buildings. It evolved from the Greek *architecton*, which means "master craftsman" or someone who controls workers and directs them in a building project. As Richard McKeon has noted, Aristotle uses the term *architecton* to describe a master craftsman "who knows the matter and makes the product" (McKeon, 1987, p. 3). However, in 1781 Immanual Kant famously appropriates the term in *Critique of Pure Reason* as a metaphor, distinguishing between "technical unity" and "architectonic unity." A unity achieved *architectonically* "originates from an idea" (Kant, 1985, p. 655). However, unity achieved without architectonics, one merely conforming technically to the requirements of a form, is more limited. In this sense, *architectonics* began to appear after the late eighteenth century in English to describe architectural or artistic elements in accordance with a single design that harmonize.

In 1919, Russian philosopher Mikhail Bakhtin responded to this Kantian concept in the first words of his first published essay, "Art and Answerability":

> A whole is called "mechanical" when its constituent elements are united only in space and time by some external connection and are not imbued with internal unity of meaning. The parts of such a whole are contiguous and touch each other, but in themselves they remain alien to each other. (1990, p. 1)

Because Bakhtin's brief essay appeared in a provincial Russian journal, his interest in architectonics received no notice until his work began to be collected and translated after his death in 1975. Even then, critics responded more strongly to his studies of the novel. His early philosophical reactions to Kant have only received some attention in recent years because scholars want to understand the role architectonics has played in helping Bakhtin to develop dialogism. But some scholars have also been interested in architectonics as a resource for composition studies.

PARTS AND THE WHOLE

As a concept, architectonics can help composition scholars understand the relationship between parts and the whole. However, with *coherence* we already have a good term that does that. Joseph Williams defines *coherence* as "a sense of the whole" (2010, p. 71): "Think of coherence as seeing what all the sentences in a piece of writing add up to, the way all the pieces in a puzzle add up to the picture on the box" (Williams, 2010, p. 72).

Architectonics goes further, however. As Bakhtin suggests, architectonic unity implies a greater sense of the whole than merely the whole of the topic. It implies an understanding of the writer's personal relation to the topic under consideration. Just as architects consider mass and the forces of gravity that push and pull on a building, architectonics as a metaphor implies the invisible social forces, primarily in language, that surround and define us. These forces push and pull us, and we are attracted to them or repelled away from them. We become defined by what we like and don't like (as any teenager knows). As individuals living in the world and as writers, we take a stand about what we like and what we don't like, arranging the items of the world in our own minds and creating our own identity by our relation to those items. In the process, we construct a personal understanding of the relationship of parts to the whole. These wholes are another word for *meaning*.

A simple example occurs in my classrooms when I ask my students to choose their own topics for writing projects. If students choose their own topics, they struggle to form architectonic wholes as they struggle to understand their topic. One essential aspect of this *architectonic* whole is the struggle itself; the other essential aspect is their own involvement in the topic. What does the topic mean to them? Without that self-awareness, the unity formed is merely mechanical, as Bakhtin calls it, or technical, as Kant describes it. With that self-awareness, however, students stand in a better position to see the relationship of parts to the whole. As a teacher, I can guide my students to that self-awareness or help them in a more practical way see relationships in the material that they have chosen. Joël Paré articulates the significance of the personal in architectonics well: "In contrast to traditional writing, architectonic writing requires the writer to understand her relationship with the subject and to become personally engaged when writing about it in order to compose an architectonically sound and thus effective text" (2007, p. 48). I would only add here, as I have elsewhere, that "Knowledge of individual parts, portions of information without a clear relationship one to the other and to the entire text, provides no true understanding" (Greer, 2001, p. 58).

Architectonics and Style

This aspect of the personal in writing is the key to understanding the relationship between architectonics and style. But this emphasis on the personal is not typically associated with style. Instead, that traditional emphasis is usually on clarity.

Williams, for example, defines style as the ability to write clearly: "it is good to write clearly" (2010, p. 2). Aristotle also feels that "the virtue of style is to be clear" (1991, p. 218). Good style, Aristotle believes, uses metaphor to make persuasion vivid by communicating "actuality" (1991, p. 238): "putting before their eyes as it has happened" (1991, p. 165). We often talk about "personal style" in subjects such as fashion or music, and in literary studies we observe personal styles of authors, but we don't always have a language to describe the significance of the personal in composition studies, unless we consider theorists like Peter Elbow and Robert Zoellner who have discussed ways to find "voice."

Joy Ritchie gives us a starting point to understand the relationship between architectonics and style when she writes, "Only as they struggle to endow the words of others with their own intentions do writers progress beyond the level of functionary or bureaucrat to develop their own style and voice" (1998, p. 135). Here she is elaborating on a point that Bakhtin explores in many of his writings, particularly "Discourse in the Novel." "Personal" does not mean merely recounting narratives about our lives or even articulating likes, dislikes, or opinions (as many first-year writers believe). The "personal" manifests itself architectonically in the intonations we give to quotations and to words of others that we embed in our own writing. As we struggle to make sense about how we feel about something, as we fit that alien language into our own creation, we create a personal, *architectonic*, style. Bakhtinan scholars Gary Saul Morson and Caryl Emerson describe this process in *Mikhail Bakhtin: Creation of a Prosaics*:

> Different forms and styles of reporting speech might usefully be regarded as different ways of "hearing" another's words. When we use indirect discourse, we do not just apply a grammatical rule, we must necessarily analyze and respond to the reported utterance and show our dialogic relation to it. (1990, p. 167)

That dialogic relation depends upon the "other." Writers need two things to create *intonation*, which is the essence of an architectonic understanding of style: (1) an understanding of their own, personal relationship to reported speech and the topic under consideration, and (2) an understanding of their relation to the "other" in their discourse. Michael Holquist explains in *Dialogism*:

> Intonation clearly registers the other's presence, creating a kind of portrait in sound of the addressee to whom the speaker imagines he or she is speaking. A common illustration of this tendency is found when we hear someone talking on the telephone to another person whose identity we do not know, but whose relation to the speaker we can guess from his or her speech patterns. Intonation is a material expression of the shaping role the other plays in the speech production of any individual self ... we always pass judgment on whatever information is contained in what we say.... " (1990, p. 61)

When we see judgment, we find intonation. Our goal as writers is to master intonation so that the attitudes we express about reported speech accurately reflect not only our relation to the topic but to every part raised in relation to that topic. When we have full control over these elements, then the parts relate harmoniously—architectonically—to the whole, and we will express an effective style.

An Example of Good Style

Let's review an example of a text that seems to express a harmonious style, as we have defined it. I choose the professional writer Gore Vidal, who, in 1993, won the National Book Award for his collection of essays titled *United States: Essays 1952-1992*. In "Novelists and Critics of the 1940s," we can see a textbook example of harmonious style. Architectonics gives us a vocabulary to name what is happening in the text.

The purpose of Vidal's essay is to criticize critics for their shallow understanding of contemporary literature. This topic alone, however, does not provide the essay with its essential unity, although every aspect of the essay illuminates that topic, even when—at the end of the essay—Vidal begins to drift into metaphysical speculations on the reasons for such shallow literary criticism. His ability to achieve this virtuoso sense of a "whole" arises from his own extremely clear relationship to the material. Such a strong perspective, something students rarely achieve, allows him to use humor like a sword. "Bookish men" have a "long historic record of bad guesses" about literary works (Vidal, 1993, p. 10); affirmative and safe novels give "warm comfort" (Vidal,

1993, p. 11); and critics who follow the crowds ignore contemporary writers to focus on safer, canonical writers "contemplated on the safe green campus of some secluded school" (Vidal, 1993, p. 14). Vidal's snarky humor amuses as it slices, a humor made possible by (1) a clear sense of the whole (he knows what he wants to say); and (2) a clear relation to his material.

As for his sense of the "other," the intonation he articulates with his reported speech adds to his topic and reaffirms his personal relationship to that topic. Clearly, he is judging! Consider the lurking sense of the "other" in this jab at a nineteenth century critic in *Blackwood's Magazine* who in 1817 thought little of Samuel Coleridge:

> Mr. Coleridge conceives himself to be a far greater man than the public is likely to admit; and we wish to waken him from what seems to us a most ludicrous delusion. He seems to believe that every tongue is wagging in his praise ... The truth is that Mr. Coleridge is but an obscure name in English literature. (1993, p. 11)

The intonation in this "reported speech" is double-voiced, a complex relationship to the "other" made possible by Vidal's own, clear perspective on the topic. On one hand, he is including the critic's comments in a list of three critics who all spoke ignorantly but with integrity about nineteenth century authors who then became canonical; therefore, the mere presence of this quotation damns it. Yet, Vidal scores points for wit by seeming to agree with the critic's attacks on Coleridge's "preciosity and obscurantism" (when, in fact, he clearly feels the opposite). We know Vidal's true feelings because the bulk of the "obscurity" falls on the 1813 critic, of course, not Coleridge. This complex intonation is exactly the sort of thing readers admire when they admire Vidal's style—and architectonics can help us see and then articulate what he is doing.

Surplus of Vision

Another, related concept contributing to good style is "surplus of vision," and before we leave Gore Vidal, I want to address it. Because of the typical emphasis in composition studies on voice (ever since the Dartmouth Conference in 1966 and throughout the 1970s), I feel the trope of vision (*sapheneia*) has been somewhat overlooked when examining style. A special kind of vision with implications for style forms when we create an architectonic, personal relation to a topic. This special vision is the result of a self-conscious understanding that we exist in a particular and unique place and time. The gift of architectonic awareness is what Bakhtin calls a "surplus of vision," defined for our purposes as the ability of an author to see more than the reader can see. As individuals, we experience a partial vision of the world. Another person, however, can sometimes see more than we can see because he or she stands in a different place and time. Bakhtin describes our poor limitations in this way:

> He does not see the agonizing tension of his own muscles, does not see the entire, plastically consummated postures of his own body, or the expression of suffering on his own face. He does not see the clear blue sky against background of which his suffering outward image is delineated for me. (1990, p. 25)

On the other hand, someone else—an outsider—can see these things because he or she has a "surplus of vision." Editors can always see errors and weaknesses because they are not as close to the text as the writers: they have "surplus of vision." The best style will arise from a writer who struggles with his architectonic relationship to his topic and then uses that perspective to see more than his reader can see. Let's return to Vidal's essay for signs that he has this "surplus of vision."

Signs of it exist in the reader that Vidal assumes for this essay, "Novelists and Critics of the 1940s," which appeared in 1953 in *New World Writing #3*. This book was a paperback anthology series featuring literary criticism that Vidal had helped to found several years earlier. The assumed reader of this article is educated traditionally, like Vidal himself, and would have known major figures of the literary canon (George Eliot, Samuel Coleridge, Charlotte Bronte) and contemporary literary critics (Edmund Wilson, Malcolm Crowley, Lionel Trilling of the 1940s and 1950s). This reader could have understood Vidal as he attacks contemporary critics by showing the disparity between the way we currently value such classics as *The Mill on the Floss* by George Eliot and the way reviewers panned it when the novel was first published:

> We do not believe any good end is to be effected by fictions which fill the mind with details of imaginary vice and distress and crime or which teach it instead of endeavoring after fulfillment of simple and ordinary duty to aim at the assurance of superiority by creating for itself fanciful and incomprehensible perplexities. Rather we believe that the effect of such

fictions tends to render those who fall under their influence unfit for practical exertion by intruding on minds which ought to be guarded from impurity the unnecessary knowledge of evil. (as quoted in Vidal, 1993, p. 10-11)

By including this quotation, Vidal expresses a surplus of vision that sees more than the contemporary reviewer could (presumably because that 1817 reviewer was narrowly constrained by a cultural bias), and Vidal expresses a surplus of vision to his own reader with his long and profound view on cultural limitations. He gives this long view to his reader almost as a gift, supremely confident in his assertions. That confidence is a key part of his style.

An Example of Weak Style

Now, let's examine a piece of student writing where almost all of these aspects of architectonics are missing. This is a paragraph from a famous text, a student essay that appears in "Inventing the University" by David Bartholomae. It is a placement essay written during a freshman orientation in response to this prompt: "Describe a time when you did something you felt to be creative. Then, on the basis of the incident you have described, go on to draw some general conclusions about 'creativity.'" Here's the first paragraph of what that student wrote:

> In the past time I thought that an incident was creative when I had to make a clay model of the earth, but not of the classical or your everyday model of the earth which consists of the two cores, the mantle and the crust. I thought of these things in a dimension of which it would be unique but easy to comprehend. Of course, your materials to work with were basic and limited at the same time, but thought help to put this limit into a right attitude or frame of mind to work with the clay. (Bartholmae, 1985, p. 624)

Bartholomae explains this essay's weaknesses in terms of limited writer agency. This student, he believes, "doesn't have the knowledge that would make the discourse more than a set of conventional rituals and gestures" (1985, p. 625). The assumption that underpins Bartholomae's position is that discourses can inhabit and control individuals. He takes that position largely from Roland

Barthes and concludes, "A writer does not write ... but is, himself, written by the language available to him" (1985, p. 631).

From a Bakhtinian perspective, Bartholomae is entirely correct when he argues that in this paragraph we can see the student struggling with language and losing. Bartholomae concludes that the student has not been inhabited by the discourses that create an "insider position of privilege" (1985, p. 645). I would differ with Bartholomae's analysis, based upon Bakhtin's concept of architectonics, in this way: Yes, we struggle with language to form architectonic wholes of meaning, but we must win that battle and not lose it to a discourse. We must make the discourse our own.

Like Lev Vgotsky, Bakhtin believes in inner speech. We appropriate elements of discourse to create intonation, accepting some and rejecting others. This acceptance and rejection can pertain to any discourse, including a dominant discourse. We are not appropriated; we gain mastery. One sign of this mastery is surplus of vision; another is intonation. We take from discourses the parts that we need to form a whole of meaning, and we communicate that clarity to our readers and listeners by telling them things they cannot see or understand themselves, given our difference in time and space.

Let's reconsider this paragraph in terms of architectonics and style in three ways:

1. **Lack of a Sense of the Whole**. No clear sense of the whole exists in this student paragraph—which makes it impossible to communicate a clear meaning. The prompt has provided no clear audience, so the student stumbles in his syntax with language. Without a clear audience in mind, the writer doesn't know how to form a whole for that audience, resulting in phrases such as "was creative was" and "but thought help to put." The concept of "creativity" does not guide all three sentences. It appears at the beginning of the first sentence ("an incident was creative"), but creativity as a topic is only implied in the other two sentences, leaving the reader to wonder about the sense of the whole. The author loses any chance of communicating meaning without that sense of the whole.

2. **Lack of personal relation to the topic**. The nonstandard word order reveals that the reader isn't communicating with anyone specifically and only weakly communicating with himself. This topic is not personal to the student. As a result, he has no strong perspective.

3. **Lack of "surplus of vision."** The author doesn't have information to communicate that the reader doesn't already know, although the reference to "mantle and crust" is promising. He doesn't follow through, however, and discussing materials that are "basic and limited at the same time" fails to advance the discussion. This lack of confident assertion is a lack of surplus of vision.

Conclusion

Before we can be persuaded that something is true, we need to feel that we have all the facts before us. F. H. Bradley, in his 1907 essay "On Truth and Copying," explains:

> Truth is not satisfied until we have all the facts, and until we understand perfectly what we have. And we do not understand perfectly the given material until we have it all together *harmoniously* [the italics are mine], in such a way, that is, that we are not impelled to strive for another and a better way of holding it together. Truth is not satisfied, in other words, until it is all-containing and one. (as quoted in Magee, 2008, p. 61)

Here, Bradley summarizes key ideas related to architectonics and style. A strong style needs to impart an understanding of a whole, and the parts of that whole must work together *harmoniously.* That harmony occurs when writers relate personally to that sense of the whole and communicate a clear perspective based upon this personal relationship. Of course the sense of the whole itself is only possible because the writer believes she has a "surplus of vision" and wants to communicate it.

The actual mechanism by which a student can obtain surplus of vision and architectonic harmony resembles some form of proximal development, as described by Lev Vygotsky. First the student must be good at one thing before she can be good at other things, including style. The teacher must lead the student through a series of steps to first see a sense of the whole, and then relate to it, and then relate to the parts with intonation, and then revise to insure a surplus of vision. Sociocultural theorists would call these steps a form of scaffolding in which the student develops greater and greater stylistic competence.

One composition scholar in this collection who describes this movement towards stylistic competence is Tom Pace in "Language Instruction at St. Paul's Grammar School and Today's Stylistic Classroom." In his article, he offers an intriguing discussion of a pedagogical approach that aligns with architectonics well. Built on Erasmus's stylistic textbook *De Copia*, and following precepts articulated by Cicero, this approach attempts to fuse wisdom with eloquence. Whether that stylistic competence is created with the traditional exercises associated with the *progymnasmata* and *declamatio*, or modern versions built on templates from *They Say/I Say*, Pace describes a methodology that demands self-awareness for the purpose of public expression. His emphasis on exercises that look at issues from multiple perspectives could almost certainly create the surplus of vision discussed by Bakhtin, and the emphasis on public expression is worthy of further exploration in terms of architectonics.

Whichever exercises are used, at each step in the process, the student should stand in the position of authority or competence, creating a history of success. This success will help develop a degree of self-awareness about his or her place in time and space. Style is the registration in writing of this architectonic understanding.

REFERENCES

Aristotle. (1991). *The art of rhetoric*. London: Penguin Books.

Bakhtin, M. (1990). *Art and answerability: Early philosophical essays by M. M. Bakhtin*. Austin: University of Texas Press.

Bartholomae, D. (2003). Inventing the University. In V. Villanueva, Jr. (Ed.), *Cross-talk in comp theory: A reader* (2nd ed.) (pp. 623-653). Urbana, Illinois: National Council of Teachers of English.

Greer, R. (2001). Toward a theory of generative rhetoric. *CCTE Studies*: 54-64.

Holquist, M. (1990). *Dialogism* (2nd ed.). London: Routledge.

Kant, I. (1985). *The critique of pure reason*. Houndmills: MacMillan

Magee, G. A. (2008). Architectonics, truth, and rhetoric. *Philosophy and Rhetoric*. 42(1), 59-71.

McKeon, R. *Rhetoric: Essays in invention and discovery* (Backman, M., Ed.). Woodbridge, CT: Ox Bow.

Morson, G. S. & Emerson, C. (1990). *Mikhail Bakhtin: Creation of a prosaics*. Stanford: Stanford University Press.

Paré, J. (2007). Writing architectonically: Applying Bakhtin's architectonics to composition. *CCTE Studies*: 47-53.

Ritchie, J. (1998). Beginning writers: Diverse voices and individual identity. *Landmark essays on Bakhtin, rhetoric, and writing*. Mahwah: Hermagoras Press.

Vidal, G. (1993). Novelists and critics of the 1940s. In *United States: Essays 1952-1992* (pp. 10-22). New York: Random House.

Williams, J. & Colomb, G. G. (2010). *Lessons in clarity and grace* (10th ed.). Boston:Longman.

MAKING STYLE PRACTICALLY COOL AND THEORETICALLY HIP

Keith Rhodes
Grand Valley State University

Style still has an image problem in composition, despite substantively strong restoration efforts like those of Paul Butler, T. R. Johnson, and Tom Pace. Certainly, scholarly interest in style has been expanding, but this expansion has had limited range. While composing this chapter, I reviewed the last four years' worth of articles in *College Composition and Communication*, finding only two regular articles directly engaged with style: Ian Barnard's "The Ruse of Clarity," and Steve Lamos' "Language, Literacy, and the Institutional Dynamics of Racism: Late 1960's Writing Instruction for 'High-Risk' African-American Undergraduate Students at One Predominantly White University." Lamos, in an argument few style advocates would dispute, demonstrates the racist effects of "emphasis on the supposed superiority of white mainstream language practices" (2008, p. 49). Certainly, any responsible approach to style will need to consider such effects and account for them. Barnard's article more directly presents the problem facing style scholarship. Barnard positions Williams, Lanham, and other advocates of "clarity" as simply old-fashioned types left behind by the postmodern, social turn. Rather than turn his advocacy for more complex writing into a vision of what "style" might be in that light, he simply claims victory for the right to defy clarity advocates, then leaves the field. Apparently, advocates of "style," reduced to being advocates of clarity, become simply stodgy enemies to be vanquished and left to our nostalgic reveries. That popular view, however, is a severe mischaracterization. Effective work on style connects with invigorating classroom practice, and theoretical work on style directly engages contemporary and progressive work on matters such as cultural boundaries and multimodal composing, as this article will demonstrate.

Nevertheless, style advocates bear the onus of changing these common misperceptions by clarifying the nature of our progressivism and making style hip and cool once more. I use "hip and cool" playfully here and throughout this article, but being hip and cool is a serious matter, and increasingly so. As Richard Lanham argues, we have entered an age of information overload, so that the ability to draw attention to a message in the first place becomes a much larger part of designing effective messages. Whether we understand the shaping of opinion as "rhetoric," or as a matter of framing (Adler-Kassner & O'Neill), or even of marketing and "branding" (Rhodes), there will be no broad revival of interest in style scholarship unless style scholars and teachers can make style practically "cool" as classroom work and theoretically "hip" as a scholarly subject. If we are to fulfill the prospects of style as the core of composition, style advocates need to recognize that style scholarship, despite capable intellectual efforts in recent years, has remained something like a stale brand or passé fashion, a message that too many potential audiences think they know fully and no longer need to hear—even when they do. Style needs reframing, rebranding, and more eye appeal—in short, to become hip and cool among composition and rhetoric scholars once more. Without sharp focus on the hipness and the cool of style, whatever it is that style advocates have to offer will not gather the level of attention that increasingly becomes the key to the rhetorical effect of any message—even scholarly publication.

Thus, I first want to focus attention on what is fresh, new, and exciting about contemporary style scholarship. It can be tempting simply to wrangle with critics like Barnard, to unpeel their reliance on the ironic hegemony of postmodernism as a silent "foundation" for their views, to examine their failure to point out what exactly is *wrong* with clarity of expression, when it can be achieved, to interrogate their unwillingness to engage carefully Joseph Williams' thoughtful arguments on the ethics of clarity in the final chapter of *Style*. More productive, however, would be to generate a new frame for style by harking back to the original senses of the word—the interestingly complex concept, beautifully explained in Lawler's article-length definition of the term (an etymological *tour de force*), of an impression that we intentionally hold out to the world to enhance our image (2003, p. 233-34). Or, in short, we need to think of style in composition in ways more like what "style" means in other contexts—the very art of the cool and the hip. Style scholars badly need to give "style" some *style*—or, as Victor Villanueva put it in his review essay on recent scholarly books on style, some "*stylin*" (2011, p. 727).

In the end, that effort might be surprisingly easy, and not merely because the groundswell has already started—or, as Villanueva notes (citing Butler), re-started, given style's hidden importance during the recent heyday of "invention" scholarship (2011, p. 736). We simply need to tap into the style that "style" still has and has always had as classroom work with students who are eager for it. My regular teaching rotation Grand Valley State University's writing major often includes a course titled "Writing with Style." Invariably, most students, innocent of our scholarly wrangling and new to the "brand," enter the class hoping that we will be wearing berets, smoking dark oval cigarettes, and writing vivid, daring prose. And indeed, at least part of the agenda for the course—a foundational course for our writing major, taken by students on both creative and professional tracks—is writing vivid, daring prose. As Crystal Fodrey explains, the rise of creative non-fiction as a form of "creative," journalistic, and academic writing brings issues of style into particular focus (this volume). More than ever, style is not, to its practitioners, a simple matter of sitting up straight and behaving well. Style-focused practices like imitation are not, to most style advocates, slavish copying, or even earnest emulation. Indeed, at its best, imitation is ironic, playful, even carnivalesque, as in Gregory Roper's imitation-based textbook (2007), a paradoxically postmodern take on classical imitation. As our students—particularly our writing majors—know, style is inherently cool. As a cool craft, it has its own instruments, like the variations in tone arising from variations in "psychic distance" between the writer and the topic (Ellis, this volume)—that is, changes in how much I am feeling the heft and texture of my own words, right now, while I write about language (to show a couple of variations on that distance). Style advocates should not have great trouble getting that message about the freshness of style out to our several audiences—even fellow scholars. In the first part of my argument, I will examine our prospects for doing that. Then I will return to how work on style with our students amply demonstrates that a progressive theoretical hipness is style's real stock in trade.

In sum, "style" needs a fresh style. Writing scholars have learned a great deal in recent years about the role of linguistic "frames" and other non-rational influences on decision-making. Such frames pre-dispose audiences to decide in certain ways rather than others. Led by prominent figures like Linda Adler-Kassner (*The Activist WPA*) and her co-author Peggy O'Neil (*Reframing Writing Assessment*), writing scholars have urged us to use the concept of frames in efforts to argue for better methods of both writing instruction and writing program administration. Of course, for even longer, writing scholars have used postmodern thought to urge that we must make the "social turn" in scholarship, acknowledging that discourse communities frame and shape our judgments about writing, language, and reality itself. We can usefully summarize much of this advice as asking us to take fashion sense seriously—to consider the hip and the cool as having weight and substance, and to consider the tactic of being a fashion leader as a part of any effort to encourage changes in practice. While few have come right out and argued for an end to rationality in writing scholarship (and fewer still have acted consistently with any such implicit faith), we must certainly grant that any argument for a significant change in view must attend to its own frame and set what is in essence a new fashion trend. Advocates of style would do well to attend to the larger issue of framing—to examine the current "stodgy" frame for style, avoid reinforcing that frame, and look for ways to reframe the discussion of style. Style advocates should invest deeply in seeing style as a progressive force in writing pedagogy, writing scholarship, and ultimately, as Paul Butler has explained so fully and well (2008, pp. 114-41), writing pedagogy's public image. I will open this section by tracking the style trends that have created our current, largely regressive, frame for discussing style. Then, I will address the kinds of new, progressive work that style advocates can use to refresh that frame and make style work stylish again.

THE OLD FRAME: STYLE GOES DOWN WITH GRAMMAR

Particularly from the viewpoint of style, we can rehearse the familiar narrative of writing education in short strokes. As Berlin usefully summarizes, the study of literature and the teaching of writing emerged in rough synchrony in the late nineteenth century, part of an impulse to teach a new wave of lower-class students the ways of the upper classes. Upper-class readers mainly noticed the grammatical error in the writing of these new students. Thus, in the spirit of the Industrial Revolution, then in full swing, colleges set about industriously to call out those errors in written "themes" and correct them. The new class of literature scholars, whose expertise included close reading of language, became the natural leaders of those efforts. But quickly the sheer volume and repetitiveness of the work generated an intermediary class of labor to do the actual work, managed by the most accomplished (or simply most advantaged) of the literature scholars (Berlin, 1987, pp. 20-57).

As we now know, the entire idea was mostly a construct of its times. Studies questioning the effectiveness of the approach appeared almost immediately and have persisted ever since (Daniels), culminating in Hillocks' pithy chart graphically showing grammar as the least effective of "treatments" for teaching writing (1995, p. 220). Even so, pockets of resistance and better ideas rose and faded like niche species in evolutionary charts. For decades, no other approaches seemed to have any power against the larger narrative that the "right" way to teach writing was to teach grammar and mark up all the errors. While it nominally focused mostly on the "style" of student writing, it converted concern for effective style almost entirely into concern for grammatical editing. In hindsight, the whole plan seems quite preposterous; faculty trained to apply interdisciplinary vision to the most challenging and exalted texts were then somehow supposed to improve the writing of every new first-year student, using the never-tested, never-proven method of grammatical study and critique. Of course, those who needed this treatment least were most likely to thrive in those circumstances, and so they became those who applied the treatment to the next round of students. This grammar-based model survived for a very long time on a combination of wishful thinking, neglect, and cheap labor; nevertheless, it never had any genuine pedagogical foundation, and it could not withstand close study.

Supposedly, a new paradigm started as far back as the early 1960s and transformed collegiate writing education. In short strokes, writing scholars finally got the news about grammar's failure, learned the benefits of writing processes, made the rhetorical turn and the social turn, professionalized writing program administration and writing teacher preparation, and grew a substantial new field of composition and rhetoric. That whole movement purported, at least, to leave "grammar" behind. While all along there has been criticism of the research opposed to teaching grammar, there has not been positive research in its favor. Furthermore, the most effective model of teaching writing requires no grammar study (Hillocks, 1995, pp. 54-57). In the new paradigm, sentences mostly take care of themselves while teachers focus on developing the rhetorical and scholarly abilities that produce the most highly valued writing.

Supposedly. In truth, a review of almost any public evidence about writing teaching shows that the grammarian paradigm has never died. Handbooks replete with correction codes have massive markets. Every composition administrator of any experience has observed that grammatical correction remains a large portion of teacher response to student writing, even in the most "enlightened" program. Anyone who spends any time, as I do, considering and ruling on transfer equivalencies knows that vast numbers of colleges have preliminary "grammar" courses for the least prepared students—despite a complete lack of evidence that these courses do more good than harm for those who take them.

This entire scuffle has had the marked effect of diminishing the role of style in talk about writing. What grammarians practiced had little if any focus on the rhetorical appeal of language, and opponents of teaching grammar tended, to paraphrase Robert Connors, to erase the sentence as a visible area of any focus. Certainly, most teachers of all kind nevertheless attended to style all along, but in mostly invisible or misunderstood ways. As a result, very little writing scholarship addresses style issues any more, and much of that which does mainly laments that we even have such concerns. Thus far, the scholarship urging the revival of style has had little impact on the larger conversation.

Despite the grim story of grammar, there has been an alternative story about style. Nobody seriously contests the stylistic advantages of sentence combining, imitation and Francis Christensen's generative sentence rhetoric, at least not since Connors' "Erasure of the Sentence" re-established that such approaches remained effective in first-year composition. As Connors reported, all of these methods have backing in our theoretical and experimental scholarship.

No mainstream textbooks make much use of them, but teachers can find well-informed niche textbooks for all of them. Somewhat like bowties, such approaches to style always seem fashionably permissible, even if never truly chic. Like a good warm parka, fleece boots, or high-function rain gear, such approaches win favor by proposing methods that simply work. Even so, such results sound mundane and weak. Sentence combining, imitation, and adding trailing modifiers will help students win higher evaluations of their writing, but they sound old-fashioned, and partial—and they probably are.

Work with written style actually does much more than just work with grammar and manipulate sentence parts. Done fully, work with style challenges boundaries of grammatical convention, genre expectation, standard usage, effective expression, aesthetic form, and the ethics of expression, all at once. As Butler has explained, style has always also been part of advanced work with invention. As my students eagerly anticipate upon entering the class entitled "Writing with Style," nothing could be cooler than style, for a writer. We already know how to start this work. Mainly, what we need is a plan, one that reframes style as a part of the progressive work of composition.

THE NEW FRAME: MAKING COOL STYLE A HOT TOPIC

Paul Butler concludes *Out of Style* with a summary plea that "compositionists redefine style in a way that is meaningful to the field and that makes the study consonant with our disciplinary vision" (2008, p. 157). I would like to expand Butler's call by pointing out three specific areas in which a rhetoric of style connects directly with very current and vital threads of composition scholarship. Loosely speaking, we can, and should, explore style through the lenses of art, philosophy, and technology, all fully informed by the social and pragmatist epistemologies to which the best-received composition scholarship currently resorts. As I will address at the end, we might also usefully connect style more visibly with the burgeoning, cutting-edge scholarship on intercultural, international, and interlingual writing. It may well be that forging this somewhat complex connection between style and culture simply requires a revival of interest in style.

No current writing scholar can step into aesthetics without recognizing that artistic impact is culturally situated, problematized by concerns about the conserving and regressive power of monologic forms of art. Yet we should also be past the naïve notion that anyone can escape the ways in which art exerts influence. The aesthetic appeal of written style remains pervasively influential. In some ways, the obviousness of this point hides it. Kate Ronald bravely addresses this dark secret openly in "Style: The Hidden Agenda in Composition Classes or One Reader's Confession." When she gets to the heart of that personal confession, she admits to student readers, on behalf of all writing teachers, that "we are still influenced by your writing style more than we admit, or perhaps know" (2003, p. 197)—and that ""I worry that I'm responding to something in my students' writing that I'm not telling them about—their style, the sound of their voices on paper" (2003, p. 197). Indeed, as Derek Soles demonstrates, writing teachers do in fact respond to particular kinds of style in first-year composition classes, in ways that we can explain in familiar and concrete terms—no matter what we might think about the ultimate wisdom of those largely unexamined results, or their likely perpetuation of social norms we might also wish to challenge. As Nora Bacon explains, the path to a genuine response, even from a writing teacher, is not "plain" style, in itself "a disappointingly anemic conception"; instead, it is the ability "to arrange words artfully, striving for beauty, wit, grace, eloquence" (2010, p. 123).

Certainly, we will find it difficult and contentious to examine which particular aesthetic aspects of written style we might emphasize in the writing of our students—or work to de-emphasize in our own evaluations. Yet prominent composition scholars have been doing similar work in closely related areas that are not as fully within the range of our direct expertise. For instance, writing scholars and teachers have heard many calls for working with visual imagery (see, e.g., Fleckenstein). As such authors stress, writing scholars need to expand our horizons to include nonlinear and affective thinking—particularly, as Fleckenstein demonstrates, if we mean to help our students take genuine social action. It should make perfect sense, then, also to work with the nonlinear and affective aspects of written style. If composition scholars can be held to the challenge of addressing visual rhetoric, we can certainly be expected to address the similarly aesthetic rhetoric of style in language, and to generate work as smart as Fleckenstein's to theorize and implement our approaches. That kind of work with language is our more natural expertise, an expertise we already have by preparation, inclination, and feel. As Butler points out, the generative work of composition scholarship in the 60s and 70s was actually intrinsically involved with this rhetoric of style, a matter misrepresented in much of the re-telling of that history within the "epistemic" narrative—as if treatments of style in those days were all about either "Romantic" voice or "current-traditional" correctness (2008, pp. 56-85). Style and invention can instead work together as the work Berthoff joins together as "forming," an act of intelligent imagination (1981, pp. 61-67). Composition scholars have already developed a thorough background in culturally informed approaches to issues of aesthetic rhetoric. Against this entire background, the dearth of intelligent, current developments in "stylistic rhetoric," the art of shaping language for effect, seem almost appallingly negligent—or at best, just downright odd. Style advocates can re-frame style as part of a fully problematized *art* of writing, addressing in particular ways the complex aesthetics of style.

In addition to the art of style, style scholarship should address the philosophy of style. I am using the word "philosophy" here to grab hold of a large and furiously active body of concerns that we might call epistemology, theory, literary criticism, cultural study, or any of the words scholars use to attempt to find some ground for metanarrative—here, metanarrative about language itself. This kind of thought that I call philosophy has been, for at least two decades now, the most compelling area of exploration in current composition scholarship. To ally style with philosophy, then, would be a powerful move toward making work with style compelling. Further, the trick is easily done. The choice of language and its forms is always entirely bound up in philosophy and never comes free of it. As Rebecca Moore Howard articulates in promoting a socially aware "contextualist pedagogy" of style, "style can become a tool for defining, analyzing, and problematizing cultural forces" and "become a way for students to understand their own stylistic choices and options" in their "sociocultural contexts" (2005, p. 55). Everything that I have lumped into "philosophy," encompassing all the most fashionable authorities used in rhetoric and composition scholarship, can legitimately be brought to bear on the careful and precise turns of style.

Perhaps nobody illustrates the philosophical possibilities of style better than critical linguist Rob Pope, whose extraordinary textbook *Textual Intervention* invites students to explore the cultural meanings of small changes, or "interventions," in the style of texts. For example, in one exercise, students reconstruct the opening of a chapter in *Robinson Crusoe* that begins with the title, "I call him Friday." The introduction to the exercise asks students to think about "who is represented as saying, seeing, and perceiving" (1995, p. 101). Pope invites a wide variety of changes in perspective, each closely tied to specific changes in language—such as the indications of power roles in the simple use of "I" in the title sentence "I call him Friday," or the use of the name for a day of the week as the name for the "othered" human being. As Pope's work displays, it should really be a commonplace that the philosophy of a text is entirely bound up in the details of its style, and that those details are themselves philosophically interesting. To do such work is to work with what Russell Greer more fully explains elsewhere in this collection as the "architectonics" of style. Too often, despite knowing better, composition scholars instead unthinkingly recreate the philosophically defunct metaphor of style as fancy dress put on meaning, escaping talk about full architectonic style to focus on the "larger" political or philosophical issues to which style becomes connected—discussing students' "right to their own language" rather than engaging deeply with the actual details of that language, how it works and what it does. As Frank Farmer notes, writing about Mikhail Bakhtin's own pedagogy, ambitious teachers might instead wish to explore how students gain a sense of "when and why ... one stylistic choice is preferable to another," and ask, "How can they understand the circumstances, or contexts, that dictate the fitness of one substitution over any other?" (2005, p. 340). At bottom, a fully philosophic approach to style pedagogy would be remarkably hip in our current theoretical contexts.

Then, of course, there is technology. Richard Lanham's *The Economics of {Attention}* begins its remarkable exploration of our still-emerging information age with an interesting cascade of points that respond to his seemingly simple question about what changes when communication moves from the page to the screen. Lanham argues most centrally that, with information overly abundant, attention to information becomes the scarce commodity, the real currency of the emerging economic paradigm of the information age (2006, p. xi). In simpler terms, it's all about the eyeballs. Lanham notes the primacy of style in this economics of attention: "The devices that regulate attention are stylistic devices. Attracting attention is what style is all about" (2006, p. xi). That is, those who best understand the rhetoric of style in emerging media will construct our increasingly virtual worlds—and control their material roots. Like many academics, Lanham wrestles with the downright sophistic implications of such powerful knowledge. What is entirely clear, however, is that rhetoric and style will have extraordinary roles in what comes next.

While one could argue that much of the emerging rhetoric will be visual, language is always completely bound up in any form of meaning-making. Those who understand the idea of manipulating language to create changes in attention will have a strong role to play in the emerging economy of attention—as perhaps illustrated by the fact that a leading thinker about this complex economics of attention happens to be a leading stylist who has chosen to write an engaging, but extended, print book (albeit with digital ancillaries). Style is the part of rhetoric where we think about why someone should attend at all to what we have written. As the world becomes increasingly awash in competing messages, it becomes clearer that whether someone will read what we write—will spend attention on our words—becomes increasingly important relative to whatever else might be better or worse about the message. In an age of information overload, a message without style is not just a bad message; it is no message. A scholarship of progressive style can explain how to drive eyeballs to words themselves, a critical matter in this emerging economics of attention.

MAKING STYLE COOL FOR SCHOOL

In the writing department at Grand Valley, "Writing with Style" has become arguably our most central course, bringing together professors with backgrounds in academic, creative, and professional writing. I must note first that my understanding relies mostly on work done by my colleagues Roger Gilles, Chris Haven, and Kay Losey, as well as discussions with many other members of our Department of Writing, though of course I have had the chance to hone my impressions with my own teaching of the course. "Writing with Style" is the one course in our curriculum taught by professors from all backgrounds; it is the most central course for our majors and minors, the one that serves best as an introduction to the field of writing as a whole. Teaching the class requires all of us to stretch, to think about style in ways that will at the same time help students to write a poem, a memo, a hyperlinked menu, even a scholarly argument—and more pointedly, to write the unfolding kinds of writing we can as yet barely imagine. While that course clearly goes beyond the normal concerns of composition and rhetoric, it helps us examine several key points about the role of style in writing education. I must avoid trying to claim too much based on our experience, since much of what we are learning is still emergent and raw, consisting largely of our intuitive answers to the problem posed by claiming to teach such a course. Yet it seems very clear that our experiences point us in the direction of style as a progressive and emerging part of writing education, rather than a regressive and merely historical one. Indeed, what is most fascinating about the course is the way in which it seems to be opening up new pedagogical territory.

As to the aesthetics of style, we have found that attention to style from the viewpoint of writing differs subtly but importantly from the kind of analysis that students do in traditional literature courses. In the words of the title of one of the core textbooks for the course, we find ourselves attending to "the sound on the page" (Yagoda, 2004), the ways in which turns of language—and the invention of contexts for that language—evoke the senses in support of aesthetic and rhetorical appeals. We also become quite fascinated by both the craft of small passages and the ways in which authors situate certain structures in larger bodies of work. As a result, we have decided to create more detailed and advanced versions of this foundational style course, focusing in greater depth on particular authors' work at both the "micro" level of passages and the "macro" level of establishing contexts for the reading of their work. While we do introduce various schematics for analysis—for instance, Williams' concepts of character, action, and modification, or the classical rhetorical figures—we find ourselves increasingly drawn to a more direct sensory description, of a kind closer to the work of art studios than literature or linguistics classes. We pore over sample passages from a wide variety of sources, try our hands at imitating the most intriguing of them, and break out by inventing our own, entirely new styles based on experimental premises and guesswork. Especially in imitation work, students regularly find themselves intuitively drawn to visual aspects of the page, a critical move that at first caught me by surprise but that I have since learned to feature prominently. The analysis of style in purely lexical terms simply doesn't cut it, doesn't get down to what makes style passionately compelling for writers or effective for readers. Even Yagoda's title does not go far enough; not just sound, but all the senses and the visceral experience of reading have a role to play in establishing the context in which readers respond to style. A writer who focuses only on turns of phrase and fails to consider all the rest considers too little of the craft.

Turning to the philosophy of style, we find ourselves directly involved in practical work with prominent theoretical contentions. Students come to us with a fascinating and diverse mix of hopes and fears. Some hope to develop something they unproblematically call "their own" style, and come prepared to fear and loathe anything that would seem to be culturally conforming. Others hope to find exactly the right formula by which to meet cultural expectations, and fear anything that smacks of interpretive uncertainty. Many seek to become stylistic chameleons, able to adapt to any writing ecosystem. But as we explore a wide variety of schemes and examples of style, students increasingly notice that this tension between the personal and the cultural has no tidy resolution. Authors whose styles had seemed Romantically individualized appear also to have been shaped by history and circumstances; formulaic visions of genre and usage turn out to depend very heavily on particular, even unique circumstances (does *your* boss think you can split infinitives?). We routinely find students duplicating the insights of critical theory before having read it. To become seriously immersed in style is to become acutely aware that language is most essentially interpretive, a never-ending negotiation between vast cultural constructs on the one hand and, on the other, the particular and often unsettling viewpoint of a writer with one unique cultural and linguistic location. "Writing with Style" becomes essentially our most central course in rhetorical theory—not mainly because we "teach" it, but because we end up living in it.

The impacts of technology get shorter shrift in our particular class because we know our majors and minors will learn a great deal more about that in other classes on document design, writing for the web, and composing for multimedia. Yet we routinely teach the class with half or even two-thirds of the sessions taking place in computer lab classrooms, and our aesthetics and philosophies of style come to be entirely infused with our awareness that much of the writing our students will do next will need to integrate visual design and information theory. To a very large extent, the strong interest some students take in a vivid, unique style has little to do with Romantic notions of voice and very much to do with the intensifying competition for attention that marks online communication. Web sites, Facebook pages and Twitter accounts gain status by attracting eyeballs, and the dull and mundane will not cut it. Current media demand concise, vivid prose in ways little has before. As Folk explains more fully, they also demand a "writing" ability that crosses symbolic and visual boundaries, a truly multimodal sense of style (this volume). A very thorough command of style, both as technique and concept, has enormous value in working with new media, in adjusting to their new blends of constraint and opportunity. Our course in style undoubtedly commands more cultural capital than we have yet considered using, opening up onto the full practice of "cultural performance" advocated and explained by Holcomb and Killingsworth. I find myself wondering whether my own aesthetics and philosophy of style would let me advertise the course ethically as the best preparation for writing effective tweets, but it probably is. Ultimately, thinking about technology is what brings thinking about aesthetics down to earth, making the sound and vision on the page a compelling topic for our most committed of professional and technical writers.

Certainly, "Writing with Style" goes beyond what we do currently in our own first-year composition program. Yet as we move forward with the more advanced course, I find myself increasingly moving the simpler parts of what I do there into my composition courses. If, as it seems to me, "Writing with Style" is something of a laboratory for enhanced work in writing, then it might well be that style can center an approach to composition that leaves behind nothing else of importance in a composition class. After all, style invokes rhetoric, culture, politics, philosophy, and technology, not to mention offering a way to consider conventions that is anything but merely mechanical.

I will raise one more such issue somewhat by way of an epilogue. Of course, the richest and most productive work on style in composition should take place in the context of what a reviewer of this article aptly expressed as "cross-cultural and cross-national concerns that surface in the contemporary classroom, particularly among ESL writers." It could not be more clear that in such discussions were are responding to what is, most fundamentally and practically, a question of style. For people concerned with writing, the rubber hits the road on intercultural matters when the style of a student's writing does not fit the expectations of readers. But that transaction also is never simply about style; scholars in the field of writing rightly address the entire context of that transaction in our scholarship. In what I see as work closely related to the teaching of style, I have begun examining whether the most productive literacy work in the area of intercultural rhetoric might not be educating readers to take on more of the work of intercultural translation, to see such translation as a normal part of any communicative process, and not merely a "problem" for the writer. That is, I see it as consistent with the discussion so far to suggest that in matters of intercultural writing, the relationship between current scholarship and style is reversed. Rather than win favor for connecting style with other scholarship for the benefit of style, as I attempt here, in intercultural rhetoric the argument must be instead to connect this other scholarship with style for the benefit of that scholarship. There is likely to be little advantage in working from the perspective of style and opening up within it a full consideration of intercultural rhetoric. The connections and interactions are simply too complex and expansive to fit under the heading of "style" itself. Rather, the vast amount of current scholarship on intercultural rhetoric would be greatly improved if its scholars had the vision to include matters of style and the teaching of style as a normal, nearly inescapable part of their own inquiry. That they typically do not I see as mainly a consequence of style's undue exclusion from the rest of our scholarly discussions. I do see that resulting deficit as a highly regrettable result, but not one much in need of complicated critique. The absence of practical approaches to teaching style in such scholarship is remarkable, but I would hope that it is a problem easily remedied simply by encouraging writing scholars generally to be thinking, more often and more prominently, about the problems of teaching style as a general topic. The connections between intercultural rhetoric and style should naturally grow much vaster if more of us, more often, think to ask, "Now, how will I teach students how to approach style in light of this problem?" Ultimately, I see this very promising, very underdeveloped area of complex research as a place where a greatly expanded study of style would converge productively with ongoing research. But that would be metaphorically a kind of running that we may well do better once they study of style itself is up and walking.

CONCLUSION

In the end, informed composition scholars teachers need to drive a simple but profound change toward framing style as progressive. Doing so will pay multiple and profound benefits, and it makes substantive sense. Those who overstress traditional concerns like "clarity"—both approvingly and disapprovingly—grossly underestimate the full concerns of style scholarship and pedagogy. Style, we need to urge, does indeed have vitality—in fact, potentially far more than any other concern in writing. Such changes in the frame for thinking about style could well have explosive potential, and style advocates should have faith that changes in the conditions in which writing is taught and studied increasingly support such a change in the best ways. A discipline of writing should not mainly look backward at what writers have done; it should look forward, toward what writers might do. At every moment of actually doing the work of writing, of going forward with both the text and the underlying ability, a writer applies concepts of style. As a discipline, we should want to offer the best advice we can about approaching that aspect of the work. Style, after all, like coolness and hipness, is always about the next big thing—not the last one.

REFERENCES

Adler-Kassner, L. (2008). *The activist WPA: Changing stories about writing and writers*. Logan: Utah State University Press.

Adler-Kassner, L., & O'Neill, P. (2010). *Reframing Writing Assessment to improve teaching and learning*. Logan: Utah State University Press.

Bacon, N. (2013). Style in academic writing. In M. Duncan & S. Vanguri (Eds.), *The centrality of style*. Fort Collins, CO/Anderson, SC: The WAC Clearinghouse/Parlor Press.

Barnard, I. (2010). The ruse of clarity. *College Composition and Communication 61*(3), 434-451.

Berlin, J. A. (1987). *Rhetoric and reality: Writing instruction in American colleges, 1900-1985*. Carbondale: Southern Illinois University Press.

Berthoff, A. E. (1981). *The making of meaning*. Portsmouth, NH: Heinemann.

Butler, P. (2008). *Out of style: Reanimating stylistic study in composition and rhetoric*. Logan: Utah State University Press.

Connors, R. J. (2000). The erasure of the sentence. *College Composition and Communication 52*(1), 96-128.

Daniels, H. A. (1983). *Famous last words: The American language crisis reconsidered*. Carbondale: Southern Illinois University Press.

Duncan, M., & Vanguri, S., (Eds.) (2012). *The centrality of style*. Fort Collins, CO/Anderson, SC: The WAC Clearinghouse/Parlor Press.

Ellis, E. (2013). Toward a pedagogy of psychic distance. In M. Duncan & S. Vanguri (Eds.), *The centrality of style*. Fort Collins, CO/Anderson, SC: The WAC Clearinghouse/Parlor Press.

Farmer, F. (2005). On style and other unremarkable things. *Written Communication 22*(3), 339-47.

Fleckenstein, K. S. (2010). *Vision, rhetoric, and social action in the composition classroom.* Carbondale: Southern Illinois University Press.

Fodrey, C. (2013). Voice, transformed: The potentialities of style pedagogy in the teaching of creative nonfiction. In M. Duncan & S. Vanguri (Eds.), *The centrality of style.* Fort Collins, CO/Anderson, SC: The WAC Clearinghouse/Parlor Press.

Folk, M. (2013). Multimodal style and the evolution of digital writing pedagogy. In M. Duncan & S. Vanguri (Eds.), *The centrality of style.* Fort Collins, CO/Anderson, SC: The WAC Clearinghouse/Parlor Press.

Greer, R. (2013). Architectonics and style. In M. Duncan & S. Vanguri (Eds.), *The centrality of style.* Fort Collins, CO/Anderson, SC: The WAC Clearinghouse/Parlor Press.

Hillocks, G, Jr. (1995). *Teaching writing as reflective practice.* New York: Teachers College Press.

Holcomb, C., & Killingsworth. J. M. (2013). Teaching style as cultural performance. In M. Duncan & S. Vanguri (Eds.), *The centrality of style.* Fort Collins, CO/Anderson, SC: The WAC Clearinghouse/Parlor Press.

Howard, R. M. (2005). Contextualist stylistics: Breaking down the binaries in sentence-level pedagogy. In T. R. Johnson & T. Pace (Eds.), *Refiguring style: Possibilities for writing pedagogy* (pp. 42-56). Logan, UT: Utah State University Press.

Johnson, T. R., & Pace, T. (2005). *Refiguring prose style: Possibilities for writing pedagogy.* Logan, UT: Utah State University Press.

Lamos, S. (2008). Language, literacy, and the institutional dynamics of racism: Late 1960's writing instruction for "high-risk" african-american undergraduate students at one predominantly white university. *College Composition and Communication 60*(1), 46-81.

Lanham, R. (2006). The *economics of {attention}*. Chicago: University of Chicago Press.

Lawler, J M. (2003). Style stands still. *Style 37*(2), 220-37. Retrieved from http://www.umich.edu/~jlawler/style.pdf

Pope, R. (1995). *Textual intervention: Critical and creative strategies for literary studies.* London: Routledge, The INTERFACE Series.

Rhodes, K. (2010). You are what you sell: Branding the way to composition's better future. *WPA: Writing Program Administration 33*(3), 58-77.

Ronald, K. (2003). Style: The hidden agenda in composition classes or one reader's confession. In W. Bishop (Ed.), *The subject is writing: Essays by teachers and students* (3rd ed.) (pp. 195-209). Portsmouth, NH: Heinemann.

Roper, G L. (2007). *The writer's workshop: Imitating your way to better writing.* Wilmington, DE: ISI.

Sledd, J. (1991). Why the Wyoming Resolution had to be emasculated: A history and a quixotism. *JAC 11*(2), 269-81.
Williams. J M., & Colomb, G. G. (2010). *Style: Lessons in clarity and grace* (10th ed.). Boston: Longman-Pearson.
Yagoda, B. (2005). *The sound on the page*. New York: HarperResource.
Villanueva, V. (2011). Reflections on Style and the love of language. *College Composition and Communication 62*(4), 726-38.

JIM CORDER'S GENERATIVE ETHOS AS ALTERNATIVE TO TRADITIONAL ARGUMENT, OR STYLE'S REVIVIFICATION OF THE WRITER-READER RELATIONSHIP

Rosanne Carlo
The University of Arizona

Traditional argumentation, with its privileging of logos and its emphasis on reasoned judgments delivered with speed, clarity, and efficiency in order to persuade an audience, is valuable in some rhetorical situations. One situation in which traditional arguments are valued is academic writing. I want us to imagine, though, a scholarly approach that values the presence of persons in argument. Imagine practicing a rhetoric and writing that asks for time, for care, for listening and understanding, a rhetoric that has the potential to be applied to scholarly writing, but more broadly, to intimate rhetorical situations which rely on person-centered appeals for identification rather than persuasion. As Richard Young has argued, rhetoric scholars need to begin to investigate and theorize dyadic and other intimate rhetorical situations in order to create a new rhetoric of argumentation, one that "breathe[s] new life into the ancient concepts of *ethos* and *pathos* and ... position[s] them within an enriched conception of rhetoric, which, like its ancient counterpart, addresses the question of how one invents arguments under the constraints of actual situations" (1992, p. 118). Many scholars in rhetoric and composition are interested in how writers and speakers invite readers and listeners into their inventive universe, especially when readers or listeners hold an opposing viewpoint and can be considered antagonistic; how writers and speakers create and foster empathy; how writers and speakers respond to informal scenes of rhetoric (e.g., among family and friends); how writers and speakers expose inquiry to readers and listeners through provisional reasoning; how writers and speakers can frame of an argument and the strategies they can use to minimize the potential threat for readers and listeners; and how writers and speakers utilize narrative in rhetorical situations.

When we begin to emphasize and value the various functions of *ethos* and *pathos* in argumentation, we realize how essential a well-theorized canon of style becomes to scholars of rhetoric and composition. We cannot begin to answer inquiries into non-traditional argument without understanding the styles that speakers and writers enact in these rhetorical situations.

This essay explores the work of Jim Corder as issuing a call to the scholarly community to value the presence of persons in making arguments. This call foregrounds ethos as fundamental and asks practitioners of rhetoric to create and embody a generative ethos, one that attempts to build time and understanding into discourse as a way to reach out and embrace audiences. This call also asks us to return to theorizing the writer-reader relationship. This relationship is fraught with complication, especially by factors such as identification and its lack, but as scholars and audience members we can begin to seek the traces of the author in his or her work; one way to do so is through stylistic analysis. Because of his focus on theorizing ethos, Corder's work opens a space in the field for a renewing interest in the teaching and learning of stylistics. It is through this type of inquiry and analysis that one's very personhood is fore-grounded as meaningful and relevant. The canon of style is connected in concrete ways to the recognition of sentence-level concerns that are essential to understanding and creating a rhetoric that closes the distance between readers and writers in a process Corder terms "enfolding." The idea of enfolding audience is a beneficial form of idealism that rejects speed, clarity, and efficiency as antithetical to generative ethos.

Enfolding, in many ways, is a performative act. As Holcomb and Killingsworth discuss in their chapter, stylistic performance is "not only [a vehicle to] present a self" but also is "an orchestration with readers, subject matters, and texts" (2010, p. 92). The authors believe that these elements, features in the rhetorical situation, relate through three arenas of interaction: the textual, the social, and the cultural. Although the framing of my essay is not organized through these three arenas, the reader can see in my analysis how Jim Corder understands his choices in unfolding his argument (textual), how he relates to his readers through his words and structures (social), and how he signals to his audience, the academic community, both his membership in, and critique of, its traditional discourses (contextual).

When scholars refocus attention on the sentence and word choice (as Holcomb and Killingsworth ask their students to do), it provides another dimension to rhetorical analysis which revives the long-lost, often-neglected canon of rhetoric: Style. Stylistics is an analytical framework that heightens scholars' awareness of language and allows us to talk about a writer's ethos in more concrete rather than impressionistic ways. Knowledge of style allows the teacher-scholar and her or his students to see the writer's varieties of *choice* in prose, the intersections of content and form, and how invention and arrangement play out before us in compositions. Style, then, is one intersection between rhetoric and composition as the writer chooses the form through which to best communicate to an audience. Richard Young, Alton Becker, and Kevin Pike's *Rhetoric: Discovery and Change* supports this claim as they define rhetoric as "a creative process that includes all the choices a writer makes from his earliest tentative exploration of a problem … through choices in arrangement and strategy for a particular audience, to the final editing of the final draft" (1970, p. xii). Young, Becker, and Pike's discussions of writer and reader relationships provide a lens through which to view Jim Corder's theory of enfolding and also his stylistic choices in writing.

Young, Becker, and Pike and Corder were all trying to define and create a New Rhetoric: one that emphasized the importance of communication among people as being essential for social change. *Rhetoric: Discovery and Change* was not merely a transactional textbook for its writers asked readers to discover and collaborate in the creation of a rhetoric that held cooperation at its center and asked practitioners to reach out to "people whose beliefs are radically different from our own and with whom we must learn to live" (Young, Becker & Pike, 1970, p. 8). These scholars all understood that confrontations often manifest between the readers of texts and the authors of texts. Style, as Corder and other New Rhetoricians believed, is a method writers use to invite readers into their inventive universes. Young, Becker, and Pike devote five chapters specifically to the writer-reader relationship; most importantly, they encourage writers to minimize any sense of threat to a reader by acknowledging opposing views and addressing the reader "as if he were intelligent, curious, honest, sincere—in short, as if he possessed the same qualities that the writer attributes to himself" (1970, p. 208). They also emphasize that the writer has a responsibility to make their image of the world visible for the reader. Corder describes writing as a process of emergence that shows a love and willingness between the reader and writer to "*see* each other, *to know* each other, *to be present to* each other, to *embrace* each other" (1985, p. 23). Style becomes essential as it is the only way for the writer to develop an ethos to be "present" to the reader, to enfold a reader into his or her inventive universe. The real magic is that the words on the page leave traces of the author who wrote them.

In this chapter, I hope to demonstrate that Corder creates a discourse that enfolds its audience through his enactment of a personal, performative style. I will explore Corder's notion of the author leaving "tracks" for readers in texts, a concept that he articulates in "Notes on a Rhetoric of Regret." Corder speaks to the writer's presence and permanence as he acknowledges that his thoughts will be referenced in future style scholarship. He admits "that if I exist, I exist over yonder, not in my own endeavors, but in other people's perceptions of my endeavors" (1995, p. 97). Although he sometimes expresses concern for the potential for his work and himself to be misread by others, Corder articulates that he is leaving his traces for future scholars to find, if we only have the patience to look hard enough.

In this sense, I agree with Wendy Bishop when she says that the end of Corder's writing is "personification" to create "a text with a real body" concluding that, "Jim Corder's essays are performative" (2003, p. 95). Corder is fully aware of his performance for readers, painfully and deliberately aware that every word he writes is in the spirit of cultivating a voice. As a speaker, he is accessible and inviting. In this same way, I am writing this chapter with an invitational tone, using the intimate pronouns "I," "you," "we," and "us" throughout. It is not my intention to interpellate and coerce you into my argument. Rather, I mean to allow for moments of identification between reader and writer, you and me; in this way, I mean to practice the style of enfolding that Corder envisioned and practiced. Corder's performative ethos, I argue, is an alternative epistemology to traditional argument that we can explore in writing; it is a way of knowing that is generative as he enfolds his audience in a discourse of his reflections.

To be effective rhetorical scholars, I believe, we must interact with the author's mind at work through a stylistic analysis of the body of the text, an analytical method I will demonstrate later in this chapter. First, though, a discussion of Corderian rhetoric is in order, one that attempts to consider his oeuvre as teaching us to see an alternative to traditional argumentation. Corder's theory of enfolding is essential in creating an alternative way to write discourse as he asks us to be cognizant of a reader of our texts; to create a space for a reader to enter a text; to create moments of identification with that reader; to hold that reader's perspective wholly in mind as we write. Corder attempts to accomplish the tasks of enfolding (no small order) through his stylistic techniques, specifically through his use of repetition, enumeration, and narrative. I then take a closer look at Corder's text "Notes on a Rhetoric of Regret;" this final section was written to both show the elements of a stylistic analysis and to further demonstrate my argument that Corder's performative style is a means through which he conveys his theory of enfolding. It is here that we see Corder's work as an answer to Young, Becker, and Pike's call for a writer who reveals his or her process of inquiry in order to create the *conditions* for cooperation and social change; Corder sees this exposure of his process of inquiry as paramount to his theory of enfolding.

WHEN THE STARS ARE RIGHT: THE THEORY OF ENFOLDING THROUGH GENERATIVE ETHOS

Jim Corder confesses a desire of displacement from traditional styles and structures of argument. In his book chapter, "Tribes and Displaced Persons: Some Observations on Collaboration," he lays bare his vision for a "scholarly sort of work but to write in a personal sort of way" that engenders a hope that his writing style would "perhaps even help to stretch out the possibilities of prose" (1993, p. 281). His lyrical repetition of "I want to be displaced" in one passage is a refrain that reinforces his conviction in a "fanatic eclecticism," a belief that through writing styles that allow for complexity and choice rather than rigidity and credo we can create voices that invite our audiences into our discourses (1993, p. 278). Many of us already practice forms of writing beyond traditional styles of argumentation, many of us want to be able to write beyond traditional styles of argumentation, some have yet to be convinced. I am of the opinion that many aims for writing are necessary—we need scholarly work that is referential and makes traditional arguments but we could also benefit from work that compliments that paradigm. And by extension, Corder's work, and his theory of enfolding in particular, reminds us that as scholars we have the opportunity to *invent* ourselves through our writing.

In an effort to legitimize and rapidly professionalize the discipline of rhetoric and composition, some scholars recall and bemoan the loss of persuasive qualities in our writing that were hastily dropped, particularly moves in writing that establish personal ethos. This decision can be seen as ironic for a discipline almost entirely based on studying the available means of persuasion (Warnock, 2003, p. 204). Corder returns us to our disciplinary roots as he writes with the intention of expanding Aristotelian concepts of ethos. Corder, like Aristotle, understood that the character of the speaker is just as important as the content of the speech:

> It is not true, as some writers assume in their treatises on rhetoric, that the personal goodness revealed by the speaker contributes nothing to his power of persuasion; on the contrary, his character may almost be called the most effective means of persuasion he possesses. (Aristotle, trans. 1926, Book 2)

Corder's focus on ethos stems from his desire to understand it as the central rhetorical appeal; he also understands ethos as Aristotle does in the sense of establishing character to induce belief through "good sense, good moral character, and goodwill" (Trans. 1926, Book 2). Corder's writing; however, is moving beyond persuasion to identification with his readers, as he searches to create a real connection that shows an openness to change one's perspective after listening to another. Hunting for ethos, both enacted through his theorizing of the term and also through his reflections of his own presence in the text as a writer, appears to be an obsessive quest for him. I think it's what draws me and others to his writings. His writing is like the speech of the prophet, Amos. It is as Corder wrote: "To own and guarantee one's words, I take it, means to be fastidiously and meticulously aware of their background, keenly thoughtful of your consequence and future; it entails giving one's words the backing of such a history of search and thinking as will stand scrutiny" (1972, p.8). His writings mirror his own philosophy of rhetoric, and this aim is to present himself as a writer who is aware of his stylistic choices in the process of creating meaning for audiences.

The desire to represent yourself for a reader is a part of the process of enfolding, a concept in rhetoric that Corder so wanted to encourage us to begin theorizing and performing; this concept is one that is only possible through a knowledge and awareness of stylistic choices. Corder's representation of self, though, is not one that assumes that a whole self can possibly be communicated through text; no matter how conscious an author is in his style, she must still slog through the imperfect medium of language. Instead, Corder shows his audience a self that is not fixed or whole; he is as an author that unfolds his personality. Unfolding is the means through which a writer can begin to enfold an audience, and style gives the author agency to begin a process of unfolding. As readers of Corder's work, for example, we learn something new about his personal life and gain a clearer understanding of his theories of rhetoric in each piece. The ideal ethos for Corder is a person who "lives in a space large enough to house contradictions" 1978, p. 79). The fragmentary self is not easy to grasp nor is it ideal. I do not know Corder the man, but Corder as an author is constructing an ethos for me as a reader. I think Tilly Warnock defines Corder's ethos succinctly and insightfully when she writes: "Through his personal, cultural, creative, critical, and ideological discourse, Corder teaches us to live with the messiness, uncertainties, and ambiguities of life [...] without denying them to make sound decisions about our *choices* of language" (2003, p. 205, my emphasis). Jim Corder is taking a risk through his presentation of self that is not "ideal," and he opens a space in scholarship where this way of being is validated and, in fact, it can be argued that it is closer to the reality of our lives.

The written act of unfolding a perspective, and by this I also mean exposing our process of inquiry for readers, through performative ethos is the *raison d'être* for Corderian rhetoric; he is risking himself before us because he believes so strongly in the possibility of one mind embracing another, even if this requires a person to hold two contradictory ideas at once, equally valuing both. There is vulnerability in this subjectivity, a vulnerability which is not appropriate to expose in all rhetorical situations,[1] but one that can be effective in terms of speaking across to an audience member who is relatively equal in terms of power dynamics to a writer. Corderian rhetoric is idealistic in this sense as it engenders a feeling of hopefulness that our words can "reach and stretch for a new Jerusalem, while we reach and stretch to make a *new* language, a language that will let us define ourselves, speak ourselves fully into existence and into relation with the other" (Corder, 1977, p. 482). Our rhetoric can lead us to identification with the other and toward creating better interpersonal relationships, and perhaps even to a better social reality. We can see Corder's construction of an ethos that houses contradictions as allowing for a collaborative process between his readers which he calls enfolding.

Enfolding a reader requires that the writer take a risk by unfolding his values and narrative to others and a willingness to begin a dialogue, even if the writer experiences resistance from her audience. It is part of a recognition that we are standing in a narrative, in a rhetoric, and that we are trying to speak out across an ideological divide to another. In perhaps his most well-known article, "Argument as Emergence, Rhetoric as Love," Corder defines enfolding when he writes: "Argument is emergence toward the other. That requires a readiness to testify to an identity that is always emerging, a willingness to dramatize one's narrative in progress before the other; it calls for an untiring stretch toward the other, a reach toward *enfolding* the other" (1985, p. 183, emphasis added). Emergence, as Corder describes, is a state of becoming; in the case of writing, he means to aim for the creation of an ethos that is developing on the page for a reader. A presentation of self as an emerging identity, in Corder's view, minimizes the potential threat that a confident, dogmatic ethos might impose on a reader. Enfolding is about vulnerability of self, a demonstration of mutual respect for the other, a coming together that is not coercive, but welcoming. One point that can be missed in "Argument as Emergence, Rhetoric is Love" is the critique that Corder is developing in response to practitioners in the field of Rhetoric and Composition who view and teach argument as a clinical, "neat" process with linear steps. Corder is challenging that anaesthetized view of argument because it often does not account for potential harm. This sentiment appears in his earlier works where we see him working toward his seminal essay. In both "Varieties of Ethical Argument" and "From Rhetoric to Grace" he includes the same passage:

> it is possible for any of us—if the stars are right and we work to make ourselves human—to enfold another whose his-

> tory we have not shared. In this act of enfolding, the speaker becomes through speech; the speaker's identity is always to be saved, to emerge as an ethos to the other, whose identity is also to be cherished. Then they may speak, each holding the other wholly in mind. (1978, p. 98; 1984, p. 26)

This is a call for making inquiry visible to a reader, of exposing the process through which one thinks and writes. This quote also asks us to envision what it might look like to emerge as an ethos, an idea that I will later discuss in terms of stylistically analyzing Corder's writing choices as a means to emerge to readers and enfold them in his history. Some of Corder's first-time readers may find his repetition infuriating, his "hedges" on offering an opinion or argument exhausting, his conflicting, schizophrenic identity to be maddening, and his personal narratives to be leading us down a path in the middle of the night without street signs. But really, these stylistic moves are intentional; they are connected to exposing his process of inquiry. Corder's stylistic techniques of repetition, enumeration, and narrative story-telling, I argue, try to accomplish this visible inquiry for readers.

Stylistic choices help an author speak and write themselves into existence; for example, Corder's use of repetition is connected to his development of ethos and presence for audiences. He writes, "I have wanted to leave tracks so that another might know where I imagine I am; for that reason, transitional passages and sections may be heavy-handed and repetitive" (1995, p. 94). Corder's repetition (sometimes of sentences, whole paragraphs and pages from one text to another), though irritating to some of his readers, is a part of his style and essential to his creation of ethos. Although Jim Corder says, "I don't expect to have too many ideas; I hold on to those I have, and repeat them" to display humility, he is fully aware that the repetition is connected to his thoroughness as writer (1993, p. 278). He wants his repetition to mirror the thorough ethos that he so admires in the prophet, Amos. He desires to make an impression on his readers, and to speak in a language that encourages understanding.

The stylistic choice of repetition can be performative; in the case of Corder's laments, he repeats lines about vanishing identities and memories in almost all his major works in order to emphasize this motif's importance. I sense that Corder is keenly aware of society rapidly changing around him, evidenced by his often nostalgic love for things past, such as the fountain pen and the typewriter. He felt that "the volume [of language] crowds our living space and our time, sometimes generating frenetic speed, sometimes a paralysis" (1978, p. 93). This paradox of speed and stasis often hinders our ability to communicate with each other, and certainly leaves little time for reflection.

Corder's awareness of the problem of time, or lack thereof, offers one way in which he can see a critique of his own theory of enfolding. He recognizes the failures that are often experienced in our communication with others. He seems to be asking in his works: What if we can't find love for another? What if all we have is really a self-love, a love that we think we feel for another but is merely a projection of ourselves onto the other? The biggest failure of communication is our inability to really hear each other, he believes. Again, this is illustrated by his repetition of the passage: "we may hear ourselves, not another; the other's words may act only as a trigger to release our own, unlocking not the other's meaning, but one we already possessed. When this happens, we are bound in space, caught tightly in our own province" (1978, p. 94; 1982, p. 134). When we do not listen to another's words, we are not able to reflect on what that person has said to us. We are not enfolding when we do not hear the other; instead, enfolding asks us to create situations in which people consciously, willingly, and trustingly allow themselves to be enfolded. This requires us to both talk across and out to another in explaining ourselves and listening to the other when they talk. In writing, since we cannot listen to our readers, we try to imagine their perspectives and to write with them in mind. As Corder says, "we have the habit of diminishing each other's words" (1978, p. 63). We not only diminish, but we ignore and talk over the other. Perhaps Corder feels the need to repeat himself because he understands our contemporary issues with listening and reflection in a world that often paralyzes us by its rapid speeds.

Another way in which writers can create ethos through their stylistic choices is through the use of enumeration in writing; in Corder's case, he uses enumeration to demonstrate his principles of enfolding. "From Rhetoric to Grace," "Asking for a Text and Trying to Learn It," and "What I Learned in School" all contain lessons that he wishes to impart to us about what he has learned as a teacher-scholar. These lessons, though, are often only parts of a whole, as he confesses to us that "there are yet other propositions I have not found" (1999, p. 57). By making his points on rhetoric tangible to readers, he offers "fragments" of truths that we can hold and reflect on about the nature of learning and life. Again, Corder argues that he cannot give us a whole, cohesive body of knowledge because such a product is an impossible ideal. He believes that "[l]anguage itself is synecdoche: we're always naming parts of things because we cannot at any given moment name the whole" (1984, p. 18). This microcosmic example of the synecdoche of language leads us to think about synecdoche in our disciplinary knowledge, and more broadly, in our self-identities. Corder is giving us parts of himself, leaving tracks and traces on the page that we need to piece together as readers. The whole, idealized body of knowledge and the whole, idealized "authentic" Jim Corder do not exist. He writes, "I have published a little about rhetoric and hope to publish more, but the rhetorics of the world swirl around me, do not come together, and I am lost. I can't find my own inventive world; it is in parts, and some escape me" (1986, p. 36). Again, Corder repeats the last line in this passage later in the paper (1986, p. 37) for emphasis. Feelings of displacement, fragmentation, loss, and lonesomeness pervade Corder's works; we can see these themes as Corder expressing his process of coming to terms and accepting that the world is synecdochic.

The re-telling of narratives also makes a writer's ethos emerge toward readers; Corder creates his narrative universe through his story-telling (the inclusions of his idiosyncratic rituals, his failed memories, his attempts to describe his relatives and the past, his humility and hedges, and his Texan sensibility). There is an epistemology of self as text happening in Corder's writing as he interrogates his memory and first lessons learned. He often explains his use of the personal as the only epistemology truly available to him: "Besides, the self is the only center I have, and I think I must use the best evidence available to me, my own experience, however I manage to misinterpret it" (1989, p. 211). There is a real (dare I say) hunger behind these statements to search through the evidence of experience and yet to be able to admit that the construction of self through memory is always a "slippery" undertaking with room for misinterpretation. Again, he often repeats the sentiment that as he writes his memories they are vanishing from him and he is also vanishing in the process: "Souls disappear. I disappear. Not all at once: we are whittled away. I diminish before my own eyes" (1995, p. 97). This lack of closure and wholeness can certainly be frustrating to a reader who is seeking an ideal self in the writings of Corder. And yet, Corder as a character is endearing, he fascinates us; he is addressing and enfolding us as readers. We learn from him and about him in the traces and the tracks, as he "manifests his own humanness" in the hope of showing us a way (1982, p. 129).

Exposure to the other through enfolding, even if this involves emerging as an ethos in texts, is a complex and ambiguous phenomena: it is loaded with difficulties. Enfolding is problematic in the sense that when we risk ourselves to emerge toward another person, as writers or readers, we open ourselves to the possibility of change. Change can be transformative and wonderful for some, but change can also be painful, hard, and for some people, unwanted. We can feel lost, unsure of our own narrative. Young, Becker, and Pike also comment on this aspect of change when they write that a writer and reader who seriously wish to practice Rogerian rhetoric, or for our case a rhetoric that values this idea of enfolding one narrative with another, the prerequisite is a willingness to change. The degree to which change affects us is subjective as our authors acknowledge: "Other changes, however, may be strongly resisted, for they affect values that we regard as essential to our identity, even to our survival. Values are hierarchically structured; some are more significant, more eminent, than others" (1970, p. 219). When two people, two families, two countries are in a conflict that spans over years for one reason or another (sometimes we often forget why we are in conflict), it may be hard to reconcile these differences, it may be too painful to approach the other, to try to understand the other. Reconciliation, in some cases, cannot be achieved for one reason or another; contrary to Corder's description of enfolding, sometimes the stars are not right and being human to each other is too complicated.

My experience reading Corder has, at times, been one of discomfort and sadness, especially reading his book, *Yonder: Life on the Far Side of Change*.[2] *Yonder* is a hybrid piece of writing, part autobiographical, part literary, and part scholarly, it is in this piece that Corder tries to write an account of what great change does to our psyche. Change, for Corder, is a battlefield that can herald great joy but also has the potential to harm. He writes, "Change is inevitable and necessary to life, but it also entails a continuous destruction and loss of worlds, great and small, a combat of old habit with new need. Identity is always about to vanish as old worlds go and new worlds come" (1992, p. 23). Corder is tackling both the changes that have happened in his personal life: a divorce, a conflict with his daughter, addiction, cancer, and public life in the twentieth century: the "dying" of Western culture, the Holocaust, the women's movement, technological advances, and so forth. This book is very difficult for me to read; it is difficult to see a mind suffering on the page; it is difficult to hear about how he lost time and memories in treatment; it is difficult to hear him give witness to the diminishing relationship between his children and his first wife. Sometimes, disclosure can be painful for a writer and a reader.

Yet, Corder's concept of enfolding is one that builds new possibilities. Its more positive facet constructs a rhetorical theory that allows scholars to practice critical reflection of self in their works, and it teaches us to reach out, enfold, and love others through our writing. We can read Corder as radical for espousing a theory of love in relation to argumentation. These writings are about compassion and reaching out to the other through encouraging an exposure to the narrative/rhetoric/argument that people compose (albeit imperfectly) through life experiences. Transparency is important to Corder, and ethos is one vehicle that we have in written expression by which we can represent ourselves (albeit imperfectly) to the other. Corder defines rhetoric as a process of love-making: "I'll still insist that argument—that rhetoric itself—must begin, proceed, and end in love" (1985, p. 185). An epistemology of inventing the self through language, risking the self through language, hearing and enfolding another through language, and perhaps even loving through language is a hopeful, ideal endeavor. We can also see this epistemology as one that offers us an alternative to traditional argumentation.

In fact, this cycle of invention and structure through language invites us to be more reflective about our ways of being and knowing, to be more subjective. An epistemology such as Corder's allows us to talk about the things we value and how we came to value them through a personal ethos in writing. Corder explains, "Ethical argument appears to be contingent upon a presence emerging in discourse, the real voice of a genuine personality that becomes understandable to us as a style, a characteristic way of moving through and among experiences" (1972, p. 7). One way Corder's theory of emergence through discourse can be discovered and explained is through a close, stylistic analysis of his work.

HUNTING PROFESSOR FOG: A STYLISTIC ANALYSIS OF "NOTES ON A RHETORIC OF REGRET"

We can be critical of Corder's writing in part because his voice is often contradictory, self-effacing, and thus his work has the potential to be read as a confession of epistemological and moral failure (Yoos, 2003, p. 123). Yoos and other readers make excellent points about Corder's writing and style. At the same time, Corder's work may also be read as an example of Young, Becker, and Pike's "Provisional writing" which is writing that "focuses on the process of inquiry itself and acknowledges the tentative nature of conclusions," a style that minimizes the threat to the reader and allows her to both understand and critique Corder's prose (1970, p. 207).

In Corder's "Notes on a Rhetoric of Regret," I find that he is working towards developing a theory for writing, one that emphasizes the affective experiences of everyday lives and celebrates personal recollections of "domestic particulars," uniting writers and readers (1995, p. 104). Corder's writing style in this piece, more importantly, is an experiment or application of his theory of enfolding. In this same vein, it is also significant to note that his article captures a spirit of inquiry, and willingness to explore personal experience that Young, Becker, and Pike so valued in *Rhetoric: Discovery and Change*. They argue that "[t]o become an effective inquirer, it is essential that you develop sensitivity and receptivity to problematic situations.... It is the best student who sees the limitations of human understanding and the need for inquiry in every aspect of human affairs" (1970, p. 91). In this piece, Corder inquires into the definition of personal writing, and explores whether or not a writer really can present his narrative to readers, more accurately, what it would look like to emerge as an ethos to readers. Corder, I think, is unsure what this means as he finds clashing viewpoints on the nature of personal writing and rhetoric. Because of this acknowledgement of a problematic situation, "Notes on a Rhetoric of Regret" has a feeling of contradiction in the opening as he asks questions about the rhetoric in which he inhabits and offers no definitive answers. Corder asks the reader: "Is there a luechocholic style?" and responds, "I expect that style can only by found by others, not declared" (1995, p. 94) and again asks, "Is there an audience for a rhetoric of regret?" surmising, "I don't know" (1995, p. 95). The uncertainty of his voice can lead the reader to think that he is tentative about his ideas, even when he describes the claiming of a self as a "chancy ground," (1995, p. 97) an interesting choice of colloquial diction for an academic essay. Yet, these moves of "tentativeness" can be seen not as a fault in argument, but as a means of identification with audiences—a presentation of ideas that is not dogmatic, but rather inviting; in other words, these are all stylistic gestures that comprise Corder's application of his theory of enfolding.

Although this chapter does not reproduce the full text of Corder's article, I encourage you to read this essay in its entirety. Indeed, there were many pieces of Corder's I could have chosen for this analysis; this is not, in fact, one of his well-known or oft-quoted works like "Argument as Emergence, Rhetoric as Love," for example. But this article has a different quality than the others in his oeuvre; I can only venture to explain this difference through a series of suppositions. Perhaps it is his desperate need to recover what might (and will) vanish. Perhaps it is his defense of personal writing that he categorized as self-serving and sinful. Perhaps it is his admission of the futility of capturing people with words. Perhaps it is his lovingly detailed descriptions of the lives of those that were long gone: his grandmother, his mother, and his father. Perhaps it is because, as a reader, I knew that he wrote this article in 1995 and he would die of cancer three years later. For all these reasons, the piece elicited a strong emotional response in me. And, perhaps, this was because Corder envisioned this piece to be one where he specifically applied his theory of enfolding. I begin my stylistic analysis, in section V, where I believe that Corder recognizes how readers, like myself, may appropriate his words for their own uses, that this appropriation was "all right: troping, I'm troped" (1985, p. 102). As a scholar sensitive to the potential for being misread in conversations and writing, Corder in his own way is telling me it is okay to hold his prose under the microscope.

Corder begins section V with a story of his mother who often represents, for him, the self-effacing attitude encouraged by the Southern Christian tradition. The assertion of the personal is identified as a sin; for example, when he asks his mother what color his hair is, Mrs. Corder tells her son it is the color of feces. He tells his audience, "It was her way of reminding me that I shouldn't be occupied with my own existence" (1985, p. 102). We know that Corder sees section V of the essay as a blasphemous assertion as he opens contradicting a preacher that his mother is with the Lord, the first simple sentences appear here puncturing the audience with self-assertion: "That may be. I think she dwells in my memory" (1985, p. 102). The argument that memory and the re-telling of experience becomes a central theme for Corder, a way of self preservation and survival in a world where we are constantly in the throes of change.

The complex sentence that follows to end this paragraph is repeated at the end of other paragraphs in variation: "If I don't remember her, and try to get her down right, she will vanish" (1985, p. 102); and when he writes of his father, "If I don't remember him, and try to get him down right, he will vanish" (1985, p. 102); and when he writes about various towns in West Texas, "If I don't remember them all, try to get them down right, they will vanish" (1985, p. 102); and when he writes of his grandmother, "If I don't remember her, and try to get her down right, she will vanish" (1985, p. 103). This repetition draws the reader to the urgency of his writing project as he begins these complex sentences with a dependent "If" clause, and completes them with an affirmative independent clause of certain extinction unless he is able to avoid their fate by completing the dependent clause of "get[ting] them down right." The brevity of these clauses also makes the reader more aware of the need to speak his relatives into existence and the stake that this section holds to his overall argument on personal writing.

Corder's real metaphor for invention and writing begins with the story about his grandmother's quilt-making which he feels scholars have misinterpreted—this stance is similar to the one he adopts toward theories of deconstruction as they view the self in writing as a fiction. A strong periodic sentence positions the reader for his critique of both sets of scholars, art historians and English: "They argue that the image of the poor needlewoman painstakingly constructing quilts out of scraps left over from important projects and stumbling upon a pleasing visual effect is a fiction" (1985, p. 103). Corder will continue to use his grandmother's quilt-making as a metaphor for the writing process as writers are often piecing together scraps of their life's experiences to form a beautiful whole.

In the following paragraphs Corder's sentences are deliberate and planned but they read in a way that seems natural and spontaneous, as if he is really speaking to us. Firstly, Corder uses an elaborated complex sentence as a stylistic device to speed the rhythm of his grandmother's life so that we will remember the image of her more: "She lived on another twenty years, lost in a world that no longer made much sense to her, entirely dependent on her children, with whom she lived, moving from one family to another every six months or so" (1985, p. 103). The next sentence is its own paragraph and slows the reader down through the repetition of the word quilt: "But she made quilts, stunning quilts" (1985, p. 103). And the next paragraph is also one sentence in which Corder uses the stylistic device of anaphora and an elaborated complex sentence as he strings together clauses repeating the phrase "to be sure that." Here he emphasizes that although these scholars believe they are empirically correct, they had no hand in the artwork of his grandmother: "She did so without the aid of authors who want to be sure that the world gets corrected, to be sure that we know how artistic artists of the quilt were, to be sure that we define the quiltmaker's art in their way" (1985, p. 103). He contextualizes these scholars as antagonistic interlocutors who only want to define his grandmother's art (literally) and personal writing (metaphorically) in one way—theirs. Yet, Corder wants to offer us an alternative to the dictates of scholarly thought on personal writing and he does so in the next paragraph through his honest, detailed, and loving description of his grandmother's quilt-making process.

The following paragraph on his grandmother is perhaps one of the most poignant in "Notes on a Rhetoric of Regret." Here he builds the prose from simple sentences to a sentence that uses the stylistic technique of asyndeton as he describes his grandmother: "She was mostly silent, withdrawn into herself, often ill-tempered" (1985, p. 103). He balances this rhythm with sentences that slow the reader down through the use of conjunctions, or polysyndeton: "She salvaged scraps of all colors and shapes and sizes," and "Then one day she'd get out her bundles of scraps and feel of them and look at them" (1985, p. 103). These sentences stylistically mirror his grandmother's process; the reader can almost feel her biding her time and rifling through the scraps and searching for the quilt that would emerge. And then, his grandmother has that moment where invention cycles into structure and she begins to work the scraps into a larger idea—a beautiful quilt. Moreover, in Corder's extended metaphor on personal writing, we can think of her work as drafting toward a beautiful composition. In fact, Corder stylistically brings us through her creative process with more elaborated complex clauses: "Then after a while, she'd start cutting, though she had no pattern. After a while, she'd start sewing. And then there would be a quilt of intricate design, beautifully rendered, lovely to see" (1985, p. 103). After that, we get three simple sentences that are arresting: "Without design, she made design. Without art, she made art. Her children are all dead" (1985, p. 103). I believe the repetition of sentence structure (from negative to positive) and words ("Without," "design," and "art") in the first two sentences adds to their affective quality (especially since they follow so many complex sentences!). We are compelled to stop and see the quilt—the completed composition—as if Corder is holding it up to the reader as a model of his theory of personal writing.

If the subtextual metaphor was not enough for some readers, in the following paragraph, Corder lays bare his opinions on personal writing. He uses a complex-compound sentence to admit that although he is aware of the then "new" and various theories of post-structuralism, just as he is aware of the scholarship on quilt-making; yet, he wants to continue to think of both his grandmother and his writing in his own way. He writes, "I know that there are other ways of thinking about personal writing and the recollection and rendition of ourselves [another example of polysyndeton here as well], and I try to honor these other views, but I'll go on thinking in this way as well" (1985, p. 103). Here, we see Corder's ethos as one that houses two thoughts on personal writing: a contradiction, but this also reveals an acknowledgement of other perspectives. Perhaps this confession can be seen as an admission that Corder was set in his ways of thinking and unable to see another perspective. But, his inclusion of the qualifier "as well" at the end of this sentence shows how he is indeed holding all these perspectives in his mind at once. In this paragraph we also experience a tone shift from first to second person when he begins to ask rhetorical questions: "Who else will tell what you remember and try to make it real but you?" (1985, p. 103). I believe these choices were made as a way to identify with the audience, to turn the essay from his familial recollections to a conversation with the reader; indeed, this is a move of enfolding his reader into his discourse.

As readers, I think we can identify Corder's position as one that is born of much reflection, and as such, we are likely to listen to his voice that speaks from experience, even if that voice is one of a maverick. In fact, he has built so much credibility in his argument thus far that his "radical individualism" is not necessarily a threatening project for us as readers. Corder is not afraid of his opinion, embracing his own heresy as he flippantly absolves himself of the sin of individualism when he utters: "I was planning to go to Hell anyway" (1985, p. 104). Yet, the note of regret creeps into his discourse just after such a brazen declaration, "I know that in trying to hold things, I too will vanish. I had hoped to be real, but I am only a vacancy in the air" (1985, p. 104). These positive-negative complex sentence constructions can be seen as undermining the previous comment about hell-fire; yet, it is not so much a subversion of the original sentiment but a way of housing contradictory feelings in one speaker, in one composition. The reader is left with a feeling of sadness as our author's hopes are not realized.

But, just as Corder has taken away any hope, he has to work to build the audience's morale to carry us to the end of the piece; the truth is, he has not yet "vanished" from the page. The following paragraphs turn into vignettes of daughters and fathers that he sees on his weekend visits to the public library.

Both these paragraphs are very descriptive as they contain a majority of complex and compound-complex sentences. Yet, he uses simple sentences to close these paragraphs such as, "She had made it" (1985, p. 104) when the girl climbs the small hill. And when he reflects on these experiences he writes a one sentence paragraph, "Not bad for early on a Saturday evening" (1985, p. 104). We get the distinct feeling from Corder that he wants to value these stories as significant, that his experience of viewing these parent-child relationships is something to be valued in writing. He implores his readers that "[we] ought to look at them. They ought to go on their way. The domestic particulars of their lives ought to be examined" (1985, p. 104). The repetition of "ought" and the string of simple sentences force the reader to slow down. His words, like a ritual on a Saturday morning, create a feeling of comfort and care—the complete opposite of hopelessness. The simple sentences that end the stories, too, offer a sort of satisfaction for the reader; they convey the message that the affective experiences of our lives are precious.

And then, Corder wants to set us right as readers; he wants to complicate our notions of authorship. He writes: "We won't, however, trap them in their words, and I won't be caught, either" (1985, p. 104). Just when we think we "know" Corder in these passages, he again wants to vanish from the page; he insists that no matter how much we analyze his words, he will never be "caught."

Corder is preparing for the conclusion; it is here where he feels he needs to reiterate his vision for the future of personal writing. Corder asserts his argument through a compound-complex periodic sentence that also has a three-part serial comma and a negative-positive construction. He writes, "The de-centering project of our time that will find us re-located after a curious, glorious, disastrous five-hundred-year journey at the center of things might lead to a new collective in which we are lost, but it needn't" (1985, p. 105). Corder establishes a tone for the reader that piques our curiosity as we wait to hear his alternative world for personal writing. Again, Corder shows us what the writing of the future will not be like: "The epic of our time, the drama, the story, the song, will not, I hope, tell of war and of the hero's triumph with the spear or gun; and surely it's unlikely that it will begin with fallen angels" (1985, p. 105). In a way, Corder is tentative about his conclusions at the beginning of the sentence entering the caveat of "I hope" but he seems more confident in the second half of the semi-colon with the qualifier "surely." Milton's fallen angels, those who are exiled or banished from heaven, could relate to his earlier references of hell and blasphemy. Corder's rebellion against the gods of academia perhaps is an unforgivable sin, and I think in a way, he understood that the revolution for personal writing and non-traditional argumentation may not be fully realized in his own work or readily accepted by academia in his time—perhaps this realization is one note on a rhetoric of regret for Corder. He reiterates his statements on the essential project of recording the present, of bearing witness to the everyday. Again, he uses polysyndeton: "We sing or tell or show or chant in the languages of the echoing past, shaped and transformed now to our uses in the forms that we can make or learn to make" (1985, p. 105). The article before us is Corder's attempt to expose the memories and the languages of his "echoing past," this dramatization before the reader is Corder's way of emerging to us in his discourse, of showing us the ways in which we can begin to view, understand, and perform the genre of personal writing. By including us in his statement, Corder reminds readers that his project extends beyond him and his thoughts on rhetoric—it is a project of inclusiveness, a project of enfolding.

Corder chooses to end the last four sentences with anaphora as he repeats "It will tell" at the beginning of each sentence. The stylistic effect is one of prophesy as he leads us to his culminating idea on writing and rhetoric. Yet, his last sentence certainly reads as a final confession as he writes: "And it will tell how, at last and after all, we came to vanish" (1985, p. 105). This prophesy leaves us with an eerie feeling as he repeats his earlier motifs of his relatives vanishing, only now he posits the idea in relation to all of us (1985, p. 105). Corder, too, has vanished but these notes remain. They are one side of the conversation Corder invites us into through his personal, performative style. He asks us to see his process of inquiry; to see how he collected scraps to create a quilt, sentences to create a whole, canons to create a rhetoric of regret.

SOME CONCLUDING THOUGHTS ON INVENTIVE UNIVERSES

Academic writing, both our own scholarship and the work we ask of students, can have many ends. One of them, as displayed in the life works of Jim Corder, is to enfold the reader into our discourses. This end is only accomplished when we work in our writing to expose the rhetoric on which we stand, where we stood, and where we hope to stand. Corder encouraged our discourse community to poke and prod at traditional writing styles because "when we set out to talk or to write about anything—about rhetoric, about writing, about anything—we are already inside a rhetoric and in fairness, we ought to show that rhetoric, even if it is sometimes as hard as learning to see and to show the back sides of our own eyeballs" (2003, p. 37). The process of enfolding is one in which we make a disciplinary rhetoric that is personal, visible, and a work in progress through writing that invites the audience to follow and collaborate in our meaning-making.

Unfortunately, I do not know Jim Corder. However, I think we have been able to speak to each other across texts largely because of his generative ethos. His voice that we as readers hear as we read; his words that translate so well into a dialogue, a commodious conversation.[3] "Generative language," Corder writes, "seeks to shove back the restraints of closure, to make in language a commodious universe, to stretch words out beyond our private universes. Extension in time and space seems to be one effort that makes this possible" (1978, pp. 94-5). Style is the means through which a writer can create this commodious universe. For a brief moment, Corder and I inhabit the same universe, enfolding toward the other, trying to work out the ideas of what it means to practice and to write in a style that creates a rhetoric of spaciousness: a place where writers and readers can think and live together.

NOTES

1. See Lassner, Phyllis. "Feminist Responses to Rogerian Argument." *Rhetoric Review* 8(2), 220-32. She provides a valid critique of a rhetoric that exposes vulnerability in the case of women speaking out against patriarchal oppression. Rogerian rhetoric, and it revised form Corderian rhetoric, would perhaps not suit a speaker or writer in a position where a power differential between audience and writer is wide as this may create a larger potential for manipulation on behalf of the dominant speaker or group. I am sure there are many other examples of critique beyond the one that Lassner forwards, and it is important to be aware of these critiques in understanding the limitations of this theory of rhetoric in action.

2. When George Yoos critiques Corder in his article, "Finding Jim's Voice: A Problem in Ethos and Personal Identity," I believe he is really concerned with the ways in which the process of enfolding can sometimes be problematic for audiences. Yoos only cites Corder's *Yonder* as evidence for his claims, asserting that Corder's style and ethos are ineffective ways of knowing. He writes, "To question one's own personal identity, to fail to find it, to lament not having it, to me is an epistemic failure of sorts. And it is also a kind of moral failure" (2003, p. 123). Yoos' fault-finding with Corder may be a result of the book's confessional qualities that draw the reader into a discourse that can elicit emotions of sadness and despair.

3. See Theresa Enos's "Voice as Echo of Delivery, Ethos as Transforming Process" for a discussion of ethos in relation to the rhetorical concept of delivery. She claims that ethos is dialogic in nature as it allows for role-playing and audience identification with the speaker; its dialogic qualities also wed it to delivery (1994, p. 188). Enos wishes to show through case study a modern-day transformative ethos: one that relies on stylistic technique to relate to their audience. She uses the writing of Jim Corder to discuss how a writer can achieve identification without sacrificing conviction through voice

(1994, p. 194), and she claims that Corder has a dialogic voice that, "is talking to us, an audience that he believes is committed to the speaker / writer's values, to his logos and pathos" (1994, p. 189).

4. I thank Theresa Enos for introducing me to Corder's work in her seminar class, "Beyond Post-Process and Post-Modernism: A Rhetoric of Spaciousness," and I am also grateful for her kind mentorship and thorough feedback.

REFERENCES

Aristotle (n.d.). *Rhetoric.* (Freese, J. H., Ed.). Retrieved from http://www.perseus.tufts.edu/hopper/text?doc=Perseus:text:1999.01.0060 (*Aristotle in 23 Volumes*, Vol. 22, translated by J. H. Freese. *Aristotle.* (1926). Cambridge and London. Harvard University Press; William Heinemann.)

Barthes, R. (1977). The death of the author. *Image-Music-Text.* 1977. 49-55.

Bishop, W. (2003). Preaching what he practices, Jim Corder's irascible and articulate oeuvre. In T. Enos & K. Miller (Eds.), *Beyond postprocess and postmodernism: Essays on the spaciousness of rhetoric* (pp. 89-101). Mahweh, NJ: Erlbaum.

Corder, J. W. (1972). Ethical argument in Amos. *The Crescent, 35*: 6-9.

Corder, J. W. (1977). Outhouses, weather changes, and the return to basics in English education. *College English 38.5.*: 474-482.

Corder, J. W. (1984). From Rhetoric to Grace: Propositions 55-81 about rhetoric, propositions 1-54 and 82 et seq. being as yet unstated; or, getting from the classroom to the world. *Rhetoric Society Quarterly 14*(5), 15-28.

Corder, J. W. (1992). Lessons learned, lessons lost. *The Georgia Review 46*, 15-28.

Corder, J. W. (1992). *Yonder: Life on the far side of change.* Athens, GA: University of Georgia Press.

Corder, J. W. (1993). At last report, I was still here. In W. Bishop (Ed.), *The subject in writing: Essays by teachers and students* (pp. 261-66). Portsmouth, NH: Boynton/Cook.

Corder, J. W. (1993). Tribes and displaced persons: Some observations on collaboration. In L. Odell (Ed.), *Theory and Practice in the teaching of writing: Rethinking the discipline* (pp. 271-88). Carbondale, IL: Southern Illinois University Press.

Corder, J. W. (1995). Notes on a rhetoric of regret. *Composition Studies/Freshman English News 23*(1), 94-105.

Corder, J. W. (1999). What I learned at school. In L. Ede (Ed.), *On writing research: The Braddock Essays, 1975-1998* (pp. 43-50). New York: Bedford St. Martin's.

Corder, J. W. (2003). On argument, what some call "self-writing," and trying to see the back side of one's own eyeballs. *Rhetoric Review 22*(1), 31-39.

Corder, J. W. (2004). Argument as emergence, rhetoric as love. In J. S. Baumlin & K. D. Miller (Eds.), *Selected essays of Jim W. Corder: Pursuing the personal in scholarship, teaching, and writing* (pp. 170-201). Urbana, Illinois: NCTE.

Corder, J. W. (2004). Hunting for ethos where they say it can't be found. *Rhetoric Review 7*, 299-316. Reprinted in J. S. Baumlin & K. D. Miller (Eds.), *Selected Essays of Jim W. Corder: Pursuing the personal in scholarship, teaching, and writing* (pp. 202-220). Urbana, IL: NCTE.

Corder, J. W. (2004). Studying rhetoric and teaching school. In J. S. Baumlin & K. D. Miller (Eds.), *Selected essays of Jim W. Corder: Pursuing the personal in scholarship, teaching, and writing* (pp. 102-38). Urbana, IL: NCTE.

Corder, J. W. (2004). Varieties of ethical argument, with some account of the significance of ethos in the teaching of composition. In J. S. Baumlin & K. D. Miller (Eds.), *Selected essays of Jim W. Corder: pursuing the personal in scholarship, teaching, and writing* (pp. 60-101). Urbana, IL: NCTE.

Corder, J. W., & Baumlin, J. (1986). Lonesomeness in English studies. *ADE Bulletin 85*: 36-39.

Enos, T. (1994). Voice as echo of delivery, ethos as transforming process. In W. R. Winterowd & V. Villespie (Eds.), *Composition in context: Essays in honor of Donald C. Stewart* (pp. 180-195). Carbondale, IL: Southern Illinois University Press.

Lassner, P. (1990). Feminist responses to Rogerian argument. *Rhetoric Review 8*(2), 220-32.

Warnock, T. (2003). Bringing Over Yonder Over Here: A personal look at expressivist rhetoric as ideological action. In T. Enos & K. D. Miller (Eds.), *Beyond postprocess and postmodernism: Essays on the spaciousness of rhetoric* (pp. 203-216). Mahweh, New Jersey: Lawrence Erlbaum.

Yoos, G. E. (2003). Finding Jim's voice: A problem in ethos and personal identity. In T. Enos & K. D. Miller (Eds.), *Beyond postprocess and postmodernism: Essays on the spaciousness of rhetoric* (pp. 117-28). Mahweh, NJ: Erlbaum.

Young, R. E. (1992). Rogerian Argument and the Context of the Situation: Taking a closer look. In N. Teich (Ed.), *Rogerian Perspectives: Collaborative rhetoric for oral and written communication* (pp. 109-121). Norwood, New Jersey: Ablex.

Young, R. E. Becker, A. L., & Pike, K. L. (1970). *Rhetoric: Discovery and change*. New York: Harcourt.

TEACHING STYLE AS CULTURAL PERFORMANCE

Chris Holcomb and M. Jimmie Killingsworth
Texas A&M University

Definitions of style generally come in two versions—one narrow, the other broad. The narrow version identifies style with *verbal* style and considers a writer's choices at the level of word, phrase, and clause, although more recently it has come increasingly to include features beyond the sentence, including point of view, discourse structure, and genre. The other version defines style more broadly as "ways of doing" and takes within its purview virtually any artifact or practice that has communicative potential: fashion, music, electronic and digital media, deportment, food, and so on. The narrow definition of style, despite its recent revival in some quarters, is often associated with the outmoded formalism of New Criticism (literary studies) or with the product-oriented pedagogy of Current-Traditional Rhetoric (composition). Meanwhile, the broader definition is more positively received in English studies because it opens wider vistas onto social and cultural criticism. Apart from a few notable exceptions, these two conceptions of style rarely overlap. Scholars working with verbal style, although they might consider stylistic features in their immediate contexts, often stop short of fully considering style's cultural dimensions. Reciprocally, those working within the broader conception of style seem eager to leave verbal form behind in order to get on to the supposedly more serious and exciting business of analyzing fashion, music, and so on, and to protect themselves from the accusation of formalism and lack of theoretical depth.

While the narrow and broad definitions of style influence the way we think about and teach style, the distinctions upon which they are based are ultimately artificial, products of disciplinary interests and specializations rather than a viable description of style's nature and operation. In questioning the dichotomy, this essay emphasizes the continuity between the two versions of style, and in doing so, it answers Keith Rhodes's call (delivered earlier in this volume) to connect scholarship and classroom work on style to broader cultural practices. Toward these ends, we offer two frameworks for teaching students to explore relationships between verbal style and culture.[1]

The first framework encourages students to begin with the particularities of verbal form and, from there, explore broader meanings and functions in terms of three "arenas" of interaction: the textual, social, and cultural. Here we focus primarily on the cultural arena, arguing that words and especially patterns of words are cultural forms just as surely as elements of fashion, music, architecture, and food are. Seeing them as such invites students to consider how their verbal styles (whether in written academic work or everyday interactions) work in concert with these other cultural elements to perform various identities.

The second framework turns the approach around and begins with cultural forms in matters like fashion and food as an entrée into the study of principles such as convention and deviation, which apply as surely to "broader" cultural practices as they do to a "narrow" interest in sentence-level matters of prose style. The suggestion is that, whichever framework the study of style employs, the important thing is to bridge the study of language and the study of the wider cultural context, or better yet, to teach students that language is one cultural practice among many, all of which can be approached together with the right conceptual tools. The frameworks, in other words, are temporary and provisional. They momentarily accept the artificial distinction of language and culture on the way to dismantling it. Before examining those frameworks more closely, we first situate them in other discussions of verbal style and culture.

STYLE AND CULTURE

Connections between verbal form and performative culture run throughout treatments of style in ancient rhetorics. Their doing so suggests just how thoroughly interdependent style and culture were in ancient rhetorical thought. Aristotle, for instance, had no technical terms, such as "figure of speech" (Kennedy, 1991, p. 242), for grouping stylistic devices or characteristics, so he improvised ones by borrowing terms either describing cultural phenomenon or carrying powerful cultural resonances. Metaphor, antithesis, and *energeia* (or vivid expression) he grouped under the more general term *asteia* or "things of the town" (Aristotle, trans. 1991, p. 244), a word that identifies these verbal forms with the elegance and refinement of the cultural center in contrast to the rusticity of geographic and cultural backwaters. Cultural resonances are also conveyed by those four qualities of style that are typically translated into English as "clarity, correctness, ornamentation, and propriety." What are their cultural associations? The tipoff is the term under which Aristotle (and his imitators) gathered them: the *aretai* or "virtues" of style. By classifying them as such, Aristotle suggests that the "virtues" do not simply describe the technical merits of a completed oration, but are instead guides to performance and action, prodding the orator to fashion his stylistic behaviors in ways that match (or at least aspire toward) criteria defining cultural excellence. The virtue of correctness is particularly revealing. The term "correctness" is a poor translation of the original Greek and Latin terms, *Hellenizen* and *Latinitas*, because it neutralizes the cultural resonances the original terms carried. Better translations—or at least, more historically accurate translations—might be "good Greek" and "good Latin." Translated as such, these phrases reveal the cultural stakes involved—that is, pitting one culture's language against those of all outsiders, incursions of which were labeled as the ultimate stylistic "vice": *babarismos* or "barbarism."

Cultural and stylistic categories also mix and overlap in the rhetorics of Cicero and Quintilian. For instance, in their discussions of jests (many of which secure their effects through stylistic devices), both authors insist again and again that the orator only use forms of joking that "befit" a *liberalis* or gentleman and avoid the gross humor of the stage clown and lowly street entertainer.[2] Their advice suggests that certain verbal forms (such as irony and oblique punning) were part of a gentleman's repertoire for expressing his social and cultural identity, while other forms (such as obscenities or overly aggressive jokes) bespoke a more lowly status. With such advice, Cicero and Quintilian present verbal style as a medium for cultural performance. Elsewhere, they use non-verbal elements of culture as metaphors for thinking about style. Quintilian, for instance, draws on several cultural practices and artifacts and, through a series of analogies, uses them to mark a difference between a natural verbal style and an overly affected one. The natural style is like a healthy body that, through wholesome exercise and training, acquires grace through such physical adornments as a "healthy complexion, firm flesh and shapely thews" (Quintilian, trans. 1972, 8.Pr.19). The affected style, however, is like a man who "attempts to enhance these physical graces" by the use of "depilatories and cosmetics" or through "effeminate and luxurious apparel" (Quintilian, trans. 1972, 8.Pr.19-20). Notice how Quintilian discusses the virtue of naturalness in verbal style by calling upon another area of culture—in this case the care of the body through exercise versus artificial beauty created via cosmetics and dress (an analogy which echoes Socrates' famous dismissal of rhetoric as cosmetics and cookery in Plato's *Gorgias*)—thus suggesting that language is one cultural practice among many, joined together by general principles of style (such as naturalness).

In more recent discussions of style in rhetorical and composition studies, this intimate relation between style and culture is often either ignored or underappreciated. In *A Rhetoric of Style*, for instance, Barry Brummett is primarily concerned with the role that style plays in the formation and reproduction of cultures, but he has very little to say, beyond a few generalizations, about how verbal style participates in these processes. Instead, he adopts what we characterized earlier as the broad definition of style and focuses, not on verbal style, but on clothing, music, cosmetics, visual media, deportment, and so on. In fact, he makes it clear early in his study that he wants to move beyond "limited view[s] of style" (2008, p. 2)—including those which identify it with "linguistic style" (2008, p. 1)—to other modes of stylistic expression: "I want to think of style as socially held sign systems composed of a wide range of signs beyond *only* language, systems that are used to accomplish rhetorical purposes across the cultural spectrum" (2008, p. 3, emphasis added). We agree that style should encompass the full "cultural spectrum," but we suspect that Brummett underestimates the importance of language and, more specifically, "linguistic style" as a force in cultural production. As the passage above suggests (particularly the modifiers "limited" and "only"), the role language plays within Brummett's conception of style is a minor one. In the book's middle chapters, that role becomes even more marginal. In other words, language ceases to be part of style altogether and, instead, serves as a metaphor (or simile) *for* style. Again and again, we come upon formulations like the following:

- "Style ... is like a language" (2008, p. 33);
- "Style ... is a kind of language" (2008, p. 45);
- "[S]tyle ... functions as does a language" (2008, p. 32);
- "A fruitful way to think of style [is] as a language ..." (2008, p. 99).

We understand what Brummett is doing here: he's taking a page from the playbook of structuralism and making a case for examining clothing, music, visual images, etc., as a system of relations (just as language is). But for those of us who study verbal style, the formulation *style is like a language* sounds profoundly odd because it suggests that the only meaningful link between style and language is, at best, a metaphorical or analogical one.

Towards the book's end, in a chapter devoted to American "gun-culture style," Brummett does consider verbal form in his discussion of the speaking style of American gun enthusiasts. But the analytical vocabulary he deploys to describe this style seems too general and impressionistic. For instance, he characterizes the speech of those who frequent gun shows and firing ranges as "plain," "reserved," and "direct and pointed" (2008, p. 159), but apart from noting that a word like "aesthetics" would be out of place in gun culture talk and that the honorifics "sir" and "ma'am" serve as markers of politeness (2008, pp. 159-160), he fails to specify what it is about their language that suggests such qualities or effects. He also fails to quote samples of their speech so that readers can either confirm or challenge his general characterization of it as "plain," "reserved," and "direct and pointed." Shortly after delivering this characterization, Brummett does include a sentence-long sample of gun talk, but it actually undercuts his previous claims about gun talk's general characteristics. The sample comes from a poster at rec.guns who is chiding another newsgroup member for taking offense from someone who was carrying a handgun. That poster writes, "you might have been a little too curious for his temperament" (Brummett, 2008, p. 160). Given its understated, euphemistic, and Latinate diction, this comment is hardly "plain" and "direct." Rather, it's a model of indirection. It's as if Brummett's earlier claims about the limits of linguistic style and about style being *like* a language were self-fulfilling prophesies. For the analysis here stops short of moving beyond its impressionistic labels to specific verbal features, and if it fails to do that, then it cannot identify connections between those features and their cultural uses and meanings.

A more promising approach to exploring relations between verbal form and culture appears in Fiona Paton's "Beyond Bakhtin: Towards a Cultural Stylistics." In this essay, Paton draws on a mostly Bakhtinian vocabulary of analysis (heteroglossia, dialogism, parody) to argue that language is "materially embedded in its cultural moment" (2000, p. 170). To illustrate, Paton offers an extended analysis of Jack Kerouac's novel *Dr. Sax*, arguing that its style internalizes, and re-inflects, the languages and even media formats of various cultural forms contemporaneous with the novel's production (such as pulp fiction, comic books, jazz, literary fiction, popular cinema, and street vernacular). The strength of Paton's analysis lies in its effort to work from the particularities of verbal form toward the broader concerns of cultural criticism, ultimately situating the novel's style in the context of Cold War discourses on nationalism and debates among American intellectuals of the 1950s over high and low culture. But where Paton could have pushed her analysis further is in understanding the stylistic features she identifies as cultural forms in their own right. Instead, she treats them in one of three ways:

1. as compositional elements borrowed from other cultural forms: for example, onomatopoeia from comic strips, or phrasings and idioms from pulp fiction or nursery rhymes (2000, p. 189);
2. as vehicles for imitating the formats of other media: for example, parataxis mimics the "sequential narrative panels of a comic strip" (2000, p. 186);
3. as instances of Bakhtin's more abstract categories: for example, parenthesis contributes to the dialogic style of the novel (2000, p. 186).

These categories certainly call attention, at least in a general sense, to the social and cultural dimensions of verbal form, but what Paton might have also noted is that devices such as onomatopoeia, parataxis, and parenthesis are themselves cultural forms. In other words, they (together with hundreds of other verbal devices) are ritualizations of language at the level of word, phrase, or clause that circulate widely, while accumulating, carrying, and shedding "cultural values and meanings independent of the content they may be used [in any given instance] to convey" (Holcomb, 2007, p. 80).

An analyst of style who does recognize such verbal patterns as cultural forms is sociolinguist Penelope Eckert. In her studies of adolescent speech at a high school in the suburbs of Detroit, Eckert charts stylistic variations within and across the school's two primary social networks: jocks and burnouts. What she finds is that features of verbal style work alongside of, and in concert with, other cultural products and practices and that, collectively, they form a richly expressive repertoire for performing identity. In other words, students perform identity by drawing on elements from *both* verbal style (variations at the level of phonology and syntax) and nonverbal style (variations in "clothing, posture and body movement, makeup, hair, territory, substance use, [and] leisure activities" [Eckert, 2005, p. 11]). Together, these verbal and nonverbal elements of style blend seamlessly in the everyday interactions of the students Eckert has observed. Theoretically, then, Eckert's study suggests that distinctions between narrow and broad definitions of style will not hold—that analyses of style (and its uses in performance) must consider verbal form working alongside (and together with) other cultural elements. Pedagogically, her study invites us to look for new ways to present and teach style to our students.

ARENAS OF STYLE: FROM TEXT TO CULTURE

To help our students explore relationships between verbal form and culture, and thus to construct a more comprehensive understanding of style, we offer two pedagogical frameworks. The first (considered in this section) moves from the textual features of verbal style through its social and rhetorical uses to its cultural meanings and values. The second framework (considered in the next section) reverses this movement and starts with stylistic activities more familiar to students (such as fashion, music, and food), activities whose social and cultural uses are more readily apparent to students.

The first framework serves as a model for helping students understand style as performance—that is, as a vehicle by which writers not only present a self, but also orchestrate relationships with readers, subject matters, and contexts. At the heart of this model is the notion of interaction. As Richard Schechner claims, "To treat any object, work, or product 'as' performance ... means to investigate what that object does, how it interacts with other objects and beings" (2002, p. 24). Building on this claim, we consider style in terms of three arenas of interaction: the textual, social, and cultural.

1. Within the textual arena, students examine how all the words on the page interact with one another to form patterns and meanings. Here students gain practice in applying different vocabularies of analysis (those from traditional grammar, linguistics, or rhetoric), and they become more accustomed to following closely the word-by-word choices of an author as they unfold in a given text.
2. With the social arena, attention turns from interactions among words and structures to interactions between writers and readers *through* those words and structures. Here we have in mind something along the lines of Rosanne Carlo's contribution to this volume where Carlo examines the interplay between a "performative ethos" and "enfolding a reader." Along similar lines, students might consider how writers use style to construct roles for themselves and their readers, to position themselves in relation to those readers (above, below, equal, familiar, or distant), and to invite readers into participatory relationships with a text, relationships that include enacting all the various rituals of social interaction (joking, flirting, sparring, instructing, and so on).
3. With the cultural arena, students consider how a word or pattern has, independent of the content it might express, a particular value or meaning to some larger community of language users. To borrow an example from Eckert, consider "negative concord," or the use of double, triple, or even quadruple negatives, as in "I ain't never done nothing to nobody." Although this feature is stigmatized in most professional and institutional contexts, among burnouts it carries the positive value of performing an "anti-school stance," and among male jocks it performs "ruggedness." (Eckert, 2005, p. 19)

A good place to start is with patterns with which students are already familiar—at least, intuitively. We're thinking here of such powerhouse tropes and schemes as metaphor, anaphora, antithesis, and tricolon. Because these figures are so ubiquitous, so much a part of our culture's repertoire for performance, students will already have at least a tacit sense of some of their cultural meanings and values. Take tricolon, for instance. It's a scheme involving a series of three words, phrases, or clauses in parallel form:[3]

- We hold these truths to be self-evident, that all men are created equal, that they are endowed by their Creator with certain unalienable Rights, that among these are Life, Liberty and the pursuit of Happiness. (The Declaration of Independence, 1776)
- There's never enough bread, never enough olives, never enough soup. (Simic, 2005, p. 85)

- Our campaign was not hatched in the halls of Washington—it began in the backyards of Des Moines and the living rooms of Concord and the front porches of Charleston. (Barak Obama, "Election Night Victory Speech," 11/4/08)
- It concludes that *The Daily Show* can be better understood not as "fake news" but as an alternative journalism, one that uses satire to interrogate power, parody to critique contemporary news, and dialogue to enact a model of deliberative democracy. (Baym, 2005, p. 261)

Students will probably have little trouble identifying the textual features shared across all of these examples (parallel series of three). They might also observe some of the social uses of this pattern—that is, how the speakers or writers in these examples are interacting with their listeners or readers through tricolon. In the fourth example, President Obama uses tricolon (a staple of presidential oratory) to reassure listeners that his goals are thoroughly democratic, springing not from the interests Beltway insiders, but from the people—the *demos*—in their most familial settings. In the final example, Baym uses tricolon to perform another kind of ritual, one common to academic discourse: previewing the organization of his article for readers.

Where students might have trouble, however, and thus need more explicit guidance, is in teasing out the cultural meanings of tricolon. We begin by asking students, "Why three items in each series? Why not two, or four, or five?" If this question doesn't ring some bells, we ask them about other patterns, objects, or activities that have three parts. If one of our students doesn't volunteer it first, we recall one of the short educational cartoons from the 1970's series *Schoolhouse Rock!*: "Three Is a Magic Number," which celebrates the virtues of three while teaching its viewers some of its multiples ("Three, six, nine ... Twelve, fifteen, eighteen ..."). Other examples we use come from Alan Dundes, an anthropologist who documents the pervasive role three plays not only in ritual, myth, and folklore but also in everyday American culture:

- Folklore (three wishes, three little pigs, three blind mice).
- Games and spectacles (tick-tack-toe, three strikes and you're out, three ring circus).
- Product sizes and appliance settings (small, medium, and large; low, medium, and high).
- Eating rituals and food (three meals per day; coffee, tea, or milk; rare, medium, and well-done).
- Common or well-known sayings ("Beg, borrow, or steal"; "Lock, stock, and barrel"; "Ready, willing, and able"). (Dundes, 1968, pp. 404-09)

To Dundes' list, we might add religion and philosophy (the Holy Trinity of Christianity; the triadic semiotics of Charles Sanders Peirce; the thesis, antithesis, and synthesis of the Hegelian dialectic).

Having established the cultural pervasiveness of three, we return to tricolon and ask students what cultural meanings and values it might have. Even if they respond, "It just feels right," that's a start because it speaks to the cultural power of three and suggests just how thoroughly this number structures our expectations and behavior. We've probably all had the experience of drafting something and jotting down two items, when a voice in our head calls to us, "You need to add one more." Apparently, Captain Jack Sparrow from *Pirates of the Caribbean* felt the same compulsion when he said, "I think we've arrived at a very special place. Spiritually, ecumenically, grammatically." His three-part list, especially the last two items, doesn't make much propositional sense, but it makes symbolic sense: he needs the three items, regardless of their semantic sense, to complete this little stylistic ritual. In fact, as Max Atkinson observes about conversational discourse, "Lists comprising only two items tend to appear inadequate and incomplete—so much so that there are various phrases that can be slotted in whenever we are having difficulty in finding a third item for a list," phrases such as "and so on," "somethingorother," and "etcetera" (1984, p. 57).

Part of what drives this compulsion towards tripartite structures has to be that, in our culture, three means stability, completeness, and (in some instances) finality. Tricolon, with its items cast in parallel form rather than dispersed over varying and irregular structures, serves as the stylistic crystallization of those meanings.[4] Thus, writers often use tricolon to deliver a well-rounded description of a person, thing, or event:

- [Colin Duffy] is four feet eight inches, weighs seventy-five pounds, and appears to be mostly leg and shoulder blade. (Orlean, 1995, p. 99)
- I require three things in a man. He must be handsome, ruthless, and stupid. (Parker, 2009, p. 19)
- Carlo, the counterman, unwrapped a Mars bar, dunked it in the universal batter, and dropped it in oil. When it floated, golden brown, on the surface, he removed it, sprinkled a little powder sugar on it, and handed it over. "Careful," said Simon. "Inside it's bloody napalm."Mmmm. I like grease. I like chocolate. And I like sugar. (Bourdain, 2002, p. 253)

Writers also use tricolon to present a representative sample of some phenomenon or class (just as Obama's tricolon [quoted above] is representative of the citizenry):

- He kept scraps of wood in a cardboard box—the ends of two-by-fours, slabs of shelving and plywood, odd pieces of molding—and everything in it was fair game. (Sanders, 2008, p. 134)
- Many of us had suspended the connections to the world we had established back home—the part-time job in the library, the graduate program, the circle of supportive friends—and we resented the loss. (Gordon, 1998, p. 121)

In all of these examples, the tricola work something like triangulation, the technique by which astronomers calculate the distance of celestial objects from the Earth and navigators determine the position of their vessels. The tricola fix and thus offer what seems a reliable description of, or sampling from, their targets. Similarly, in academic discourse (even in the humanities), we often hear of "triangulating" data—that is, confirming some observed phenomenon by finding at least three instances of it, or examining a single phenomenon from three methodological perspectives.

In public oratory, tricolon often serves the performance function of cuing listeners to applaud (Atkinson, 1984, pp. 57ff.). Stephen Colbert capitalized on this power in a comedic segment, way back when he was just a correspondent on *The Daily Show with Jon Stewart*.[5] In the segment, Colbert is supposedly on-the-scene in D.C., reporting on the previous night's State of the Union address, and while anchor Stewart is trying to get Colbert to report on the substance of the speech, Colbert's responses keep culminating in tricola delivered in tones and rhythms of presidential oratory. These tricola are followed by cut-shots to file footage of the House floor with members standing and applauding—as if Colbert were the President. Here are several of Colbert's tricola (reinforced by anaphora):

- The State of the Union is a celebration of democracy, a night when Washington and the entire country can reaffirm their faith in the nation—not as Democrats, not as Republicans, but as Americans.
- If we do go to war, there's no one I'd rather have defending me than the brave men and women of the armed forces. We're proud of you. We believe in you. And we will prevail. (Holcomb, 2007, pp. 71-75)

Finally, when the exasperated Stewart asks if Colbert can "tell us about the actual substance of the speech," Colbert responds, "Why, Jon? That won't get applause."

This segment implicitly confirms tricolon's status as a cultural form (Holcomb, 2007, p. 74). The humor wouldn't work if viewers failed to recognize as such. It wouldn't work, that is to say, if listeners failed to register how Colbert was using tricolon (along with other elements of performance, such as vocal tone and pacing, the cut-shot to the House floor, etc.) to signal a shift between performing (and comedically confusing) two cultural identities—journalist and politician.

The three-arenas framework can be applied to other verbal devices—not only to the figures of speech, but to any pattern or feature whose meanings exceed the subject matter that, on any given occasion, it might express. For instance:

- The intentional misspellings and typos of geeks and gamers ("teh suc," "pwned," and "pr0n").
- The heavily nominalized and jargon-filled prose of academics.
- Passive voice in scientific writing.
- The esoteric (and overworked) diction and metaphors of wine connoisseurs ("with notes of honeysuckle and a strong, oaky finish").

All of these features (and so many more) are little rituals of language that circulate relatively widely, get rehearsed again and again, and assembled (along with other non-verbal elements) into fresh combinations as writers and speakers orchestrate their interactions with audiences and perform various selves. Exploring these possible functions requires students and teachers to treat verbal form as an object of serious (and deep) cultural analysis.

PRINCIPLES OF STYLISTIC PERFORMANCE: FROM CULTURE TO TEXT

In *Performing Prose*, we introduce stylistic principles like convention and deviation, voice and footing, tropes and schemes, through the close study of language—that is, to use the terms in the last section, we begin with the textual arena and work toward the cultural arena—finishing in our last chapter by showing how, once these concepts are worked out in language, they can be demonstrated as evident in all strata of cultural activity. Our point is that the concepts of culture and language are thoroughly interdependent, and that language itself is one of many such activities. Unlike the search for food, water, and habitat, the primary activities of existential life, or even sex, on which the perpetuation of species depends, language is a secondary activity that, by facilitating social interchange, supports and enlivens the primary work of survival and reproduction. The same trends found in linguistic style—convention and deviation, for example—are at work in other stylistic performances: in fashion, food, art, sport, technology, and other areas that are partly rule-governed and partly based on decisions, whether by individuals or groups. More significantly for the study of style, concepts like convention and deviation can help to form bridges between the understandings of style in various cultural activities. Here, we'd like briefly to consider a second approach or framework for studying style. Instead of moving from language outward to the larger cultural arena, with the help of these conceptual bridges, we might well turn things around and begin with an area more familiar to the average student—fashion, for example—thereby applying the old premise of behaviorism in education: always move from the most familiar to the least familiar material (see Zoellner, 1969).

In matters of clothing, as in cultural practices, people depend partly on rules or laws, partly on conventions, and partly on personal choices. In the west, required clothing includes a top (shirt, blouse, etc.), a bottom (pants, skirt, etc.), and footwear (shoes, boots, sandals). At some public places, like the beach or the swimming pool, the rules are more relaxed unless you want to go into the snack bar for a hot dog ("No shirt, No shoes, No service"). Even at this most basic level, however, culture intervenes. In hot, moist climates like the tropical rain forest, some cultural groups wear nearly nothing (the rules are more like a perpetual trip to the beach), while in many desert climates, more elaborate rules for covering prevail—full-length robes and head scarves and veils, for example, many of which elements have been codified in religious law, such as that of Islam. Covering in one way or another becomes a matter of religious duty—and a matter of identity politics in global society, where requirements for dress become issues of confrontation and legislation. For any given society, the law becomes the foundation of required behavior. The law says what must be covered and to what extent. Despite the so-called sexual revolution and the vaunted freedom of expression in American life and art, laws against indecent exposure remain on the books. It is against the law for women to go topless on most U.S. beaches, for example, but not on most European beaches; and at least one well known political commentator on the European scene has expressed wonder over the prudery and hypocrisy of Americans on this score (see Zizek, 2010, pp. 121-22). The law may also require *un*covering, as in the case of some European countries that have tried to institute anti-veiling laws on the argument that public safety depends upon the police being able to identify the faces of citizens.

Beyond the law, dress is governed to some extent by *conventions*. We "dress up" for weddings and funerals and "dress down" for ball games and college classes. The occasions for dressing up have changed over the years—people used to dress up for air travel, for example, and Sunday church—as has the meaning of dressing up. (Do men dress up in tuxedo, dark suit with necktie, or just slacks with ironed shirt; must women wear a full-length gown, "little black dress," or skirt and blouse with low heels?) Along with historical shifts, regional and national customs cause variation in the definition of dressing up—the relaxed west coast versus the more formal east coast in the U.S., for example.

Finally we come to style—deviations from, or personal variations within, dress codes and conventions. East-coast businessmen might express themselves with a colorful tie, or businesswomen with a bright scarf, while still following the convention of wearing a dark suit to work. The daring may flaunt convention entirely, leaving off the tie or jacket, and thereby engendering expectations of rebelliousness or special creativity (that they better live up to).

Students can bring plenty of their own examples along these lines. The key is to make the transition to language via the conceptual bridges to the more familiar cultural practice. Once the concept of rule-governed, conventional, and deviant behavior is established, we can get at some key definitions in the basic study of language:

- **Grammar** is the set of rules by which a language functions. The rules change over time, but are relatively stable.
- **Style** comprises the choices a writer makes within that system. Style is often defined as deviation from a norm.
- **Convention** is the shifting ground of linguistic restriction between grammar and style, between definite rules and clear choices.

A great place to begin working with these distinctions is the kind of restrictions that often get codified as rules when they are in fact matters of choice or community preference. An injunction that every student will recognize, for example, is *never use the first-person pronoun*. What grammar (the law) actually says about use of the first-person is that, like all pronouns, it must agree in person, number, and case with its antecedent and with any verb to which it serves as subject. Avoiding the use of the first-person *I* or *we* is not a law or a rule, but a convention. For one thing, it is a convention of formality, like wearing a tuxedo to the prom. Drawing attention to oneself—whether by the use of *I* or by the wearing of flamboyant clothing—can be considered bad manners in some situations or in some cultures. One must become a student of the culture to know the conventions and codes, the manners and mores. Avoiding the use of the first-person *I* or *we* can also be a badge of identity—like the businessperson's dark suit, the head scarf of Moslem women, or the uniform of the soldier. Writers in science and engineering avoid the first person to suggest the objectivity and reproducibility of their work. It doesn't matter that *I* get one result in my lab; by following these procedures, *anyone* can get such a result. The emphasis thus falls on the methods and the findings rather than on the interpretations of any individual. In forthrightly using *we* in the famous paper announcing the structure of DNA, Francis Crick and James Watson flouted convention and emphasized the originality of their discovery and the daring quality of their interpretation (see the discussion in Holcomb & Killingsworth, 2010, pp. 50-53).

Students may grasp the analogies between language and other cultural practices quite quickly, but still have trouble crossing the bridge between them. Ultimately they must be convinced that it is in their best interest to know the inner workings of language as well as they know the intricacies of fashion, sports, or music. To that end, we rely on performance. Performance is the moment when language goes into action, when the writer puts the stylistic repertoire to use with a rhetorical awareness of audience and context. Good performance finally requires mastery of rules (grammar), knowledge of conventions (norms, audience expectations), and the informed practice of style (good decisions about deviations).

Performance will also reveal continuities (and thus bridge the divide) between the two definitions of style with which this chapter began: narrow definitions which identify style with verbal style, and broad definitions which identify it with fashion, music, food, etc. Narrow definitions often fall short because they measure style in terms of its efficiency in transmitting information (for instance, the whole prescriptive tradition on clarity and concision), or because they are too invested in the representational function of language (style may depict behavior—may even enhance depictions of behavior—but is not a form of behavior itself). In either case, style is defined (sometimes exclusively) as a relation to content and usually as content's subordinate partner. As a result, narrow definitions leave style vulnerable to charges of formalism. Broad definitions, by contrast, often ignore or underestimate the role verbal style plays in the production and reproduction of culture, and their selection of objects of analysis seem driven by a misguided assumption: if you want to examine relations between style and culture, you can't get there through verbal form.

If, however, we approach style as performance—as a medium for social and cultural interaction—then doing so will dismantle distinctions between narrow and broad definitions by treating the objects each traditionally analyzes as belonging to the same set. Reconfiguring them as such invites us (and our students) to consider patterns at the level of word, phrase, and clause as performative set-pieces—that is, as ritualizations of language that work alongside of (or sometimes in tension with) ritualizations in deportment, dress, food, visual design, sport, etc.—all of which play a role in structuring and orchestrating interactions not only between style and content, but also (and more importantly) among performers, audiences, and the contexts they inhabit. More generally, this reconfiguration invites students to marshal the strengths of both linguistic and cultural analysis in developing a practice of composition that addresses the deep motives of writers and readers in the widest possible context.

NOTES

1. These frameworks originally appeared in our textbook Performing Prose: The Study and Practice of Style in Composition. Here we elaborate on their pedagogical uses and explore their theoretical implications more fully.

2. See, for instance, Cicero's De Oratore (2.60.244; 2.60.247; 2.61.251-52; and 2.67.270) and Quintilian (6.3.17-18; 6.3.29; 6.3.46-47; and 5.3.83).

3. The following discussion of tricolon is based on our analysis of the same scheme in Performing Prose (pp. 151-154).

4. Our thinking here is influenced by Jeanne Fahnestock's Rhetorical Figures in Science where she argues that several key figures exemplify or "epitomize" particular lines of reasoning (pp. 23-24).

5. The following is based on Holcomb's analysis of the same segment (pp. 71-75).

REFERENCES

Aristotle. (1991). *On rhetoric: A theory of civic discourse*. Trans. George A. Kennedy. Oxford: Oxford University Press.

Atkinson, M. (1984). *Our masters' voices: The language and body language of politics*. London: Routledge.

Baym, G. (2005). The Daily Show: Discursive integration and the reinvention of political journalism. *Political Communication. 22*: 259-76.

Bourdain, A. (2002). *A cook's tour: Global adventures in extreme cuisines*. New York: Harper Perennial.

Brummett, B. (2008). *A rhetoric of style*. Carbondale: Southern Illinois University Press.

Cicero. (1977). *De oratore*. (E. W. Sutton & H. Rackam, Trans.). Loeb Classical Library 349. Cambridge, MA: Harvard University Press.

Colbert, S. (2003). Live from D.C. *The Daily Show with Jon Stewart*. Comedy Central. 29 Jan.

Declaration of Independence. (1776). *National Archives*. Retrieved from http://www.archives.gov/exhibits/charters/declaration_transcript.html

Dundes, A. (1968). The number three in American culture. In A. Dundes (Ed.), *Every Man His Way* (pp. 410-24). Englewood Cliffs, NJ: Prentice-Hall.

Eckert, P. (2005, Jan). *Variation, convention, and social meaning*. Paper presented at the Annual Meeting of the Linguistic Society of America, Oakland, CA. Abstract retrieved from http://people.pwf.cam.ac.uk/bv230/lang-var/

eckert%202005%20variation%20convention%20and%20social%20meaning.pdf
Gordon, E. F. (1998). Faculty wife. In P. Lopate (Ed.) *The Anchor Essay Annual: Best of 1998* (pp. 115-32). New York: Anchor.
Holcomb, C. (2007). "Anyone can be President": Figures of speech, cultural forms, and performance. *Rhetoric Society Quarterly 37*, 71-96.
Holcomb, C.& M. J. Killingsworth. (2010). *Performing Prose: The study and practice of style in composition.* Carbondale: Southern Illinois University Press.
Obama, B. (2008). Election night victory speech. Grant Park, IL. 4 Nov. 2008.
Orlean, S. The American man at age ten. In N. Sims & M. Kramer (Eds.), *Literary journalism.* New York: Ballantine.
Parker, D. & S. Y. Silverstein (Ed.). (2009). *Not much fun: The lost poems of Dorothy Parker.* New York: Scribner, 2009.
Paton, F. (2000). Beyond Bakhtin: Towards a cultural stylistics. *College English 63*: 166-93.
Quintilian. (1972). *Institutio oratoria.* Cambridge, MA: Harvard University Press.
Sanders, S. R. (2008). The inheritance of tools. In R. Atwan (Ed.), *Best American essays: College edition* (5th ed.) (pp. 131-139). Boston: Houghton.
Schechner, R. (2002). *Performance Studies: An Introduction.* London: Routledge.
Simic, C. (2005). Dinner at Uncle Boris's. In L. Gutkind (Ed.), *In Fact: The best of Creative Nonfiction.* New York: Norton.
Zizek, S. (2010). *Living in the end times.* New York: Verso.
Zoellner, R. (1969). Talk-write: A behavioral pedagogy for composition. *College English 30*, 267-320.

INVENTIO AND ELOCUTIO: LANGUAGE INSTRUCTION AT ST. PAUL'S GRAMMAR SCHOOL AND TODAY'S STYLISTIC CLASSROOM

Tom Pace
John Carroll University

INTRODUCTION

Ever since the publication of Robert Connors's 2000 article "The Erasure of the Sentence," compositionists have reconsidered that "dirty" word of post-process writing instruction—style. This reconsideration is a good thing, in part, because near the end of his essay, Connors was pessimistic about the teaching of stylistics as a part of the field's future:

> Many people still professionally active today have deep background as generative rhetoricians or imitation adepts or sentence-combining pioneers, but they have lost most of their interest; they do not do that much anymore. They have cut their losses. We all must. (2000, p. 122)

This pessimism appears to have been short-lived, however, as the last decade in composition studies has witnessed a mini-renaissance of interest in stylistics. Two of the emerging issues in this resurgence of style include, one, style's role in public debates about writing instruction, and, two, the role of style as a tool of invention. In his 2008 book, *Out of Style: Reanimating Stylistic Study in Composition and Rhetoric*, Paul Butler argues that that the loss of stylistics from composition in recent decades left it alive only in the popular imagination as a set of grammar conventions. Additionally, Butler uses Michael Warner's argument about counterpublics—publics, e.g., the discipline of composition studies itself, which are defined in tension with the larger public sphere—to contend that it is through style that scholars in the field can find a needed entry into public discussions about writing, stressing that the field of composition and rhetoric should re-energize stylistic study in a concerted effort to dislodge popular public perceptions of writing instruction. In doing so, Butler also stresses the importance of style as a tool of invention to help students generate ideas for these public audiences. Butler's work suggests that the book has not closed on style, that there is much more to be done in re-establishing style as a subject of inquiry in composition, particularly in its role to prepare student writers for public audiences and to explore the inventional possibilities of style. Ultimately, this focus on public audiences and the interplay between style and invention suggests that the teaching of style is often synonymous with teaching composition.

In this chapter, I argue that the teaching of style, often discarded variously as prescriptive, decorative, and intellectually deadening, can and should be reconfigured as a vital element of current rhetorical instruction on the historical grounds that stylistic considerations are integral both to rhetorical invention and to rhetoric's public function. As the editors of this collection suggest in their introduction, style "creates and reflects knowledge, and allows us to access the ideology and cultural values of a text" (Duncan & Vanguri, this volume). Indeed, while the recent research in style has argued that style is an inventive canon tied to the public turn in composition, style as a source of invention historically been tied to public writing. Here, I explore the teaching of style in early modern England, making specific connections between the canon of style and its role in providing access to dominant forms of discourse in early modern English society. Specifically, I focus on the curriculum at St. Paul's grammar school in London and the role Erasmus played in developing its curriculum. I focus on St. Paul's because it is arguably the most important preparatory school in early modern England, educating generations of scholars who later exercised a profound effect on English culture and society through literature, the law, politics, commerce, and the clergy. By revisiting some of the pedagogical practices in early modern England, we can gain useful insights about how to teach style today.

St. Paul's Grammar school became the model for almost every subsequent English grammar school for the next two hundred years, and at its educational core was the teaching of style based largely on Desiderius Erasmus's stylistic textbook *De Copia*. Early modern writing curricula, as exemplified by St. Paul's incorporation of *De Copia*, was infused with the study of style as a source of invention and as preparation to write for the public sphere. As a review of Erasmus will explain, a dialectic exists in early modern rhetoric between the understanding of style as decoration and style as a tool to help rhetors invent arguments. Style in this period, therefore, was not just a simple matter of adding words to ideas—far from it. The canon of style during the early modern period emerged as a division of rhetoric that allows the ideas themselves to take flight and affect the way knowledge was constructed for both listeners to a speech and readers of a text. The teaching of style at St. Paul's, then, acts as an important site for this chapter because the curriculum did not divide style from other areas of writing instruction, notably the invention of ideas and the preparation of students for the public sphere. By reminding ourselves of this important moment in the history of style, we can begin to see the pedagogical possibilities of style as a tool of composition instruction that prepares students to write for public audiences as well as a site for the discover of ideas.

This chapter is divided into three parts. The first part explores the role of stylistics in the curriculum at St. Paul's grammar school in London, a curriculum developed by humanists John Colet and Desiderius Erasmus that linked the teaching of style with the teaching of invention. The chapter's second part shows more specifically how style and invention were taught together in Renaissance grammar schools via the *progymnasmata* and the *declamatio*, exercises designed to train rhetors the art of invention and style. Finally, the last section of the essay describes a first-year composition course I teach that draws on some of the stylistic work from early modern England, including using imitation, using style as a source of invention, and other stylistic pedagogies. This style-based first-year writing course, at its core, uses Gerald Graff and Cathy Birkenstein's *They Say/I Say* to teach students how to use elements of style to create rich, sophisticated prose for public academic audiences. Specifically, Birkenstein and Graff's book offers writing teachers a kind of mini-progymnasmata and declamatio, reinforcing for students the interplay of style and invention. Although they never talk overtly about style and invention in their book, Graff and Birkenstein teach students to use numerous sentence-level and paragraph-level conventions designed to assist students to develop and generate ideas for writing. They stress as much in their introduction, suggesting that focusing on stylistics help students lead to discovery of ideas:

> Our templates also have a generative quality, prompting students to make moves in their writing that they might not otherwise make or even know they should make. The templates in this book can be particularly helpful for students who are unsure about what to say, or who have trouble finding enough to say, often because they consider their own beliefs so self-evident that they need not be argued for. (2010, pp. xx-xxi)

Much like the early modern grammar school classroom that used style as a tool of invention, the templates and lessons from *They Say/I Say* are designed to use style as a generator of ideas. As such, using style as a generator of ideas allows students to develop their prose style for various public audiences. Indeed, Graff and Birkenstein reinforce for students the public function of style in *They Say/I Say*, noting that "Working with these templates can give you an immediate sense of how to engage in the kids of critical thinking you are required to do at the college level and in the vocational and public spheres beyond" (2010, p. 2).

Ultimately, this chapter shows how style is not a reductive, rigid, surface-only concern. Rather, style forms the very heart of rhetorical education and reinforces the connection between elocutio and inventio. Early modern grammar schools, like St. Paul's, act as a historical precedence to reimagining style as a core feature of the composition classroom, one that plays a central role in a student's rhetorical training.

ERASMUS AND THE RISE OF ST. PAUL'S GRAMMAR SCHOOL

The teaching of style in early modern England fostered a humanist education, including preparing students for the public sphere. Even if the broader goals of an early modern rhetorical education were humanistic, using language in public contexts was very much on the minds of Renaissance educators. Many of these educators, of course, were heavily influenced by the Greek and Roman education models and used those models in their own early modern classrooms. As Teresa Morgan argues in her book Literate Education in the Hellenistic and Roman Worlds, most of the language instruction in the earlier periods focuses more on training bureaucrats rather than teaching stylistics as preparation for the public sphere (1998, p. 198-226). Likewise, Wayne Rebhorn reminds us in his book Renaissance Debates on Rhetoric that Renaissance writers see rhetorical training in the early modern period as preparation for the public realm. Rebhorn insists that, "Renaissance writers about rhetoric characterize the orator a ruler, label him a prince or king or emperor, and identify the audience he controls in a complementary manner as being his subjects" (2000, p. 4). Here, Rebhorn argues that rhetorical education in the Renaissance, and hence the textbooks on rhetoric that were produced during this period, was designed to prepare students for careers in which they would interact with the public on public matters. In other words, students who studied rhetoric in early modern grammar schools did so under the assumption they would use their training for public ends.

The most important grammar school in England to develop this type of curriculum was St. Paul's of London. Indeed, St. Paul's Grammar School became the model on which almost every other grammar school in early modern England would be based. T. W. Baldwin points out that "anyone who wishes to understand the principles upon which the sixteenth-century grammar school was founded in England would be very unwise to begin anywhere else than with Erasmus" (1944, p. 77). Humanist John Colet, who was Dean of St. Paul's Cathedral and a close friend of Erasmus, wanted to apply classical-influenced education to his new school at St. Paul's. In 1504, Colet became Dean of St. Paul's Cathedral in London, and a year later inherited his father's fortune, a fortune that enabled Colet to expand upon and re-build the school at St. Paul's, which had been in disrepair for several years. It also gave Colet the impetus he needed to apply Erasmus's ideas about rhetoric and education to his own grammar school. In a letter to Erasmus, Colet envisioned starting a grammar school based on Erasmus's methods of teaching eloquence, expressing fondness for his friend's "genius, art, and learning, and copiousness, and eloquence," going so far as to express his desire for Erasmus to teach at his own school (Nichols, 1962, p. 94). Colet never did get Erasmus to teach for him, but he did start his own grammar school in London establishing, as the school's curricular foundation, Erasmus's ideas about teaching eloquence as preparation for the public sphere.

St. Paul's School in London opened in 1511 and became a place where style formed the centerpiece of a young student's education. This education did not just focus on eloquence for the sake of artifice only—although that did occur—but rather teaching the public function of style. Specifically, students at St. Paul's learned eloquence to help them gain access to careers in the law, politics, the clergy, and other early modern professions. In his study of John Milton's education at St. Paul's, *John Milton at St. Paul's*, Donald Lemen Clark outlines the curriculum at St. Paul to show how the education in style students like Milton learned there went beyond mere artifice to prepare students for public careers. Clark insists that "the whole of grammar school education was devoted to language and literature, not as sciences to be known, but as arts to be practiced" (1942, p. 130). By practice, Clark means that an education in style went beyond rote memorization and was designed specifically as rhetorical training for public careers in politics, law, and clergy.

Consequently, the main educational thrust of Colet's school, indeed of English grammar schools in general, would be the acquisition of style, based primarily on Erasmus's *De Copia*. In his statute on "What shalbe taught" in his grammar school, Colet clarifies this focus on eloquent expression, noting that the teaching of style does not just mean artifice but rather a marriage of eloquent expression and public function, based on the Roman model of preparing students to use rhetoric publically, "as have the very Roman eloquence joined with wisdom specially" (Colet, 1909, p. 278). Here, Colet echoes Cicero's declaration of the role of the true rhetor found in Cicero's *De Inventione*: "wisdom without eloquence does too little for the good of states, but that eloquence without wisdom is generally highly disadvantageous and is never helpful" (Cicero, trans. 1949, p. 3). Humanists such as Colet and Erasmus took Cicero's argument about eloquence and wisdom and designed grammar school curricula intended to teach eloquence for public careers, so that students were taught to use eloquence not just for artifice only but to use eloquence in public functions. Erasmus's rhetoric, as outlined in *De Copia*, is a reaction to ornamentation for mere artifice. He argues that the good style should not be ostentatious and grandiose for its own sake, but rather it should have a rhetorical purpose.

For Erasmus, as with most sixteenth-century humanists, this purpose meant persuasion within the public realm. Of course, he does not shun stylistic polish and rhetorical decoration. Rather, he believes that the most accomplished and useful rhetorician was one who could turn from amplitude to terseness as the situation required, an understanding of figurative language that is echoed by William FitzGerald elsewhere in the collection. Erasmus, for instance, argues in *De Copia* that education in eloquence prepares students for various public audiences, and thus, he is concerned with the characteristics that enable success in that public function:

> To take compression of language first, who will speak more succinctly than the man who can readily and without hesitation pick out from a huge army of words, from the whole range of figures of speech, the feature that contributes most effectively to brevity? And as far as for compression of content, who will show the greatest mastery in setting out his subject in the fewest possible words if not the man who has carefully worked out what are the salient points of his case, the pillars so to speak on which it rests, distinguishing them from the subsidiary points and things brought in merely for embellishment? No one in fact will see more swiftly and surely what can be omitted without disadvantages than the man who can see where and how to make additions. (Erasmus, trans. 1978, p. 300)

Here, Erasmus spells out for his reader the usefulness of an education in style as a tool of invention, especially in pubic contexts. He points out the necessity for learning the figures of speech in order to "pick out from a huge arm of words" those linguistic features that lead most to brevity. Erasmus also points out how stylistic education helps students summarize material quickly and efficiently, pointing out "the salient points of his case." In other words, Erasmus assumes that being able to use brevity and to point out the important points of a case are meant to be used in the public sphere and, as a result, showcase the public function of style.

Since so many of the grammar school students would use their education as stepping stones into the arenas of politics, law, commerce, or clergy—all social realms in which they would be asked to argue public issues—their education in eloquence would have a decisive political bent. Erasmus would articulate his vision of rhetorical education for the public sphere further in *De Ratione Studii*. In this text, Erasmus proposes a course of study that would serve as the foundation of the English grammar schools. In *De Ratione*, Erasmus takes his ideas about rhetoric and style that he developed in *De Copia* and applies them to pedagogy. Erasmus begins *De Ratione* with a discussion of epistemology, arguing that knowledge is "of two kinds: of things and of words" (trans. 1978, p. 666). For Erasmus, the knowledge of words comes prior to the knowledge of ideas, yet ultimately the knowledge of ideas is more important: "a person who is not skilled in the force of language is, of necessity, short-sighted, deluded, and unbalanced in his judgment of things as well" (trans. 1978, p. 666). Ideas can only be truly created or conveyed to an audience if they are accompanied by eloquent, precise language. In other words, Erasmus maintains that whatever figures of speech the rhetor uses, whatever trope or scheme a speaker employs, it must be done in conjunction with the rhetorical constraints that the situation demands. More often than not, those rhetorical demands were made in the public sphere. Ultimately, Erasmus's theory of rhetoric, the application of eloquence to wisdom for a public audience, would be adapted by Colet and applied wholesale in his grammar school at St. Paul's.

THE PROGYMNASMATA AND DECLAMATIO

Elocutio at St. Paul's was taught in conjunction with inventio. Donald L. Clark writes that schoolboys at St. Paul's were "taught the same arts of eloquence as if [their] masters had chosen to call it all rhetoric instead of calling part of it rhetoric and the other part logic" (1942, p. 15). Students did not study these subjects separately, but rather they intersected and built upon one another in the schoolboy's course of study and were seen as one process of mental action. In other words, the teaching of logical arguments went hand-in-hand with the teaching of language. St. Paul's used Erasmus's ideas about *copia* and brought it together with the traditional divisions of classroom practice: One, the elementary level was known as the *progymnasmata* and, two, the advanced level was known as the *declamatio*. Again, these two levels come from Greek and Roman educational methods which had changed little over the centuries.

The *progymnasmata* refers to the exercises designed to train rhetors in the art of invention. Specifically, at St. Paul's and at other grammar schools in early modern England, the *progymnasmata* was used to teach students to invent arguments for public functions. In "The Very Idea of a *Progymnasmata*," David Fleming insists that one of the primary virtues of the *progymnasmata* was how prepares students to a wide variety of rhetorical elements, most specifically for a public function: "some are deliberative, others are forensic or epideictic; some practice the student in introductions and epilogues, others in proof and refutation" (2003, p. 116). Fleming reminds the reader that the exercises in the *progymnasmata* train students for the whole of public rhetoric: the three purposes of public discourse: forensic, deliberative, and epideictic, as well as how to support arguments and refute others. In his essay on the uses of the Greek *progymnasmata* for teaching invention in modern classrooms, John Hagaman points out that "The exercises are based on analyses of prose passages, memorization, imitation, and students' own compositions" (1986, p. 24). Hagaman stresses that the teaching of the *progymnasmata* took into consideration the context of discourse, and not just mere rote memorization, and as such trains students to explore ideas from various perspectives, ultimately for public purposes. These exercises were not used simply as prescriptive measures to teach a young rhetor how to formulate an argument. The exercises in the *progymnasmata* were used as a teaching heuristic to explore the tensions between the instructor's desires for the student and the student's own desire for freedom of learning. For instance, Richard Enos points out that the *progymnasmata* was designed by classical rhetoricians not to be used in a prescriptive, rigid manner.

> One of the most important tasks for historians and theoreticians of classical rhetoric is to introduce, refine, and possible modify the heuristic ... process of classical rhetorical theory for the resolution of contemporary communication problems so that the benefits of rhetoric, which have been evident for centuries, can continue to be made apparent through scholarly research. (Enos, 1983, p. 30)

In other words, the *progymnasmata* was used as a tool for students to learn how to eventually create arguments on their own, based on the rhetorical constraints they encountered. Indeed, early modern rhetoricians adapted the *progymnasmata* to fit their needs.

At St. Paul's, for example, school masters used the *progymnasmata* as a site where instruction in style was used as a tool of invention, designed to train students to develop their style for a variety of public roles. The *progymnasmata* was in fact aimed very squarely at public use. For example, the narrative sequence involved a retelling of a story from poetry or history and was aimed not so much at eloquence—although that was the goal as well—as it was at knowledge. Thus, as schoolboys retold a tale from history, they practiced how a story was told: point of view; what was accomplished; the time when it was accomplished; the place; how it was done; and the cause. Another example involves the *chreia*, in which students drew from a proverb and amplified it. For example, students might take a saying such as "Socrates said the root of learning is bitter, but the fruit is pleasant" and develop an essay based on its theme. Thus, such a saying is a rhetorical trope in which students would learn how to craft a piece of writing based on the precept of a proverb. In other words, they learned to develop eloquence, to explore an idea, and to arrange it appropriately all at once. For instance, Hagaman stresses that the sequenced exercises in the *progymnasmata* are meant to help students develop their rhetorical skills so that they are able to progress from concrete tasks to more abstract ones, thus training students to use a variety of rhetorical elements to help them address their instructors and classmates, as well a more public audiences. "The *progymnasmata*," Hagaman claims, "progresses from the concrete, narrative tasks to abstract persuasive ones; from addressing the class and teacher to addressing a public audience such as the law court" (1986, p. 25). To that end, students at St. Paul's were instructed in the *progymnasmata* as a means of teaching them to develop style based on a number of rhetorical situations they may eventually encounter in their professional and scholarly lives.

At the advanced level of grammar school, students were expected to showcase all of this learning as part of the *declamatio*. Toward the end of the students' grammar school career, they were expected to demonstrate their knowledge of rhetoric with a prepared speech (*declamatio*). In his *Handlist of Rhetorical Terms*, Richard Lanham defines the *declamatio* as "The elaborately ornamented and rehearsed speech on a fictional situation or hypothetical lawsuit which formed a central part of Roman rhetorical discipline" (Lanham, 1984, p. 44). If the *progymnasmata* were the smaller-scale exercises, the *declamatio* was a full-scaled rhetorical performance in which the student was expected to showcase all he learned and accomplished during his tenure in grammar school. Together, both the *progymnasmata* and the *declamatio* worked together to prepare students for using eloquence as a public function. In his *Roman Declamation in the Late Republic and Early Empire*, S. F. Bonner points out that the *declamatio* began as exercises in voice training, as rhetors learned to adjust their voice and pitch to fit whatever rhetorical situation they faced (Bonner, 1949, pp. 277ff.). Early modern education adapted the practice in their grammar schools, and it soon became a central part of the curriculum. Lanham points out that *declamatio* was significant to the young boy's education because it allowed the student to receive a fairly broad education: not only in history and mythology, law and political science, but in psychology, sociology ... and, above all, in decorum, the appropriate adjustment to social situations of all sorts. Declamation provided what we might call a centrifugal educational technique, a single central (we would say interdisciplinary) exercise out of which training of declamation provided, that is, a model for a core curriculum in miniature (Lanham, 1984, p. 44).

Lanham raises an interesting point about the usefulness of the *declamatio* in early modern education. The point about the *declamatio* as an interdisciplinary exercise is significant because it shows how language instruction was fundamental to a student's education in early modern grammar classrooms. Instruction in language, in eloquence, went hand-in-hand with teaching students how to think, how to learn their subject matter, and how to understand how to use language in a variety of public situations. This interdisciplinary curriculum, with the *progymnasmata* and the *declamatio* at its core, leads students use style and to develop eloquence as a tool for becoming participants on the stage of public life.

TEACHING STYLE IN TODAY'S CLASSROOM

Much of what the early modern stylistic classroom addressed can be applied to today's writing classrooms. Recently, I taught a first-year writing course where my writers explored the intersection between style and invention, used imitation as a tool of developing their style, and wrote their projects for a public audience, both academic and non-academic. The students in this course were all first-year students attending the university on a service and social justice scholarship and, as a result, many of the writing projects asked students to write about issues of service for public audiences. In all, students wrote four major essays. I asked them to revise three of their projects for submission in their final portfolios. In addition to the portfolio, my writers also worked in small groups throughout the semester developing, planning, writing, editing, and producing their own academic journal. The journal contained essays written by each group member that explored issues of social justice and service that students and faculty at the university would find relevant and noteworthy. At the end of the semester, the groups' journals were reviewed by an outside team of writing specialists: the university's Writing Center director and two of her consultants—an English department graduate assistant and an undergraduate junior marketing major. These readers came to class on the last day of the semester and discussed with the writers the strengths and weaknesses of each journal. Thus, throughout the semester, my writers became cognizant of the notion that they were developing their writing style for a real audience of academic readers in a way they normally would not if they were just writing for me or for their class colleagues.

While many of the assignments asked students to perform a variety of academic tasks—summary, making claims and supporting them with research, connecting personal experience to public contexts, among others—the main thrust of the course was exploring stylistics as a tool of invention. This interaction between style and invention was accomplished mainly through using Graff and Birkenstein's *They Say/I Say*. This book is an accessible introduction to the various sentence-level rhetorical moves that academic writers make in argumentative writing. The authors present dozens of model templates that students can incorporate into their own prose in an effort to see how academic writing is often writing done in response to other people's ideas. The book helped my writers unpack the vagaries and mysteries of academic discourse. As such, the exercises and lessons from *They Say/I Say* act as a mini-*progymnasmata* and *declamatio*. By this, I mean that the lessons on academic style the book teaches build on one another, showing how the different academic conventions and rhetorical moves can be used as tools of invention. Students use the templates to imitate various academic conventions, with an eye toward generating sophisticated prose for public academic and non-academic audiences. Ultimately, building on these lessons and stylistic elements allow students to showcase their learning at once in their final projects.

Each of the four major essays students wrote corresponded with a lesson from *They Say/I Say*, stressing the role style plays in the invention process. The first essay asked them to write a clear, well-organized summary of one of the essays from the course reader. In doing so, students were asked to establish some kind of connection between the article and its impact on their thinking about their education and what they hope to accomplish as a service and social justice scholar at the university. The second essay asked writers to pick one of the course readings and make a claim about whether they agree or disagree, or both, with the main claim of the reading, using library research to support their claims. In this essay, students were introduced to Cicero's arrangement scheme and expected to use it in their paper. The third essay asked students to pick an issue about which they are passionate and write three different letters to three different public audiences advocating for that issue. Finally, their last project asked them to write a personal narrative about their experience with service and social justice and to connect their experience with a larger social context. In this final project, students were expected to showcase their stylistic learning, much in the spirit of the early modern *declamatio*. As such, the sequence of assignments in this course, using the exercises and lessons from *They Say/I Say*, mirrors the step-by-step process of the *progymnasmata* and *declamatio*.

For all four assignments, students were asked to use a number of the templates and the lessons on style from *They Say/I Say* to help them generate and develop their ideas in their papers and to further develop a more sophisticated prose style. Indeed, I would suggest that the stylistic lessons and templates from *They Say/I Say* reflect Butler's argument in *Out of Style: Reanimating Stylistic Study in Composition and Rhetoric* that the teaching of style appears in places where many of us in composition studies do not expect it. Specifically, Butler argues that is often mistaken to believe that style disappeared completely following the social turn and is no longer a part of the field. Rather, Butler implies that "style is often hidden, having dispersed into a 'diaspora of composition studies,' where it is being used in important ways" (2008, 24). Specifically, Butler locates this "diaspora" in such categories as genre theory, rhetorical analysis, personal writing, and theories of cultural difference. To these categories, I would add the various elements of academic discourse that Graff and Birkenstein's book address, since *They Say/I Say* works from the assumption that all good argumentative writing, including academic writing, makes claims in response to other claims.

Now, I would like to share some of my writers' reflections on how imitating and using the templates from *They Say/I Say*, how focusing on the interplay between style and invention, and how writing for various public academic and non-academic audiences helped them develop their own prose style. Imitation, of course, is nothing new in writing instruction, as Denise Stodola argues in this collection, noting that the medieval focus on imitation helps current writing instructions break down the form-content binary. This collapsing of the form-content binary is one of the strengths of *They Say/I Say*. One of my writers, Melissa, noted how focusing on the templates from *They Say/I Say* helped her write a more sophisticated academic style than she had before entering college. "The templates in *They Say/I Say* actually helped a lot," Melissa claimed, "because when I would be stuck with what transition to use or how to introduce a thought, the templates gave me great ideas to incorporate." Here, Melissa suggests that imitating the templates in her academic writing led her to develop ideas in her writing, not just use the templates for artifice or surface decoration. Indeed another student, Abbey, also suggested the importance of style in her writing, not just for her composition course but for other first-year courses as well. "Most of my classes required me to write a significant amount," she asserts, "so I took what I was learning about style and applied it to my other writing assignments. I found it easier to take on opinions in speech, political science, and religion when writing with style in mind." Both Melissa and Abbey were able to use their lessons in style for other academic assignments outside the composition classroom, thus reinforcing the public function of style in writing instruction.

Here's an example of Melissa's prose in an early draft of her first assignment, where students summarized a reading and connected it to their personal experiences as students. The audience for this essay was the university community, so students had to write for an audience outside the classroom—a more public audience, if you will. In her essay, Melissa summarized Kate Ronald's essay on the importance of style and connected it to an experience from high school. Here's the opening of Melissa's first draft:

> In Kate Ronald's "Style: The Hidden Agenda in Composition Classes or One Reader's Confession," style is described as a necessity in writing. Without it every paper blends together and the reader awaits the end. Ronald argues against the age-old theory in schools: "it is what you say and not how you say it." Throughout my years of service before becoming an Arrupe Scholar and working with others I have learned that the way you connect with someone and interact with others has everything to do with the style of how you present the information therefore agreeing with Ronald's argument.

Melissa's opening is problematic. She does not clarify clearly Ronald's argument, nor does she clearly show how Ronald's essay connects to her own experiences from high school—though, she begins to make those moves. These moves are a bit clumsy, and she moves much too fast from Ronald's essay to her own experience.

> By the time Melissa submitted this essay in her final portfolio, she had revised it several times, using the stylistic advice from They Say/I Say. Her prose grew more confident, stronger, and she was able imitate the templates in a way that allowed her to generate ideas in her opening that were missing in the first draft, ideas that allowed her slow down and take the reader point by point to establish connections between Ronald's essay and Melissa's personal experiences. Here's the revised first paragraph:In her essay, "Style: The Hidden Agenda in Composition Classes or One Reader's Confession," Kate Ronald

argues that while most writing instructors do not teach style, most of them do grade a student's writing style. Style, according to Ronald, is the sense that "someone is home" when writing (Ronald, 1995, p. 95). One feature of style that she elaborates on in her essay is the element of entertainment that shows the reader a focus on style. Ronald points out that if writers do not interest their audience, then the reader will have a hard time paying attention or remembering anything from the writing. This element of entertainment goes along with the importance of style in writing. Ronald argues that style is the most important part of writing and that personal experience is a great way to add outside experience to a paper and make it more interesting. I agree with Ronald's stance that style is the most important asset in conveying a message because I have seen style act as a significant asset in my own experiences, both academic and extracurricular.

This revised version not only shows that Melissa holds a firmer grasp of Ronald's argument, but she also displays a more eloquent style. The sentences are more cohesive with one another, and Melissa slows down her connection between Ronald's essay and her experiences so that the reader is less confused about how Melissa arrives at those connections.

But writing for an audience was not the only public audience these writers addressed. In their third project, students were asked to write three letters to different audiences outside the university, advocating for an issue. Jessica, one of the strongest students in the class, chose to advocate for clean water in her small Ohio town, writing to an audience of high school students urging them to begin a clean water advocacy club, as well as to an audience of local business owners. Jessica is an interesting example because she came to the class already a strong writer. As she noted in her final portfolio letter, "As skeptical as I was coming in to this class (I thought that since I had tested out of it with my two AP English classes, I didn't need to take it), I have learned a lot in the last few months." Later, she told me that the course's focus on style made her more conscious of how elements of style, imitation, and the templates from *They Say/I Say* led her to be more aware of the interplay between style and invention, especially as it relates to the stylistic elements cohesion. "The way I believe style consideration has most impacted by writing in the last semester was through the idea of cohesion," Jessica insists. "When I edit my papers, I now try to make sure all of my sentences flow with the sentences that precede them." In her letter to the local business owners, Jessica demonstrates how this focus on cohesion leads her to write more eloquent prose for a public function. In this section of the letter, Jessica appeals to the business owners' awareness of cost, showing how clean water does not have to be as expensive as they may fear:

> As dismal as these statistics may be, the solution is hopeful. A mere $20 can provide one person with clear water for 20 years. One well, to supply an entire village with clear water, costs only $5,000. Last year, our group organized an end-of-summer dance for high school students in order to raise awareness and money for this cause. We succeeded in raising $6,312—more than enough to build an entire well and change the fate of a village community.

Her use of the templates from *They Say/I Say*, as well as her conscious use of the stylistic element cohesion, leads Jessica to develop ideas for her writing in a public sphere that she may not have been able to do otherwise. For instance, the first sentence in the above example uses a dependent clause to connect to the previous paragraph and to set up the argument about expense in this paragraph. Also, Jessica uses numerous transitions from sentence to sentence to reinforce cohesion from one idea to the next. As such, Jessica's heightened awareness of style in a public sphere echoes many of the stylistic exercises and purposes in the early modern grammar school.

Another student, Matthew, also recognized the power of sentence-level rhetoric in helping him generate ideas in his writing, for both academic audiences and non-academic public readers. Before coming to college, Matthew had not considered style much at all in his writing, noting that "My style before EN 111 had been sufficient for previous assignments in high school. However, I realized that I needed to be able to develop a more scholastic style for my years in college." Matthew learned how to generate ideas more fully and to connect more clearly to his audience. Here's an example of Matthew's prose, where he consciously uses the templates from *They Say/I Say* not only to imitate academic styles to produce more sophisticated prose but to help him generate ideas to write about. This passage comes from an essay in which Matthew responds to arguments made by Graff about the role of public schools fostering intellectualism through the use of students' personal interests, such as popular culture:

> Personal interests can indeed be the foundation for the understanding of intellectualism. In his essay "Hidden Intellectualism" Gerald Graff makes the claim that too often we associate intellectualism with common areas of study and

that instead we should incorporate individual interests and passions to motivate the intellect. Graff uses personal experience to back this belief, citing the analysis he and his friends made between "sport teams, movies, and toughness" (Graff & Birkenstein, 2010, p. 300). According to Graff these interests are legitimate areas for intellectualism to thrive, "It was in these discussions with friends about toughness and sports that I began to learn the rudiments of intellectualism" (Graff & Birkenstein, 2010, p. 300). It is clear then that, at least to Graff, personal interests can be the foundation for counterarguments, arguments, and the composing of beliefs.

As this passage illustrates, Matthew imitates numerous academic moves and conventions, allowing him to create a more "scholastic style" to write a fluid summary of Graff's position. That is, Matthew incorporates various transitions and phrases, uses connecting elements to show cohesion from sentence-to-sentence, and he frames his summary around different templates from *They Say/I Say*, including such phrases as "According to," "It is clear that," and "Not only did," among others. In his final portfolio letter in which he reflects on his writing throughout the semester, Matthew acknowledges that "using style ... for the first time with an understanding of ethos and pathos made the essay a more interesting one to write and gave me a new perspective and form to use in writing subsequent papers." The understanding of style that Matthew reveals in this letter suggests the interplay between style and invention, as well as the public function of style when students are required to consider audiences beyond the classroom, as he was asked to do in the previous assignment. Actually, Matthew himself says as much later when he observes the role style now plays in his writing for other academic audiences. "I am more conscious of when and how I insert my opinion and keep in mind the prompts and field of study," he asserts. In other words, a conscious understanding of style and its role in the writing classroom leads students like Matthew, as well as others cited in this chapter, to consider how style helps them develop ideas, to consider how imitating other styles improves their own academic prose, and to consider how style makes them more aware of their writing in the public sphere.

CONCLUSION

My students' writing demonstrates how style is not a reductive, rigid pedagogy that teaches standards of form and rules of usage, but rather style is a dynamic part of the writing process that can be seen as synonymous with composition. This understanding of style as a vibrant element of the writing classroom locates a historical precedent in the early modern grammar classroom. The education that students received at St. Paul's grammar school, for instance, points to the high place that style held in the early modern curriculum. For scholars and educators such as Erasmus and Colet, training in eloquence was hardly naïve, but this focus on eloquence led to careers in public oration, in the law, in commerce, in the clergy, and in other early modern professions. Students who read and imitated classical authors and who practiced and learned the *progymnasmata* and the *declamatio* did so with an eye toward public practice of their art. Accordingly, style formed the very heart of rhetorical education and reinforced the connection between elocution and *inventio*. This lively interplay between style and invention emerges in the contemporary writing classroom through the use of Graff and Birkenstein's *They Say/I Say*, a book that offers students opportunities to strengthen their own style by imitating numerous academic conventions, through using their templates as sources of invention, and through following a revised *progymnasmata* and *declamatio*. The early modern grammar schools, therefore, act as a historical precedence for contemporary writing classrooms to re-imagine style as a central feature of writing instruction.

REFERENCES

Baldwin, T.W. (1944). *William Shakespeare's small Latine and lesse Greek*. Urbana, IL: University of Illinois Press.

Bonner, S. F. (1949). *Roman declamation in the late republic and early empire*. Berkeley: University of California Press.

Butler, P. (2008). *Out of style: Reanimating stylistic study in composition and rhetoric*. Logan, UT: Utah State University Press.

Cicero. (1949). *De inventione*. H.M. Hubbell. Tran. Cambridge: Harvard University Press.

Clark, D. L. (1942). *John Milton at St. Paul's School*. New York: Columbia University Press.

Connors, R. (2000). The erasure of the sentence. *College Composition and Communication 52*: 96-128.

Fleming, J. D. (2003). The very idea of a progymnasmata. *Rhetoric Review 22*(2), 105-120.

Graff, G. & Birkenstein, C. (2010). *They say/I say: The moves that matter in academic writing* (2nd ed.). New York: W.W. Norton.

Hagaman, J. (1986). Modern use of the 'progymnasmata' in teaching rhetorical invention. *Rhetoric Review* 5(1), 22-29.

Horner, W. B. (Ed.) (1983). The classical period. *The present state of scholarship in historical and contemporary rhetoric*. Columbia: University of Missouri Press.

Lanham, R. (1991). *Handlist of rhetorical terms* (2nd ed.). Berkeley: University of California Press.

Lupton, J. H. (1909). *A life of John Colet*. London: G. Bell and Sons.

Morgan, T. (1998). *Literate education in the Hellenistic and Roman worlds*. Cambridge: Cambridge University Press.

Nichols, F. M. (1962). Epistles of Erasmus. Epistle 223. New York: Russell and Russell.

Rebhorn, W. A. (Ed.). (2000). *Renaissance debates on rhetoric*. Trans. Wayne A. Reborn. Ithaca, NY: Cornell University Press.

Thompson, C. R. (Ed.). (1978). Collected works of Erasmus (Vol. 24). Toronto: University of Toronto Press.

THE RESEARCH PAPER AS STYLISTIC EXERCISE

Mike Duncan
University of Houston-Downtown

There is a major theoretical and pedagogical consequence of recognizing that style is central to composition; namely, all the writing done by student writers in composition courses must be re-conceptualized as some form of stylistic exercise. By "stylistic exercise," I mean an activity that allows a student to explore the myriad of rhetorical options that style offers. This exploration is typically accomplished through exposure to a new writing genre, with the accompanying expectation that students will acquire increased skill and fluency within that genre, as well as genres that they have yet to encounter.

One of the oldest common stylistic exercises in American colleges and high schools is the so-called "research paper," which has been widely assigned in some form since the 1920s. Direct descendants of the assignment continue to appear on American college syllabi nationwide, despite numerous criticisms over the last seventy years over its form and even the need for such an assignment. Most versions of this creature do not exist outside the composition classroom, for example, in direct conflict with their professed purpose of teaching students how to do "research." The length requirements, too, can be arbitrary and counter-productive. The difficulty the assignment presents for students is considerable, perhaps even unfair.

But I am not writing here to bury the research paper. Rather, I think the assignment—or, rather, the *idea* of the assignment as much as any particular execution—is an ideal candidate for demonstrating the pervasiveness of the claims of this collection.

At every step of its nearly hundred-year career as a secondary and college-level pedagogical tool, the "research paper" has taught a certain kind of writing that is difficult and laborious enough to persuade countless students to have someone else write it for them. It tends to represent one style—the "right" or "correct" style for performing "research." And in that form, it has guided many a student to better writing.

But there is another way to conceptualize it, and that is as a door to a multitude of other demanding styles. This approach, of course, requires that the research paper exist not only in the mind of the student, but in the mind of the instructor, as an exploration of style, even as it seemingly hews to one specific path.

To explain what I mean by this claim—namely, that the research paper can be profitably viewed as a stylistic exercise that leads to increased control over many styles, rather than just an artificial "research" style—I offer three origin stories for the research paper in American education. These three stories agree with each other more than they disagree, but the portraits are sufficiently different to give them voice individually as accounts of the assignment's instructional genesis. Together, these three stories form a historical pathway toward a style-based way of reconceptualizing the assignment.

ORIGINS

One origin story is told in Robert Connors's *Composition-Rhetoric*, revised from an earlier appearance in his 1987 "Personal Writing Assignments" article. Connors holds the genre arose in composition around 1920 out of three needs: 1) instructors wanting to "transcend the personal writing" paradigm that was prevalent, 2) the desire for a corrective response to the increasing availability of secondary and tertiary source materials, namely a packaged, gentrified solution to increasing concerns over intellectual property, and 3) a hunger for more formalized, efficient instruction. Furthermore, Connors concludes that the assignment teaches "the research attitude," synonymous with "the modern attitude," where the rhetor is a "medium, not an originator"—the student collectively merges with the secondary research rather than create new knowledge (1997, pp. 321-323).

In this first tale, the research paper is an ironic and flawed entity that meets institutional needs rather than student ones; any student benefits are secondary precipitate. The assignment was not wielded without good intent, or completely ineffectual, but it failed on an epistemic front and as part of the larger current-traditional pedagogy.

A second origin story is told in David Russell's *Writing the Academic Disciplines*. Russell holds that the genre is a mixture of the research ideal of German universities and the British oral thesis tradition (2002, pp. 78-79). "Course theses" appeared, beyond the usual shorter themes, in the 1860s, evolved into "graduating theses" by the 1880s, and eventually became class-specific papers simultaneously with the introduction of German-style seminars. This rapidly forming tradition, originally intended to model scholarly activity to students and improve writing skills, migrated to lower-level courses and secondary schools, losing much of its scholarly idealism on the way. In the

1910s, the assignment "begins to harden into its familiar form" as an empty exercise in formality (Russell, 2002, pp. 83-88). Suffused through Russell's account is the social function of the assignment. To scholarly idealists, it was an apprenticeship lesson for bright students in conjunction with a seminar. To more "egalitarian" forces, it functioned as a doorway to college success for all students, even in secondary settings, which quickly led to "research papers" being taught in junior high schools (Russell, 2002, p. 86).

In this second tale, the research paper is an emancipating entity that did not always succeed in its promise, decaying rapidly as it drifted down to the secondary level. The portrait is more positive than the one offered by Connors, but it, too, is a story of failure.

The third origin story is mine, and a bit longer. It is a story of a central institutional debate about student teaching that recurs every decade or so in journal or book form, with the sides taking on new avatars and new sites of battle, and with the concept of the research paper serving as one of the favorite battlegrounds. The military metaphor is not accidental, as World War II seems to have had a significant hand in its development.

Narrowing down the time periods of its presence is crucial to understanding that development. The research paper was "established custom" (Angus, 1948, p. 191) in 1948, with a division between the "high school term paper" and the college "research paper" present in 1943 (Arms, 1943, p. 24) that goes back at least to 1936, with the secondary version preparing for the latter version (Bader, 1936, p. 667). Taylor's 1929 *A National Survey of Conditions in Freshman English* (Brereton, 1995, pp. 545-562), reviewed in *The English Journal* in 1930 by Stith Thompson, does not give any details on assignments; Thompson, though, refers to it in passing as "the project" at his institution, where it concerns "the proper handling of bibliography, notes, and planning in the large" (Thompson, 1930, p. 555).

However, Ralph Henry's 1928 survey of twenty-seven American colleges reveals, in response to a question about the length of assignments, that themes were still the dominant assignment, with an average of one per week assigned, with "longer themes assigned 'occasionally'":

> These longer themes are from 1,500 to 2,500 words in length and fall due "once a month," "three per semester," or in a larger number of institutions, "one each semester." ... In general the program agreed upon by the large majority is as follows: a theme of about 300-500 words (three or four pages) each week, with one long paper of 1,500-2,500 words due each semester. (Dr. Shiperd reports an average assignment of

155

> 1.7 themes per week, an average length of 4+ pages, and an average of two longer themes per semester. (1928, p. 306)

The "longer theme" of 1928 would then be, by the modern 300-word page, a 5-8 page paper. "Long theme" seems to be the preferred term in this period; high school students speak poorly of such a "long theme" in a 1913 survey (Hatfield, 1913, p. 318). It is unclear, however, when it became a freshman college requirement across the board, as opposed to something reserved for junior or senior level classes, as it seems to be in an elective class in 1902 (Hart, 1902, p. 370) and in a 10,000 word form in 1916 (Harris, 1916, p. 502). It is also unclear when it became "long"—the high school "long theme" of 1915 is only 750 words (Rankin, 1915, p. 196). In 1922, Fred Newton Scott complained (at length) about pointing out errors in themes in the *English Journal* (Scott, 1922, p. 463), but made no mention of long themes.

While the early 1920s seems a reasonable time frame for it to be a widespread requirement from college freshmen, the assignment does not become a focus of recorded debate until the 1940s. Angell Matthewson's 1941 "Long Compositions Based on Research" and Annette Cummings' 1950 "An Open Letter to Teachers of English," could be considered at first to be odd choices to represent poles of conflict; one is a high school teacher just before WWII; the other is a junior college teacher after the war, nine years later. But their opinions are antithetical products of the earlier forces described by Connors and Russell, as well as the world war that happened between the two essays.

Matthewson, in 1941, held that senior high school students of the time needed to write at least one long paper (1,500 to 3,000 words) involving research. His reasoning was that longer rather than shorter assignments tended to challenge and motivate students to do more, and prepared them better for college work, which would involve similar assignments.

Not long afterward, the educational world shifted with the war. Shortly after the attack on Pearl Harbor in December, an editorial in the January 1942 *English Journal* opined it was the job of teachers of English to build war morale and support social service among students (Hatfield & De Boer, 1942, pp. 67-68). The NCTE quickly followed in February with a statement on "The Role of the English Teacher in Wartime," championing American values and ideals while rejecting the xenophobia and excessive patriotism that had appeared during the Great War. It includes the following injunction:

> e) As teachers of English, we can develop those skills essential to participation in democratic life (1) through classroom practice in grouping thinking and decision, (2) through

teaching the techniques of public and panel discussion, and (3) through emphasis upon the need for precision and honesty in the use of language in reading and reporting and in the expression of ideas in speech and writing. (NCTE, 1942, p. 88)

These idealistic wartime NCTE standards hang over the thoughtful review of faculty and student views of the college "term paper" in the *Journal of Higher Education* in June of the same year. The assignment is taught unevenly at the lower level and often overburdens students across courses, but when carefully supervised and possibly saved for junior and senior level classes, it is a "worthwhile" assignment (Rivlin, 1942, p. 342). It would seem, then, that the research paper met patriotic muster in the 1940s; Angus' aforementioned description of it as "established custom" becomes even more ironclad.[1]

"An Open Letter to Teachers of English," however, appears in 1950, five years after the war is over, from a junior college in Michigan, after the G.I. Bill of 1944; over a third of junior college students are veterans. Cummings holds that research papers in undergraduate classes are a hypocritical waste of time. Most students, she states, cannot handle logical thinking, and therefore the research paper is lost on them; the assignment is an artifact of colleges gunning for more graduate students, and high schools gunning for more college enrollees. She would prefer assignments based on "experience and observation" for teaching logic (1950, p. 39).

Cummings' critique is notable in that she critiques the assignment as an assignment, rather than how it is taught. Earlier criticism focuses on pedagogical cautions such as plagiarism and padding (Woods, 1933, pp. 87-89) or a lack of "scientific" standards (Ahl, 1931, p. 17). The assignment itself is spared and its value, when taught well, is championed. Arms, in 1943, for example, is typical; he has major issues with topic selection, but thinks the assignment is "the real center of freshmen English in that, like little else in much college work, it gives an opportunity to set up a problem and find a solution" (Arms, 1943, p. 25).

The concept of the research paper becomes, thus, a focus point for professional opinions of the transforming student body and the nature of ideal "college work." If, as Matthewson, you believe students tend to rise to a structured challenge presented by an enthusiastic and organized instructor, and it meets the moral and political demands of the age, it's the best stylistic exercise since sliced bread. If, however, as Cummings, you believe that many, if not most, students in your classroom are not suited for logical thinking by intelligence or temperament, the research paper tends to only be an exercise in futility for both student and instructor.

Notably, despite the distance between their opinions, both Matthewson and Cummings largely pass over the content of the assignment. Cummings is worried about command of "logic," and Matthewson is worried about "argument"—both of which must be displayed within the genre. These are critical concerns about any writing. But looking back to the assignment's early origins and accounts of its teaching, the assignment is all about meeting genre expectations—documented secondary sources, library protocols, formatting, scientific method, appropriate topic selection (probably the most pressing concern of instructors up until Cummings)—argumentation and logic are necessary, of course, for these tasks, but not as emphasized.

The remainder of my tale of the assignment is cyclic. The assignment changed under the influence of abolitionist thought, but it did not go away. In 1961, 83% of all colleges required a research paper in the freshman composition program (Manning, 1961). In 1982, when Richard Larson attacked the very concept of the assignment in *College English*, it was 84% (Ford & Perry, 1982, p. 827). Larson's attack is different from that of Cummings; he too sees the assignment as hypocritical, but not because it is beyond the students. Rather, the concept of the assignment—as much as he is willing to allow its existence[2]—tends to produce a kind of "non-writing" that cannot but fail to teach research. Furthermore, the job of teaching the writing styles of other disciplines should not fall to English (Ford & Perry, 1982, p. 816). Concerns about writing across the curriculum aside, Larson's is still a critique kin to those seen before the 1940s, which concerned themselves with the value of the assignment to teaching research.

These three stories suggest something very interesting about our discipline—namely, one of its central, traditional assignments is a murky, multi-definitional entity that isn't even universally agreed upon as pedagogically useful, even though four-fifths of programs use it in some form. The question, then, is not so much about the assignment, but what model of writing is preferred; are we to teach argument and logic, with the rest trappings, or are we to focus on genre demands and research methods, in which case argument and logic will come? Is there another way? The format of the traditional research paper offers a clue; namely, it forms a genre that is plastic and generic enough to be molded into other styles.

BENEFITS OF THE "GENERIC" STYLE

The generic research paper simultaneously displays all the weaknesses of a rhetoric reduced to ornament, and all the strengths of a rhetoric grounded in genre. It can be an empty and frustrating exercise in formalism, and it can be an empowering stepping-stone that leads to linguistic flexibility, which in turn allows the absorption and mastery of a multitude of other genres. It is the latter way of thinking—the stepping-stone model—that I want to describe here, but that will require dissecting the prevailing versions discussed thus far. One problem rests in the word "research," and the other in the word "paper."

In composition studies, "research" is generally talked about either as a skill (something you do) or as a genre (how a skill is used in a particular locale). We can talk about writing skill in general, a sort of under-writing that changes for the occasion, or writing skill in the context of a certain field or occasion, say psychology. The generic research paper is neither quite an English literature analysis, nor a publishable psychology journal article; its method of inquiry is not precisely the same as either and would be rejected by peers in both, at least until it bent to the will of genre. In its final form, with a research method, topic selection, and citational demands, without particular disciplinary ties, it is a sectioned, preliminary, sketchy shadow of a "real" writing genre that is socially connected. This is the point from which Larson started his critique, and where I depart.

I depart from Larson because there are benefits to socially isolated writing. The WAC job that the paper often takes on, rightly or not, demands a generic approach, even if that generic feel coming from picking a topic or theme for the entire course and deriving writing principles from that topic. Either way, an isolated paper is a safe space in which to experiment with stylistic conventions, at least if it is taught in the light of revision. More time can be spent working on generic argumentative moves. An audience beyond the instructor could be provided, as I can do in professional writing courses, to add the social aspect, but this puts a lie to the authority of the instructor, as well as the fact that there is a social aspect to the paper already—the university as a whole, and their fellow students.

The word "paper," implying a fixed and formal product, also has problems; this is why I favor "project," like Thompson did in 1930. For students to see the research paper as a stylistic exercise, it must be equated with revision. Projects are ongoing works-in-progress; papers are physical entities. If students can screw up citations without fear and see them as the parenthetical helpers for the reader that they are, then they are in the stylistic mindset. If they see citations as hurdles they must clear before arguing, then they are in a research mindset. The former is vastly preferable for teaching writing.

The project (leave "research" and "paper" behind for now) must be eased up to carefully rather than demanded all at once; breaking into individual sections or drafts reinforces its constructed, temporary nature. Above all, though, it must be constantly portrayed as preliminary practice, rather than a certificate of achievement that says the writer now knows how to conduct "research." Doctoral degrees perform that role well enough. A spirit of inquiry, though, can be instilled without going that far. There is no right way to write the project, any more than there is a right way to write a memo; an "A" on a project should not mean mastery of research. It must should, rather, a mastery of a style, a way of arguing.

All college freshmen need is the simple confidence that when they encounter new writing genres—and they will—that they have a basic stylistic template to draw from through experience with a project of inquiry that has given them a model for how knowledge is constructed. Thinking about the research paper in terms of stylistic play drains persuasive power from its sideshow horror elements of length and complexity and focuses, rather, on how language affects change. It is when they move to the sophomore level without a stylistic template for large documents, however, that ethical issues appear.

LENGTH AND ETHICS

A March 2011 op-ed in the New York Times called "Teaching to the Text Message," by Andy Selsberg, an adjunct professor at John Jay College, begins with the following three sentences:

> I've been teaching college freshmen to write the five-paragraph essay and its bully of a cousin, the research paper, for years. But these forms invite font-size manipulation, plagiarism and clichés. We need to set our sights not lower, but shorter. (2011)

The rest of the piece, which is about 470 words, is a case for assigning smaller writing assignments to college freshmen—some two lines long, some the length of YouTube video comments or Amazon book reviews, topping off at the length of a cover letter or a networking email. Selsberg does not advocate eliminating longer writing projects from English courses, but he would prefer to set them aside for the second semester or later. Doing what he calls "rewarding concision first," he suggests, "will encourage students to be economical and inventive with language," as this is more, "in tune with most students' daily chatter, as well as the world's conversation."

I do not like bullies, but I do not think the research paper is a bully. On the contrary, I think the research paper, or, rather, the stylistic project I have described thus far, is a close friend—a sometimes boorish, anal-retentive, nerdy, and verbose close friend, but a friend nevertheless, and sometimes a quickly neglected friend when new ideas for teaching writing come along.

Namely, it is a friend that serves a special and central ethical function in the teaching of writing at the college level. For if, as scholars and teachers, we believe that well-constructed arguments require evidence, and not just evidence, but warranted evidence—if we believe that the intellectual work of others must not only be referenced to make informed arguments, but cited for easy reference—and if we believe that stylistic conventions of academic discourse must be respected (if not followed lockstep) in order to facilitate communication and learning, then it follows, necessarily, that when we teach college students how to write, we must teach and demonstrate to them the best practices for presenting complex arguments that we have available. In this way, the "learning research" goal merges with the "better writing" goal for the assignment.

This necessitates an assigned paper of sufficient length that has the metaphorical and literal breathing room to develop complex, warranted arguments that require parenthetical citation, and exhibit the stylistic forms common to what we ourselves recognize as learned discourse. Break it up into smaller assignments first if you would, but eventually, it must be performed in total to satisfy the ethical charge that I have just outlined.

My concern with Selsberg's position, even as I sympathize with it and see how it responds obliquely to the research paper tradition, is that our mission as university and college instructors cannot be primarily to teach students how to replicate and value soundbite discourse, web discourse, twitter discourse—pick whatever new medium you prefer, including ones yet to emerge. We must understand these emerging forms, yes. Be fluent with their conventions, certainly. Critique and analyze them, definitely. But we should not fall prey to fetishizing new mediums, no matter how current or hip or tantalizingly brief they are. We have an ethical charge to expose students to the existence of complex and nuanced argumentation that requires extended forms to develop ideas. Furthermore, we have a charge to show them how to construct these structures. We can value concision while knowing quite well that argumentation cannot always be reduced to, say, 470 words, or 140 characters.

The research paper is difficult work for both students and instructors. It is so difficult to grade that many professors eschew it for smaller assignments. It is so difficult to write that students see even modest page requirements as torture. The research paper is one of the reasons that the composition course is sometimes dryly called the course taken by students who do not want to take it and taught by teachers who do not want to teach it. The assignment is ultimately frightening for many students because it confronts one of our greatest fears as social humans, which is that we have nothing to worth to say of any *length* on a topic. This is a fear so frightening that students will try to circumvent it through plagiarism and padding without close supervision. Getting past that fear is worth it, though, and this point cannot be stressed enough. Once a student has the genre in hand, they have something far better than the skill that Selsberg favors, "to express one key detail succinctly and eloquently"—and that something is the form of good questions, which returns to the praise of Arms in 1943: the assignment, when taught well, shows how to state a problem and seek a solution, in that order.

Eloquence and succinctness are wonderful qualities. But they will not enable a student to provide a nuanced answer that requires more than a few sentences to explain. In order to write an extended argument, one must read a great deal, understand what one has read, reflect on that reading through analysis, and then reconsider all that has been done. All academics know this task can't be done "succinctly," let along quickly, if quality is desired. Even the books written by academics for general lay audiences, rather than for other academics, are still books—they don't become 470-word articles through a skillful application of eloquence and succinctness. Succinctness demands a harsh price in the form of context and complexity, and eloquence can be a distracting lacquer.

I am not arguing against the value of style here—on the contrary. Style and content are the same thing. The form of the discourse empowers its content, which is why it is extremely hard to say anything very meaningful in a five-paragraph essay, a form that is almost entirely consumed by its maddening redundancy. Constraints like those of the sonnet can empower writers, of course, but the research paper has its empowering constraints, too. An insistence on a thesis, on a specific question of interest, on warranted evidence for claims, on supporting citations, on accurate (not necessarily succinct) summary and synthesis—all these add power. Once a student knows how these work—a state only possible by fitting them together themselves—they become old friends. Cranky, nerdy friends, but friends nonetheless—and ethical friends, too.

I do not want to make a straw man out of Selsberg because as I mentioned before, he does not want to get rid of research papers. But I have seen college curriculums that have done so in the name of meeting students where they are—a noble and practical idea—and yet the very point of meeting students where they are is to get them closer to where the instructor is, not to pull them up about halfway and then let them go. If an undergraduate student cannot write a developed, thesis-driven argument of ten pages or more by the time they graduate, the university that granted their degree has done them a disservice in a myriad of ways. I could also argue the same if they cannot do so by the beginning of their sophomore year.

CONCLUSIONS

There is no reason the assignment has to be called a "research paper" to serve a sound pedagogical purpose. I have assigned plenty of rhetorical analysis papers, textual analysis papers, analytical reports, reader-response papers, proposals, exploratory papers, compare-contrast papers, feasibility reports, linguistic analyses, articles, you name it—but I cannot recall ever telling an undergraduate or graduate class that they needed to write a "research paper," save casually or absentmindedly. All of that writing that I have assigned requires some kind of specialized method of inquiry, so I have always thought most of these assignments as "research papers" to some extent, part of my ongoing pedagogical crusade for the civil right of being able to think about and express one's positions in written form. I do not think most of my colleagues call it by its 1950s name, either—the buzzphrases I've heard lately at recent conferences are "extended argument" or "extended thought"—either way, the length is both metaphorical and tangible.

As someone who primarily teaches junior-level and senior-level professional writing more so than composition, there is a similar assignment in my classes—the proposal. It requires research, though not research that can be done entirely in library or online—it requires making phone calls, interviewing people, going to places to find physical records. Its written product is also quite different. And yet the students who do well on such an assignment are the ones who understand from the beginning that it is all a stylistic dance; certain sections of the proposal do certain maneuvers, which in turn support other sections—they must look a certain way in order to persuade visually, and content presented must leap a certain bar to establish authority. It is a game we are playing in which learning how to play is the goal. The actual proposal is a mere byproduct of the style-driven process. Likewise, "the research paper," printed and stapled for review, should not be the final arbiter of learning "research" or "writing" in a course; it can at best reflect dimly on what has occurred within the student's mind as a result of stylistic play.

I have taken a historical approach here, as Tom Pace did in the previous chapter, rather than that of a shorter and more sermonic piece for two reasons. First, the research paper is an old assignment, and an old topic; to praise or blame, at this point, is as much of a tradition as the assignment itself, and stories are easier to follow from the beginning. Second, it seemed a shame to praise the old research-imprinting mission of the research paper and reframe it as stylistic exercise in 470 words, when I could enact the "long paper" myself, and thus demonstrate the form and value of the extended argument.

NOTES

1. There is a non-epistemic slant to the university mission in these years; Edward Hamilton's idea of the function of higher education in 1944 as "training youths to find, formulate, test, and evaluate ideas" or, rather, "to read intelligently and critically, to think, and to express ideas properly, logically, and forcefully" (p. 164) tends to skip right past invention.

2. See Doubleday's response (pp. 512-513).

REFERENCES

Ahl, F. N. (1931). The technique of the term Paper. *The High School Journal 14*(1), 17-19, 53.

Angus, D. (1948). Avoiding the pseudo-research paper. *College English 9*(4), 191-194.

Arms, G. (1943). The research paper. *College English 5*(1), 19-25.

Bader, A. L. (1936). Independent thinking and the "long paper." *The English Journal 25*(8), 667-672.

Brereton, J. C. (Ed.) (1995). *The origins of composition studies in the american college, 1875-1925*. Pittsburgh: University of Pittsburgh Press.

Carpenter, H. S. & Elder, V. (1928). Objective teaching in the library. *The English Journal 17*(2), 121-128.

Clark, W. (2006). *Academic charisma and the origins of the research university*. Chicago: The University of Chicago Press.

Connors, R. J. (1987). Personal writing assignments. *College Composition and Communication 38*(2), 166-183.

Connors, R. J. (1997). *Composition-rhetoric: Backgrounds, theory, and pedagogy*. Pittsburgh: University of Pittsburgh Press.

Cummings, A. (1950). An open letter to teachers of English. *The English Journal 39*(1), 38-39.

Ford, J. E. & Perry, D. R. (1982). Research paper instruction in the undergraduate writing program. *College English 44.8*: 825-831.

Hamilton, E. W. (1944). Let's teach composition! *College English 6*(3), 159-164.

Harris, L. H. (1916). A proposed course in advanced exposition for college students. *The English Journal 5*(7), 501-503.

Hatfield, W. W. (1913). What the graduates of our high schools think. *The English Journal 2.5*: 318-322.

Hatfield, W. W. & De Boer, J. J. (1942). Teaching English in wartime: An editorial. *The English Journal 31*(1), 67-69.

Hart, S. C. (1902). In the college. *The School Review 10*(5), 364-373.

Henry, R. L. (1928). Freshman English in the Middle West. *The English Journal 17*(4), 299-310.

Larson, R. L. (1982). The "research paper" in the writing course: A non-form of writing. *College English 44*(8), 811-816.

Manning, A. (1961). The present status of the research paper in freshman English: A National Survey. *College Composition and Communication 12*, 73.

Mattewson, A. (1941). Long compositions based on research. *The English Journal 30*(6), 457-462.

McCaslin, D. (1923). The library and the department of English. *The English Journal* 12.9: 591-598.

Moulton, M. R. & Holmes, V. L. (2003). The research paper: A historical perspective. *TETYC*: 365-373.

NCTE. (1942). English instruction and the war. *The English Journal 31*(2), 87-91.

Rankin, C. S. (1915). After "Pilgrim's Progress". *The English Journal 4*(3), 196-200.

Rivlin, H. N. (1942). The writing of term papers. *The Journal of Higher Education 13*(6), 314-320, 342.

Russell, D. R. (2002). *Writing in the academic disciplines: A curricular history* (2nd ed.). Carbondale, IL: Southern Illinois University Press.

Selsberg, A. (2011, March 7). Teaching the text message. *The New York Times*. Retrieved from http://www.nytimes.com/2011/03/20/opinion/20selsberg.html

Scott, F. N. (1922). English composition as a mode of behavior. *The English Journal 11*(8), 463-473.

Thompson, S. (1930). A national survey of freshman English (Review). *The English Journal 19*(7), 553-557.

Woods, R. C. (1933). The term paper: Its values and dangers. *Peabody Journal of Education 11*(2), 87-89.

PART TWO: APPLYING STYLE

INTRODUCTION TO PART TWO: APPLYING STYLE

Mike Duncan and Star Medzerian Vanguri
University of Houston-Downtown and Nova Southeastern University

While Part One of this collection presented a variety of conceptions of style that were both theoretically and pedagogically informed, the essays in Part Two concentrate more on how style can be presented as a central aspect of composition in the classroom. The diversity of methods and genres offered here again assume the centrality and importance of style, regardless of the nature or the disciplinary site of pedagogical presentation. In particular, however, teachers of composition, as well as those teaching technical writing, linguistics, literature, creative writing, nonfiction, and fiction will find much of interest in this second half of the collection, given the focus on assignments, example texts, techniques for stylistic analysis, assessment, and terminology that enables increased student conceptualization of style. Also, much like the collective argument formed by Part One, these eight essays, when read together, suggest strongly that these different pedagogical sites have, in common, the potential for a pedagogically profitable incursion by style due to its centrality to composition.

The first essay, "Style in Academic Writing" by Nora Bacon, argues for a pedagogy focused on stylistic variation, rather than that of mere clarity of concision. This pedagogy can teach students to make and appreciate stylistic choices in various genres of academic writing across the curriculum. Bacon debunks the commonly-held assumption that academic writing does not embody style, and also provides an historical account of the influence of the Plain Style on academic writing. She concludes her essay with the claim that teaching stylistic variation can allow students to develop rhetorical awareness of their stylistic choices, as well as that of others. Bacon's essay reflects Greer's emphasis on awareness in Part One, though her location of this awareness in academic writing places this essay more firmly within the demesnes of the classroom.

Zak Lancaster's "Tracking Interpersonal Style: The Use of Functional Language Analysis in College Writing Instruction" also argues for a stylistic approach, placing such approaches within the recent trend of rhetorical genre studies. He argues that systemic functional linguistics (SFL) and appraisal theory can bridge the global concept of genre, with local methods of analyzing textual language patterns. Lancaster's skillful link between style, composition, and linguistics reminds us of the cross-disciplinary nature of style and the value in such interdisciplinary work.

The growing presence of multimodal texts in composition classes is also addressed here through the lens of style. In the third essay, "Multimodal Style and the Evolution of Digital Writing Pedagogy," Moe Folk calls for a production-centered style pedagogy. Accounting for the material dimensions of style within computer-mediated contexts, Folk presents three iterations of multimodal style—style as technical prowess, style as difference, and style as subservience. These three iterations are then examined in an analysis of a digital retelling of the fairy tale *Little Red Riding Hood*. As editors, we would be remiss to not include an essay such as this one that addresses how style is, too, central to emerging mediums as well as existing ones.

Creative writing is yet another area where attention to rhetorical style can be highly beneficial. In "Voice, Transformed: The Potentialities of Style Pedagogy in the Teaching of Creative Nonfiction," Crystal Fodrey argues for a rhetorical approach to creative writing pedagogy that has as its core rhetorical style. Fodrey presents several iterations of style as it is discussed in creative nonfiction craft texts to illustrate the writer-centered, rather than audience-centered, stance that dominates these texts. She then presents a style-focused creative writing curriculum as a demonstration of how the two seemingly disparate disciplines' pedagogical approaches can work together. In addition to placing style in yet another academic context, Fodrey performs an important service by offering a middle ground between style-focused and audience-focused composition.

Luke Redington's "Fighting Styles: The Pedagogical Implications of Applying Contemporary Rhetorical Theory to the Persuasive Prose of Mary Wollstonecraft and Mary Hays" claims that effective writing style begins with "stylistically-aware" reading. Redington outlines a pedagogy that has students first read and identify stylistic elements in published prose before employing these techniques in their own writing. Redington stylistically analyzes the writings of Mary Wollstonecraft and Mary Hays, as an example of his argument, to illustrate how their styles relate to their identities as women in eighteenth-century Great Britain. This analysis leads into a heuristic that further explains the analysis and can be adapted for other classroom contexts. Redington's ordering of awareness before enaction, again, stresses the imitative nature of effective composition instruction.

While much of the recent scholarship on style pedagogy is situated in composition courses, the parallel field of professional writing is another important context for style-focused approaches to writing. Jonathan Buehl's "Style and the Professional Writing Curriculum: Teaching Stylistic Fluency through Science Writing" offers a stylistic approach to teaching science writing. In this chapter, he presents a curriculum for a professional writing course whose goal is to address the challenges of multiple audiences (expert, non-expert, general). Because workplace writing genres are tailored to audiences beyond the classroom, the audience expectations and stylistic conventions may be more varied than in composition courses. Buehl's curriculum seeks to make stylistic fluency transferable to these multiple contexts. This flexible fluency has long been a goal of composition, though it is not always, as it is in Redington's essay, characterized as style.

In "Toward a Pedagogy of Psychic Distance," Erik Ellis borrows the concept of "psychic distance" from creative writing to describe the "felt" metaphorical distance between reader and text. Ellis suggests that when students can internalize an awareness of psychic distance, they can become more audience-aware in their writing and more aware of the craft of their own and others' writing. Perhaps more importantly, the concept of psychic distance allows students to reconceptualize readers as an audience to be invoked, rather than directly addressed. While traditional rhetorical approaches to identification ask students to anticipate an audience's needs (which a student may or may not have access to), psychic distance makes students aware of how their language choices define roles for their readers. Ellis gives Ede and Lunsford's work on audience construction a stylistic turn toward ethos and awareness.

Star Medzerian Vanguri's "What Scoring Rubrics Teach Students (and Teachers) about Style" argues that while style is not explicitly taught in many composition classrooms, rubrics (which may be created departmentally and used by teachers with little modification) often contain a category for style and, therefore, communicate to students certain expectations for stylistic effectiveness that may be decontextualized from classroom teaching. From an analysis of scoring rubrics collected nationwide, Vanguri culls the conceptions of style that the rubrics communicate, and develops from them four evaluative criteria for style: readability, appropriateness, consistency, and correctness. By exploring style's relationship to grading, this chapter illustrates the ubiquity of style in our everyday practices as teachers of composition and the significance of the role it plays in defining "good" writing for students.

STYLE IN ACADEMIC WRITING

Nora Bacon
University of Nebraska at Omaha

There can be little doubt that a central goal of first-year composition is to teach academic writing; this commitment is visible in our professional literature and in the mission statements of countless first-year writing programs. We promise to help students make the transition to college writing and succeed in their other classes because that is the purpose for which first-year composition courses were created, and it's the reason our courses continue to be required in almost every American college and university.

But teachers who embrace this mission find that it sits awkwardly with our commitment to teaching style. First, we recognize that many academic genres allow limited room for stylistic play. Is style an important enough feature of academic writing to deserve a place in our overcrowded curriculum? Second, we know that style varies across the curriculum: the styles preferred by mathematicians may be quite different from those preferred by historians or social workers or chemists. If we integrate style instruction into a general education course designed for students who are headed toward dozens of different majors, which style do we teach? Even if we could know the whole range of academic styles, we could hardly teach all of them in fifteen weeks. Is there a generic, teachable "academic writing style"? Is it the plain style?

In the paragraphs that follow, I challenge two widespread assumptions about academic writing that have obscured our view of its style(s): the notion that academic writing is impersonal and formulaic (essentially style-free) and the notion that the only characteristics of academic style worth teaching are clarity and conciseness. I suggest that a central insight of Writing Across the Curriculum—that academic discourse practices vary—provides a guiding principle for style pedagogy: at the heart of the enterprise is analysis of stylistic variation, with attention to the rhetorical choice-making that accounts for it and with opportunities for imitation, experimentation, and play.

THE DICHOTOMY: WRITING WITH STYLE VS. WRITING FOR THE ACADEMY

Perhaps because it addresses an audience of students, Kate Ronald's 1995 essay, "Style: The Hidden Agenda in Composition Classes or One Reader's

Confession," describes style's uncertain place in composition instruction in particularly clear and accessible language with a focus on the practical consequences for students. Ronald explains that

> different eras have emphasized different parts of composition. Plato and Aristotle were upset by what they saw as an enchantment with style; they worried that writers could dazzle audiences without caring much about telling them the truth. And so they focused on invention, on figuring out issues by thinking and writing. (Ronald, 1999, p. 170)

In the 1980s and 1990s, she says, composition teachers informed by the writing process movement similarly focused on content rather than form and thus on invention rather than arrangement or style.

But there's a problem:

> Your teacher, and I, and all the others who were part of this latest revolution in rhetoric, haven't been exactly honest with you about the matter of style. We say we aren't overly interested in style ... but we are still influenced by your writing style more than we admit, or perhaps know... . I'm still rewarding and punishing my students for their writing styles. And here's the worst part of my confession: I'm not sure that I'm teaching them style. (Ronald, 1999, pp. 170-71)

When teachers don't address style in their classes, students are judged by a standard that's hidden from view, and they are expected to demonstrate stylistic skills that they are never taught. One student will write vivid, lively sentences and another won't; the first student's success and the second's relative failure will be reflected in their grades, but the matter of how one *achieves* an effective style will remain mysterious.

If Ronald is correct—and I believe she is—then composition teachers have, in our neglect of style, done our students a disservice. But for all her honesty and wisdom, Ronald takes her argument down an unfortunate path. She accepts the dichotomy that has plagued our thinking about style pedagogy for too long, suggesting that writing with an effective style is one thing, writing for the academy quite another.

Ronald defines style in terms of the presence of the author; the writing she admires is "writing where somebody's home." She speculates that students sometimes write as if "nobody's home" because they're playing it safe, writing to avoid mistakes or distancing themselves from their prose in order to protect themselves from criticism, and sometimes they write dry, lifeless prose because they think they have to in order to sound "collegiate." And, she implies, collegiate writing does indeed require that the writer leave home. While English teachers may like writing with style—"we have a real bent for the literary element, the metaphor, the clever turn of phrase, the rhythm of prose that comes close to the rhythm of poetry" (Ronald, 1999, p. 174)—teachers in other disciplines are likely to prefer author-evacuated prose:

> Many professors believe that you should be learning to write one certain kind of style in college, one that's objective, impersonal, formal, explicit, and organized around assertions, claims, and reasons that illustrate or defend those claims. You know this kind of writing. You produce it in response to questions like "Discuss the causes of the Civil War," or "Do you think that 'nature' or 'nurture' plays the most important role in a child's development?" (Ronald, 1999, p. 175)

The example that follows is stiff and verbose, easily recognizable to any composition teacher as the work of a young writer trying on an overly formal, alien "academic" voice. Observing that the passage has "no authentic voice," Ronald observes, "I don't like this kind of writing very much myself.... I prefer discourse that 'renders experience,' as Peter Elbow (1991) puts it, rather than discourse that tries to explain it" (Ronald, 1999, p. 175).

The assumptions behind this analysis warrant scrutiny because they are so very widespread in our profession. Like many others who have written about academic discourse, Ronald writes as if the qualities we see in the most unappealing academic writing—awkwardness, wordiness, excessive formality, impersonality, a naïve aspiration to objectivity—were what defines academic writing. If the writing performs an academic function, such as explaining experience, the writer must be away from home; the writing will be stale, and while reasonable people may write such stuff because they have to (on an exam, for example, or in a publication required for tenure) and other people may read it because they have to, they can hardly expect to like it. Only if the writing performs a different function, "rendering experience" as literary works do, can a text convey the writer's voice and give pleasure. The academy harbors a few people who write, appreciate, and reward clever, well-crafted prose—Ronald suggests that all English teachers fall into this category while others limit the group to "creative" writers—but for the most part, the academy insists on thesis-driven essays written in plain, utilitarian prose by uncreative writers. You can have academic writing or you can have style, but you can't have both. You can teach academic writing or you can teach style, but you can't teach both.

This dichotomy is easy to see in "Style: The Hidden Agenda in Composition Classes" because Ronald, writing for an audience unfamiliar with debates in composition pedagogy, necessarily simplifies the issues. Others who criticize academic writing acknowledge that academic styles vary widely (in "Reflections on Academic Discourse," Peter Elbow is particularly specific and persuasive on this point; see pages 138-140). Nevertheless, the essential terms of the dichotomy inform most of our thinking about style in composition studies, so that teachers feel compelled to choose between teaching academic discourse and teaching the delights of style. The choice is imposed on us not only because we have so little time that we have to make difficult choices about where style might fit but because style has so little relevance to academic writing as it is usually conceived.

THE PLAIN STYLE

With her reference to Plato and Aristotle, Ronald points to ancient articulations of the tension between style and substance, between language that "dazzles" and language designed primarily to express truth. In seventeenth century England, Thomas Sprat addressed the same tension, writing a forceful condemnation of eloquence. In *The History of the Royal Society*, Sprat urges a spare, unadorned style as necessary to scientific inquiry. Volubility, *copia*, eloquence—these are the enemies of the plain style, and Sprat reports that in the interest of science, members of the Royal Society sought to avoid them:

> They have therefore been most rigorous in putting in execution, the only Remedy, that can be found for this extravagance: and that has been, a constant Resolution, to reject all the amplifications, digressions, and swellings of style: to return back to the primitive purity, and shortness, when men deliver'd so many things, almost in an equal number of words. They have exacted from all their members, a close, naked, natural way of speaking; positive expressions; clear senses; a native easiness: bringing all things as near the Mathematical plainness, as they can: and preferring the language of Artizans, Countrymen, and Merchants, before that, of Wits, or Scholars.(Tillotson, Fussell, & Waingrow, 1969, p. 27)

The ideal of matching the number of *things* to the number of *words* is telling, for the theory of language underlying the plain style is a correspondence theory. The goal of writing is to reflect external reality. The best writing is transparent, permitting a clear view of the phenomenon being described or analyzed without excess, without distortion, without distraction.

The influence of the plain style on writing pedagogy can hardly be overstated. Among Sprat's descendents are the authors of the two most widely adopted books on style, Strunk and White's *The Elements of Style* and Joseph M. Williams's *Style: Ten Lessons in Clarity and Grace*.

As many readers have observed, *The Elements of Style* is as idiosyncratic and inconsistent as it is charming. In the final chapter, "An Approach to Style," White seems to be having a wonderful time fooling around with language, creating a string of aphorisms and extended metaphors even as he recommends "turning resolutely away from all devices that are popularly believed to indicate style—all mannerisms, tricks, adornments. The approach to style is by way of plainness, simplicity, orderliness, sincerity" (1959, p. 55).

His own indulgences notwithstanding, White cautions against calling attention to oneself or one's craft: *Place yourself in the background; write in a way that comes naturally; do not overwrite; do not overstate; avoid fancy words; avoid foreign languages; use figures of speech sparingly; prefer the standard to the offbeat*. Throughout the book, Strunk and White highlight the importance of clarity and conciseness. Among the "Elementary Principles of Composition" is the admonition to *omit needless words*:

> A sentence should contain no unnecessary words, a paragraph no unnecessary sentences, for the same reason that a drawing should have no unnecessary lines and a machine no unnecessary parts. This requires not that the writer make all his sentences short, or that he avoid all detail and treat his subjects only in outline, but that every word tell. (1959, p. 17)

To illustrate Strunk's most famous injunction—*use definite, specific, concrete language*—White turns to that other well-known advocate of the plain style, George Orwell, quoting his translation of Ecclesiastes ("I returned, and saw under the sun, that the race is not to the swift ...") into gobbledegook ("Objective consideration of contemporary phenomena compels the conclusion that success or failure in competitive activities exhibits no tendency to be commensurate with innate capacity ...") (1959, p. 17).

In *Style: Ten Lessons in Clarity and Grace*, Joseph Williams offers dozens of similar translations, and his exercises invite students to transform wordy, awkward, or indirect sentences into lean, clear prose. The stylistic virtue that he stresses from beginning to end is clarity; his specific suggestions—to use the subject and verb positions to identify actors and actions, to avoid nominalization, to prune out redundancy—are offered to this end. And like Orwell, he weighs the ethical and political consequences of clarity on the one hand, obfuscation on the other. We have an ethical duty, Williams argues, to write prose as clear as the prose we wish to read. And we have a right to insist on clarity from people in positions of power: "We must simply insist that, in principle, those who manage our affairs have a duty to tell us the truth as clearly as they can. They probably won't, but that just shifts the burden to us to call them on it" (2005, p. 186). To Orwell and to Williams, clarity matters because the workings of democracy depend upon clear thinking and honest communication.

The plain style seems perfectly congruent with the goals of scientific discourse. The knowledge-making mission of the academy would seem to be well served by the effort to describe, explain, analyze, and evaluate the world with as much clarity as we can muster. For this practical reason, as well as the ethical and political reasons suggested by Orwell and Williams, the plain style endures. To the extent that style has any presence in composition theory and pedagogy, it consists mostly of lessons encouraging clarity and conciseness.

This approach to style pedagogy is problematic, however, for at least two reasons. First, there's the epistemological problem. While some scholars may proceed from a positivist view of language, seeking words that map onto a pre-existing, describable reality, others question such a project. In *Style: An Anti-Textbook*, Richard Lanham raises this point as an objection to privileging clarity above all. Characterizing style textbooks and handbooks together as "The Books," he identifies a "fundamental error":

> In Western philosophy's long-standing quarrel between idealism and realism, The Books remain realists. Reality is "out there" and words must remain loyal to it.
>
> A complete theory of prose style need not settle this endless dispute [between idealism and realism]. But it should chart the whole dispute. It should account for a prose loyal to a preexistent reality and it should account for a prose loyal to words themselves as a final reference point.... The Books omit half the process.... They thus ground themselves on

> both a false theory of knowledge and a false theory of perception. They assume both a neutral observer whom psychology has long ago disproved and a neutral language that even science has now discarded. (1974, p. 39)

In the forty years since Lanham wrote those words, the "realist" view has continued to lose ground in the academy.

The second problem with reducing style pedagogy to instruction in the plain style is an aesthetic one. It's easy enough to grant that clarity and conciseness are generally desirable qualities in writing. When I read Orwell, Strunk and White, or Williams, I nod in agreement; when these writers offer "before" and "after" examples of revision, with a profusion of nominalizations or a string of prepositional phrases in the first sentence and taut, lean syntax in the second, I always prefer the sentence as revised. And yet. While clarity and conciseness may be necessary to an effective style, surely they are not sufficient.

Pedagogy that privileges the plain style cannot teach style as Kate Ronald has defined it for us. To Ronald, writing has an effective style if it is infused with the personality of the writer, making use of those literary devices English teachers love ("the metaphor, the clever turn of phrase, the rhythm of prose that comes close to the rhythm of poetry") (1999, p. 174). To write with style is to arrange words artfully, striving for euphony, wit, eloquence. Twentieth-century advocates of the plain style may not reject artful language with the vehemence of Thomas Sprat, but they don't encourage it, and they don't offer much help to the young writer who hopes to achieve it.

What this discussion has, I hope, demonstrated is that conceptions of "academic writing" and "style" that prevail in composition studies make it difficult for us to see where style fits into a course in academic discourse. The academic/creative dichotomy creates one kind of difficulty: when we accept the view of academic writing as inevitably dry, stiff, and impersonal, academic writing and style must live in different homes, presumably the dutiful, dogged first-year writing program and the happily sybaritic creative writing program. Privileging the plain style creates another difficulty: while the plain style seems generally well suited to the purposes of academic writing, the goals of clarity and conciseness constitute a disappointingly anemic conception of style.

VARIATION IN ACADEMIC WRITING

Let us return to the rather obvious observation that academic writing is not all the same. It varies, in structure and in style, in many respects: the shape taken by a text, or by particular paragraphs and sentences within a text, will depend upon factors associated with the writer—his or her personality, mood, knowledge, experience, professional status, ethnicity, gender, proficiency with language, and so on—and other factors associated with the context—the practices of the discipline, the conventions of the genre, with these in turn shaped by the culture in which the discipline is situated and the history in which generic conventions have evolved.

Given the breadth of this variation, and given the complex personal, social, and political dynamics that account for it, what sort of instruction in style might be useful to a writer at the point of entry into the academic discourse community?

This question is nested in two larger issues that composition theorists have wrestled with at least since the early 1980s. First is the issue of what it means to become part of a discourse community. Ever since Patricia Bizzell's 1982 article introducing the term, composition teachers have taken seriously the responsibility to initiate students into the academic discourse community. The issue that never really goes away, and that seems particularly pressing when we think about style, is that "initiation" slides so easily into "assimilation": we worry that as students learn to sound like members of academic discourse communities, they will sound less like members of other communities they care about, less like themselves.

Second is the issue of transfer. To a surprising degree, knowledge seems to be context-bound; people who learn a skill in one setting do not easily operationalize it in other settings, and the more pronounced the differences between the two settings, the less likely that transfer will occur (Ellis, 1965; Perkins & Salomon, 1992; Smagorinsky & Smith, 1992). Some years back, an "abolitionist" argument gained some traction among composition scholars with the claim that since discourse practices vary within the academy, since academic writing is not one thing, first-year composition courses cannot teach a universally applicable set of "general writing skills" and therefore have no function (Petraglia, 1995). If this argument is extended to style instruction, it leads to the conclusion that since style varies within the academy, it is fruitless to try to teach academic style.

The abolitionist argument has largely disappeared from view, to be replaced by a commonsense approach informed by Writing Across the Curriculum theory. We aim to teach not only those skills that seem broadly useful in the academy but also rhetorical awareness, alerting students to the fact of discourse variation and teaching them to analyze the rhetorical demands of new disciplines and other new contexts. Specifically, we aim to teach a critical rhetorical awareness, inviting students not only to try their hands at academic writing but, at the same time, to stand at a distance from it, to see how it compares to other kinds of writing, to think about why it has the characteristics it has, what values it reflects and perpetuates, whose power it reflects and perpetuates, and where, in light of that analysis, they choose to stand in relation to academic discourse.

DIRECTIONS FOR STYLE PEDAGOGY

What, then, does a first-year writer need to know about style? What might he or she expect to gain from style pedagogy in a composition course focused on academic writing? Guided *analysis* of style in academic texts can help students recognize the stylistic preferences of successful writers; appreciate variation across writers, disciplines, and occasions; and understand the factors that account for variation. Guided *practice*—deploying specific syntactic/stylistic options to achieve desired rhetorical effects—can help novice writers take the step from appreciating to producing effective style in academic texts. The three passages below are examples of academic texts that could function as objects of analysis and resources for practice with style.

The passages represent different genres and disciplines—*Programming in Prolog* is a textbook in computer science, *The Freedom of the Streets* a monograph in history, "On Beauty and Being Just" a lecture in philosophy—but each is the product of an academic writer doing academic work.

> It is a dark and stormy night. As you drive down a lonely country road, your car breaks down, and you stop in front of a splendid palace. You go to the door, find it open, and begin looking for a telephone. How do you search the palace without getting lost, and know that you have searched every room? Also, what is the shortest path to the telephone? It is just for such emergencies that maze-searching methods have been devised.
>
> In many computer programs, such as those for searching mazes, it is useful to keep lists of information, and search the list if some information is needed at a later time. For example, if we decide to search the palace for a telephone, we might need to keep a list of the room numbers visited so far, so we don't go round in circles visiting the same rooms over and over again. What we do is to write down the room

numbers visited on a piece of paper. Before entering a room, we check to see if its number is on our piece of paper. If it is, we ignore the room, since we must have been to it previously. If the room number is not on the paper, we write down the number, and enter the room. And so on until we find the telephone. There are some refinements to be made to this method, and we will do so later when we discuss graph searching. But first, let's write down the steps in order, so we know what problems there are to solve. (Clocksin & Mellish, 1984, p. 142)

In 1888, twelve-year-old Ollie Kreps lived with her parents in a house on East Second Street in Davenport … . She was the oldest child in a crowded, poverty-stricken home. Her parents, married thirteen years, had nine children. Ollie and her father were the family's sole wage earners. Albert Kreps worked as a laborer at the Davenport Lumber Company. His work, though poorly paid, was probably steady in the warm months, when river men floated huge rafts of logs down the Mississippi from the timberlands of Wisconsin for processing at riverside lumber mills. But in the winter months, when the central events of this story took place, the river froze and traffic dwindled to a standstill. Lumber milling and virtually all other work depending on the river came to a halt, and Albert Kreps joined hundreds of other seasonally unemployed men in Davenport, waiting for the spring thaw, when the river opened, the mills turned, and plowing and planting began again. (Wood, 2005, p. 111)

Beauty brings copies of itself into being. It makes us draw it, take photographs of it, or describe it to other people. Sometimes it gives rise to exact replication and other times to resemblances and still other times to things whose connection to the original site of inspiration is unrecognizable. A beautiful face drawn by Verrocchio suddenly glides into the perceptual field of a young boy named Leonardo. The boy copies the face, then copies the face again. Then again and again and again. He does the same thing when a beautiful living plant—a violet, a wild rose—glides into his field of vision, or a living face: he makes a first copy, a second copy, a third, a fourth, a fifth. He draws it over and over, just as Walter Pater (who tells us all this about Leonardo) replicates—now in sentences—Leonardo's acts, so that the essay reenacts its subject, becoming a sequence of faces: an angel, a Medusa, a woman and child, a Madonna, John the Baptist, St. Anne, La Gioconda. Before long the means are found to replicate, thousands of times over, both the sentences and the faces, so that traces of Pater's paragraphs and Leonardo's drawings inhabit all the pockets of the world (as pieces of them float in the paragraph now before you). (Scarry, 1998, p. 3)

The three passages serve as counterexamples to the idea that academic writing is dry, dull, objective, passionless, or merely utilitarian. These writers have made stylistic choices in the interest of giving pleasure, and for me as a reader, they succeed. Each passage is quite different, stylistically, from the others. Of the three, Scarry's lecture strikes me as being most self-consciously styled: the language itself commands our attention as images "glide" into an observer's field of vision, as traces of an image "float" in a paragraph, as the writer shatters the fourth wall in the final clause. The paragraph is typical of Scarry's long lecture; it is a virtuoso performance, both as an instance of philosophical reasoning and as cleverly crafted prose. In the other passages, the language does not call attention to itself. Nevertheless, all three texts demonstrate stylistic choices that would be fruitful to discuss in a course on academic writing.

Sample Stylistic Analysis: Choosing Subjects

Consider, first, the human presence in each of the passages. None of these writers uses "I"; none seeks to render the writer's own experience. Nevertheless, the passages are decidedly populated, a point students could discover by analyzing the focus, or choice of subjects, in the clauses.

The Clocksin and Mellish passage is the easiest to analyze. In the first paragraph, there are ten subject-verb pairs; in five of them, the subject is "you." Student writers are sometimes advised to avoid the second person in academic writing, so it's worth asking why Clocksin and Mellish use it. What does the use of "you" accomplish? What tone does it set? (Other questions naturally follow: What else do these writers do to set an informal tone? Why would they want such a tone in a textbook? Would they be likely to make similar choices in other academic contexts?) In the second paragraph, there are twenty subject-verb pairs; in twelve, the subject is "we." To whom does "we" refer? Presumably to the reader and writer. In the first few sentences, the search for the telephone continues, so Clocksin and Mellish could easily have continued to use the second person. But with "we," they insert themselves into the paragraph, and so "we" search for the telephone together and, in the final sentences, "we" write down our steps in order so that "we" can see what problems there are to solve and what refinements might be made when "we" discuss graph searching. Having walked through the castle with me, Clocksin and Mellish are by my side as I learn to write code for maze-searching programs. When I return to my day job as a writing teacher, I might ask students to comment on the effect of the pronoun choice on the chapter's tone or on the appropriateness of the stylistic choice to its rhetorical context.

Like the Clocksin and Mellish passage, Sharon Wood's paragraph introducing Ollie Kreps's family illustrates the general preference of published writers for human subjects. Writing students picking out the subject-verb pairs would find that seven clauses have human subjects: *Ollie Kreps, she, parents, Ollie and her father, Albert Kreps, river men, Albert Kreps*. The non-human subjects are concentrated in the last two sentences: *events, river, traffic, milling, work, river, mills, plowing and planting*. The list of subjects captures the movement of the paragraph, from Ollie to the social group that shaped her (her family), from her father to the social group of which he was a part (river men), from river men to the forces that governed their economic circumstances (the river traffic, milling, work, plowing and planting). Because Wood is a colleague of mine, I was able to ask her, in a discourse-based interview, about the reasons for her stylistic choices. She explained that, as a labor historian, it is important to her that Albert Kreps's unemployment and Ollie Kreps's prostitution be understood not only as the plight of individuals but as social phenomena. In crafting sentences, she responds quite intentionally to concerns about both content and style. In this passage, she chose concrete subjects and active verbs in the interest of keeping the prose clear and direct; human subjects in the interest of telling an engaging story; and subjects naming natural or economic forces in the interest of accurately representing the historical context in which her "characters" lived.

The stylistic principle of preferring concrete, preferably human, subjects is one that I like to teach: I want my students to know that using human subjects can help them achieve clarity in their sentences and cohesion within their paragraphs. But because academic writing often focuses on natural phenomena or abstract concepts, academic writers do not always have a cast of characters available to serve as subjects. The Scarry passage is an interesting example because not only is the writer discussing an abstract concept, but her purpose is to attribute agency to this abstraction. Not surprisingly, the passage has more non-human than human subjects, with beauty itself serving as a subject in the opening sentences: "*Beauty* brings copies of itself into being. *It* makes us draw it, take photographs of it ... Sometimes *it* gives rise to exact replication ... ." In the fourth sentence, people begin to appear on stage as a face "glides into the perceptual field of a young boy named Leonardo." Words referring to Leonardo (*boy, he*) become subjects in the next clauses, though Scarry still manages to present the artist as being acted upon: as images come before him, he reproduces them, over and over, repeatedly, almost robotically. Finally, it is a description of Leonardo's practice that assumes agency—clause subjects include Walter Pater's *essay*, *traces* of his paragraph, *pieces* of his text—as beauty replicates itself in the work of Leonardo, then Pater, then Scarry. This passage cannot illustrate a simple lesson like "prefer human subjects." But it surely demonstrates the importance of the subject position in establishing agency. The presence of Leonardo and Pater (and, perhaps, the entrance of an angel, a Medusa, a woman and child, etc.) may reflect an accomplished stylist's impulse to populate her prose.

SAMPLE STYLISTIC ANALYSIS: SENTENCE VARIETY

When advised to keep their sentence subjects consistent, students often worry that the sentences will sound too much the same, that the style will be boring. The three passages above, or others like them, could be used in lessons on sentence variety. Taken together, the texts have 33 sentences containing 643 words. The average sentence length is 19.5 words, a bit shorter than the norm for academic writing. But the range of sentence lengths is strikingly wide, and the sentence structure varies in other ways as well.

Of the three texts, the Clocksin and Mellish passage has the least variety in sentence length: the average length is 17.6 words, and nine of the fifteen sentences fall close to the mean. This passage also has the most consistency in its sentence subjects, relying heavily on "you" in the first paragraph and "we" in the second. But I think it's a rare reader who would find the passage choppy or dull. The sentences vary in type—in addition to declarative sentences, there are two questions and an imperative—and the writers have varied their sentence openers. In the second paragraph, for example, although "we" is used as a subject of eleven clauses, it never begins a sentence. Instead, the writers begin sentences with transitional expressions, free modifiers, and subordinate clauses: *For example, if we decide ... What we do is to write down ... Before entering a room, we check to see ... If it is, we ignore the room ... If the room number is not on the paper, we write down ... And so on until we find the telephone.*

In the Wood and Scarry texts, the sentences vary more dramatically in length. These sentences are, overall, longer than Clocksin and Mellish's, with means of 19.8 words in the Wood passage and 22.0 words in the Scarry passage. But the ranges are wide (Wood's sentences range from eight to 45 words, Scarry's from six to 52 words) and in each passage, only two sentences fall near the mean. In other words, both writers create a mix of short, medium-sized, and long sentences. While all the sentences are declarative (excepting one fragment in the Scarry piece), their structure is varied: some are developed by means of pairs or series, others with subordinate clauses, others with free modifiers. In a composition class, these passages would work well to introduce medial modifiers, phrases that interrupt the sentences to provide detail or, in some cases, drama. Novice writers don't often use medial modifiers, but when they give them a try, they find them easy and natural. So students would benefit from noting, and imitating, sentences like these:

> Her parents, married thirteen years, had nine children.

> His work, though poorly paid, was probably steady in the warm months ...

> He does the same thing when a beautiful living plant—a violet, a wild rose—glides into his field of vision ...

Analysis of sentence variety in effective academic writing can give students motivation and specific strategies for developing their own sentences.

SAMPLE STYLISTIC ANALYSIS: FIGURES OF SPEECH

A time-honored approach to teaching style is to identify figures of speech. The Clocksin and Mellish passage is an extended metaphor, using the story of hunting through a castle in search of a telephone to explain the logic of maze-searching. The story is entertaining, but Thomas Sprat's worries can be laid to rest: the pleasure does not distract us from the point or short-circuit our ability to comprehend. On the contrary, the strategy of explaining a new concept by analogy to a familiar one is common in academic writing because it aids comprehension; in this case, the metaphor is so essential to the explanation that it is difficult to imagine how maze-searching could be explained without it.

The three passages offer a wealth of resources for teaching schemes of balance, particularly parallelism. Again, Clocksin and Mellish's use of parallelism contributes to the clarity of their explanation:

> Before entering a room, we check to see if its number is on

our piece of paper. If it is, we ignore the room, since we must have been to it previously. If the room number is not on the paper, we write down the number, and enter the room.

The two sentences beginning with "if" describe alternative scenarios in grammatically similar constructions: If X, we ignore the room; if—X, we enter the room. It is important that the sentences be grammatically similar so that readers immediately recognize the two options as a pair, just as they would recognize two arrows on a flowchart.

Lessons in parallel structure, simply showing that items in a list should have the same grammatical structure, begin with series like these:

> You go to the door, find it locked, and begin looking for a telephone.
>
> It makes us draw it, take photographs of it, or describe it to other people.

More complex series illustrate how effectively a parallel list can draw a picture, establish a rhythm, create a mood:

> Lumber milling and virtually all other work depending on the river came to a halt, and Albert Kreps joined hundreds of other seasonally unemployed men in Davenport, waiting for the spring thaw, when the river opened, the mills turned, and plowing and planting began again.

Student writers can hear the beauty of a sentence like that one. They appreciate the sense of motion, of water flowing and wheels turning in response to the thaw, and they understand how the alliterative phrase "plowing and planting" calls to mind ancient, earth-bound cycles in which the men of Davenport participate.

Elaine Scarry relies heavily on parallelism and repetition, as well she might in a paragraph about replication. Almost every sentence contains an echo, whether she is setting out an array of possibilities in matched phrases ("sometimes it gives rise to exact replication and other times to resemblances and still other times to things whose connection to the original site of inspiration is unrecognizable") or repeating exactly the same words ("The boy copies the face, then copies the face again. Then again and again and again.") In her final sentence, Scarry, like Wood, plays with the sound of the words. Read the sentence aloud, listening for for the echo of *faces* in *traces* and *pieces*, or for repeated use of words beginning with *p*:

> Before long the means are found to replicate, thousands of times over, both the sentences and the faces, so that traces of Pater's paragraphs and Leonardo's drawings inhabit all the pockets of the world (as pieces of them float in the paragraph now before you).

If Elaine Scarry can have this much fun with her academic writing, then so can the rest of us. More to the point, so can our students.

FROM ANALYSIS TO PRACTICE

I come, in the end, to the recommendation that we teach style by relying on familiar methods: analyzing the work of excellent stylists; introducing principles like sentence focus, sentence variety, and balance; designing exercises that prompt students to imitate the stylistic moves they admire; encouraging students to experiment with style in their own writing. I believe this work can and should be done in the context of courses focused on academic writing. There is no shortage of exemplary academic writing: if you pause for a few minutes, you'll think of academic texts that you would like to bring into the classroom, and if you spend an afternoon browsing through your bookshelves, you'll find dozens more.

Such texts deserve analysis not only in our classrooms but in our scholarship. Are the stylistic features observed in the three sample passages above characteristic of their disciplines? My impression is that computer scientists are often playful in their writing and that historians are typically good storytellers, but I suspect Scarry's writing is unusually lyrical for a philosopher. I wish I could give you more than impressions and suspicions; I wish I had studies to cite or findings to report. Stylistic variation in academic writing is a research area begging for further exploration. Close attention to style would be a useful extension of current scholarship in writing in the disciplines; ideally, the work would be performed with sophisticated analytical tools such as those afforded by systemic functional linguistics (see Lancaster, this volume). Students who are invited into the investigation will find a window into the values and mores of the academy.

Reflecting on the place of style in composition classes, we do not have to conceive of style and academic writing as competing topics vying for our limited time. Academic writing is writing. Its style is sometimes ugly, sometimes lovely, sometimes almost invisible—but if the writer is making choices about how to arrange words in sentences, the prose has style. It must be acknowledged that different kinds of discourse permit different degrees of stylistic experimentation and play. A dissertation has less room for eloquence than a poem or a memoir. But doesn't a dissertation have *some* room for stylistic play? Couldn't it have more? If we look for style in academic writing, we may find more pleasure and beauty than we expected, or we may find that we—or the next generation of writers, taught to appreciate and experiment with prose style—can create more room by pushing at the edges of academic genres. Whether they are "rendering" experience or "explaining" it, they should know that they can strive simultaneously for clarity and elegance, for truth and beauty.

REFERENCES

Bizzell, P. (1982). College composition: Initiation into the academic discourse community. *Curriculum Inquiry 12*, 191-207.

Clocksin, W. F. & Mellish, C. S. (1984). *Programming in Prolog* (2nd ed.). Berlin: Springer-Verlag.

Crowley, S. (1998). *Composition in the university: Historical and polemical essays.* Pittsburgh, PA: University Pittsburgh Press.

Elbow, P. (1991). Reflections on academic discourse: How it relates to freshmen and colleagues. *College English 53*, 135-155.

Ellis, H. C. (1965). *The transfer of learning.* New York: Macmillan.

Lanham, R. A. (1974). *Style: An anti-textbook.* New Haven: Yale University Press.

Perkins, D. N. & Salomon, G. (1992). Transfer of Learning. *International encyclopedia of education, second edition.* Oxford: Pergamon Press.

Petraglia, J. (Ed.). (1995). *Reconceiving writing, rethinking writing instruction.* Mahwah, NJ: Lawrence Erlbaum.

Ronald, K. (1999). Style: The hidden agenda in composition classes. In W. Bishop (Ed.), *The subject is writing: Essays by teachers and students* (pp. 167-82). Portsmouth, NH: Heinemann.

Scarry, E. (1998). On beauty and being just. The Tanner lectures on human values. New Haven: Yale University.

Smagorinsky, P. & Smith, M. W. (1992). The nature of knowledge in composition and literary understanding: The question of specificity. *Review of Educational Research 62*, 279-305.

Strunk, W. & White, E. B. (1959). *The Elements of Style.* New York: Macmillan.

Tillotson, G., Fussell, P., & Waingrow, M. (Eds.). (1969). *Eighteenth-Century English literature.* New York: Harcourt

Williams, J. (2005). *Style: Ten lessons in clarity and grace* (8th ed.). New York: Pearson.

Wood, S. (2005). *The freedom of the streets: Work, citizenship, and sexuality in a Gilded Age city.* Chapel Hill: UNC Press.

TRACKING INTERPERSONAL STYLE: THE USE OF FUNCTIONAL LANGUAGE ANALYSIS IN COLLEGE WRITING INSTRUCTION

Zak Lancaster
Wake Forest University

INTRODUCTION

Rhetorical Genre Studies, or RGS, has had much influence in recent years on reconceptualizing the goals of college level writing instruction in North America, both in the contexts of first-year composition (FYC) and upper-level writing in the disciplines. One broad goal for FYC specifically has been conceptualized as helping students gain "genre awareness" (see the work of Beaufort; Devitt; Johns) or "awareness of the social and ideological aspects of genre production and consumption" (Cheng, 2007, p. 304). By assisting students to develop a nuanced awareness of genre—and not just familiarity with particular genres—it is hoped that students will be better equipped to examine samples of a genre they are working in with a keen rhetorical eye, approach unfamiliar writing situations with greater confidence in their existing store of genre knowledge, and learn to make more deliberate genre choices in their own writing—which may include motivated disruptions of genre expectations. A key instructional method for fostering this kind of nuanced genre awareness is to train students to analyze genres, tracking how textual choices shape, and are shaped by, contextual dynamics. This approach is discussed by, among others, Amy Devitt, Anis Bawarshi, and Mary Jo Reiff ("Materiality"), who argue that RGS informs a discourse analytic approach that "links patterns of language use to patterns of social behavior" and thus "allows students and researchers to recognize how 'lived textuality' plays a role in the lived experience of a group" (2003, p. 542). The advantage of the approach, as Devitt et al. explain, is that it "focuses on the actual uses of texts, in all their messiness and with all their potential consequences" and "ties that use to actual language, to the smaller bits of language that alert analysts to underlying ideas, values, and beliefs" (2003, p. 543).

As suggested by the focus on language and text in the above explanation, undertaking genre analysis in FYC has the potential to place stylistic analysis back on composition's center stage in a theoretically-grounded manner, enabling instructors and students to track textual patterns in a way that is sensitive to contextual dynamics. Nevertheless, I'd like to suggest in this chapter that the approach has not been as fully operationalized for the classroom as it could be if the textual aspects of genre analysis were considered with more systematic attention to language use. As Devitt notes ("Refusing"), RGS has largely distanced itself from matters of form, and so the "smaller bits of language" referred to above have not been foregrounded in published genre analyses, nor have specific analytic constructs that students and instructors can use to guide the process of noticing these bits of language, connecting them to other bits of language, and discerning their socio-rhetorical purposes in samples of genre under analysis. My argument in this chapter is that systematic approaches to text analysis are necessary if writing instructors are to support students' analyses of genre in ways that help them to identify subtle patterns of text that connect to context. Starting from this initial position, I'd like to suggest that genre-register theory in systemic functional linguistics, or SFL, can offer one very useful way to get started connecting genre as an abstract concept to the nuts and bolts of analyzing genre samples systematically and in detail.

SFL is a theory of language developed from the work of the linguist Michael Halliday (see, e.g., "Explorations"; "An Introduction") that explores how our choices in language reflect, and work to realize, key contextual variables that are always at play in situations where language is used. These are the field (the topic of the text, the nature of the social action), the tenor (the relationship between participants, i.e. writer and reader), and the mode (the part that language plays, and what the participants expect the language to do for them in the situation). According to this theory, stylistic qualities of a given text are constructed through patterns of language choices that are motivated by the field, tenor, and mode. For example, as Jonathan Buehl's chapter (this volume) helps us to understand, science discourse is the way that it is (lexically dense and highly nominalized) because the discourse has evolved over time to accommodate the expression of new kinds of knowledge (field) and interpersonal relationships (tenor).

Williams' lessons in *Style: Ten Lessons in Clarity and Grace* draw liberally from Halliday's meaning-based grammar and from Halliday and Hasan's work on textual cohesion. Building on this earlier work in SFL, James R. Martin and David Rose, among others, have recently developed a set of discourse-based tools for "tackling a text" (Martin & Rose, 2007), and these tools enable analysts to explore how meanings (ideational, interpersonal, and textual) are constructed in discourse. Because these analytic tools do not assume prior knowledge of

SFL, they are ideal for use in composition classrooms when the goal is to unpick how a text's abstract qualities—such as its "flow" or "style"—are constructed through language.

In this chapter, I focus specifically on the SFL-based Appraisal framework (developed most fully in Martin and White) in order to discuss how patterns of language use construct a text's interpersonal style. Building from the clause-level resources described by Halliday ("An Introduction"), the Appraisal framework is useful for tracking how a particular "voice" or persona is constructed in a text; how other voices and perspectives are brought into play; how affect and judgment are encoded; how evaluative meanings are scaled up and down in force and focus; and how community-recognized knowledge and values are signaled. As an analytic tool, Appraisal helps to explore how these meanings may be infused in a text below readers' and writers' consciousness, patterning together in certain ways to construct the text's interpersonal style. In this way, the analysis is useful for getting students and instructors to think concretely in terms of the frequently cited dictum that stylistic choices are meaningful.

In order to motivate the use of SFL-based discourse analysis in composition instruction, I begin with a very brief explanation of composition's relationship to linguistics and then turn to recent work in rhetoric and composition studies on rhetorical grammar. I place emphasis on aspects of that approach that seem to be working toward the goal of operationalizing rhetorical genre analysis for the composition class and those aspects that do not. I then use this critique to demonstrate how key analytic concepts from SFL, including genre, register, and interpersonal meanings, can aid in the stylistic analysis of academic texts. This discussion builds on Nora Bacon's general point (in this volume) that style is very much present in academic discourse, and that analysis of stylistic choices in academic writing is of high educational value for FYC instruction.

THE BACKGROUNDING OF LANGUAGE IN COMPOSITION STUDIES

Because I am suggesting that students and instructors take up linguistic analysis to analyze stylistic patterns in genre samples, a brief discussion of composition's relationship to the field of linguistics seems relevant. Composition's distancing from linguistics has been well documented (see, for example, Barton and Stygall; Johnson and Pace; and MacDonald), and it is more than partly justified. It has to do with at least three interconnected phenomena: the shift from a product to process-oriented view of writing, which had the effect of positioning questions about textual patterns as representative of a "product" or static view of writing; the increasing awareness that the structuralist and generative linguistics of the sixties and seventies had little to offer either our teaching of writing or our study of the production and reception of actual texts; and, perhaps most importantly, the increasing use of social constructionist theories to examine texts, which had the effect of shifting attention away from the texts themselves to their larger social contexts. This latter move, referred to widely as "the social turn," has been important for bringing about a de-centering of language and text in favor of a stronger focus on the social patterns of activity revolving around the interpretation and (re)production of texts.

This de-centering of language is understandable given composition's past privileging of form without consideration of context, as seen in older formalist approaches. It is also understandable given the field's past focus on the individual writer engaged solely in a cognitive process of problem-solving, a point of view reflected in much work on text linguistics (e.g., Beaugrande and Dressler). I'd like to suggest, however, that the "social turn" has succeeded so well in directing the field's gaze upwards and outwards, above and beyond the linguistic features of texts, that most compositionists nowadays tend not to think about meaning as construed through the language we use to construct texts but rather as residing in the activities that surround and govern the workings of texts. As a result, the field's theoretical understanding of language and how it functions as a meaning-making resource has been under-explored.

This de-centering of language is evident in Devitt, Bawarshi, and Reiff's genre-based textbook *Scenes of Writing*, which is geared toward training students to analyze genres and raise their genre awareness. To analyze a genre, the authors outline four analytical steps:

1. Collect Samples of the Genre
2. Identify the Scene and Describe the Situation in Which the Genre is Used
3. Identify and Describe Patterns in the Genre's Features
4. Analyze What These Patterns Reveal about the Situation and Scene (2003, pp. 93-94)

These four steps provide a useful overarching direction for analysis. They do not, however, provide the type of detailed support needed to account for salient patterns in language use that are not apparent after initially scanning a text. Under the third step, students are prompted to consider "patterns in the genre's features," for example whether sentences are long or short, complex or simple, and whether they are in passive or active voice. Students are also prompted to consider whether the sentences "share a certain style" and "what diction is most common" (Devitt, Bawarshi, & Reiff, 2003, p. 94). This level of analysis, I'd like to suggest, is not as nuanced as it could be to guide students toward analyzing how "smaller bits of language" can reveal "underlying ideas, values, and beliefs," as suggested above, and so a number of questions arise. For one, what advice can we give students if they cannot identify recurring patterns in the texts they are analyzing? What analytic tools are available to guide students' process of identifying recurring and co-occurring patterns—ones that may not stand out after initial scans—and then connecting those patterns to larger rhetorical functions? How can students develop an analytic vocabulary, or meta-language, for talking about word/phrase, clause, and text level features in genres under examination in meaningful and concrete ways?

RHETORICAL GRAMMAR

Rhetorical grammar is one approach to analyzing word/phrase, clause, and text level features of discourse that is potentially valuable for students' genre analysis projects. Laura Micciche defines rhetorical grammar as "using grammatical devices that enable us to respond appropriately and effectively to a situation" (2004, p. 719). As opposed to analyzing "style," which Micciche defines as the "'extraordinary' use of language," analyzing rhetorical grammar means tracking the rhetorical purposes of seemingly minor choices in "the 'ordinary' use of language—grammar" (2004, p. 717). In this way, Micciche endorses a pedagogical goal that rings familiar with Devitt's goal of alerting students to "purposes behind forms" (2004, p. 197). As Micciche writes:

> The grammatical choices we make—including pronoun use, active or passive verb constructions, and sentence patterns—represent relations between writers and the world they live in. Word choice and sentence structure are an expression of the way we attend to the words of others, the way we position ourselves in relation to others. (2004, p. 719)

Instruction in rhetorical grammar, Micciche points out, can assist learners in coming to see the rhetorical effects of particular syntactic and lexical choices. For this reason, rhetorical grammar is "just as central to composition's driving commitment to teach critical thinking and cultural critique as is reading rhetorically, understanding the significance of cultural difference, and engaging in community work through service-learning initiatives" (2004, p. 717).

A concrete method that Micciche explains for sharpening students' sensitivity to rhetorical grammar is to have students keep commonplace books in which they record grammatical patterns from their readings that are of interest to them and then practice using those patterns to construct texts of their own. This method encourages students to "tinker with language, seeing how it is crafted and directed rather than as simply 'correct' or 'incorrect'" (Micciche, 2004, p. 724). Further, by tinkering with grammatical choices, students can begin to take notice of how subtle manipulation of language can have important political ramifications. Micciche demonstrates, for example, how an analysis of "hedging" devices such "likely" and the verb "believe" in George Bush's 2002 speech to the United Nations—as in Bush's claim that "U.N. inspectors *believe* Iraq has produced two to four times the amount of biological agents it declared"—can open up a discussion with students about standards for providing evidence when making a case for declaring war (2004, p. 725). Keeping commonplace books, therefore, pushes students "to think in unfamiliar ways about texts to which they have developed familiar responses" (Micciche, 2004, p. 727). In this way, instruction in rhetorical grammar can arm students with concrete ways of looking at and talking about language and, potentially, can enable them to home in on subtle ways that arguments are built up through language in particular texts. Micciche's discussion of rhetorical grammar, therefore, goes a long way toward revealing the tension between formal constraint and choice that gives rise to creative expression and nuanced rhetorical decisions.

One potential limitation of the approach, however, is that it is not clear how rhetorical grammar analysis is informed and shaped by considerations of genre. In particular, neither Micciche's article, nor Martha Kolln's widely used textbook, treats explicitly the ways in which genre acts as a superordinate constraint on the array of possible grammatical choices speakers/writers can make in a given rhetorical context, or the ways genre serves as a guidepost for directing the process of rhetorical grammar analysis. To return to Micciche's example of Bush's speech, an important sequence of questions for analyzing this speech from a genre and rhetorical grammar perspective include: What are the communicative purposes of U.S. presidential speeches to the U.N.? Under what circumstances are they typically delivered? What are some typical rhetorical moves used in other crisis speeches? How does Bush's particular speech relate to these genres and how is its structure similar to or different from typical organizational stages in these other genres? Then, we may ask: in which moves do "hedging" devices, or expressions of modality, accumulate most abundantly? What rhetorical work do these devices accomplish within the context of a particular move or argumentative stage? What language features accumulate and pattern together with other language features in other moves?

In pursuing questions such as these, rhetorical grammar and genre analysis can be brought together so that instructors and students can track ways that grammatical choices accumulate and pattern together in particular phases of a text as it unfolds; students and instructors can discuss how these patterns create waves of meaning that achieve generic purposes and perhaps give rise to a particular style for the sample of the genre under investigation.

A second limitation of rhetorical grammar analysis—one that is characteristic of most other linguistically oriented approaches to discourse analysis—is that the discussions of grammatical/rhetorical "choices" do not specify what exactly it is that is chosen when a grammatical or rhetorical choice is made. In other words, making a choice suggests that a speaker/writer is at least tacitly aware of multiple other available options for producing related meanings in a particular situation, but those other available options tend not to be discussed explicitly. The usefulness of the SFL approach to discourse analysis, to which I now turn, is that it proposes networks of increasingly delicate levels of options that are available in various linguistic systems (for example the system of mood) to achieve particular discourse level meanings. These system networks help analysts track the choices that speakers/writers have made from a network of other choices they could have made but did not.

LOCATING STYLE IN SFL GENRE/REGISTER THEORY

As mentioned above, SFL explores language choices in terms of the meanings they realize. As Mary Schleppegrell explains,

> Every language offers its speakers/writers a wealth of options for construing meaning. SFL facilitates exploration of meaning in context through a comprehensive text-based grammar than enables analysts to recognize the choices speakers and writers make from the linguistic systems, and to explore how those choices are functional for construing meanings of different kinds. (2011, p. 21)

These choices and meanings are analyzed at the most general level through the connected concepts of *genre* and *register*.

GENRE

Genre in SFL has been defined as "staged, goal-oriented social processes" (Martin, 1998, p. 412). Importantly, genre in this view operates at the broad context of culture, which is a point of view somewhat at odds with the RGS view of genre as socially situated. Specific differences in perspectives and purposes of SFL and RGS approaches to genre have been discussed in detail elsewhere (see, e.g., Bawarshi & Reiff; Devitt; Hyon; Martin & Rose, 2008), but primarily it should be noted that, in the RGS view, genres are fluid modes of action that can be located within particular communities (i.e., they are socially situated); this is because they regularly facilitate communicative purposes among participants in a particular social group. In the SFL perspective, genres are recurring text types that grow out of social purposes within the culture at large; *narratives*, for example, are used to resolve complications in a story and *critical responses* are used to challenge the message of a text.

It is conceivably possible to reconcile the RGS and SFL views of genre, as others have noted, by casting the SFL conceptualization as "elemental" genres that pattern together in particular ways to construct larger "macro" genres. Tenure and promotion reports, for example, are socially situated genres that are comprised of *accounts, explanations, narratives, personal responses*, and so on, and these elemental genres are realized through recurring textual stages. Attempting to reconcile the two approaches in this way has merit, but to proceed with genre analysis it is arguably more important to understand the SFL concept of *register*. Register is the crucial component in SFL genre theory that tends to be under-discussed in others' accounts of SFL genre theory and pedagogy.

Register

Analyzing the schematic structure of elemental genres like *accounts* and *expositions* does little in and of itself to help forward our understanding of how genres are infused with meanings, or how meanings vary in specific instances or realizations of a genre in a particular context. Register, therefore, is a specific theory of social context that helps to answer these questions. Register analysis explores how three contextual variables are both reflected and realized in every situation where language is used. These variables are, as identified above, the *field* of discourse (the topic of the text, the nature of the social action), the *tenor* of discourse (the relationship between participants, i.e., writer and reader), and the *mode* of discourse (the part that language plays, what the participants expect the language to do for them in the situation). Using this linguistically oriented theory of context, we can talk, for example, about how interpersonal meanings are realized through specific lexico-grammatical choices that both reflect and shape the tenor, or participant relations, in a given context.

As illustration of this last point, consider the case of the *critical response* genre. Critical responses are one of many response genres frequently assigned in school contexts (on response genres, see Christie & Derewianka; Martin

& Rose, 2008). The critical response is realized through the stages of *evaluation, deconstruction,* and *challenge.* Generally, the author(s) first evaluates a text (evaluation), then breaks the text down by explaining how it works (deconstruction), and then challenges some aspect of the message in the text (challenge). When an individual author constructs a critical response in a given situational context—for a particular group of readers, on a particular topic, through a particular mode of discourse—his or her specific choices in language range in degree of formality, commitment, explicitness, and other factors related to the interpersonal context. To illustrate, consider the following two versions of an excerpt from a *challenge* stage of a published *New Left Review* article by Joshua Cohen and Joel Rogers. The one on the left is the actual published version and the one on the right is my modified version.

Published Version by Cohen & Rogers	**My Modified Version**
Chomsky presents reams of evidence for the [propaganda] model.... Nonetheless, Chomsky's view of the media and the manufacture of consent seems overstated in three ways. First, the claim that business people and state managers are in the main relatively "free of illusion" seems overdrawn, at least when that claim is offered (as Chomsky usually offers it) without substantial qualification....	Evidence is presented for the [propaganda] model.... Nonetheless, in three ways Chomsky overstates the argument that the media manufacture consent. First, he completely overdraws the claim that business people and state managers are in the main relatively "free of illusion"; he certainly overdraws this claim when he offers it without substantial qualification, as he frequently does....

One similarity between the versions is that they are both relatively formal. They both use diction appropriate for scholarly journalistic discourse (e.g., *nonetheless, overstates, overdraws, substantial qualification*). In addition, the length and complexity of clauses are comparable, and they both use a mix of active and passive constructions. But the differences in meaning are important, and they are accomplished through language in two basic ways.

First, there is a difference in the kind of nouns that serve as the theme for the forthcoming evaluations. As Nora Bacon notes in her chapter in this volume, academic writing often cannot use persons as grammatical subjects because of the frequent need to deal with abstract concepts. The use of abstract sentence subjects (rather than personal ones) can become even more complex when the task at hand is to critically evaluate others' work. In Cohen and Rogers's text (the published one), only the first clause and one parenthetical clause toward the end of the passage thematize a person, *Chomsky*, whereas the second clause and each remaining clause thematize abstractions, *Chomsky's view* ..., *the claim* ..., and *that claim*. The pattern is reversed in my modified version, where the first clause thematizes an abstraction, *Evidence,* and the second and remaining clauses thematize a person, *Chomsky, he, he,* and *he*. The choice, then, about what to take as the point of departure for the message turns on whether the forthcoming evaluation can be interpreted as praise or as critique. In other words, that there is evidence presented for the propaganda model can be understood as a positive appraisal, while the other appraisals can only be understood as critiques (*overstated, overdrawn*). The difference in theme selection here therefore bears on the degree of interpersonal alignment with the subject of the evaluation: Chomsky and his views on the media. Cohen and Rogers' grammatical choices, that is, are at least partly guided by their purpose of constructing a critically distanced stance when engaging in critique of Chomsky's work on the media.

Second, there is a difference in the way the authorial voice modulates its commitment to the evaluations being put forth. In the published version, the authorial voice reduces the level of commitment when putting forth critiques. This is accomplished through the use of the expressions *seems* and *usually*, while the authorial voice amplifies the proposition that *Chomsky presents evidence*. (Compare <u>reams</u> *of evidence* with <u>much</u> *evidence*). The opposite pattern obtains in my modified version. The authorial voice is highly committed to the critiques (<u>*completely*</u> *overdraws,* <u>*frequently*</u> *does*), while the passive construction of the first clause works to construct a more reluctant concession regarding the existence of evidence.

Through this brief register analysis, then, we can be very explicit about how Cohen and Rogers construct a textual voice that is at once critical of Chomsky's views on the media and committed to the basic set of value configurations that many *New Left Review* readers are likely to associate with Chomsky's point of view. This positive positioning is accomplished by placing *Chomsky* in theme position and amplifying the positive evaluation—that this person, Chomsky, *presents* <u>*reams*</u> *of evidence*. In terms of negative evaluations, the textual voice is more distant; this distance is accomplished by backgrounding the human participant, thematizing abstractions, and using the appearance-based evidential *seems* to signal willingness to reconsider the critique. In my version, the interpersonal positioning is the opposite. Choices in wording frame the textual voice as interpersonally involved and committed to the *critiques* of Chomsky's views on the media, but distant from Chomsky as a person (or, the values he represents) when it comes to saying anything positive. A close examination of Cohen and Rogers' article reveals, in addition to many other complex rhetorical strategies, recurring patterns in these configurations. Here are further examples (positive/negative appraisals are in *italics*, and appearance-based evidentials are shaded):

Positive evaluation
- With *copious* documentation, he *effectively* makes the case that …

Negative evaluations
- Second … the model's claim that … seems *exaggerated* …
- The "Backroom Boys" example just given indicates *otherwise*

This brief analysis, then, challenges the view that these textual patterns represent some stylistic "tic" that is characteristic to Cohen and Rogers as individual authors. Rather, I am suggesting that we can account for these patterns in terms of the register variables of field, tenor, and mode. Specifically, the difference in meanings between the original version and my modified one can be best analyzed in terms of tenor, in this case the interpersonal distance between the authors and the subject of the critique (Chomsky and his media analyses) and also, importantly, the ways the authors choose to position themselves in relation to their readers' perspectives on Chomsky and his work. The particular set of values that the *New Left Review* represents and that its readers are likely to bring to their reading of the article factor into Cohen and Rogers' (perhaps tacit) choices for what to place in theme position and how to construct an interpersonal stance in regard to those values. We could imagine register configurations where my modified version would be more interpersonally effective, for example contexts where Chomsky's work on the media tends to be met with more committed resistance.

Through this type of analysis, students can come to see how particular stylistic choices—for example, the choice to be dialogically expansive (*this seems to be the case*), dialogically contractive (*this is definitely the case*), or dialogically disengaged (*this is the case*)—may vary within instances of the same genre (e.g., a critical review article) in light of particular contextual variables. To make increasingly subtler shades of distinctions in interpersonal positioning, and begin to home in on a particular text's or author's style of interpersonal positioning, SFL-based Appraisal theory is useful for tracking the choices that speakers/writers make to encode attitudinal meanings, adjust degrees of evaluations, and contract and expand dialogical space. As Martin and White explain, the framework explores "how writers/speakers construe for themselves particular authorial identities or personae, with how they align or disalign themselves with actual or potential

Table 1: Engagement resources in excerpts from economics and political theory term papers

From challenge stage of A-graded critical response in economics	*From challenge stage of A-graded critical response in political theory*
(1) The result of this kind of market structure is a system in which insurance firms control significant market power, as a monopsony to medical practitioners and a monopoly to patients. (2) The Supreme Court rejected the argument that the Federation's actions were designed to protect patients from insufficient dental treatment, stating that the idea of the provision of information leading to adverse outcomes was directly against the spirit of the Sherman Act. (3) However, their reasoning that insurance companies act almost as simple representatives of patients is not upheld by the current situation. (4) The object of the health insurance company is to maximize profit, not to maximize the health of the patient. (5) If insurance were purchased directly by the patient, competition among providers could equate the objects of both provider and patient. (6) However a perfectly competitive market clearly is not available to many of the consumers who purchase insurance directly.	(1) With his theory established, I think Rawls' first response to Fraser would be that the cultural injustices she believes require recognition are already accounted for in his "fully adequate scheme of equal basic rights." (2) Rawls proposes that one way of forming a list of basic rights and liberties is to consider what is essential to "provide the political and social conditions essential for the adequate development and full exercise of the two moral powers of free and equal persons." (3) It seems obvious that persons are unable to adequately develop and exercise their moral powers under conditions of extreme cultural disenfranchisement. (4) If a person is "routinely maligned or disparaged … in everyday life interactions", then it is unlikely that they will be able to participate in the means of acquiring the moral powers and will certainly be unable to fully exercise their moral power. (5) For example, if a woman is unable to go to school and be educated, then it is unlikely she will be able to adequately develop her moral power. (6) Further, if she is then unable to fully participate in society, she will be limited in the exercise of her moral power.

respondents, and with how they construct for their texts an intended or ideal audience" (2005, p. 1).

TRACKING INTERPERSONAL STANCE-TAKING

Appraisal theory makes use of three interrelated sub-systems to track choices in interpersonal meaning. Attitude, Graduation, and Engagement. *Attitude* tracks meanings related to feelings and affect, judgment of people (their motives and behavior), and appreciation of the aesthetic quality of things. *Graduation* tracks meanings related to raising or lowering the force and focus of propositions (in terms of intensity, quantity, preciseness, and protypicality). And finally *Engagement*, inspired as it is by Bakhtinian notions of heteroglossia and dialogism, tracks meanings related to engagement with others' voices and perspectives. Appraisal analysis is useful for systematically tracking how the sequencing and configuration of various interpersonal resources of language vary depending on the genre under analysis.

To illustrate, the following paragraph is from a second year student's argumentative essay written in a political science course. This paragraph demonstrates how particular configurations of Appraisal resources can cluster together to create a distinct interpersonal style. (Resources of Attitude are in underlined and resources of Graduation are in SMALL CAPS.)

> (1) Firstly, Zakaria's implication that the forces that moved into power in Bosnia were counterproductive ones to the American ends is TOTALLY <u>irrelevant</u>. (2) If America found democracy to TRULY be such a <u>noble</u> cause to spread, then SURELY it would not <u>violate a nation's sovereignty</u> in an attempt to preserve its democratic status. (3) Although ostensibly this would tie into his greater thesis regarding liberty as a lesser need than democracy as ideals America has worked to spread, his <u>generous</u> usage of the term democracy here and his <u>inability to PROPERLY hold it true to its definition</u> TOTALLY <u>undermines</u> his insistence in conceptual exactness and differentiation between democracy and liberty in the first place.

This paragraph makes use of many Appraisal resources. The meanings that overwhelm the paragraph, however, have to do with, on the one hand, *Attitudinal* resources of judgment (*noble, violate, generous, inability to properly hold it true to its definition*) and appreciation (*irrelevant, undermines*), and, on the other hand, *Graduation* resources of force (*totally, surely*) and focus (*truly, properly*). In terms of sequencing, the high force appreciation in the first sentence—that Zakaria's claim is "totally irrelevant"—sets up a wave of strongly negative meanings that spread through the remainder of the paragraph. This general spreading-through partly explains why the use of the conditional structure in the first part of sentence 2 (*If America found* …) works to reinforce the negative meaning by ironically reconsidering Zakaria's claim after having just forcefully rejected it. This ironic meaning is carried through in the second part of sentence 2—*then SURELY it would not* …—by strongly negating a proposition that we can assume the author in fact endorses, that "America" has violated a nation's sovereignty. Finally, the ironically and forcefully critical stance is carried through in the lengthy third sentence by the sarcastic judgment of Zakaria's use of the term "democracy" as *generous*, combined with the more explicitly negative judgment, his *inability to properly hold it true to its definition*. This student's critiques of Zakaria's reasoning, then, are expressed in a style of stance-taking that is explicitly evaluative, strongly committed, and dialogically contractive.

Appraisal analyses of undergraduate student writing (Coffin; Derewianka; Tang; Wu) show that the style of stance-taking displayed in this critique of Zakaria is not always rewarded in university contexts calling for "critical discussion" of texts. Particularly as students progress into upper-level writing courses in the disciplines, they are expected to construct stances that are at once critical, authoritative, and dialogically expansive. Beverly Derewianka found, for example, that writing from more advanced students tended to construct stances that were "explicitly open to other voices and possibilities" (2009, p. 162). Through the use of various *Engagement* strategies, more advanced and proficient writers tend to encode in their texts "an awareness of the problematic, constructed and intersubjective nature of meaning-making" (Derewianka, 2009, p. 163). Unlike the critique of Zakaria above, which uses heavily ramped up and ironic judgments, the texts Derewianka analyzed in her study of student writing worked to carefully juxtapose "other voices [that] are explicitly drawn into the discussion, interpreted, analyzed, critiqued and played off against each other" (2009, p. 163).

The particular choices explored by the Appraisal sub-system of *Engagement* involve the way writers/speakers engage with other voices and perspectives by directly acknowledging them or by denying, countering, conceding, or entertaining those perspectives. Dialogically contractive wordings work to boost the speaker's/writer's commitment to the proposition being put forth; in so doing, they contract space for the inclusion of alternative perspectives. Options for contracting the dialogic space include:

pronouncing an assertion (I am convinced that …)

affirming a proposition (clearly, certainly, obviously it is true/is the case)

disclaiming alternative views (It is not the case … rather …).

conceding and countering alternative views (It is true that …, but …)

Dialogically expansive wordings, in contrast, lower the speaker's/writer's commitment to the proposition being put forth and thus expand space for the inclusion of alternative perspectives. Available options for opening up the dialogic space include:

suggesting (one way to proceed is …)

conjecturing (perhaps, probably, it is likely …)

evidentializing (it seems/appears that …)

hypothetical reasoning (if we grant that …, then we …)

attributing views to others (Chomsky states that …, according to experts)

The options of conjecturing and evidentializing have been viewed in the linguistics literature on hedging, or displaying uncertainty and/or "deference, modesty, or respect" (Hyland, 2000, p. 88). In the *Engagement* framework they are seen more as functioning to open up space for the inclusion of alternative views and, as Martin and White explain, to extend offers of solidarity to imagined readers who are not already aligned with the author's point of view (2005, p. 126). Through the use of this framework, analysts can make explicit the specific choices in interpersonal stance-taking that speakers/writers have made and track the ways those choices pattern together to create a particular interpersonal style.

USING ENGAGEMENT TO ANALYZE DISCIPLINARY STYLES OF STANCE-TAKING

One useful project that students and instructors can explore in the context of FYC is the ways in which similar genres across disciplines may be characterized by different stance-taking styles. For example, how might argumentation in the contexts of classroom genres calling for "discussion" or "critical reasoning" assume subtly different and discipline-specific ways of positioning the textual voices vis-à-vis anticipated readers?

Before proceeding with illustrations, let me concede that such a project is a complex undertaking. One finding from Chris Thaiss and Terry Zawacki's *Engaged Writers, Dynamic Disciplines* is that the causes for miscommunication between students and faculty about good writing often result from five largely unexamined contexts at work in the design and evaluation of any writing assignment: "the academic; the disciplinary; the subdisciplinary; the local or institutional; and the idiosyncratic or personal" (2006, p. 138). Many or most instructors have difficulty stepping outside their own "ways of knowing, doing, and writing" (Carter, 2007, p. 385) to reflect on which of these contexts are at play when they design writing assignments and develop evaluative criteria. When it comes to talking about stylistic patterns at work in student writing, therefore, analyses of student-produced classroom genres may point to valued features of a general academic style (as opposed to a journalistic or conversational style), a broad disciplinary style (economics discourse), a sub-disciplinary style (discourse in economic regulation and antitrust policy), a sub-disciplinary style favored at a particular institution, or an author's idiosyncratic style. For this last context, Bacon (this volume) lists such factors as the writers' "personality, mood, knowledge, experience, professional status, ethnicity, gender, proficiency with language, and so on." When an interpersonal style is unpicked, then, any of these contextual variables may be seen as relevant, and making these complex interpretations can be a valuable exercise for student writers in the context of FYC.

Pursuing this line of analysis, I used the *Engagement* framework discussed above to code two undergraduate students' argumentative essays, one in economics and the other in political theory. The two paragraphs presented below are comparable because (a) they are both from the critical response sections of the respective papers, which called for evaluation and reasoned argumentation; (b) they were both written by fourth year students at the same large public university who were majoring in the respective disciplines; and (c) they both received A's and were praised by the instructors for sophisticated "critical reasoning." The economics text was written in an upper-level undergraduate course focused on economic regulation and antitrust policy, and in this passage the student is challenging the reasoning of the Supreme Court. The political theory text was written an upper-level undergraduate course on twentieth century political thought, and in this passage the student is using John Rawl's concept of justice as fairness to challenge Nancy Fraser's argument in her paper "From Redistribution to Recognition." (Dialogically expansive resources are set in shaded text and contractive resources are underlined. As with my analysis of the student's critique of Zakaria above, I have highlighted here the lexico-grammatical "triggers" for discourse semantic options.)

An important similarity between the two excerpts is that both authorial voices are highly engaged dialogically. Both texts, that is, use strategies of attributions (e.g., *argument, stating, proposes*) and hypothetical reasoning to expand dialogical space, subtly allowing for alternative views, and they use pronouncements (*clearly, obvious, certainly*) to contract that space and guide the readers toward their own points of view. What this heteroglossic engagement suggests is that both authors are aware that, in academic contexts, writers are expected to negotiate assertions with an imagined reader who is not already aligned with the author's point of view but rather "is coolly rational, reading for information, and intending to formulate a reasoned response" (Thaiss & Zawacki, 2006, p. 7). Furthermore, the juxtaposition of perspectives accomplished by alternating between expansive and contractive wordings may be characteristic of academic writing valued for "critical" reasoning. In her study of the ways experts in anthropology evaluated student writing in a general education course, Mary Soliday found that readers tended to reward a "reflective stance," which involves a "student's ability to appreciate diverse positions and then to commit to a judgment within [that] context" (2004, p. 74).

In the two paragraphs in Table 1, we can see that such appreciation, or at least awareness, of diverse positions is subtly infused throughout the texts as the writers open up dialogical space by acknowledging and entertaining other points of view before committing to a stance. For example, in the economics paragraph, the direct denial in sentence 4 (*not to maximize the health of the patient*) is followed by an expansively worded elaboration in sentence 5 that works to entertain a concession (*If insurance ... could equate ...*); the dialogic space is then once contracted in sentence 6 through the use of a counter (*However*) and pronounced denial (*clearly is not available*).

In terms of differences, the paragraph from economics generally takes a more committed stance. It makes use of dialogically contractive options that the political theory text avoids, namely the strategy of directly disclaiming other views (e.g., *However ... is not upheld by the current situation*). It also grounds its propositions in a more objective voice, as seen in the bare assertion in sentence 1 and the lack of self-mentions. In contrast, the excerpt from political theory uses more expansive options to build its argument, particularly the option of entertaining alternative views, which is accomplished not only through the use of attributions and hypothetical reasoning, which the economics text makes use of as well, but also conjecturing (*I think; it is unlikely*) and evidentializing (*it seems obvious*). Through the use of these strategies, the student author gently challenges Fraser's views rather than directly countering or denying them.

One pedagogical question raised by this type of analysis, then, is whether or not argumentative writing in economics is more highly valued when it adopts a direct and committed stance-taking style, and whether argumentative writing in political theory is more highly valued when it adopts a less committed style. Obviously, there is no way to give a generalized answer to this question on the basis of two students' essays. We certainly would not want to over-estimate the value of committed and direct argumentation in economics, especially in light of the economist Deirdre McCloskey's suggestion that "the economist looks always at other possibilities in a world of imagination, the opportunity cost, the alternatives foregone by the actions in question" (1998, p. 94) or Trine Dahl's recent finding that writers of research articles in economics excel at constructing knowledge claims that "achieve the optimal balance of caution, modesty, and self-promotion" (2009, p. 385).

Perhaps, then, we need to consider the sub-disciplinary contexts. For the economics paragraph, this context is the field of economic regulation and antitrust policy, and thus the course material (and likely style of argumentation) shunts back and forth between the discourses of economics and law. In this regard, the frequent disclaim moves found in the economics paragraph may be more characteristic of the "lawyerly" rhetoric identified by McCloskey in the economist Robert Coase's discourse (McCloskey, 2009. p. 90). Furthermore, on a personal/idiosyncratic level, we might consider the fact that the graduate student instructor (GSI) who graded the papers in the course was pursuing a joint PhD in law and economics and that, as stated in an interview, he valued explicit counter-argumentation.

Likewise, it would be unfair to conclude that the dialogically expansive style evident in the political theory paragraph represents a political scientist's mode of argumentation. The particular context is political theory, and the professor of the course, who was trained in philosophy, remarked in an interview that the writing assignments in his courses tended to be more "humanities oriented" than social science. At the same time, however, another possible understanding of this paragraph, one suggesting a more "idiosyncratic" stylistic reading, is that the dialogical positioning in the paragraph is too complex and thus the writer misses an opportunity to align the reader with his/her own point of view. In particular, it seems that the writer could have wrapped-up the paragraph with a more contractive move rather than ending with the hypothetical examples. Yet another reading, one which rings with the skillful use of dialogically contractive language that appears in the conclusion of this paper, is that the writer is trying out a "voice" perceived to be appropriate for a political theory discussion, in which critical argumentation should not be carried out in a heavy handed manner but through the careful juxtaposition of various positions and evaluation of them with respect to one another.

CONCLUDING REMARKS

In this chapter I have discussed ways that SFL-based genre/register theory and Appraisal theory can guide the textual dimensions of genre analysis projects in the context of college writing instruction. Through the type of systematic attention to the interpersonal dimensions of texts that I have illustrated in this chapter, students and instructors can trouble some of the hard and fast stylistic principles that many students bring with them to their FYC courses, principles such as "be assertive, use active verbs, be clear and concise, eliminate 'filler' words, avoid repetition," and so on. What I would like to suggest, then, is that my discussion of texts in this chapter can serve as a model for the types of discussions that can take place in the context of FYC instruction that is focused on analyzing classroom genres across the curriculum. What drives my discussion is the general question of what sorts of interpretations can be made about fine-grained language choices in academic writing. What enables me to have this discussion is a concrete analytic framework and robust meta-language for talking about linguistic choices as they are related to meaning, in this case interpersonal interaction and dialogical stance-taking.

Use of an analytic framework allows students to adopt a critical distance from the texts they are analyzing. In this way it can facilitate the process of observing and tracking recurring patterns of language use that are otherwise difficult to notice from more casual scanning. Research from English for Specific Purposes contexts shows that students equipped with concrete analytic constructs for analyzing texts are better able to engage in reflection on their own rhetorical choices. Cheng, for example, discusses the gains graduate students made when reflecting on their rhetorical "moves" and "steps" when writing research article introductions (after John Swales' CARS model). Cheng's main argument is that in order to recontextualize discursive/rhetorical strategies from one genre to another, novice academic writers need a set of concrete analytic constructs that allows them to notice recurring patterns in the texts they read and then articulate their meta-reflections about their own use of such patterns. This process of noticing and reflective articulation can support a rhetorically sensitive transfer of genre features as students learn to use generic features "with a keen awareness of the rhetorical context that facilitates its appropriate use" (Cheng, 2007, p. 303). This argument makes sense when we consider that, in order to engage in meta-reflection about writing strategies and discursive choices, especially very fine-grained strategies and choices, learners need a specific language of reflection.

In short, I have argued in this paper for particular conceptual and methodological tools of text analysis with the goal of enabling students to conduct genre analysis with control and authority. The larger goal of enabling students to do close, text-based genre analysis, however, is to help them to foster sensitivity to the relations between textual forms and rhetorical effects as they learn to write in various and complex rhetorical situations. As Devitt et al., put it, the idea is to "teach students how to gain knowledge of scenes and genres and how to use that knowledge to make more critically informed and effective writing decisions within various scenes" (2004, p. xvii). This knowledge and sensitivity can be the driving force behind the transfer from successfully analyzing to successfully writing genres, a process whereby students come to read as writers and to write as readers.

REFERENCES

Barton, E., & Stygall, G. (Eds.). (2002). *Discourse studies in composition*. Cresskill, NJ: Hampton Press.

Bawarshi, A., & Reiff, M. J. (2010). *Genre: An introduction to history, theory, research, and pedagogy*. West Lafayette, IN: Parlor Press and the WAC Clearinghouse. Retrieved from http://wac.colostate.edu/books/bawarshi_reiff/

Beaufort, A. (2007). *College writing and beyond: A new framework for university writing instruction. Logan*: Utah State.

de Beaugrande, R., & Dressler, W. (1981). *Introduction to text linguistics*. London: Longman.

Carter, M. (2007). Ways of knowing, doing, and writing in the disciplines. *College Composition and Communication 58*(3), 385-418.

Cheng, A. (2007). Transferring generic features and recontextualizing genre awareness: Understanding writing performance in the esp genre-based literacy framework. *English for Specific Purposes 26*, 287-307.

Christie, F., & Derewianka, B. (2008). *School discourse*. London and New York: Continuum.

Coffin, C. (2002). The voices of history: Theorizing the interpersonal semantics of historical discourses. *Text 22*(4), 503-528.

Cohen, J., & Rogers, J. (1991). Knowledge, morality and hope: The social thought of noam chomsky. *New Left Review 187*, 5-27.

Dahl, T. (2009). The linguistic representation of rhetorical function: A study of how economists present their knowledge claims. *Written Communication 26*, 370-391.

Derewianka, B. (2009). Using appraisal theory to track interpersonal development in adolescent academic writing. In A. McCabe, M. O'Donnell, & R. Whittaker, R. (Eds.), *Advances in language and education* (pp. 142-165). New York and London: Continuum.

Devitt, A. J. (2004). *Writing genres.* Carbondale: Southern Illinois University Press.

Devitt, A. J. (2009). Refusing form in genre study. In Giltrow, J., & Stein, D. (Eds.), *Genres in the Internet: Issues in the theory of genre* (pp. 27-46). Amsterdam, NLD. John Benjamins.

Devitt, A. J., Bawarshi, A., & Reiff, M. J. (2003). Materiality and genre in the study of discourse communities. *College English 65*(5), 541-558.

Devitt, A. J., Bawarshi, A., & Mary Jo Reiff, M. J. (2004). *Scenes of writing: Strategies for composing with genres.* New York: Pearson Longman.

Halliday, M. A. K. (1973). *Explorations in the functions of language.* London: Edward Arnold (Explorations in Language Study Series).

Halliday, M. A. K. (1994). *An introduction to functional grammar* (2nd ed.). London: Arnold.

Halliday, M. A. K., & Hasan, R. (1976). *Cohesion in English.* London: Longman.

Hyland, K. (2000). *Disciplinary discourse: Social interactions in academic writing.* London: Longman.

Hyon, S. (1996). Genre in three traditions: Implications for ESL. *TESOL Quarterly 30*(4), 693-722.

Johns, A. M. (1997). *Text, role, and context: Developing academic literacies.* New York and Cambridge: Cambridge University Press.

Johnson, T. R., & Pace, T. (2005). Introduction. In T. R. Johnson & T. Pace (Eds.), *Refiguring prose style: Possibilities for writing pedagogy* (pp. 1-2). Logan, UT: Utah State University Press.

Kaplan, M. L., Silver, N., Meizlish, D., & Lavaque-Manty, D. (n.d.). Using metacognition to foster students' disciplinary thinking and writing skills. Ongoing research study, University of Michigan, Ann Arbor.

Kolln, M. (2003). *Rhetorical grammar: Grammatical choices, rhetorical effects* (4th ed.). New York: Longman.

MacDonald, S. P. (2007). The erasure of language. *College Composition and Communication 58*(4), 585-625.

Martin, J. R. (1998). Linguistics and the consumer: The practice of theory. *Linguistics and Education 9*(4), 411-448.

Martin, J. R. & Rose, D. (2007). *Working with discourse: Meaning beyond the clause* (2nd ed.). London: Continuum.

Martin, J. R. & Rose, D. (2008). *Genre relations: Mapping culture.* London: Equinox.

Martin, J. R. & White, P. R. (2005). *The language of evaluation:* Appraisal *in English.* New York: Palgrave Macmillan.

Micciche, L. R. (2004). Making a case for rhetorical grammar. *College Composition and Communciation* 55(4), 716-737.

McCloskey, D. (1986). *The rhetoric of economics.* Madison, WI: University of Wisconsin Press.

North, S. (2005). Disciplinary variation in the use of theme in undergraduate essays. *Applied Linguistics 26*(3), 431-452.

Schleppegrell, M. J. (2011). Systemic functional linguistics: Exploring meaning in language. In J. Gee & M. Handford (Eds.), *The Routledge handbook of discourse analysis* (pp. 21-34). London: Routledge.

Soliday, M. (2004). Reading student writing with anthropologists: Stance and judgment in college writing. *College Composition and Communication 56:1*: 72-93.

Swales, J. M. (1990). *Genre analysis.* Cambridge: Cambridge University Press.

Swain, E. (2009). Constructive an affective "voice" in academic discussion writing. In A. McCabe, M. O'Donnell, & R. Whittaker (Eds.), *Advances in language and education* (pp. 166-184). New York and London: Continuum.

Tang, R. (2009). A dialogic account of authority in academic writing. In M. Charles, D. Pecorari, & S. Hunston (Eds.), *Academic writing: At the interface of corpus and discourse* (pp. 170-190). New York and London: Continuum.

Thaiss, C., & Zawacki, T. M. (2006). *Engaged writers, dynamic disciplines: Research on the academic writing life.* Portsmouth, NH: Boynton/Cook.

Williams, J. (1997). *Style: Ten lessons in clarity and grace.* New York: Addison Wesley.

Wu, S. M. (2007). The use of engagement resources in high- and low-rated undergraduate geography essays. *Journal of English for Academic Purposes 6*, 254-271.

MULTIMODAL STYLE AND THE EVOLUTION OF DIGITAL WRITING PEDAGOGY

Moe Folk
Kutztown University

Notions of style—particularly the idea of multimodal style—are key in the ever-evolving digital composition framework. If indeed composition is undergoing a multimodal turn (see Faigley; George; Kress; Kress & Jewett; Kress & van Leeuwen; Lanham; Lankshear & Knobel; New London Group; Porter; Selber; Selfe; Selfe & Hawisher; Takayoshi & Selfe; WIDE Collective; Wysocki, 2001; Wysocki, 2004; Yancey), understanding the connection of multimodal style to production and analysis is paramount. Digital composition, in calling forth the use of multiple meaning-making modes, places stress on the existing logocentric composition framework, thereby placing stress on logocentric conceptions of style. In a period when digital compositions constantly evolve, conceptions of style evolve as well, and the boons and banes of multimodal style in digital realms are all related to boundless iterations. After all, if the act (and enactment) of style is difficult enough to grasp when dealing only with words that it has sustained scholarly inquiry for thousands of years, what happens when style is no longer bound by the printed page, bound by the essayistic traditions of composing for delivery on 8.5 x 11 white sheets of paper? As Collin Brooke wrote, it is important to discover what happens in digital composing when "style escapes the cage that print technology represents" (2002).

At the most basic level, if style is seen as a composer making choices, ultimately revealing patterns and providing style in the sense of a distinct manner of composing something, then the choices open to a digital compositionist are simply exponentially greater when working in multiple modes than in a singular mode. For example, although stylistic inquiries in an alphabetic text *could* have focused on some overall visual elements (e.g., font, use of bullets, paragraphing, etc.), they usually just focused on elements related to words and sentences (e.g., sentence variation, schemes, tropes, and figures, not to mention the various application of static abstractions). In contrast, a stylistic look at a digital video could involve numerous static visual elements, moving visual elements, audio components, and textual components, not to mention how they are all mixed together (or separated). This proliferation of choices is similar to what Kress argued about the complexity of multimodal composing:

> [T]here are now choices about how what is to be represented should be represented; in what mode, in what genre, in what ensembles of modes and genres and on what occasions. These were not decisions open to students (or teachers or textbook makers) some 20 years earlier. (2003, p. 117)

Although one could read Kress's concerns merely as inventional choices, they eventually translate to production choices, and style is part and parcel of every step of the digital composing approach. Similarly, if we believe that changes in style result in changes of meaning (Beardsley, 1969, p. 7), then there is much at stake when there are multiple modes with their own styles to consider, especially in the consideration as to whether our digital invention reach exceeds our digital composing grasp. The ability to craft something rhetorically effective with a digital text, then, depends on one's ability to grasp style on a deep analytical and productive level.

In a multimodal work, a singular mode could stand out from the intended multimodal whole and thus greatly affect the perceived meaning of the entire work. In other words, whether you're a dualist or not, a singular mode can be separated from the whole and greatly affect the meaning of a text because of how one perceives the stylized content of the mode in question. For example, if a composer constructed a webtext that focused on persuading people to adopt a pro-life abortion view, that webtext would be perceived quite differently by its audience—regardless of identical textual and visual content—if the audio playing over the webtext was AC/DC's "Highway to Hell" versus Albinoni's "Adagio." This is not to say that the classical piece represents a more "highbrow" Ciceronian style and is therefore more rhetorically effective, but simply to illustrate that the attitude, stance, and lyrics of the AC/DC song would be taken completely differently within the context of the multimodal whole of the pro-life argument and thus change the meaning of the webtext itself. "Adagio" might strike a somber note that reinforces the seriousness of the topic, but "Highway to Hell" could be taken as a chastising, religious-oriented rebuke to those who do not share the views of the webtext's creator. In addition, playing the songs softly would not translate to some kind of "lessened" rhetorical effect. It also points to the intellectual recklessness of privileging the icono-textual aspects of the argument like many of the field's multimodal textbooks and scholarly approaches do. In another vein, there will be people who abandon the pro-life webtext (and thus its argument) on the production level simply because it had a song playing that could not be stopped or interacted with, a choice in and of itself that betrays a lack of audience awareness within dominant social consumption patterns of webpages revealed by prolonged use. In some sense, the use of the two songs mentioned above would be noteworthy because they already have an established ethos that can be elicited (or counteracted).

This notion recalls the idea of available designs in the multimodal composition process as formulated by the New London Group. The composer accesses existing designs that carry some sort of meaning and during the process of design, transforms them into the redesigned and re-deploys them for different semiotic purposes.

Similarly, other scholars address the complex diffusion of style in various meaning-making modes by examining how style is distributed throughout modern cultural constructs. Barry Brummett, for example, argued for the importance of understanding style and how it functions because it is "the basis for organizing the social today" (2008, p. xiii). Brummett identifies the importance of style to both individual and collective meaning in contemporary society:

> [S]tyle creates tensions between social allegiance and individuality, tensions likely to increase under conditions of postmodern complexity. The social organization of style is never value free. Style's aesthetic organizes such value-laden dimensions of the social as gender and sexual identity, class, time, and space. (2008, p. 43)

In a similar vein, Brummett argued "there are cohesive clusters of style—movement, gesture, speech, vocabulary, decoration, and the like" that can be read and utilized in certain social ways. Providing one of what could be countless examples, Brummett noted how "'Hippie style' may or may not be currently fashionable, but it nevertheless remains a style that is available to be mined for its signs and meanings, and it may go in and out of fashion over the years" (2008, p. 4). In other words, what digital style accesses is a slew of social patterns, histories, and technological patterns. Ewen also implicated the immense importance of style to the social when he defined style as "a way that the human values, structures, and assumptions in a given society are aesthetically expressed and received" (1988, p. 3). Taken together, a view of style in the larger societal sense espoused by Brummett and Ewen is important for the enterprise of digital composition. For one, if style is such an intrinsic part of social formation, if it is indeed powerful enough to be simultaneously repellant and attractant, it cannot help but be implicated in the rhetorical effectiveness of digital texts in every stage of the composing process.

In addition to needing to understand the distribution of multimodal style in established and evolving social contexts, digital composition's embrace of other modes naturally recalls other disciplines' concepts of style. After all, other notions of style have developed in disciplines that have traditionally been much more multimodal than English studies. The opposing tensions between style in English studies and just one discipline, art history, for example, could fruitfully complicate notions because multimodal style cannot be shoe-horned into a lone discipline's previous understandings. For example, the influential early art scholar Wölfflin categorized an "expressive" base for style rooted in personal, national, and period representational tendencies, which congeals many English studies theories of author, text, and genre into one notion. Also, what Milic identified as psychological monism is mirrored in art history by what Genova called the "signature view"—"a distinctive ensemble of the characteristic ways an artifact is made in order to place greater emphasis on the individual maker" (1979, p. 315) and elevate the innate characteristics of the artist. Additionally, Genova claimed the signature view is damaging because it denies the vital role style "plays in creating and discovering meaning" (1979, p. 315), which is basically opposite of the arguments against monism. Similarly, art history has provided new schemas, such as having perfected style as a cataloging tool (see Elsner, 1996, p. 106) in order to make some sense of the vast amount of artistic works. I argue this is what students, teachers, and citizens of the digital age do (whether consciously or unconsciously) in order to make sense of the proliferating digital texts around them—we align ourselves with certain styles as a means of sifting through and determining what should be focused on and recalled, what should be discarded and remembered. Art history also has the "meaning-expressing model," where meaning is the primary function of style but still plays a role in identification (Genova, 1979). In some ways, this view is like a hybrid of the monistic views Milic identified (psychological monism and Crocean aesthetic monism); in a digital composition where more modes are capable of being styled, this meaning-expressing model can become a powerful concept.

The aforementioned art history concepts are not alone in holding promise; important digital composition behaviors and predilections could also be understood by examining stylistic conceptions rooted in psychology (see Brummett, 2008, p. 2) anthropology, and biology (see Bang, 2000; Kress & van Leeuwen, 2001; Postrel, 2003, p. 32). However, despite the possible contributions other disciplines' ideas hold for developing multimodal style, approaching beneficial contemporary theories of style in digital composition means discerning complex notions of style that dovetail with, and also rupture, dominant existing conceptions of style within the framework of English studies.

EVOLVING CONCEPTIONS OF MULTIMODAL STYLE

Using traditional composition textbooks as an example, Woodman (1982) pointed out prevailing conceptions of style, thus illustrating a proliferation of implied practices even when only working with alphabetic texts:

> Be sure to follow the style of academic documentation (style as format); Standard edited English is the style likely to be acceptable to your readers (style as grammaticality); Try to write in a clear and readable style (style as precision); Varied sentence patterns promote a pleasing style (style as syntactic variation). Density of embedding is characteristic of a mature style (style as syntactic complexity); Modern readers prefer a plain style (style as linguistic register). (1982, para. 6)

While the guises Woodman pointed out cover much stylistic ground and are still quite common in contemporary textbooks and pedagogical approaches, the complexity that multimodal style adds to the equation means that other iterations of style are missing or under-theorized. The viewpoints and attitudes applicable in the spaces where composers use computers and various semiotic modes to form new types of digital compositions give rise to ever-evolving notions of style. What follows are existing iterations of multimodal style that I have developed, a process that included years of teaching multimodal composition, years of analyzing and creating a variety of digital texts, and years of collecting what amounts to thousands of students' rhetorical reflections about their own multimodal works. One of the things that spurred my interest in multimodal style was the importance I noted that students placed on multimodal style across all aspects of the composing process, as discussed in their rhetorical reflections. For example, when prompted to discuss why they chose a particular topic, students often cited a desire to approximate the style of a particular work they had admired, or they chose a particular style they identified with a positive, professional ethos, but one they could nonetheless definitely pull off with their multimodal composing skills. While some of these existing/evolving iterations of multimodality might recall previous notions of style, all are still under-theorized from our established iterations of style in digital compositions, but transcending these entrenched notions is important because of the integrated nature of multimodal style to the analysis and production of digital texts.

STYLE AS TECHNICAL PROWESS

In this iteration, style is primarily defined and achieved by expressing mechanical superiority/expertise. *Style as technical prowess* privileges how technologies meld with existing semiotic systems to create new artifacts or the ways technology is used to foster new expression (similar to the idea of the redesigned from the New London Group). In short, an individual's expertise with digital composing technologies (e.g., software) allows for a certain type of production, which in turn allows for a particular style that is not within the digital composing repertoire of most people. Indeed, the style often becomes the text in the eyes of the audience who cannot make it—and in many cases the actual technical style ends up being valued above content by the composer and thus becomes the marker for the audience. However, it is important to note that the advanced technical style is neither patently positive nor negative; its rhetorical effect, as noted before, is bound up in evolving technologies and the multimodal style conventions that change as the social practices associated with those technologies change. In short, *style as technical prowess* recalls the social recognition captured in Holcomb and Killingsworth's definition: "[S]tyle is a performance of identity using a recognized form within a cultural context" (2010, p. 168).

An early example taken from the Web would be the use of animated GIFs, which showcased a certain technical capability on the part of the composer (particularly for those unfamiliar with how to make them), thus imbuing pages with a certain sense of style, and often becoming the marker of "wow" technical factor even when the animated GIF was rhetorically inappropriate. Nowadays, the animated GIF is often seen as *the* marker of a cheesy second-generation site or is used to mark an ironically bad web page. For example, The Geocities-izer, a website that promises to make any other website "look like it was built by a 13-year-old in 1996," relies heavily on placing animated GIFs in the mirrored site. While the field tends to suspect that an unyielding focus on technical prowess is damaging because it supersedes "higher order" critical and rhetorical concerns, *style as technical prowess* nonetheless shows how important advanced digital composing can be to digital text production, and how a wide range of rhetorical critical possibilities are thus opened up for production and analysis alike.

STYLE AS DIFFERENCE

Although style as difference has long been covered under the aegis of doing something with distinction, or of simply being a matter of unteachable essence (as in psychological monism), the digital iteration may rest simply with actual difference. However, *style as difference* is intrinsic to current digital compositions, particularly if we are indeed suffering from an abundance of information and it becomes more difficult to attract attention (as Lanham argues). In addition, there is also the issue of what Schilb has called rhetorical refusals, instances where a composition purposefully elides the expectations associated with its particular intention; this notion seems apt for digital compositions, where what is often engaged with and shared with others amounts to novel constructions.

Using style as the means to attract attention, though, also presents a problem, for as Lanham suggested, purposeful self-consciousness is not highly regarded within our culture (2006, p. 142). Furthermore, *style as difference* is not tied to text alone, as Sonya Foss's definition of visual novelty attested: "[S]ome dimension of the form, structure, or construction technique of the image stands out as exceptional or extraordinary" (1993, p. 215). The elements Foss refers to could include such things as exquisite detailing, superb craftsmanship, or a finely finished surface—elements that stand out in this age of mass-produced and often poorly crafted objects. The technical novelty may result from a different scale than usual—miniature or grand—so that it generates awe and admiration (1993, p. 215).

In connection, I would argue a notion of digital composition pedagogy expertise is intended to help students and scholars avoid producing more ho-hum "mass produced and often poorly crafted objects." (Even though, sometimes, as in the case of Prezi versus PowerPoint, audiences can be so negatively overwhelmed by the paradigm of one form, they react positively to something in a novel form no matter how well the new is done.) Also, Foss's ideas are tied to the technical and thus recall *style as technical prowess*; however, novelty is the ultimate goal in *style as difference* and even though that may be achieved through technical ends, *style as difference* is more outwardly focused on attracting audience and differentiating itself from what's out there now on the whole. *Style as technical prowess* is more focused on attracting audience by promoting self-ability and achieving novelty through technical ends. What unites them, however, is the importance of digital production capabilities in fully achieving either.

STYLE AS SUBSERVIENCE

In contrast to ideas of style that center on individual expression, this notion posits style as a result of boundaries erected and enforced by groups with rigid attention to context. This notion also supposes that composing pleasure (and stylistic impact) is rooted in the familiar, not the novel, and often attempts to enforce the familiar with stylistic "technological barricades" such as character limits, image-size limits, and text boxes. This is to be found, for example, in the case of most content management systems, which usually limit the number of stylistic "interruptions" available to the author-designer severely (perhaps the most widespread example would be course management software like WebCT and Blackboard). *Style as subservience* is thus related to notions of compositional efficiency by limiting or eliminating traces of the individual (see Katz) and intractable notions of genre (see Bawarshi; Kress & Van Leeuwen, 2001, p. 55-56). However, within this stylistic mode, opportunities for *style as difference* still present themselves, but the composer can risk much by not keeping to convention. There may be rigidly enforced conventions associated with the existing practices that can cause trouble when broken. The other downfall is that *style as subservience* can be implied when it is not meant to be, and subservience can be read as the opposite of *style as difference* when implicated in a good way.

MULTIMODAL STYLE CASES IN POINT: MEDIAWIKI AND LITTLE RED RIDING HOOD

To illustrate the ways these multimodal style iterations overlap, compete with, and co-extend each other with regard to rhetorical benefits and drawbacks, I will look at examples related to digital composition. One example is related to a platform for building a digital text, and the other centers on the retelling of a traditional tale in digital form.

To begin, a digital text produced in MediaWiki provides a brief example of how the benefits and drawbacks of these three approaches are mediated by production aptitude. Students or teachers without the means to approach *style as technical prowess* would, most likely, have an external person set up the wiki. No matter what the text is being built, then, the text will have the same default design to start. If the students or teachers hope to enact *style as difference* with their digital text, they would not be able to do so without a more developed knowledge of digital production. That is, they would need to be able to access the backend of the database hosting the wiki to effect any rhetorical changes. Those who do not access the background (or lean on the expertise of the system administrator or some such person to do it for them), would—regardless of whatever the written style of the wiki text—end up calling forth the multimodal style of Wikipedia, which exists using the same open-source MediaWiki software default with only a few minor tweaks. Thus, some technical production expertise is needed to manipulate the backend to move beyond the default settings that give Wikipedia its main look and stylize the author's content instead of re-perpetuating the defaults. If not, the wiki will have the default picture of a sunflower in the upper left, be unable to upload certain file attachments, and use the defaults for color and font as well. Thus, the text on such a wiki would fall under the heading of *style as subservience* whether that was what the author intended or not, with the audience reacting to a similar way as well. While some audience members might view the hypothetical MediaWiki text as trustworthy because it resembled such a known commodity as Wikipedia, still more people would react negatively to it, particularly in academia, where its ethos is colored less by its enormously helpful use as a heuristic device and more by negative concerns about reliability and mutability. In short, the entire process of building and maintaining the wiki—regardless of whatever the actual content is—is mediated by digital production expertise, which in turn translates to a style, which ultimately determines if the text is perceived as subservient, transcendent, successful, or rhetorically inappropriate. Such a range of possibilities points to the importance of understanding multimodal style on a deep level in digital pedagogy.

The next example centers on the popular fairy tale *Little Red Riding Hood*, which is found in variants all over the world, with the variant that took root in the United States popularized by the Grimm Brothers. I have selected a tale with multiple variants in order to better interrogate the connection between stylistic variant and stylistic value: Holcomb and Killingsworth, in adapting Leech and Short, posit that "Stylistic variant refers to alternate expressions for roughly the same thing, while stylistic value refers to the consequences (what is gained and lost) by choosing one alternate over another" (2010, p. 2). What I argue based on looking at variants of *Little Red Riding Hood* is that stylistic value in contemporary digital composition terms is largely a consequence of multimodal style, especially the text's perceived novelty as accomplished through technical prowess. In other words, the more work that seemingly went into a text, and the more it transcends the digital composition capabilities of the average person and those of other texts they have seen, the more likely the stylistic value will resonate strongly. After all, a well-worn tale such as *Little Red Riding Hood* would seem to hold no further surprises. However, on March 7, 2009, Tomas Nilsson uploaded a re-interpretation of the classic tale as part of a university assignment. Within a month, the Swedish graphic design/communication student's video had attracted more than 500,000 views and almost all of the comments run along the lines of the following: "Oh my God!"; "How long did that take to make?"; "I hope you got an A for this!"; and some combination of "awesome" modified by swear words.

Given that the story (the content) is so well-known as to be almost blasé at this point, what has attracted people to Nilsson's video is the stylistic value of its re-telling, especially when a look at the video reveals that pieces added to the original story are more in line with elements of style I have spoken of in the preceding section on iterations of multimodal style rather than extending the story's content in any meaningful way. Ultimately, these additional elements reshape the meaning of the text itself because of the stylistic values attached to them by the audience.

The approach established in the beginning of Nilsson's video is the dominant one taken throughout: (1) The viewer's focus is constantly moved along different planes (i.e., right to left, top to bottom, from the edges to the middle, middle to the edges, etc.) (2) The focus switches constantly between large-scale and small-scale views of similar places, and (3) Diagrams, particular many employed as a type of visual footnoting, are employed throughout. The video begins with a "book" coming out of a bookshelf and ends with that book closing and returning to the bookshelf (Figure 1).

Multimodal style offers an interesting lens to view this piece as an instructor. For one, this video illustrates problems that occur when instructors purposefully or unknowingly privilege text within a multimodal work. Though primarily reliant upon visual storytelling, there is still plenty of text involved, and much of it is illegible given the piece's spatial elements and its delivery through YouTube. In other words, if the instructor is assessing how such a text works by looking at the text, this piece would suffer, even though the visual elements provide the

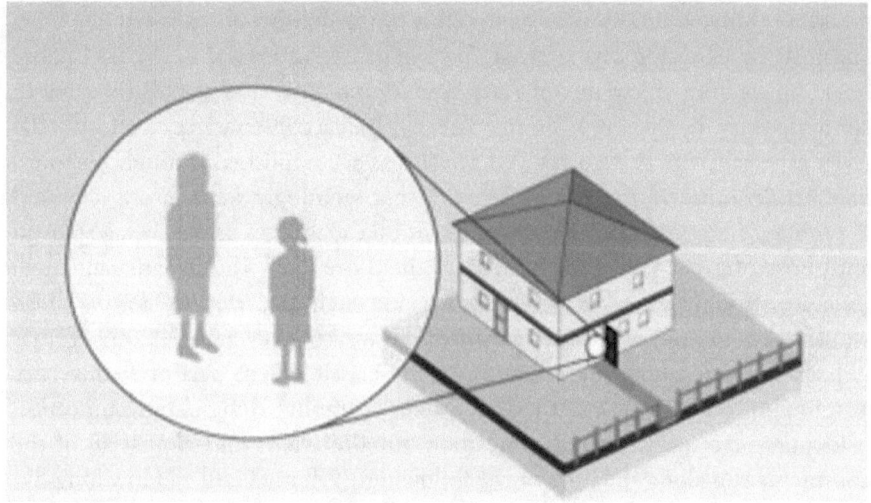

Figure 1: Beginning of cut-out view of Little Red Riding Hood and Mother.

containers for text in the form of a diagram and are more readily recognizable as such.

In addition, if classical stylistic approaches were the only means of interrogating style here, some things could be illumined sharply while other important stylistic elements reside in the shadows. For example, some classical rhetorical constructs are directly applicable to this piece. The constant switching between parts and wholes, for examples, recalls synechdoche, metonymy, and metalepsis. The part where close-up squares of two eyes, shoes, and a canine-looking nose are on the screen, the part in the story where the main characters first meet, is an example of synechdoche (Figure 2). However, there is a temporal complexity in this example that the synechdoche is situated within but cannot adequately address: this scene carries more meaning and suspense by not having all four elements emerge simultaneously—Red Riding Hood's feet are shown first walking, then stopping, leading to her widened eye, then the Wolf's widened eye, and then finally the twitching nose.

The video engages in visual exergasia (repeating the same idea changing words/delivery) in the constant use of diagrams. Also, there is visual antanaclasis (the repetition of a word in two different senses, usually for comic effect): Red Riding Hoods meets the Wolf, who questions her about where she is going, and a comic talking bubble appears above Red Hiding Hood that contains an image of her Grandmother; almost immediately, comic thought bubbles emanate from the Wolf to Red Riding Hood's bubble containing Grandmother, and a complete listing of nutrition facts appears right next to the old woman. In other

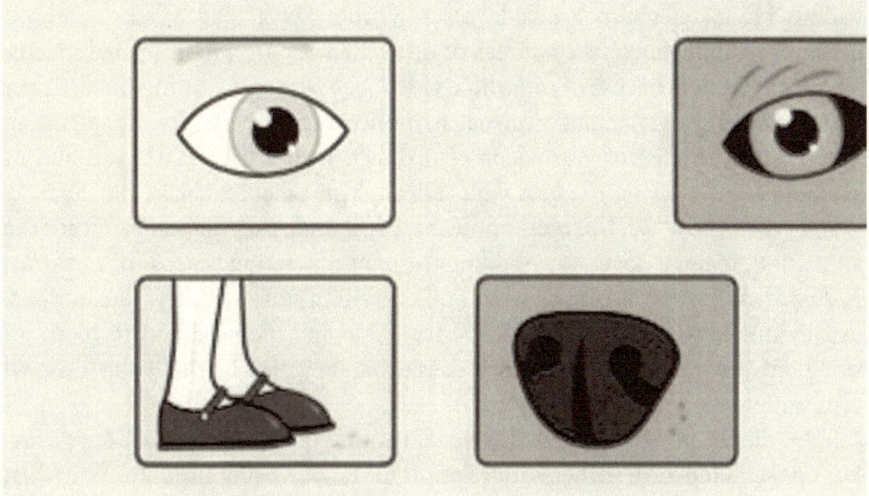

Figure 2: Synechdoche with Little Red Riding Hood and the Wolf.

words, Grandma is conceived of as a sickly old relative by Red Riding Hood and as food by the Wolf. Taken together, these few examples show how classical stylistic strategies are adaptable to digital texts and can offer some significant rhetorical nuances that can aid with analysis and production; however, the examples also show there is a lot more going on in this text than the classical tropes can make sense of.

For one, the elements of multimodal style that I identified and developed previously in this chapter, *style as technical prowess*, *style as difference*, and *style as subservience*, all play a large role in the understanding of the video. As viewer comments attest, most people are wowed by the technical prowess involved with making the video and routinely inquire how long it took to make. With that in mind, there are elements of the video that, on the surface, seem to support the viewpoint that the whole reason behind creating the text was to represent *style as technical prowess*. A look at some of the elements introduced to the story by Nilsson would seem to bear this out. The Volkswagen bus, for example, was certainly *not* in the original story but it receives a rather long view (especially in the context of how the piece was edited) of 10 seconds. That view is mostly devoted to showing the aerodynamics of the VW (Figure 3), then a cutaway view from the side to expose its innards (Figure 4). These views do not contribute significantly to what would classically be deemed the content of the story, but these views contribute mightily to the *style as technical prowess* of the piece, which in turn affects the overall content of the piece as perceived by readers. (Again, this is borne out by almost 7,000 comments in the piece.)

The video also makes use of *style as difference*. A brief look at existing Red Riding Hood tales also available on YouTube shows that Nilsson's version definitely stands out in the context of other Red Riding Hood-related videos, and not even in the sense of the whole video, but within the listing hierarchy of its chosen delivery system. For instance, if one were searching for a Red Riding Hood video, the list of videos comes up, each with a still frame, and almost all show a girl wearing red or a wolf. Nilsson's still picture shows the cutaway side view of the VW. The method, using Flash and After Effects to create the animation, is also a novel way of doing the reinterpretation because of *Little Red Riding Hood*'s status as primarily an oral or written story with few illustrations, usually quite representational. In a sense, removing the narration to focus on using only images to carry the story, thus using images to be the "voice" instead of to supplement the voice, is novel in itself.

Despite the novel aspects of the video, it also is bound by *style as subservience*. For one, as alluded to earlier with relation to the text being illegible even when viewed in full-screen mode, the video suffers quality loss in being distributed by YouTube. Ultimately, the style of the video becomes subservient to the rendering algorithms that support YouTube's ability to upload and stream content. So, despite what many people would read as an adept technician crafting the story, a technician who seemingly has the ability to create almost anything, that technician's content is ultimately mediated by YouTube in what amount to stylistic constraints on the viewer's end. If all of Nilsson's text were legible, as it might be in other formats and venues, that would change the viewing experience of the consumer and alter the conception of the meaning as a whole.

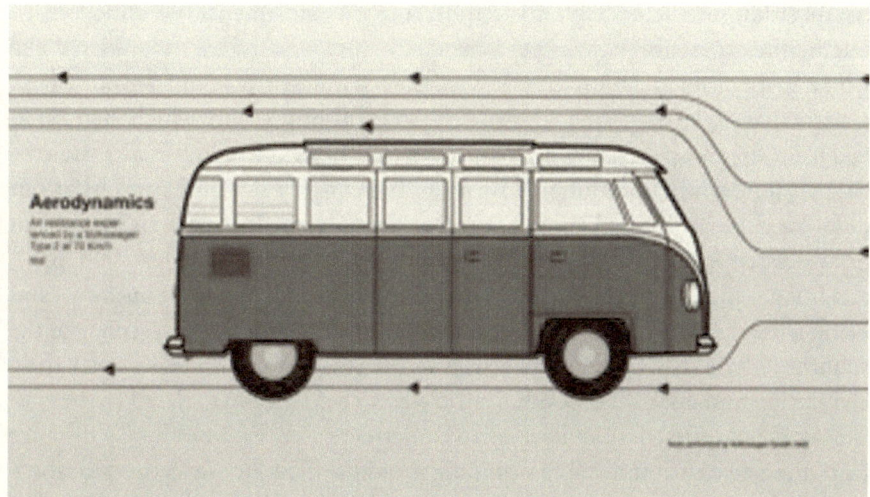

Figure 3: View of VW bus showing aerodynamics.

Figure 4: Cut-away view of VW bus.

In other words, the viewer would probably spend more time reading and making connections between the words and images, rather than concentrating on just the images. Thus, *style as subservience* was enacted on Nilsson's video because it was forced to confine to the realities of YouTube's system.

Though those previous distinctions help shed further light on the video's style, there are still elements missing, particularly as to how style is embedded in social constructs and how that adds to the video's content. The VW, for example, might be picked up on as a repetitive design element by a multimodal composition instructor (e.g., it is red because it complements the protagonist), but neither that nor its existence as *style as technical prowess* would tell the whole story of its inclusion. The VW bus is a particular type of transport, with a particular style that itself agent-lessly seeks a group, and which in turn is taken up by groups seeking a particular style. Thus, one could make the case its inclusion/symbolification will be read differently by not only the author but different cultures. In the United States, for example, the idea of the VW bus can be associated with the cluster of signs Brummett called hippie style (2008, p. 4), and it is a vehicle that is associated with a lifestyle of embracing the outdoors and being a free spirit. As such, it is not associated with the rigid complacency of the suburbs (where Red Hiding Hood lives in the video) but with being away from civilization and out in the woods. In the video, then, the style related to the VW is a marker of the rural and serves to underscore Red Riding Hood's distance from the safe and comfortable stomping grounds of her house in the suburbs.

Another social style that is included, and which "updates" the tale, is the use of video game information style. Although related in some sense to the constant use of the diagrams, the video game elements differ from the diagrams and more closely resemble game play elements. For example, after the Wolf and Red Riding Hood meet, a graph reading "Live Stats" appears, allowing us to track how they have split up but the Wolf circles back to Grandma's house. Another example appears later when Grandma and Red Riding Hood are rescued from the Wolf's belly. They are shown together, each with her own "Status" represented by a number of stars and bar graph elements depicting differing levels of "Health" and "Happiness." Though people of all ages play video games, their inclusion in what is in essence a children's fairy tale shows a novel way of skewing the style for a modern audience of children. In addition, video games are often associated with play and not being serious (despite the many games that revolve around killing people), and the game play moments in the video are humorous in light of their novel inclusion in the narrative of an old story.

Other social aspects that come into play in constraining and extending audience resonance with the video's style are related to pre-existing "templates" that are yoked, in a sense, to *style as subservience*. For one, the video is, in essence, a remix of a video by the Swedish band Slagsmålsklubben, which in turn seems to have been inspired by a ubiquitous series of Flash animation ads for the Scandinavian company Nokia by Australian animator Steve Scott. Both rely on the interplay of close-up and long shot and diagrammatic info and patterns. There is a direct relation in the comments to Nilsson's video as to its positive "wow" effect whether or not people are familiar with the Slagsmålsklubben video beforehand or not.

In the end, the differing conceptions of multimodal digital style in Nilsson's video contribute greatly to the meaning of the piece and make it quite difficult to ascertain previous stylistic areas of debate, such as where form and content begin and end. It may be more accurate in this case to ascertain the content as the story that pre-existed the author and the form as everything he did to it, which in turn both became and reshaped the entire content.

To further situate how iterations of multimodal style resonate in Nilsson's approach, it is illustrative to examine another digital variant of *Little Red Riding Hood* (Figures 5 and 6). As part of the practical element for a Masters in Design, Donna Leishman created "RedRidingHood" in 1999-2000, published it on her website in 2001, and her variant was more widely publicized in 2006, when it was included in the first volume of the *Electronic Literature Collection*. Leishman's variant of Little Red Riding Hood is radically different from the popularized Grimm variant, making Nilsson's variant seem almost a one-to-one retelling

Figure 5: Leishman's Red getting the basket from her mother.

despite his introduction of modern items to the storyline. Both are virtually wordless and rely on visuals and music to engage and carry meaning; Leishman's "RedRidingHood" also hinges on clickable interactivity to uncover additional elements of the narrative. The narrative here involves a complex storyline with hidden content (a diary), a (possible) dream sequence, a pregnant Red Riding Hood, and a Wolf-boy with a gun. As Leishman said, "RedRidingHood is a non-textual animated exploration into engaging the viewer in a recognizable narrative experience, combining the utterly and moderately linear alongside random non-authored sequences (the dream section)" ("Interview"). Leishman also mentioned how important style situated within digital technology was in affecting the invention and planning of "RedRidingHood," which was created using Flash: "A goal of this project was to be interesting to both male and female readers. A highly stylised comic imagery helped serve this and bypass the technical limitations of dial up speed Internet connection typical circa the late 1990's" ("Dissonance"). In other words, just as Nilsson's video is subject to *style as subservience* because of YouTube's realities, Leishman's was subject to *style as subservience* based on the realities of file speeds and how they had formulated audience expectations in 1999/2000; however, whereas the primary repercussion

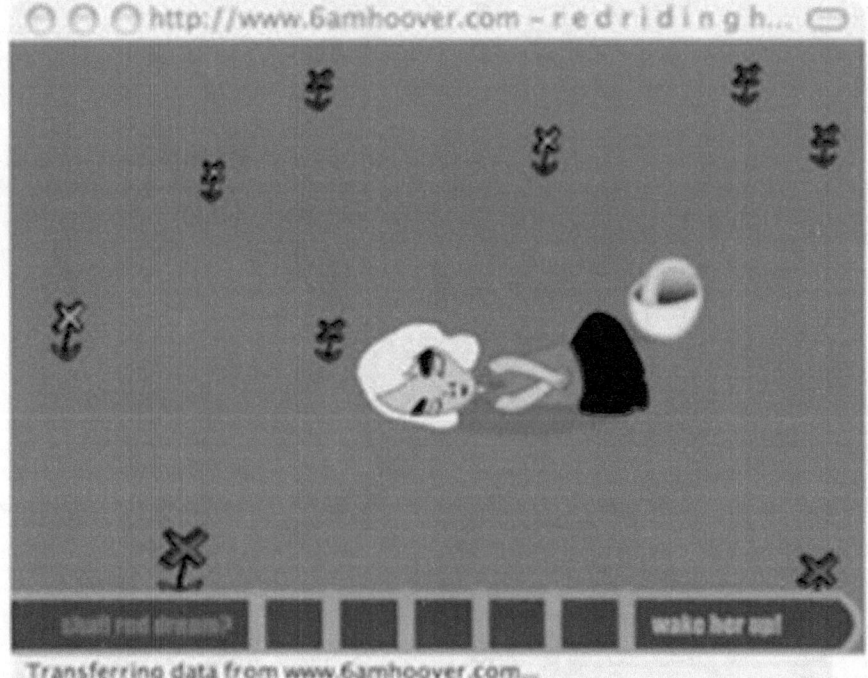

Figure 6: The screen that allows readers to enter the dream sequence (or not)

to Nilsson's video may have been losing rendering quality, Leishman had to make a conscious decision to render the entire story in a more simple style than she perhaps otherwise would have chosen.

Similar to the reception given Nilsson's work, Leishman's variant met with strong positive reactions upon its initial publication. For example, the introduction to the piece on the *Electronic Literature Collection* states, "Leishman's playful retelling of the Little Red Riding Hood fairy tale makes use of comic book vernacular, limited forms of explorative interaction, optional narrative paths, and a jazzy soundtrack. *RedRidinghood* is the type of Flash piece that suggests the potential for complex forms of interactive storytelling without typographic text." Just as the enthusiastic reception for Nilsson's variant was primarily tied to the stylistic value attributed to its technological prowess, early reaction to Leishman's piece was primarily based on the pathos that its novelty and technological prowess aroused. In a review that accompanied an early author interview, Kendall Pata said, "The animation of these drawings is superb" and "flawless"; moreover, Pata noted, Leishman's tale "may be an adaptation, but it is so original and relevant that the older story easily becomes yesterday's news." In fact, a term seen often in early pieces that reference Leishman and her work is "Flash Goddess."

However, it is important to remember that Leishman's was made public in 2001 and Nilsson's video was made public in 2009, and despite a difference of only eight years, the stylistic difference in the way technology is related to understanding and appreciating each digital text is about as pronounced as the stylistic difference between Faulkner and Hemingway. Indeed, those who experience "RedRidingHood" in 2011 rather than 2001 seem to have a much more negative take on it in comparison to early opinions. For one, the entire genre of the clickable Flash narrative is one that seems to be unknown to many users, or at least transcend their currently operating patience levels. The animation itself may have been revelatory in 1999 when it was being built, but advances in speed and attendant image-rendering capabilities have affected what audiences expect. For example, Claudia Cragg, who maintains a blog called "The Writer's Game," talks about the results of testing Leishman's work on her own family:

> [T]he three novice DF [Digital Fiction] readers who test-drove RRH [RedRidingHood] did not appreciate all the facets of Leishman's production quite simply because they failed to open the right doors. This may not make them idiots. Instead it means that they came at the project with different levels of gaming and computing exposure, which led them to

make choices that even Leishman may not have anticipated. Only the very youngest, 12, was willing to keep having another attempt to see what had been missed and only she fully appreciated the "Secret Diary" with its Satanic aspirations and the protagonist's dream sequence for another hidden life as a player in the meat market. (2007)

As Cragg notes, contemporary context is important in considering how people will respond to the text, but what is implied to the test subjects here is that there *is* more to the text, which influences their expectations. On a personal note, I only realized the various facets to this text after becoming frustrated that nothing worked, born out of frustration with the dream sequence. In an unanticipated bit of *style as subservience* that I interpreted as *style as technical prowess* (or lack thereof), I assumed the text was broken because nothing ever came up when I clicked on "shall Red dream?". Only when I tried it on a different computer whose pop-up blocker actually prompted me about continuing was I able to explore the dream. After reading the intro to the piece on the Electronic Literature Collection, I knew I was missing vast swaths of content but felt I had clicked everywhere I could; I ended up having to research how other people found the content. Thus, while Nilsson's video was able to take advantage of much improved streaming capacity and wide distribution available through YouTube and the faster connection speeds that support them, Leishman's work is still stuck in the parameters of the file size that shaped it in 1999/2000 and is further impacted by advances browsers have made to deal with the ubiquity of Flash pop-ups that characterized a previous generation of webtexts and advertising. Thus, through no fault of her own at the time, Leishman's work suffers in contemporary reception because of the ways current technological realities shape the *style as subservience* of her text.

The other problem lies with *style as technical prowess* related to visuals. For one, the parts of the narratives that might most suggest style as technical prowess are often hidden away in the clickable narrative (i.e., the dream sequence, the diary, and the title sequence). The title sequence where Red's name grows in dagger-like images, for example, is impressive, and all of the little flourishes of the flowers are not uncovered unless a reader explores. A misreading of Nilsson's video might mean the viewer skews the analysis even more toward technical prowess; a misreading of Leishman's clickable narrative means the *style as technical prowess* objects are hidden instead of open as with Nilsson, thus affecting the value of the text. Thus, a viewer who couldn't find/open those aspects would probably not even develop any sense of *style as technical prowess* when looking at it through a contemporary lens. The one aspect of the main narrative that does stand out is the ultimate bedroom scene (Figure 7), although that might be more aptly described as *style as difference* because the scene evokes mystery and a rupture to the predominant narrative of *Little Red Riding Hood*: the viewer sees Red in bed, cradling her stomach (which, when clicked, reveals a spinning baby that resembles the Wolf-boy), and the Wolf-boy emerges from behind a wall with a gun. He strokes Red's hair, then she looks directly at the audience, and the piece is over.

With the exception of the bedroom scene, the other piece that jumps out in the main narrative in a *style-as-technical-prowess* sense is the city scene (Figure 8). The window that is lit up needs to be clicked on to continue the story, but just about every window in every building lights up when scrolled over. It creates a fascinating diversion once one finds out there are clickable places hidden in parts of the text, and detracts from the *style as technical prowess* once one realizes no content is hidden behind any of these other windows. While the amount of detail in the buildings themselves may not be enough to create "wow" factor on behalf of the audience, they nonetheless stand out compared to the other buildings and some of the animation that feels clunky by contemporary standards (i.e., Red moving around on her knees among the flowers). While

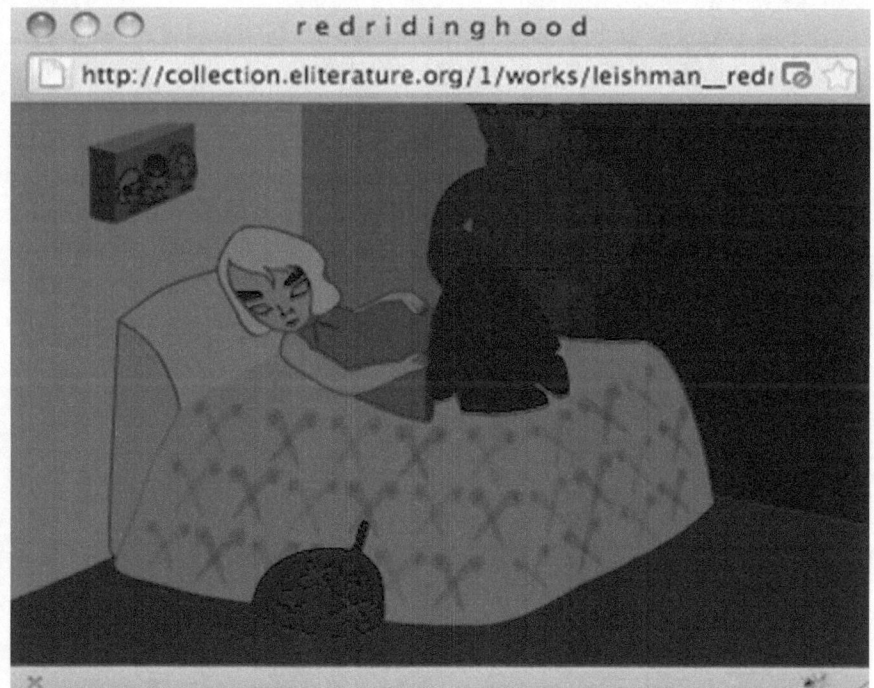

Figure 7: "RedRidingHood" Bedroom Scene

Nilsson's video did not exactly have stellar character animation (that effort seems to have gone into the VW), as witnessed by the way his Red Riding Hood moves from the house, the facial features in close ups are well done. Looking at "RedRidingHood" today involves seeing it not as it was meant to be seen in 2001 but, constructed as we are by multimodal style and social contexts, seeing it through the lens of 2011 digital texts. As part of Cragg's experiment to have people navigate through Leishman's work, one of her reviewers called it "pretentious," but the main complaint was that "the graphics aren't up to it; this generation is used to video game graphics that are absolutely terrific, so if you're gonna have a sort of computer animated story, really it has to be pretty high quality to keep people's interest" (Cragg, 2007). Cragg's experiment dated from 2008, and it must be added that while Leishman's "RedRidingHood" is fixed in time, the graphics and animation (among other elements) that color our perception of digital texts are constantly evolving toward complexity, not simplicity. As such, it's hard to imagine, given the constraints of bandwidth in 1999, how forward thinking Leishman's text was at the time, but it's difficult, if not impossible, to read through that lens today (with the possible exception of a novel kind of *style as difference* in adding plenty of subversive and feminist wrinkles to a well-established tale).

The iterations of style I have mentioned earlier in this chapter and have applied to the two *Little Red Riding Hood* variants all relate to each other in complex ways in the contemporary moment, and will relate to each other in even more complex ways that may be difficult, if not completely impossible, for a composer to conceive in the future given the inter-related effects of technology and society on texts. While a composer cannot prepare for every eventuality

Figure 8: Cityscape in "Red RidingHood"

relative to the reception of a text in the future, the fact remains that having a hope for a successful text in the future means creating a successful text today, and that involves an intense understanding of the multimodal style of the kinds of texts one wants to make on an analytical and production level, realities that need to be considered on a deep pedagogical level by composition instructors.

CONCLUSION

Taken, together, the iterations of multimodal style point out the importance of digital style as more than a means of personal expression, more than a means of emotion, more than a cultural construct, more than a matter of taste, and more than an individual choice. Digital style is embedded in material constructs, economic constructs, historical events, and technological production. In short, style is a complex adaptive system (Holland). On the wider scale of style as a complex adaptive system, the powerful use of style in the Nilsson video is now "out in the world," and it can emerge within a multitude of texts by a multitude of authors (even though it may have been based on two different pre-existing texts). Its style is not a stable form, then, but will lead to a co-evolution of differing styles, which ultimately will re-shape the idea of style within the original video. The video itself might be "fixed" in its place on YouTube, but the elements of its style are not fixed because they transcend containers and taxonomies. There could very well be a "redundant flow" from this video, but it will probably occur in an intriguing web of non-linear objects related to the original video.

On the whole, these iterations of multimodal style point to the necessity of instructor expertise in digital production and analysis when fruitfully engaging issues of digital composition. For example, what others with more knowledge in the audience might see as "mistakes" that detract from rhetorical effectiveness could be falsely construed by the instructor as personal idiosyncrasies beyond the realm of instructor mediation. There is also the issue of an instructor seizing on something as brilliantly conceived by the student that is actually a well-worn default or template without much stylistic cachet. Thinking of how this example would apply in traditional terms, it is doubtful that stylistic aspects in a traditional "text-only" writing teacher's wheelhouse would have been dismissed as personal idiosyncrasy—i.e., penurious or superfluous use of commas was not seen as a stylistic peccadillo so much as a rhetorical deficiency. This is not to argue that digital pedagogical expertise means adhering to prescriptivism when it comes to style, only that instructor understanding of a wide swath of composing elements is needed when it comes to composing and teaching sophisticated texts with digital underbellies. This, unfortunately, is not easy to develop in an area that covers a broad range of meaning-making elements and evolves daily.[1]

However, unless instructors can freely engage with digital style on a deep production level, I fear the most common pedagogical approach (because it is easiest to replicate in the current departmental system of most colleges) surrounding digital texts will ignore the need for digital production expertise whatsoever, ultimately meaning composers will be unable to produce what they set out to produce, relying instead on written documents to explain exactly what the composers were trying to accomplish rhetorically. This becomes a detrimental method of communication, cutting the composer off from not only the realities of digital texts but the complex realities and affordances of style: "[O]ne cannot wear or do whatever one likes and declare to the world that the garment or action mean what the individual says they mean" (Brummett, 2008, p. 34). In other words, when relying on a separate text to make the case for the digital text, the latter is severed from reality and given birth by a textual document that never accompanies it in its actual existence, and the nature of the digital text is thus conceived of as vastly different from the composer and actual audience perspective alike. This is dangerous if composition instructors intend to help students become truly active participants who can handle the complex realities of their social, civic, and economic lives. Understanding multimodal style is paramount in the move toward digital composing complexity because it provides the connection to a sophisticated production that resonates with contemporary, and perhaps future, audiences.

NOTES

1. One way for instructors to approach the complexity of digital texts might actually occur during that most inevitable step of teaching: assessing student work. As Star Medzerian Vanguri argues in this collection, "grading style is teaching style." Multimodal style is at once global and local, and it recruits so many different semiotic systems (all of which are both static and constantly in flux) that assessing digital work provides ongoing challenges for novice and experienced instructors alike. Vanguri's chapter "What Scoring Rubrics Teach Students (and Teachers) about Style" offers a way for instructors to start wrapping their heads around the dizzying complexities of multimodal style by thinking more deeply about how style is constructed on rubrics, which can be used to approach the complex aspects of multimodal style in a way that is feasible yet not reductive. The synechdochal aspects of multimodal style provide particular challenges in assessment (e.g., "extracting" words, sound, and/or images from the whole and grading them separately); accordingly, Russell Greer's "Architectonics and Style" chapter in

this collection could be very helpful in constructing rubrics because he channels ideas from Bakhtin and others to interrogate the intricate relations of parts to wholes in style.

REFERENCES

Bang, M. (2000). *Picture this: How pictures work*. New York: Basic Books.
Bawarshi, A. (2000). The genre function. *College English 62*(3), 327-52.
Beardsley, M. (1969). Style and good style. In G. A. Love & M. Payne (Eds.), *Contemporary essays on style* (pp. 3-14). Glenview, IL: Scott, Foresman & Company.
Brooke, C. (2002). Perspective: Notes toward the remediation of style. *Enculturation: Special Multi-journal Issue on Electronic Publication 4*(1). Retrieved from http://enculturation.gmu.edu/4_1/style/
Brummett, B. (2008). *A rhetoric of style*. Carbondale, IL: Southern Illinois University Press.
Cope, B., & Kalantzis, M. (Eds.) (2000). *Multiliteracies: Literacy learning and the design of social futures*. London: Routledge.
Cragg, C. (2007, December 10). One writer's view of "Leishman's RedRidingHood." [YouTube Video, *The Writer's Game*]. Retrieved from http://www.youtube.com/watch?v=ZJ761yb2jCQ
Elsner, J. (1996). Style. In R. S. Nelson & R. Shiff (Eds.), *Critical terms in art history* (pp. 98-109). Chicago: University of Chicago Press.
Ewen, S. (1988). *All consuming images: The politics of style in contemporary culture*. New York: Basic Books.
Faigley, L. (1998). Visual rhetoric: Literacy by design. In L. Bridwell-Bowles, & B. Peterson (Eds.), *Proceedings of Center for Interdisciplinary Studies of Writing, Speaker Series No. 9, 1998,* University of Minnesota. Retrieved from http://writing.umn.edu/lrs/assets/pdf/speakerpubs/Faigley.pdf
Foss, S. K. (1993). The construction of appeal in visual images: A hypothesis. In D. Zarefsky (Ed.), *Rhetorical movement: Essays in honor of Leland Griffin* (pp. 210-224). Evanston, IL: Northwestern University Press.
Genova, J. (1979). The significance of style. *The Journal of Aesthetics and Art Criticism 37*(3), 315-324.
George, D. (2002). From analysis to design: Visual communication in the teaching of writing. *College Composition and Communication 54*(1), 11-39.
Holcomb, C. & Killingsworth, M. J. (2010). *Performing prose: The study and practice of style in composition*. Carbondale, IL: Southern Illinois University Press.
Holland, J. (1995). *Hidden order: How adaptation builds complexity*. Reading, MA: Helix Books.

Katz, S (1992). The ethic of expediency: Classical rhetoric, technology, and the Holocaust. *College English* 54(2), 255-275.

Kress, G. (2003). *Literacy in the new media age.* London: Routledge.

Kress, G., & Carey Jewitt, C. (Eds.) (2003). *Multimodal literacy.* New York: Peter Lang.

Kress, G., & van Leeuwen, T. (2001). *Multimodal discourse.* New York: Oxford University Press.

Lanham, R. A. (2006). *The Economics of Attention: Style and substance in the age of information.* Chicago: University of Chicago Press.

Lankshear, C., & Knobel, M. (2003). *New literacies: Changing knowledge and classroom learning.* Philadelphia: Open University Press

Leishman, D. (2009). Dissonance in multi-semiotic landscapes in the work of Donna Leishman. *HYPERRHIZ.06: Special Issue: Visionary Landscapes.* Retrieved from http://www.hyperrhiz.net/hyperrhiz06/24-artist-statements/77-dissonance-in-multi-semiotic-landscapes

Leishman, D. (2011, February 13). RedRidinghood. Retrieved fromhttp://www.6amhoover.com/redriding/red.htm.

Leishman, D. (n.d.). Interview by Grace Sterns. *Histories of Internet art: Fictions and factions-net practice 3.0.* University of Colorado, Department of Art and Art History. Retrieved from http://art.colorado.edu/hiaff/interview.php?id=83&cid=3

Milic, L. T. (1969). Theories of style and their implications for the teaching of composition. In G. A. Love, & M. Payne (Eds.), *Contemporary essays on style: Rhetoric, linguistics, and criticism* (pp. 15-21). Glenview, IL: Scott, Foresman and Company.

Nilsson, Tomas. (n.d.). Slagsmålsklubben—Sponsored by Destiny. YouTube. Retrieved from http://www.youtube.com/watch?v=Y54ABqSOScQ

Pata, K. (n.d.). Fern Hill. *Histories of Internet art: Fictions and factions-net practice 3.0.* Retrieved from http://art.colorado.edu/hiaff/sound/kendall_fern_hill.mp3

Porter, J. (2002). Why technology matters to writing: A cyberwriter's tale. *Computers and Composition 20,* 375-394.

Postrel, V. (2003). *The substance of style: How the rise of aesthetic value is remaking commerce, culture, and consciousness.* New York: HarperCollins.

Schilb, J. (2007). *Rhetorical refusals: Defying readers' expectations.* Carbondale, IL: Southern Illinois University Press.

Selber, S. (2004). *Multiliteracies for a digital age.* Carbondale, IL: Southern Illinois University.

Selfe, C. L. (1999). *Technology and literacy in the 21st Century: The importance of paying attention.* Carbondale, IL: Southern Illinois University Press.

Selfe, C. L., & Hawisher, G. (2004). *Literate lives in the information age: Narratives of literacy from the united states*. Mahwah, NJ: Lawrence Erlbaum Associates.

Takayoshi, P., & Selfe, C. (2007). Thinking about multimodality. In C. Selfe (Ed.), *Multimodal composition: Resources for teachers* (pp. 1-12). Cresskill, NJ: Hampton Press.

The WIDE Research Collective. (2005). Why teach digital writing? *Kairos: A Journal of Rhetoric, Technology, and Pedagogy 10*(1). Retrieved from http://www.technorhetoric.net/10.1/binder2.html?coverweb/wide/index.html

Wonder Tonic. (2011, February 2). The Geocities-izer. Retrieved from http://wonder-tonic.com/geocitiesizer/

Woodman, L. (1982). Teaching style: A process-centered view. *Journal of Advanced Composition 3*(1/2), 116-125.

Wysocki, A. F. (2004). Opening new media to writing: Openings and justifications. In A. F. Wysocki, J. Johndon Johnson-Eilola, C. L. Selfe, & G. Sirc (Eds.), *Writing new media: Theory and applications for expanding the teaching of composition* (pp. 1-42). Logan, UT: Utah State University Press.

Wysocki, A. F. (2001). Impossibly distinct: On form/content and word/image in two pieces of computer-based interactive multimedia. *Computers and Composition 18*, 137-162.

Yancey, K. B. (2004). Made not only in words: Composition in a new key. *College Composition and Communication 56*(2), 297-328.

Wölfflin, H. (1915). *Kunstgeschichtliche grundbegriffe: Das problem der stilentwicklung in der neueren kunst* (M. D. Hottinger, Trans., 1932). London: G. Bell and Sons, Ltd.

VOICE, TRANSFORMED: THE POTENTIALITIES OF STYLE PEDAGOGY IN THE TEACHING OF CREATIVE NONFICTION

Crystal Fodrey
University of Arizona

At the end of her "Voice as Echo of Delivery, Ethos as Transforming Process," Theresa Enos asks a question that I, too, have sought to answer in every composition pedagogy I've developed, modified, or discarded over these first seven years of my teaching career: "Can we show [students] that their essays, even "academic" essays, can be ... affirmations that rest on demonstrated openness and comprehensiveness—all this expressed by a transformed voice that seeks identification without sacrificing conviction?" (1994, p. 194). We most often encounter such a voice in writing that situates the self, the sort of writing published in *The Best American Essays* with a lineage that goes back to Montaigne, essays that are usually only assigned in a handful of "creative" English courses that privilege the personal. But we encounter this voice, too, in the writings of scholars like Jim Corder, Wendy Bishop, bell hooks, Victor Villanueva, Gloria Anzaldúa and others who incorporate strong but fallibly human selves who strive toward greater understanding of whatever issues they choose to explore. After using a style-based pedagogy in an advanced composition course focused on creative nonfiction,[1] I think I might finally be able to answer Enos's question (at least tentatively) with a yes. I've found that a style-based pedagogy has the potential to show students ways to transform their voices into the type of open, comprehensive ones Enos describes; such voices in the context of rhetorically-conscious essays have the potential to affect wide-reaching audiences.

However, a problem arises from the insufficient style resources available for those who teach creative nonfiction themed classes. When I first started conceptualizing the creative nonfiction themed advanced composition course I will later describe, I found plenty of instructive craft essays in textbooks and other craft publications like *The Writer's Chronicle* that touched on style in a broad sense, but, as to be expected, I had a difficult time finding texts positioned from a creative writing standpoint that would aid students in understanding sentence-level style from a rhetorical standpoint.[2] These discipline-based perspectives, though, are not as disparate as they might seem because in the end those who offer instruction all want the same result: good writing that fits the given genre. It's just that most style-related creative nonfiction craft essays that instructors, and thus, students, likely come across provide unproblematized impressionistic criteria to judge and explain style but do not give writers the tools to learn how to make stylistic decisions, an essential skill to producing good creative nonfiction.

From my both/and position as a degree holding, aspiring creative nonfiction writer and a degree seeking, aspiring composition scholar, I find myself serendipitously situated to speak to the need for greater stylistic guidance in nonfiction prose courses. I see the relative silence and ambiguities regarding style in anthologized creative nonfiction craft essays as an opportunity, as potentially useful uncharted territory for both teachers and students; therefore, I'd like to explore how anthologized creative writing craft essayists—who so readily share their writing experiences and thoughtful suggestions with those who might follow their lead—attend to or avoid the more technical, sentence-level aspects of writing, or what Chris Holcomb and M. Jimmie Killingsworth refer to in their chapter as the textual arena. Based on Tim Mayers's discussion of core assumptions about creative writing that permeate the discipline, he would likely point to the idea that "[s]tudents, assuming they're motivated enough, can learn to master craft, but they either have or do not have the other essentials of a 'serious writer,' and nothing a teacher of creative writing does can change this" (2005, p. 13). This assumption, if indeed widely held by those who identify with the dominant ideologies of creative writing over those of composition, might explain why instructional value of the textual arena is diminished. It is at the word and sentence level where writers distinguish themselves; this is where unique voices emerge. But this micro level of writing is also viewed as expression, as genius, as the man himself. Mayers refers to this idea of genius—that writers either have it or they don't—as part of the problematic "institutional-conventional wisdom of creative writing" (2005, p. 13). Style works to demystify "genius" by upholding the idea that all writers make rhetorical choices, whether conscious or internalized, that have certain effects on their audiences.

Undergraduates studying essayistic composing—especially typical non-geniuses at the beginner or intermediate level—can benefit from stylistic instruction just as other composition students can.[3] Regardless of whether a creative nonfiction course is housed in composition or creative writing,[39] style study in such courses has the potential to demystify what makes flash essays, travel memoirs, literary journalism, nature writing, and so on, different from the more traditional forms of academic writing to which they are accustomed. Yes, style is only one aspect of creative nonfiction, only one fifth of the rhetorical canon to emphasize in a class that can cover so much else. But teaching the importance of style analysis and production helps students new to the form understand what it means when they are asked to write in an open, identification-seeking, literary way. Vivian Gornick explains to writers in *The Situation and the Story: The Art of Personal Narrative* that "[e]very work [of literature] has both a situation and a story. The situation is the context or circumstance, sometimes the plot; the story is the emotional experience that preoccupies the writer: the insight, the wisdom, the thing one has come to say" (2001, p. 13). I tell my students that the "stories" in creative nonfiction pieces emerge in part from the style of the writing that begins at the sentence level and moves outward.

Chris Anderson also makes an important connection between style and creative nonfiction in *Style as Argument* in which he analyzes works by Tom Wolfe, Truman Capote, Norman Mailer, and Joan Didion to defend his claim that "[o]ur experience reading contemporary nonfiction is an experience of style," style for him meaning the rhythms and textures of language use (1987, p. 1). If reading nonfiction prose is "an experience of style," then we can assume 1) that students have much to learn from studying the styles of published creative nonfiction writers and 2) that writing creative nonfiction can also be "an experience of style" since writing precedes reading. Yet style instruction is not being privileged or even much explored in creative nonfiction pedagogy if the content of the technique-driven craft essays students encounter in popular textbooks is any indication.

What I'm proposing is a pedagogy through which students learn to analyze "the deployment of rhetorical resources, in written discourse, to create and express meaning" (Butler, 2008, p. 3) in order to demystify the pleasurable aesthetic qualities or "literariness" of creative nonfiction at the sentence level, give students a rhetorical vocabulary to discuss works in progress, and help students develop their writerly voices in an effort to bridge the gap between writers and various publics. The idea behind the approach is this: If writing students study published flash essays, literary journalism, memoirs, and other personally situated prose through a rhetorical lens, study "the use of written language features as habitual patterns, rhetorical options, and conscious choices at the sentence and word level" in those writings (Butler, 2008, p. 3), and study how audiences receive and discuss the writings, then those students just might be able to learn through this mimetic, analytic process to make similar or better moves in their writings, for their audiences, for their purposes.

Those who write in literary genres, just like any other language users, have the capacity to improve and have the agency to affect diverse audiences, to move people to action if they so choose. In undergraduate creative nonfiction themed courses, a pedagogy grounded in rhetorical theory with an emphasis on style can aid students in recognizing and using that agency. My fall 2010 advanced composition students, whose writings and reflections I will discuss later in this chapter, are a testament to the possibilities of this style pedagogy. But before bringing their voices into the conversation, I first need to shed some light on the ways style is currently discussed in creative nonfiction craft essays.

REPRESENTATIONS OF STYLE

Style is either something we name but do not value or value but cannot name.
— Star Medzerian, 187

In *Out of Style* Paul Butler briefly discusses the renewed interest that a growing contingent of compositionists has in personal writing. He notes that this interest "is imbued with the study of style, even though it is not acknowledged or recognized in that way" (2008, p. 107). I agree with this assertion as well as his observation that:

> [t]he dispersion of style into personal writing suggests that style, while manifested locally in sentences, has important impacts on the broader form of discourse. It seems that the attention to ... creative nonfiction in composition is focused primarily at that broader level. What is clear, however, is that those features of the broader form of discourse ... become most important through the stylistic features enacted in sentences. (Butler, 2008, pp. 107-108)

To say this another way: compositionists who publish scholarship on creative nonfiction tend to conflate sentence-level style with form when discussing the various genres like the personal essay, memoir, or literary journalism. We ask, what are essayistic forms capable of that other forms are not? How and why do we teach students to write in these forms? We focus on the importance of expression, reflection, introspection, uncertainty, and exploration, and we weigh the pros and cons of the writing's self-centeredness versus its usefulness. This deliberation is relevant and necessary to our scholarship, and even though I may be critical of the way those who identify themselves as creative writers discuss issues of style, let me state for the record that I am equally critical of those discussions (and lack thereof) in composition studies.

Most any writing class with a focus on types of creative nonfiction like the essay, memoir, or literary journalism spend a fair amount of time on the important issues of genre definitions, memory, truth representation, narrative construction, public exposure of private details, broad characteristics of various essay forms—the usual suspects. Those technique and concept-related topics are covered in most craft sections of creative nonfiction textbooks and in the creative nonfiction craft articles that appear in prominent magazines like *The Writer's Chronicle*. Yet, anthologized creative nonfiction craft essays rarely emphasize the sentence level where meaning is made (or obscured). Stylistic terminology becomes conflated with impressionistic, inadequately-defined concepts like "voice"[4] and "authenticity." My initial familiarity with those terms comes from my years as a creative writing undergraduate and master's student when I never thought to problematize their meanings. My essays apparently displayed these qualities, and, therefore, I was labeled a talented writer. While the part of me that remembers this culture of genius quite well can see the appeal of using such terms in order to maintain the institutional-conventional wisdom, the part of me that thinks writing can be taught, the rhetoric and composition teacher-scholar part, insists that there's a better way to learn about style. That way is linked to how well students understand style from a rhetorical standpoint.

In the fall of 2009, I had a critical encounter with a creative nonfiction craft article that, at first, bothered me because the title invoked authenticity, a concept I do not buy into. I opened up my new copy of *The Writer's Chronicle* to Sebastian Matthews's article "Stepping Through the Threshold: Ways to Achieve Authentic Voice in Memoir," read it from a rhetorical perspective, and didn't quite know what to make of the advice. The strategies he explains to his audience were largely helpful—

> Strategy 1: Create an occasion for speech
> Strategy 2: Speak through the mask of the first person "I"
> Strategy 3: Engage history
> Strategy 4: Become your project
> Strategy 5: Ground in place and time
> Strategy 6: Separate character from narrator
> Strategy 7: Imagine a listener for your story
> (Matthews, 2009, pp. 72-80)

—but I found them unsettling because of the purported end result: authentic voice. While I think, as Enos does, that a personal *ethos* can emerge through one's stylistic choices, I have a hard time believing that a self-constructed written version of oneself can *be* absolutely true or authentic. At best a voice can only *seem* true or authentic based on how a writer chooses to arrange and word his sentences within the context of the topic and the form of the piece. So when I look at that list, especially strategies 1, 2, 3, 5, and 7, my mind immediately goes to rhetorical situation. Who am I writing for and why? How do I want them to respond? How will I situate myself for that intended effect? What historical and cultural contexts am I working within? Am I responding to an opportune moment? These questions sync up with many of Matthews' "authentic voice" (*ethos*) building strategies; therefore, this illustrates one way that rhetoric can be applied to the teaching of creative nonfiction. Matthews may not be using rhetorical terminology, but he is still talking about craft in a way that could be construed as rhetorical, especially if the end result from taking his sage advice would be similar regardless of how the strategies are worded.

Likewise, the creative nonfiction textbooks I'm analyzing here—*Contemporary Creative Nonfiction: I &* Eye, *Fourth Genre: Contemporary Writers of/on Creative Nonfiction*, 5th edition, and *Creating Nonfiction: A Guide and Anthology*—contain many writings on craft that at times use a parallel discourse with rhetoric and composition theory and practice to describe certain conventions writers of creative nonfiction might follow. And in most of these texts, the fact that writers use accessible language to discuss strategies that ultimately can help writers plan writing projects and build *ethos* works well because anthologized essayists are some of the best writers of our time. They're engaging. They create identification with their readers through their use of psychic distance, a concept Erik Ellis thoughtfully explores in this collection. However, these positive qualities become somewhat irrelevant when published creative writers write rather ambiguously therefore unhelpfully about what I have been referring to throughout as style. The writers I discuss in the upcoming sections address macro level writing issues but rarely touch on the sentence level where style-talk would be valuable. I've grouped their depictions of style into three categories—style as genre, style as magic, and style as voice—based both on the ways that the term "style" is used as well as how concepts related to style are described. Closer examination of these depictions illuminate the need for a more direct, pragmatic approach to the explanation of style in creative nonfiction.

STYLE AS GENRE

Lee Gutkind is the only writer in *Contemporary Creative Nonfiction: I & Eye* to use the word "style" in a craft context. In "The Creative Nonfiction Police" he says, "Of course, I am a creative nonfiction writer, 'creative' being indicative of the style in which the nonfiction is written so as to make it more dramatic and compelling" (Gutkind, 2004, p. 349). Here "creative" differentiates the "style" of writing Gutkind does from other "styles" of nonfiction. "Style" could be changed to the word "technique" or "method" or "way," and the sentence would maintain a very similar meaning. "Genre" might be the most precise word to show the relationship between "creative" and "nonfiction," and that appears to be what he's getting at, his own approach of taxonomizing creative nonfiction by naming its attributes: "dramatic and compelling," what other "styles" of nonfiction are not.

Style does indeed play a large role in making any piece of writing dramatic and compelling, boring and pedantic, or somewhere in between. If a writer learns how to analyze the stylistic decisions her favorite author makes at a sentence level and gains a vocabulary to articulate that analysis, she can then imitate these and integrate them into her compositions if she so chooses. When Gutkind continues in his article, saying that "[w]e embrace many of the techniques of the fiction writer, including dialog, description, plot, intimacy of detail, characterization, point of view" a reader would learn what is possible in creative nonfiction—an important lesson—but that reader would not learn about style in the rhetorical sense, which, to me, is every bit as vital to their later success as a writer.

STYLE AS MAGIC

This next set of style depictions seem impractical as style depictions, no matter how beautifully they're written, simply because a student would not likely be able to glean stylistic lessons from them. Craft essays are meant to serve at least a partially pragmatic purpose. When André Aciman explains "I write to give my life a form, a narrative, a chronology; and, for good measure, I seal loose ends with cadenced prose and add glitter where I know things were quite lusterless," I know that he's talking about style after the semicolon, but he doesn't *teach* readers anything concrete about style (Aciman, 2005, p. 134).[5] What does he really mean when he says "seal loose ends with cadenced prose"? How does he do that? And how does he go about "add[ing] glitter"? What constitutes glitter? Don't get me wrong, I enjoy reading his impressionistic imagery, and I suppose I could ascertain suitable answers to these questions by stylistically analyzing his craft essay, "A Literary Pilgrim Progresses to the Past." That seems to defeat the point of a craft essay, though.

Style theorist Winston Weathers would likely agree. In "Grammars of Style: New Options for Composition," Weathers essentially explains the style of creative nonfiction as "Grammar B," an alternative discourse with the "characteristics of variegation, synchronicity, discontinuity, ambiguity, and the like" (2010, p. 221). He might tell Aciman that one who writes using Grammar B "must still be concerned with a rationale for his composition, a rationale that informs the composition, if not with 'order and sense,' then certainly with 'interest and effectiveness' in a kind of drama imperative" (2010, p. 237). However, we have no way of knowing Aciman's writing rationale unless he shares this with us more explicitly.

Another example of style-talk in a magical context comes from Cynthia Ozick's craft essay "She: Portrait of the Essay as a Warm Body." Ozick's title informs readers that they will be gaining greater insight about the essay form through an extended metaphor of the body, so I anticipate this move. She writes that "the essay is by and large a serene or melancholic form. It mimics that low electric hum, which sometimes rises to resemble actual speech, that all human beings carry inside their heads—a vibration, garrulous if somewhat indistinct, that never leaves us while we are awake" (Ozick, 2005, p. 204). This description, housed in a loose, complex, interrupted sentence, leaves readers with a poetic impression of style. I read the sentence, let it wash over me, and try to recreate the metaphor in my mind. Style as a "low electric hum." For those who think best in abstractions, this might be a fruitful way to understand style, as something intangible and just out of reach. I can appreciate that point of view for having once lived it, but I'm now convinced that rhetoric offers us a better way. Students don't have to be content to cull a concrete lesson from an impressionistic stylistic description that tells them the lyric essay "is held together by the glue of absence, the mortar of melody, the threnody of unspent inspiration" (Kitchen, 2009, p. 366). Instead, after gaining a stylistic vocabulary from completing style activities in class or from studying a book like Holcomb and Killingsworth's *Performing Prose: The Study and Practice of Style in Composition,* they could appreciate Judith Kitchen's lyrical sentence as one that expertly showcases the use of anaphora, asyndeton, and balance. Then they could write their own sentences that exhibit similar qualities. Through this inventive process, some may stumble upon ideas for future essays in which they can use their Kitchen-inspired sentences.

STYLE AS VOICE

As is true in Matthews's article explaining techniques to achieve authentic voice in memoir, when other published craft writers discuss "voice" or the production of "sound" in creative nonfiction writing, I find that they come closest to describing style (or at least a concept directly connected to aspects of style) in concrete terms that student writers might be able to find useful. For example, In "The Singular First Person," a craft essay in which Scott Russell Sanders analyzes the rhetorical effectiveness of prominent essayists without using rhetorical terminology, he explains, "[o]nce you have heard [Wendell Berry's] stately, moralizing, cherishing voice, laced through with references to the land, you will not mistake it for anyone else's. Berry's themes are profound and arresting ones. But it is his voice, more than anything he speaks about, that either seizes us or drives us away" (Sanders, 2004, p. 79). From this, we learn possible characteristics of what voice/style can be—"stately, moralizing, cherishing"—and we learn possible options for what voice/style can do—"seiz[e] us or driv[e] us away." If a student read Sanders's essay in tandem with Berry's "The Long-Legged House," that student could gain a deeper understanding of the effects of Berry's style choices. This knowledge, in turn, could prove generative when the student sits down to invent or draft a nature-themed essay of his own even though Sanders does not demystify style at the sentence level.

Voice also features prominently in Steven Harvey's "The Art of Self," located along with Sanders's piece in *The Fourth Genre* textbook. Harvey's use of "voice" could be directly substituted with either "style" or "discourse," as it is discussed here: "Each of us has many voices—the voice for a friend, a colleague, a student, a lover—and each voice is different. Personal essayists ... must constantly adjudicate the voices in their hearts and choose the right language" (Harvey, 2009, p. 345). This process of judging and choosing the best voice for a particular essay is a key part of what he refers to as "shaping" or "fashion[ing] a text," the way in which an "artist creat[es] a surrogate self" in writing (Harvey, 2009, p. 344). By acknowledging the conscious language decisions one must make in order to put the most relevant and appropriate version of oneself forward in a piece of personal writing, Harvey implies the rhetoricity of the process even as he denies the importance of audience concerns. Even though his article discusses style on an impressionistic level without many specific helpful examples, he does manage to quickly yet eloquently combat the idea of an unfiltered creative voice.

The strong connection between voice and *ethos* development is undeniable even in the most impressionistic descriptions, like Aciman's "cadenced prose" critiqued above or Vivian Gornick's description of George Orwell's "persona" as "something genuine that he pulled from himself, and then shaped to his writer's purpose" (2004, p. 139). Enos explains that from antiquity to modern times, the perception of "voice" in rhetoric has moved from that which presented the truth to an audience to that which can facilitate "the acceptance of belief" (1994, p. 187). Looking at voice in this historical context, we can call pure authenticity into question, but that doesn't mean voice itself is a defunct concept. The facilitation of belief for an audience comes from an *ethos*-generating voice. Enos notes that "ethos cannot be separated from audience consideration because part of the ethical appeal is one's stance, a textual manifestation of an attitude and what Aristotle calls goodwill, the benevolent attitude of the writer toward readers" (1994, p. 188). A writer does not need to have the primary goal of persuasion in mind for this benevolent *ethos* to yield advantageous results; Rosanne Carlo effectively argues this point in her chapter "Jim Corder's Generative Ethos as Alternative to Traditional Argument." Indeed, voice, which emerges from stylistic choices, as Enos demonstrates via a stylistic analysis of Jim Corder's personal essayistic prose in her article, can allow a writer to engage in "dialogic action, where both writer and reader are aware of, and enjoy, the engagement" (1994, p. 194).

This type of voice/style-privileging composition can indeed facilitate a powerful identification that, in turn, can create the potential for certain audiences to respond favorably to the writing at hand. Such a move in the way we talk about the development of voice would broaden its scope in both composition and creative writing. As Mayers explains:

> "Voice" ... might be viewed not as the enactment in language of unique self-qualities or an individual's artistic vision, but rather as a rhetorical device developed through conscious or unconscious absorption of, or resistance to, other such rhetorical devices. "Finding one's voice," then—the dream of many dedicated students of creative writing—may be a rhetorical rather than a spiritual exercise. (2005, p. 120)

With a toolbox of, as T. R. Johnson calls them, "renegade" rhetorical and stylistic devices in tow—"concrete strategies" that incite a "highly pleasurable practice in which selves, texts, and worlds are experienced as dynamic, interanimating processes"—students can control their muses instead of letting their muses control them (2003, p. 344).

I'm still critical of voice-talk in creative nonfiction craft essays, though, because of the instances when writers insinuate or unproblematically explain a process by which words flow freely from a true self onto the page, thereby upholding what Louis T. Milic refers to as "psychological monism, which finds its most common expression in the aphorism that the style is the man," a theory that has long since been rejected by contemporary style theorists (1965, p. 67). One of my favorite pieces of recent craft writing to share with students is the "Style" chapter in Becky Bradbury and Doug Hesse's *Creating Nonfiction* textbook because of the numerous helpful examples and analyses they share of interesting punctuation usage, sentence rhythm, repetition, and point of view; however, I pause every time I read the following excerpt from the chapter:

> Whatever the mode, whatever we create, our style expresses who we are at that moment in time. While we can't avoid being aware of an audience (the reader, the viewer, the judge), we need to try to push that observer out of our mind's eye while we are working. (2009, p. 78)

Part of me wonders if that passage promoting writer-based prose is included in the chapter as a nod to dominant creative writing ideology before offering suggestions on ways for students to vary their style even though that seems to directly contradict the sentiment that "our style expresses who we are at that moment in time." I shouldn't speculate, though. Even in this collection, Ellis, who also claims a creative writing background, argues that "language can be rhetorically fitting regardless of how well it matches audience expectations." I will, however, fundamentally disagree that style choices should be made to please the writer above all others because that is not a sustainable practice, and I disagree even more so with the idea that it is a helpful pedagogical strategy to both purport self expression and teach methods of stylistic improvement due to the incongruence of these ideas. As Milic warned us in 1965, "the monistic view of style ... cannot be allowed to infect the teaching of our subject, for it vitiates all the available pedagogical resources of rhetoric" (1965, p. 126). From my experience, it seems that students come into introductory creative nonfiction themed classes—likely more often than they come into a "less creative" composition class—with something like a monistic mindset, determined that the point is to produce expressive writing for the self instead of personally-situated writing for an audience or at least as some blend of expression and rhetoricity. There's nothing inherently wrong with either point of view, but the distinction between them is one upon which so much depends, especially for "non-genius" students who have the most to gain from writing instruction.

STYLE PEDAGOGY IN ACTION

In the first week of my Fall 2010 Advanced Composition class, I asked my students in a short writing assignment to define style as a reaction to how published writers have defined style, prior to our first class discussion on the issue. They read the Bradbury and Hesse chapter as well as Milic's "Theories of Style and Their Implications for the Teaching of Composition," Weathers's

"Grammars of Style" cited earlier, and an excerpt on style from Book III of Aristotle's *Rhetoric*. What Dawn, one of the students, wrote in response to Milic's explanations of psychological monism and rhetorical dualism[6] highlights the dominant response of her classmates as well, over half being creative writing majors or minors like her and the rest a mix from other majors:

> A definition of style that I am comfortable with would be finding the way with syntax, tone, and word choice. It's the voice that readers hear when they read the work written on the page. The voice will change depending on how the writing develops, but like a personality, the voice is always there …
>
> I believe that good writing is something that cannot be taught but is something that is inherent. We are either good writers or we are not cut out from the correct cloth to be a writer. There are no workshops that can teach a bad writer to become a better writer nor are there books that can be written to mold someone. (Dawn, Short Assignment #2)

Just as many of the aforementioned craft writers demonstrated, Dawn too is able to eloquently articulate the possibility that someone can both be born a good writer and somehow "[find] the way with syntax, tone, and word choice." You either have the gift and know what sounds best or you don't have the gift and, therefore, should not pursue a future in writing. It should come as no surprise that I encountered a fair amount of resistance when I started to play the audience card, made connections between rhetoric and creative nonfiction, and asked them to write in "voices" not their own.

I'm going to focus here on how I framed style for my students in the first weeks of the semester, as that framing provided the foundation for all of the style work and essay composing they did throughout the course. In order to maintain the dual objectives of teaching the basic tenets of creative nonfiction and sentence-level style from a rhetorical standpoint, I started lightly with the "what is creative nonfiction" talk under the assumption that we could create a dynamic list of sometimes contradictory characteristics as a class throughout the semester (which we did). We spent a week on recognizing and practicing the different sentence types (fragment, simple, compound, complex, compound-complex) in class, which proved to be no easy task even for writers at an advanced level. Simple sentences can at times be quite long through the connection of many prepositional phrases and complex sentences can be quite short so long as a dependent and independent clause exists; that is a lot for a student to wrap their mind around if they haven't had much formal grammar instruction. These lessons on sentence types became reinforced as students completed a series of copy and compose exercises for homework.

Copy and compose is a style activity created by Winston Weathers and described in his 1969 book *Copy and Compose: A Guide to Prose Style*. Students are asked to copy a sentence by hand (my students type their sentences if that is their preferred method) and then compose a sentence of similar length and structure. Copy and compose practice gave students a chance to imitate with the intent to internalize common grammatical structures and rhetorical schemes found in some of the flash essays they had been reading from the anthology *Short Takes: Brief Encounters with Contemporary Nonfiction* and the online journal *Brevity: A Journal of Concise Literary Nonfiction*. They also worked in groups to count the number of each sentence type in some of those under 1,000 word essays. All of this was in preparation for their first assignment: 1) to conduct and write a stylistic analysis of a published flash essay of their choosing that looks specifically at how both sentence and essay-level choices come together to work well in the piece as a whole, and 2) to write their own flash essay about a place of personal significance that imitates the sentence and essay-level style (but not the content or overall theme) of the essay they analyzed.

Because students analyzed and wrote only flash nonfiction pieces in this first five-week unit, they were able to concentrate their efforts on interpretation of published writing, on form and language quality, and on the calculated transformation of their voices, instead of lengthy text production. Hans Ostrom had a similar experience when he asked his fiction students to engage in an imitation of microstories. He explains that "students are invited by a particular text to manipulate language in a similar way" and it is partially this conscious shift in positionality and the resulting emphasis on language choices that makes the activity such a fruitful one (1998, p. 168). In my class, asking students to focus on places significant to them—topics they know intimately in most cases—allowed me to maintain a location-based class thematically, moving from personal spaces to community spaces to publication spaces over the semester, but spend a significant amount of time on style in the first unit.

In a reflection piece written directly after his submission of Unit 1 essays, Larry, another student, said:

> [n]ot only has [the study of style] helped me to understand how others package and deliver meaning to the readers, but it has given me the ability to put this understanding to immediate and practical use. My writing in other classes has been

> dramatically improved. (L., Process Comment on Imitation Assignment)

I agreed with this assessment even within the context of the relatively few weeks that I had gotten to know his work because he initially did not vary his sentence constructions very often or develop details in his writing beyond basic descriptions. Because of his background in journalism, he had a tendency to pack as much information as quickly as possible into his prose. But then he turned in his flash essay about his visit to a slave house in Senegal, imitating Salman Rushdie's "Water's Edge." In the essay he's standing in a room in the Maison des Esclaves "designed to break the spirit and weaken the mind" of America-bound African slaves. Of this space he writes, in part,

> Because these places were devised to physically, emotionally and psychologically prepare the captives for the harsh, inhumane conditions in the ship's cargo bay, they were purposefully designed to be cramped in space, barely tolerable in comfort with very little to no light. At the rear of the house, there was a single door of ominous foreboding. Slaves going through this portal knew it to be their last in Africa. Not a single person who passed through this door returned to their homeland, hence the proverbial name—The door of no return. (L., "Maison Des Esclaves.")

Rushdie dwells on the details in "Water's Edge" with long complex sentences mimicking the motions described like

> [b]efore that first creature drew that first breath there would have been other moments when other creatures made the same attempt and fell fainting back into the waves or else suffocated, flopping fishily from side to side, on the same seashore and another, and another. (2005, p. 65)

So Larry had to make similar moves in order to write a successful imitation. Although the writing is not in what Larry might consider to be his own voice, he was obviously still happy with the end result, and so was I.

Not everyone had such a positive experience. Nicole, another student, immediately noted at the end of the unit that "[o]verall, I am glad we did this assignment so I can incorporate some of [Ann] Daum's stylistic devices into my writing, but I am looking forward to having my own voice again." (N., Process

Comment on Imitation Assignment). Daum's tone in "Those Who Stay and Those Who Go" is, as Nicole describes, "stoic," but Nicole picked a funny place of significance to write about: her British grandmother's favorite Applebee's. During the revision process, Nicole struggled to transform her lively prose into something quiet and contemplative. In her case, the rough drafts were decidedly better than what she submitted as her final because in each subsequent draft the divide between form and content grew wider. Like lines delivered from a poorly casted actor, the style from which her voice emerged created an ill-fitting *ethos* for the topic at hand. She learned an important lesson from the process, though: She should have picked a David Sedaris essay to imitate.

I walked away from this unit with some lessons learned as well. Perhaps one of the most surprising is that when students understand the rhetorical effects of certain schemes like asyndeton and polysyndeton—speeding up or slowing down a sentence, respectively—they will start using those schemes all of the time—even in pass/fail short writing assignments—to achieve those effects, and their writing as a whole becomes more enjoyable to read (the exception being those who use the figures ad nauseum). Many students feared the fragment at the beginning of the semester, claiming that it would hurt their *ethos* due to its ungrammaticality. That is, until they realized many essayists use fragments quite often to achieve writing that sounds more like the way people talk. Or think.

I also wanted to see if some relevant claims made recently by contemporary style scholars manifested themselves in practice. For instance Butler asserts that "memory can be recalled, and focused, through stylistic resources" (2008, p. 148). I used this idea to inform how I introduced copy and compose, asking students to hold their places of personal significance firmly in mind when they created their sentences. Many of the sentences found a way into their prose, sometimes exactly, sometimes in altered form. One student even created an outline for their essay from their copy and compose sentences and built around those sentences to compose their rough draft. Likewise, I found what Medzerian argues in "Style and the Pedagogy of Response" to ring true to me, that "[t]o adequately articulate our expectations to students through our commentary, we must use language that is text-specific and that treats student writing as comprised of conscious choices" (2010, p. 191). I found that I was able to engage with student texts at a deeper analytical level than I had been able to in the past and my students were able to understand my commentary and critiques because we shared the common language of style.

In the units that followed, the spatial elements of my pedagogy became more prominent: My students became new journalists, researching by immersing themselves in local spaces outside their comfort zones, and finally they became publication-seeking writers, locating spaces for their work and creating pieces appropriate for the rhetorical situations of those spaces. With an understanding of style, and using sentence-level stylistic analysis as a revision exercise, the majority of my students were able to meet these challenges and at times exceed my and their own wildest expectations. For her final project, Dawn created a deeply personal blog that documented her ongoing battle with postpartum depression, and she shared it with other women online dealing with similar issues. Larry wrote a series of flash essays with the goal of "shin[ing] a flashlight on the Dark Continent so [his] readers can see the cultural diversity and fascinating curiosities that can be discovered in Africa," and he won a creative writing scholarship with one of those essays the following semester (L., "Final Exam Essay"). Nicole created the "Ubuntu Memoir Project," on tumblr.com, the "story of [her] life and who [she] is told through the stories of other people. An autobiography of biographies" with the purpose of "showing the world that we, as people, have such a great influence on one another, that we should use that influence for good" (N., "Ubuntu Memoir Project").

Starting with style, my students were able to see the importance of language in terms of audience, and by the end of the course the majority of them were not producing merely self-expressive writing. They were producing effectively self-situated writing with voices that did not say "me, me, me" but "look at this injustice I've seen and want to do something about" or "look at what I've done and learned in my life that I can share with you so you can learn something and do something in the world." Voices that "seek identification without sacrificing conviction." Maybe my fall 2010 class was an anomaly and I will never again feel the palpable energy of a group of writers creating something bigger than the sum of their parts, but I will strive to regenerate that energy in every class I teach.

CLOSING THOUGHTS

The growing popularity of creative nonfiction is undeniable. Creative nonfiction may not be central to English studies, but it does stand at the nexus of creative writing, composition, and literature because it is increasingly studied (and sometimes produced) in all three. According to the *AWP Guide to Writing Programs*, as of March 2012, 127 MFA programs offer concentrations in creative nonfiction—a significant rise from the thirty-five that Hesse reported from the same guide in 1999 (2003, pp. 252). This seems to imply that more students are becoming interested in writing fact-based prose that privileges narrative, personal situatedness, and a literary style, which also means that more students are reading and appreciating this type of writing. If students are demanding more courses in creative nonfiction, a variety of effective pedagogical options should be available for those who are called upon to teach it. I've offered style pedagogy as one such option.

If style's reemergence into composition theory and practice takes hold, which I sincerely hope it does, then style should logically emerge in creative nonfiction as well in ways that highlight the rhetorical effects of stylistic decisions. Writing in the various genres of creative nonfiction, after all, thrives on sentences that *sound* authentic, like a human voice speaking. When students, especially at the undergraduate level, understand how to analyze, imitate, and successfully employ the devices utilized by their favorite writers in ways that position those students as writers who could be published, as writers who can imbue prose with the rhythms and figures of "creative" writing, they also realize that they don't have to be literary geniuses to produce polished, engaging essays. Composing this way is not magic, despite how it might feel.

NOTES

1. Like many who teach this type of writing, I do not particularly like the term "creative nonfiction," a term that defines the genre by what it is not and accomplishes little beyond securing its province in creative writing instead of composition. I use it, though, because "creative nonfiction" is currently the dominant way to describe fact-based prose that privileges narrative, personal situatedness, and literary style. Also, I see the writing process is an inventive, creative process, regardless of the end result, so I reject the idea that some writing is inherently creative while other types are not.

2. A notable recent exception to this, which I read long after I designed the class described herein, is Emily Brisse's "The Geography of Sentences" published in the March/April 2012 Writer's Chronicle.

3. Dennis Rygiel first made an argument similar to this in his 1989 "Stylistics and the Study of Twentieth-Century Literary Nonfiction." In this article Rygiel argues for students to use a practical stylistic form of analysis, one that "derives its aim of systematic description of language use" rather than impressionistic description when analyzing nonfiction prose (30). He models this approach through an analysis of two E. B. White essays and notes that his students routinely made the comment that they improved as writers after studying stylistics. I see myself building on Rygiel's pedagogical ideas using style theories from Enos, Winston Weathers, Paul Butler, T. R. Johnson, and others.

4. For more on the composition/creative writing split that landed creative nonfiction more dominantly in creative writing programs than in composition ones, see Douglas Hesse's "Who Owns Creative Nonfiction?"

5. I subscribe to Enos's definition of voice as that which emerges from style and has the potential to create a transformative ethos; however, this definition comes from rhetorical scholarship and is not used in creative writing craft texts where the idea of "voice" is generally shrouded in ambiguity. See Bizzaro and McClanahan's "Putting Wings on the Invisible: Voice, Authorship, and the Authentic Self" for a historical recounting of the perception of authentic self and voice in creative writing and composition since the late 1960s.

6. As a reader of this essay in the context of the anthology Contemporary Creative Nonfiction: I & Eye, I do not know for certain whether Aciman's primary purpose was to write a craft article or something else perhaps more lyrical or exploratory. However, because his essay has been placed with other craft articles, I make certain assumptions about the sort of demystifying information the writer is expected to divulge.

7. Milic explains that the view of rhetorical dualism " has always implied that ideas exist wordlessly and can be dressed in a variety of outfits, depending on the need for the occasion" (1965, p. 67).

REFERENCES

Aciman, A. (2004). A literary pilgrim progresses to the past. In B. Nguyen & P. Shreve (Eds.), *Contemporary creative nonfiction: I & Eye* (pp. 133-36). London: Longman.

Anderson, C. (1987). *Style as argument: Contemporary American nonfiction.* Carbondale, IL: Southern Illinois University Press.

The Association of Writers and Writing Programs. (2011, June 13). Official guide to writing programs. Retrieved from http://guide.awpwriter.org

Bizarro, P., & McClanahan, M. (2007). Putting wings on the invisible: Voice, authorship, and the authentic self. In K. Ritter, & S. Vanderslice (Eds.), *Can it really be taught: Resisting lore in creative writing pedagogy* (pp. 77-90). Portsmouth, NH: Boynton/Cook.

Bradbury, B., & Hesse, D. (Eds.) (2009). *Creating nonfiction: A guide and anthology.* Boston: Bedford/St. Martin's.

Brisse, E. (2012). The geography of sentences. *The Writers Chronicle 44*(5), 84-93.

Butler, P. (2008). *Out of style: Reanimating stylistic study in composition and rhetoric.* Logan, UT: Utah State University Press.

Daum, A. (2005). Those who stay and those who go. In J. Kitchen (Ed.), *Short takes: Brief encounters with contemporary nonfiction* (pp. 54-59). New York: W. W. Norton & Company.

Dawn. Short assignment #2, August 31, 2010.

Enos, T. (1994). Voice as echo of delivery, ethos as transforming process. In W. R. Winterowd, & V. Gillespie (Eds.), *Composition in context: Essays in honor of Donald C. Stewart* (pp. 180-95). Carbondale, Il: Southern Illinois University Press.

Gornick, V. (2004). The situation and the story. In B. Nguyen & P. Shreve (Eds.), *Contemporary creative nonfiction: I & eye* (pp. 136-39). London: Pearson.

Gornick, V. (2001). *The situation and the story: The art of personal narrative.* New York: Farrar, Straus and Giroux.

Gutkind, L. (2004). The Creative Nonfiction Police. In B. Nguyen & P. Shreve (Eds.), *Contemporary Creative Nonfiction: I & Eye* (pp. 349-54). London: Pearson.

Harvey, S. (2009). The art of self. In R. L. Root, Jr., & M. Steinberg (Eds.), *Fourth genre: Contemporary writers of/on creative nonfiction* (5th ed.) (pp. 344-345). Boston: Allyn and Bacon.

Hesse, D. (2003). Who owns creative nonfiction? In T. Enos, & K. D. Miller (Eds.), *Beyond postprocess and postmodernism: Essays on the spaciousness of rhetoric* (pp. 251-66). Mahwah, NJ: Lawrence Erlbaum Associates.

Holcomb, C, & Killingsworth, M. J. (2010). *Performing prose: The study and practice of style in composition.* Carbondale, IL: Southern Illinois University Press.

Johnson, T. R. (2003). *A rhetoric of pleasure: Prose style and today's composition classroom.* Portsmouth, NH: Boynton/Cook.

Kitchen, J. (2009). Mending wall. In R. L. Root, Jr., & M. Steinberg (Eds.), *Fourth genre: Contemporary writers of/on creative nonfiction* (5th ed.) (pp. 364-367). Boston: Allyn and Bacon.

Kitchen, J. (Ed.) (2005). *Short takes: Brief encounters with contemporary nonfiction.* New York: W. W. Norton & Company.

Larry. (2010). Process comment on imitation assignment, September 23, 2010.

Larry. (2010). Maison des esclaves. Imitation essay assignment, September 23, 2010.

Matthews, S. (2009). Stepping through the threshold: Ways to achieve authentic voice in memoir. *The Writers Chronicle 42*(2), 72-80.

Mayers, T. (2005). *(Re)writing craft: Composition, creative writing, and the future of English studies.* Pittsburg: University of Pittsburg Press.

Medzerian, S. (2010). Style and the pedagogy of response. *Rhetoric Review 29*(2), 186-202.

Milic, L. T. (1965). Theories of style and their implications for the teaching of composition. *College Composition and Communication 16*(2). 66-69+126.

Nicole. (2010). Process comment on imitation assignment, September 23, 2010.

Nicole. (2010). Ubuntu memoir project. Final project. Retrieved from http://theubuntumemoirproject.tumblr.com

Nguyen, B. M., & Shreve, P. (Eds.) (2004). *Contemporary creative nonfiction: I & eye.* New York: Pearson.

Ostrom, H. (1998). "Carom shots": Reconceptualizing imitation and its uses in creative writing courses. In D. Starkey (Ed.), *Teaching writing creatively* (pp. 164-71). Portsmouth, NH: Boynton/Cook.

Ozick, C. (2004) She: Portrait of the essay as a warm body. In B. Nguyen & P. Shreve (Eds.), *Contemporary creative nonfiction: I & eye* (pp. 200-05). London: Pearson.

Root, R. L., Jr., & Steinberg, M. (Eds.) (2010). *The fourth genre: Contemporary writers of/on creative nonfiction* (5th ed.). New York: Longman.

Rushdie, S. (2005). Water's edge. In J. Kitchen (Ed.), *Short takes: Brief encounters with contemporary nonfiction* (pp. 65-67). New York: W. W. Norton & Company.

Sanders, S. R. (2004). The singular first person. In B. Nguyen & P. Shreve (Eds.), *Contemporary creative nonfiction: I & eye* (pp. 73-80). London: Pearson.

Weathers, W. (1969). *Copy and compose: A guide to prose style.* Upper Saddle River, NJ: Prentice Hall.

Weathers, W. (2010). Grammars of style: New options in composition. In P. Butler (Ed.), *Style in rhetoric and composition: A critical sourcebook* (pp. 219-38). Boston: Bedford/St. Martin's.

FIGHTING STYLES: THE PEDAGOGICAL IMPLICATIONS OF APPLYING CONTEMPORARY RHETORICAL THEORY TO THE PERSUASIVE PROSE OF MARY WOLLSTONECRAFT AND MARY HAYS

Luke Redington
Purdue University

I. WOLLSTONECRAFT AND HAYS: THE NEED FOR A STYLE-CENTERED READING AND A PROPOSED METHODOLOGY

For centuries, Mary Wollstonecraft was stigmatized and her pupil Mary Hays was largely overlooked. Even though reformers borrowed directly and abundantly from her ideas from the moment they appeared, nearly a hundred years passed from the publication of Wollstonecraft's works until it became common to cite her as an authority. Of Hays' place in history, M. Ray Adams says, "Soon after the time of the French Revolution she became enveloped in an obscurity which has never lifted" (Adams, 1940, p. 472). Writing in 1940, Adams could hardly have guessed the robust return both authors would make to the public consciousness. The past thirty years have seen exponential growth in the amount of scholarship on both authors; Wollstonecraft's work alone has been the subject of over 500 journal articles in the past twelve years. Although Hays' writings may not be experiencing the same crescendo of scholarly attention, she is now a fixture, along with her mentor, in at least three academic disciplines. Literature studies, communication studies, and women's studies all find rich and rewarding material in the fiction and creative non-fiction of both pioneering authors.

The relationship between Wollstonecraft and Hays has also sparked immense interest. Much biographical scholarship has addressed Wollstonecraft's mentoring of Hays and the subsequent advocacy role Hays would go on to play for her mentor. Consequently, scholars such as Katharine M. Rogers have undertaken comparisons of their work. Although their novels *Maria, or the Wrongs of Woman* and *The Victim of Prejudice* are frequently compared works, a large and growing body of criticism exists on each author's primary work of persuasive non-fiction, Wollstonecraft's *A Vindication of the Rights of Woman* and Hays' *An Appeal to the Men of Great Britain in Behalf of Women*. Such criticism tends to compare the works' remarkably similar ideologies. I concede the existence of significant similarities in their ideologies, but I seek to augment current assessments of *Vindication* and *Appeal* by drawing attention to the vastly different writing styles the two works utilize. Very little work to this effect has yet been done. Miriam Brody has lucidly examined the social ramifications of Wollstonecraft's stylistic choices, but scholarship that compares the two authors' styles as a means of refining our conclusions about their ideologies is still a pioneering endeavor.

The absence of a comparative stylistic analysis is more remarkable given that in the past forty years, style has become a major topic in rhetorical theory. Especially in composition studies, renewed debates about writing style have resulted in the overturning of ideas championed since the time of Aristotle. Once thought a superficial matter of presentation, style is now largely considered a politically potent, ideologically substantive feature of any carefully crafted text. From this perspective, differences in style between these two early feminists become very important. Since Wollstonecraft and Hays are back in the spotlight and likely to remain, it is both inevitable and beneficial that their centuries-old writings will be re-examined and assessed against the canons of contemporary rhetoric. The stylistic re-assessment I undertake in this chapter will evidence the value of the current emphasis on style by exemplifying the sorts of discoveries this emphasis makes available. But more specifically, I want the method of discovery to evidence my assertions about needed adjustments in the pedagogy of writing style in college courses.

In terms of contemporary scholarship, the leading work comparing the form and content of *A Vindication* and *An Appeal* is Katharine M. Roger's 1987 article "The Contribution of Mary Hays." Rogers overviews the structures, strategies, and styles of both authors' main works of persuasive prose with occasional reference to their fiction for additional examples of their argumentative techniques. Rogers' purpose is two-fold. First, as the title of her article implies, she wants to ensure that Hays not be "dismissed as a lesser Wollstonecraft" but is instead recognized as an important feminist rhetorician in her own right (Rogers, 1987, p. 131). Second, she contends that Hays' approach to argumentation not only differs but also complements Wollstonecraft's. Whereas Wollstonecraft critiques institutions and social systems, seeking to overturn injustice on a macroscopic level, Hays focuses on domestic and relational concerns. Wollstonecraft, Rogers notes, operates in the realm of the abstract. Wollstonecraft hopes that if virtue can be defined similarly for both genders, life will improve for men and women alike (Rogers, 1987, pp. 131-132). Hays, though, consistently favors a pragmatic and specific approach. She concerns herself with "how oppressively the double standard actually operates in married life" (Rogers, 1987, p. 133). Rogers laments that specificity and pragmatism did not remain flagship concerns in Hays' fiction, where Hays instead tended toward sentimentalism and "a stupefyingly stilted style" (Rogers, 1987, p. 140). Rogers concludes her comparative investigation succinctly:

> Hays's feminist works, then, complement the Vindication. She fleshes out Wollstonecraft's analysis with examples from daily life and lowers her rhetoric to a familiar no-nonsense tone. Together the two authors make the points that need to be made on the theoretical and domestic level. (Rogers, 1987, p. 139)

Rogers makes a compelling case. She shows that Hays' techniques, which might appear overly simplistic to a modern reader, were the result of an adept awareness of her audience. Rogers also rightly credits Hays for having a sense of which arguments to simply dismiss, as she does with the essentialist pronouncements found in the conduct literature of her time (Rogers, 1987, p. 135).

However, there are several challenges I would like to pose to Rogers' conclusion about the complementary nature of Wollstonecraft's and Hays' agendas. First, Rogers makes an unjustified assumption about authorial intention. Certainly, one must grant that, taken together, the two authors cover a range of both theoretical and practical concerns. But there is no evidence that Wollstonecraft and Hays collaborated to create, between the two of them, a farther reaching treatise than either would have produced alone. Instead, the little that is known about the life circumstances from which both authors wrote the works in question suggests that they set out, independently and simultaneously, to perform roughly the same task and yet produced two books that differ greatly in their style. Perhaps a more useful question than whether the works are complementary is whether they are compatible. That is, are the ideals and goals Wollstonecraft and Hays promote sufficiently harmonious to allow both agendas to be pursued without infringing on one another?

I posit that their agendas are not as compatible as Rogers suggests, as an application of current rhetorical notions of style will show. However, I would like to address two possible objections to this methodological approach to reading centuries-old texts. First is the charge of anachronism. It is reasonable to wonder about the fairness of retroactively projecting today's stress on style backward to the end of the eighteenth century. New literary theories frequently inspire wildly divergent readings of venerated texts. A new theory is likely to do this insofar as the assumptions on which it is based are accepted as valid within pertinent discourse communities. It is on this basis that feminist critics offer radically different readings of literary texts that have been commented upon for millennia. Their readings are based in part on the premise that women have consistently been slandered and objectified in literature and have also been largely excluded from literary production and criticism. Therefore, literary texts produced and read in any culture where these assumptions hold true ought to be reconsidered, no matter how old or reverently canonized. Hélène Cixous' 1976 treatise "The Laugh of the Medusa," derives much of its force from its delineating and decrying of the various ideological biases that have undergirded the repression and exclusion of women. Not surprisingly, this leads Cixous to a consideration of how women are taught to write. She admonishes women to find their own way of writing that frees itself from the confining binaries and prejudices of the male dominated literary establishment. "Woman must write woman," she demands (Cixous, 1976, p. 877). Cixous' historical generalizations about the treatment of women have become widely accepted in many academic discourse communities, and interpretations based on this framework have likewise grown in acceptance. In fact, in 2008, Oxford University Press published an anthology of feminist re-interpretations of Greek myths appropriately titled *Laughing with the Medusa*.

Thus, the argument about the applicability of a modern notion of style should turn on the validity of its underlying premises. The foundational premise in view here is that experienced writers skillfully affect their message through their rhetorical techniques. Their style and their meaning are too closely related to be considered separately. This view is discussed by rhetorician Louis T. Milic in his 1965 article "Theories of Style and Their Implications for the Teaching of Composition." Milic's only caveat about aesthetic monism is its tendency to problematize pedagogy for beginning writers. They may need help, he cautions, in coming to grasp the range of choices available to them for conveying nuances of meaning. But the two masterful writers whose persuasive prose this chapter treats certainly do not fall into this category. Their style is inseparable from their meaning.

The second objection is most likely to arise from critics familiar with Milic's theory of style. Milic's 1965 essay is by no means a manifesto in favor of aesthetic monism. In fact, it sounds almost like the opposite. Writing at a time when composition teachers in American higher education were considering major changes to the Aristotelian approach to teaching rhetoric, Milic feared that compositionists would blindly adopt "organic" theories of writing which essentially claimed that students should write whatever they feel, and that all expressions of feeling were inherently meaningful. Milic warned that this view of writing, called aesthetic monism, would render teachers helpless to their students. Novice writers, Milic argues, will be the first to claim they need help expressing what they feel, and compositionists must not hesitate to introduce them to techniques from classical rhetoric that have aided writers and speakers for millennia. But regarding the analysis of literary texts, Milic makes a key concession. He sees the need for a theory that can account for the effect of the author's subconscious on his or her art and yet also assumes the author's choice of style was deliberate (Milic, 1965, p. 20). That is, Milic grants that the work of mature authors should indeed be regarded as the skillfully rendered expression of what they feel, and thus meaningful in every aspect. If even this most vociferous opponent of aesthetic monism admits its place in literary analysis, then the case for using it in this fashion becomes quite compelling.

Not only does Milic function as an important if unintentional advocate for aesthetic monism, he also provides a useful definition of style. He describes style as, "the relationship of the thing to idea and idea to word [which] is left unexpressed" (Milic, 1965, p. 17). In other words, style is the holistic communicative value of a literary text arising from the interrelation of what is said, how it is said, and what is not said. Authors announce their content, but they enact their style. Milic therefore offers a key insight by describing style as a thing/idea/word relationship *that is left unsaid*. This view of style opens the possibility that the most important component of a work may be the attitude the author displays toward the audience or toward the subject matter. Reading any text, but especially a rhetorically charged text, with Milic's definition of style in mind, reveals aspects of embedded ideology that, paradoxically, may go unnoticed when one is reading a text primarily to discern its ideology. This view of style also suggests that methodologies for reading and writing pedagogy can converge with beneficial results; Milic's particular argument shifts from a question of student's frustrations with college writing assignments to ruminations about their stylistic sensitivity as readers. The following style-centered reading and analysis is intended to exemplify such a convergence.

II. A STYLE-CENTERED READING OF WOLLSTONECRAFT AND HAYS

With the case for aesthetic monism articulated and its view of style defined, I would like next to look at the stylistic features of *Vindication* and *Appeal,* particularly the ways in which differences in style may suggest differences in meaning. Rogers began efforts along this vein in her discussion of what she calls tone. She notes, as a matter of course, the differences in tone between both authors but sees them merely as such (Rogers, 1987, p. 138). Since it is outside the scope of this project to offer a stylistic analysis of both book-length texts in their entirety, this essay will focus on passages from both that exhibit great similarities in their announced content.

Chapter 2 of *Vindication*, entitled "The Prevailing Opinion of a Sexual Character Discussed," and Chapter 5 of *Appeal,* entitled "What Women Are," stand out as particularly apt passages for this type of comparison. Both chapters describe women in eighteenth-century England as caught in a vicious cycle. Women are acculturated to be childish—to feel rather than to reason—and thus furnish proponents of status quo patriarchy with examples of the unfitness of women to govern themselves or advance in society. Both chapters argue that this cycle can and must be broken by offering women access to education. Finally, both chapters outline specific ways that all of society would benefit from women's education. (One of the later chapters of *Vindication* even includes remarkably detailed plans for how coeducational schools should operate.) Wollstonecraft and Hays shift the frame of reference for the debate about women's education from the supposed intellectual ineptitude of women to the actual oppression of the patriarchy. Thus, the passages I will discuss are remarkably similar in the logical trajectory of their argument.

Stylistically, though, the excerpts differ greatly. For example, each author takes a very different tone when employing arguments based on historical precedent. Wollstonecraft immerses herself in the debates about the nature of women that had passed among English and Continental philosophers in the two centuries leading up to her time, including the contributions of Bacon, Milton, and Rousseau. The history that concerns her is the relatively recent history of western thought about women's nature and role in society. She wants to address the "many ingenious arguments [that] have been brought forward to prove, that the two sexes, in the acquirement of virtue, ought to aim at attaining a very different character" (1974, p. 39). That is, she wants to counter the arguments that were used to bar women from education. Virtue, in the context of Wollstonecraft's Enlightenment-laden lexicon, means something very much like agency or self-actuation and is thus linked to the attainment of education.

Having stated her main premise, Wollstonecraft frames the argument around a sharp conjecture: "If then women are not a swarm of ephemeron triflers, why should they be kept in ignorance [of the means of attaining virtue] under the specious name of innocence?" (Wollstonecraft, 1974, p. 39). She next reviews a number of passages from the aforementioned writers who her audience would likely have held in high regard. She focuses especially Milton's *Paradise Lost*. She challenges the representation of Eve as subservient by design and sees Milton as having inadvertently helped her case. Milton certainly stresses the eternality and spirituality of women in his rendering of the creation of Eve (Wollstonecraft, 1974, pp. 41-42). Milton's ontological view of women, then, suggests that they stand equally ready with their male counterparts for education, or "the betterment of one's soul," as it was often described in Enlightenment discourse.

In its announced content, Wollstonecraft's passage simply calls for women to be allowed access to education. However, the dexterous, erudite, polemic style in which this passage is written accomplishes much more than this. Wollstonecraft's style serves as her credentials to enter this discussion as an Enlightenment intellectual. It puts her opponents on notice that she has raided their rhetorical arsenal. Her style is thus one of the most important evidences she can offer for her case that women can benefit from education as much as men. Her style displays her acumen; it issues a challenge; it demands an answer. She could have chosen any topic as the announced content of this discourse, and written in this style, it would still pose the same challenge to educated men who want to exclude women from their ranks.

In stark contrast to Wollstonecraft's sophisticated style is the straightforwardness of Mary Hays' persuasive prose. Here is a passage that offers a wide-sweeping historiography of the detrimental effects of a civilization denying education to a large portion of its society:

> We have for examples of this, only to contemplate the characters and conduct of the descendents of Egyptians, the Greeks, the Romans, and other nations, living under the same climates, and upon the very same soil, where their renowned ancestors flourished in arts, and triumphed in arms; and to consider to what a state of degradation and humiliation they are now reduced! (Hays, 1974, pp. 69-70)

The social and historical essentializing found in this passage undermines its validity as an argument based on historical precedent. Can any cogent, pertinent analogies be drawn between the role that education (and exclusion from it) played in the classical cultures Hays lists and the role it played in Enlightenment England?

So if the argument Hays forwards here is to succeed, it must do so more on the basis of style than content, a style characterized by enthusiasm and earnestness. Not only is the exclamation mark a clue to the high emotional pitch of this prose, but the extended list of adverbial clauses that modifies "living" gives the sentence a hymn-like rhythm. Furthermore, it is a relatively long sentence but a short paragraph. This is typical of Hays' style throughout the *Appeal*. By comparison, Wollstonecraft's sentences are longer, more complex, and grouped into paragraphs whose relationship to one another plays a greater role in advancing the linear progress of her argument. And, as noted, this sentence's length is a function of the adverbial clauses. This is among the most ideologically simple ways to achieve long sentences. In academic prose, sentence length usually proliferates because of long noun clauses in the subject position and the frequent use of other forms of subordinate clauses to reflect complicated and contingent relationships among ideas. The communicative effect of Hays' long but fairly simple sentences is reflected in her work's title; she is indeed, from the stylistic perspective, making an appeal, a supplication. As Rogers notes, the hallmark of Hays' stylistic strategy is repetition. Rogers sees Hays as tapping into "the persuasive power of earnestness and gravity" (1987, p. 134). Whereas Wollstonecraft bursts into the conversation on her own intellectual merits, Hays politely but persistently knocks on the door.

From these two passages, then, one can see that even when Wollstonecraft and Hays address similar topics, their styles achieve different communicative effects. Already this suggests a significant difference in their respective agendas for women's rights. The question of how an underrepresented group can gain an audience is sometimes the most important issue it faces. The agendas of Dr. Martin Luther King, Jr. and Malcolm X, for example, differed sharply enough on this point to prevent their working together toward common goals, since the latter condoned violence under certain circumstances as a means of garnering attention.

I propose that there are also differences in the content of the agendas proposed by Wollstonecraft and Hays. They may be considerably less compatible than is commonly thought. For example, the following excerpt from Hays reveals, both in its content and delivery, demure attitude toward oppression hardly imaginable in Wollstonecraft:

> Women therefore, generally speaking, act a wiser and a better part as individuals, to keep within that boundary prescribed by their lawgivers. Within it they often contrive to do mischief enough; without it who can pretend to say where the mischief might end? For, candidly speaking, perhaps it would be dangerous to trust women all at once, with liberty in that extent which is their due.
>
> But it is to be regretted, that the temperance and good sense

shewn by women, in submitting with so good a grace to injuries, which though they cannot redress, they nevertheless feel very severely; it is much to be regretted, that this temperance and good sense, is not attended with better consequences to themselves. (1974, p. 71)

Here is incontrovertible evidence of Hays' gradualism; how would this ever have operated smoothly alongside her mentor's revolutionary ardor? It is outside the scope of this project to explore this and all other possible divergences in agenda between Hays and her mentor, eminently useful as such an undertaking would be. Instead, I wish to emphasize what the style of the proceeding passage says about Hays' approach to alleviating women's suffering. The style of this passage demonstrates Hays' unwavering resolve to remain civil at all times. In light of the panoramic extent of the "injuries" Hays must have in mind, it is very telling that she understatedly laments that this suffering "is much to be regretted" (1974, p. 71). If there were ever a time that merited an unrestrained outburst, this qualifies. Hays' choice to maintain her suppliant, long-suffering tone even under these circumstances suggests that her commitment to civility tops of her list of ideological priorities.

Wollstonecraft's tone, by contrast, is the stylistic equivalent of a call to storm the Bastille. In response to Rousseau's assumption that, "with respect to the female character, obedience is the grand lesson which ought to be impressed with unrelenting rigor," she exclaims, "What nonsense! When will a great man arise with sufficient strength of mind to puff away the fumes which pride and sensuality have thus spread over the subject!" (1974, pp. 50-1). This is an *ad hominem* attack in the most literal, gendered sense of the term—an attack against man. Wollstonecraft accuses her opponents of hubris, not merely faulty logic. But the strategy works. It succeeds in part because the erudition of her style has earned her the right to take an occasional jab at her opponents. Furthermore, she follows this attack with a reiteration of her watertight postulation that if men insist on defining the quest for virtue as a natural outworking of human nature, they must include all humans in this quest.

This comparison of their style shows that Wollstonecraft and Hays differ in agenda because they differ so greatly in their relationship to their chosen audiences. Wollstonecraft, of course, addressed *Vindication* primarily to Talleyrand in the hopes that the French Revolution would result in advances in the wellbeing of France's women in general and their access to education in particular. Her choice to write in a high register of English, though, suggests that Great Britain's educated elite is her primary audience, and these she feels comfortable addressing as her equals. Rogers suspects that Hays' style is an adaptation of the women's conduct literature with which the middle class would have been familiar (1987, p. 135). This is an interesting choice on Hays' part, given that her invoked audience is specifically the men of Great Britain. The value of applying the perspectives of aesthetic monism to these texts is that it allows an author's choice of agenda, choice of audience, and choice of style to be seen as different facets of the same choice. The author decides who has the power to positively modify the problem at hand and also how to present himself or herself to that audience. Wollstonecraft and Hays differ in style in part because they differ in their conviction of which segment of England's population should take up the feminist cause. Style is never merely style.

This perspective has numerous implications for the college writing classroom, two of which I would like to delineate in the interest of incorporating style more effectively into curriculum. First, the means through which conclusions were drawn about the role of style in Wollstonecraft's and Hays' writing may evidence why discussions of style can seem inaccessible, even esoteric to students. If stylistic analysis typically utilizes, as it has here, historical context, literary context, reader response criticism, audience analysis, rhetorical theory, and grammatical scrutiny, then students can hardly be blamed for not knowing what instructors have in mind when referring to style. If style truly arises from all these factors, it is a more advanced concept than typically billed. To teach style as a mere adjunct to the rudiments of grammar (as is often then case in middle school) is therefore a curricular miscalibration. To teach style as a component of audience awareness (common at the collegiate level) comes closer to the mark, but still under-represents its complexity and value.

Related to this issue of miscalibration is a question of curricular sequencing, and it can be explained by making use of Benjamin S. Bloom's *Taxonomy of Educational Objectives*. As writing teachers, we tend to feel most assured that students are advancing in their understanding of style when we see its techniques used with creativity and dexterity in their own writing. A cursory reference to Bloom's taxonomy would seem to confirm this; to employ style in one's own writing is to create, and creation is a part of synthesis, the second highest form of learning. But a closer look at the taxonomy prompts two further questions: Can the student explain her or his success? Can the student reproduce success in a variety of topics and genres, and in relation to diverse audiences?

Explaining one's own success requires a panoply of specialized vocabulary, since style draws upon many facets of literary and linguistic analysis. Bloom contends that possessing specialized vocabulary is a basic, foundational form of learning; he groups it with "knowledge" at the bottom of his taxonomy. The rationale for doing so, articulated in the following quote, seems directly applicable to the question of how stylistic aptitude should be taught and assessed. Perhaps Bloom's own style—his nearly belligerent use of repetition—indicates a suspicion that educators will not initially share his emphasis on the foundational importance of vocabulary:

> Each field contains a large number of symbols, either verbal or non-verbal, which have particular referents. These represent the basic language of the field—the shorthand used by workers in a field to express what they know. In any attempt by workers to communicate with others about phenomena within the field, they find it necessary to make use of some of the special symbols and terms they have devised. In many cases it is impossible for them to discuss problems in their field without making use of some of the essential terms of that field. Quite literally, they are unable to think about many of the phenomena in the field unless they make use of these terms and symbols. (1956, p. 64)

If Bloom's sweeping generalizations seem reliable, then students need to be supplied a vocabulary of style as early as possible. This vocabulary could eventually provide students with a framework that helps them to evaluate (Bloom's highest form of learning) a variety of rhetorical situations and make appropriate stylistic choices. In contemporary pedagogical terms, this would be the level of development at which transference could reasonably be expected. Even if Bloom's taxonomy is not taken as precisely reflective of a writer's development, we may still do well to accept the premise that the accumulation of vocabulary precedes (and provides) the ability to assess sophisticated challenges and consistently reproduce results.

III. WRITING STYLE, IDENTITY, AND ETHOS

Students may not feel particular enthusiasm for memorizing lists of Greek and Latin vocabulary, but there may be a way to utilize their affective development to foster cognitive development. Curriculum that highlights connections between writing style and a sense of identity can show students that they already have a vested interested in this topic by raising concerns they are likely to have considered previously in history and social studies classes and in their own interpersonal experiences. Wollstonecraft and Hays elaborate on the relationship between their choice of writing style and notions of gender in their society in ways today's audiences are likely to find interesting, even estranging.

Consequently, they are useful for helping scholars and students see the recursive connection between identity and style as both enduring and current.

Wollstonecraft lays out what she sees as the connection between style and conceptions of gender in the introduction of *Vindication,* and she announces her plan to trample these notions:

> I shall disdain to cull my phrases or polish my style;—I aim at being useful, and sincerity will render me unaffected; for, wishing rather to persuade by the force of my arguments, than dazzle by the elegance of my language, I shall not waste my time in rounding periods, or in fabricating the turgid bombast of artificial feelings, which, coming from the head, never reach the heart. I shall be employed about things, not words!—and, anxious to render my sex more respectable members of society, I shall try to avoid that flowery diction which has slided from essays into novels, and from novels into familiar letters and conversation. (1974, p. 23)

So for Wollstonecraft, much is at stake in style. She posits herself as a spokeswoman for all women (at least in Great Britain), and the respectability of their collective reputation will rise or fall based on her ability to eschew fancy talk for substantive ideas. Language practices in general are at stake, too, in her view. She believes essays set the standard that should be emulated by authors of other genres and then by casual speakers; therefore, the style of her essay is a question of national importance.

Wollstonecraft can be forgiven for overestimating the immediate social impact of the style of her essay, but she did not underestimate the extent to which her society viewed writing style as inherently gendered. In her 1996 essay "The Vindication of the Writes of Women: Mary Wollstonecraft and Enlightenment Rhetoric" Miriam Brody documents the pedagogical influences Wollstonecraft would both appropriate and react against in crafting *Vindication*. First, Brody notes that the gendered notions of style that pervaded Enlightenment rhetoric have their roots in classical rhetoric. Ancient rhetoricians beginning with Aristotle described good writing in exclusively male terms, praising its force and productivity as its highest merits, Brody contends. Their metaphors were also gender-laden, such as a builder making effective use of his tools and as a legislator making good use of his wisdom. Brody puts special emphasis, though, on the contributions Quintilian made to this notion. He made explicit the correlation of good persuasive prose and natural masculinity in an extended metaphor that describes ornamented, affected language as a well dressed eunuch.

He contrasted this with plain language, which he likened to the attractiveness, strength and productivity of a virile man (1996, pp. 107-108).

Brody contends that these gendered notions of rhetoric prevailed for centuries, and most importantly for Wollstonecraft, they influenced the Enlightenment thinkers under whom she studied. Thus, Wollstonecraft faced not only the challenge of being a woman writer at a time when very few were published, but in *Vindication* she participates in the most "masculine" category of discourse: persuasive prose intended for the public arena.

Brody sees Wollstonecraft as having met this challenge in three ways. First, Wollstonecraft not only adopts but draws attention to her forthright style, as seen in the previously quoted excerpt from the introduction of *Vindication*. Second, she joined with her rhetorical predecessors in the condemnation of affected femininity. She mitigates this attack, however, by focusing it particularly on the habits and attitudes of upper class women. In Brody's view, this distinction paves the way for Wollstonecraft's third technique, that is, the description of the healthy, effective, unaffected woman who matches men in their ability to wield the "masculine" traits of persuasive language. This new category or "genus," into which she implicitly places herself, she calls "the exceptional woman" (Brody, 1996, pp. 112-113). To Brody's analysis, I would add that Wollstonecraft uses style to distance herself from women in general and to align herself more closely with the men with whom she seeks an audience. She saw style as central to gender, and she chose to adopt a socially solitary role for the sake of her rhetorical mission.

Hays does not theorize about her style, but she does apologize for it. Worried that her style, so conciliatory by comparison to Wollstonecraft's, will distance her from men, she explains:

> I have heretofore, it is true, been pretty free in my observations upon the conduct of men, where I think it absurd and capricious with regard to women; but I hope without acrimony, for I am sure I feel none towards them. On the contrary I love them with all my heart as individuals. (1974, p. 93)

It is possible to see the effects of gender and style operating in quite the opposite ways here as in Wollstonecraft's text. The assumption that women must be peacemakers (presumably at any cost) underlies the preceding excerpt, as does the assumption that women must avoid even the appearance of acrimony. Women are embodiments of pure love, in Hays' view, and this must be reflected in their writing style. Many of the rhetorical techniques Wollstonecraft employs become necessarily off limits in this view. The sarcastic pronouncement of acquiescence, the bombastic rebuttal, and certainly the *ad hominem* attack do not fit within Hays' construct of femininity.

Although contemporary feminist rhetoricians would have much to say about this patriarchal construction of womanhood, they too question the ethics inherent in classical rhetoric. In her 1979 article "The Womanization of Rhetoric," Sally Miller Gerhart goes as far as to claim that "any intent to persuade is an act of violence" (1979, p. 195). She lists several tendencies within the classical rhetorical tradition, many of which persist to the present day, that she sees as inherently patriarchal and destructive. These include a proclivity for conquest and competition, a disregard for the feelings and opinions of others, and the assumption that one should value victory as a higher good than personal growth and change. While Gerhart's equating persuasion with violence never caught on—perhaps it was recognized as an attempt at persuasion—her critique of the inherently patriarchal nature of Western rhetoric sparked a discussion that continues to this day. Especially prominent in this conversation are Sonja K. Foss and Cindy L. Griffin. Wanting to explore further the notion that rhetors should embrace a willingness to grow and change as a result of argumentation, they developed a framework called invitational rhetoric. Their 1995 article "Beyond Persuasion: A Proposal for Invitational Rhetoric" includes recommendations for maximizing the personal developmental potential inherent in exchanging the classical, conflict-oriented model of rhetoric for a model that is "rooted in equality, immanent value and self-determination" (1995, p. 5). Invitational rhetoric has immediate implications for style. It necessarily favors conciliatory word choices over inflammatory ones, for example. The use of a rhetorical question meant to force an opponent to abandon his or her position, a stalwart of classical rhetoric, has no place in the invitational approach.

Wollstonecraft and Hays, then, fare very differently in an assessment of the extent to which they embody the values of invitational rhetoric. With Wollstonecraft, we arrive at an ethical impasse. Many of the stylistic techniques invitational rhetoric eschews as hegemonic are commonplace in Wollstonecraft's repertoire. But ironically, she adopted and co-opted these techniques from classical and Enlightenment rhetoric on ethical grounds of her own, namely, because they were the right tools to accomplish a worthy task that she was in an exceptional position to undertake. If Wollstonecraft has a methodological advocate among contemporary feminist rhetoricians, it may be Cixous, who claims that women should consider themselves free to take anything that works from the male-dominated world of writing and use it in their own way: "We've been able to possess anything only by flying; [in French, "to fly" has the double meaning "to steal"] we've lived in flight, stealing away, finding, when desired, narrow passageways, hidden crossovers" (Cixous, 1976, p. 887). Writing two centuries after Wollstonecraft, Cixous likewise collapses the question of ethics into one of pragmatic necessity for the advancement of women. But Hays, from the standpoint of invitational rhetoric, generally exhibits the conciliatory tone that accords with a concern for the feelings of all participants in a debate. She could be said to anticipate and embody this aspect of invitational rhetoric. The premium she places on civility as exemplified in her ever hopeful, never spiteful tone, also seems to accord with these principles.

By overtly commenting on the rhetorical aims of their stylistic choices, both authors highlight the functioning of the "economies of attention" William Kurlinkus describes in this volume. Hays and Wollstonecraft both employ style in an attempt to "get the audience to pay the right kind of attention." The ethical components of "economies of attention" Kurlinkus outlines can readily be demonstrated to college-level writing students. Even without exposure to classical or contemporary rhetorical theory, they can appreciate the conundrums these feminist authors faced as they sought the best styles to suit their purposes. Certainly, students can describe instances of feeling that they had to alter or fabricate a sense of self for the sake of a writing assignment. Even in an age when educators seek to root prejudice out of language instruction, we cannot help sending inadvertent messages about which dialects, preferences, and attitudes are most welcome on the page. It is important to acknowledge, then, the ethical advancement inherent in supplying students the agency to shape their own written identities.

IV. THE TRANSITION FROM A STYLE-CENTERED READING METHODOLOGY TO A STYLE-CENTERED WRITING PEDAGOGY

Rhetoricians and experienced writers will likely recognize the implications for writing of this style-based reading methodology. Many may find in it echoes of their own experiences when immersion in a body of literature helped them find their voice(s) on the page. But college students, especially first and second year students in mandatory composition courses, will need a manageable process by which a guided reading experience can equip them to be style-conscious authors. The following heuristic therefore seeks to encapsulate this article's methodology into four sequenced steps that can be applied to a wide range of artifacts in a writing classroom.

In terms of preparation, the first two questions entail choosing an old document whose stylistic features students will analyze. The instructor's choice should be calibrated around the student's linguistic dexterity; the sample document should be old enough to seem entirely removed from the student's place and time, but not so old that the vocabulary and syntax significantly obscure comprehension. Next, the instructor should be ready to offer an historical overview of the artifacts' circumstances of origin.

1. WHAT IS THE CULTURAL AND LITERARY CONTEXT OF THIS DOCUMENT?

Writing instruction about the persuasive prose of Mary Wollstonecraft should probably begin with guided readings in Edmund Burke. As his speeches are less intricate (by Burkean standards) than his essays, and since they take greater care to explain their purpose and occasion, they provide an entry point for helping students understand the social shifts and tensions of late eighteenth century Great Britain. It would also show students the stylistic standard Wollstonecraft adopted and then determined to exceed. When studying the persuasive prose of Mary Hays, the obvious starting point is the conduct literature that proliferated during her day and that established the style Hays would emulate.

For first and second year students, I recommend choosing a document from within approximately the past fifty years. The dearth of history instruction generally in secondary education and the specifically rare use of primary documents effectively preclude the possibility that any landmark essay will be too familiar to play its role in this heuristic. In teaching Martin Luther King Jr.'s "A Letter from the Birmingham Jail" at the university level, I have found that a basic review of the challenges faced by the Civil Rights movement in the early 1960s is necessary. In any instance, the historical overview should eventually focus on a discussion of the rhetorical situation that immediately surrounds the document.

2. HOW SHOULD THE AUTHOR'S STYLISTIC CHOICES BE SEEN IN LIGHT OF THE HISTORICAL AND LITERARY CONTEXT?

I have found that students' appreciation of King as an author and rhetor elevates dramatically when they compare his letter to the pedantic style of "A Call for Unity," the open letter from Alabama clergymen that prompted his response. Without this comparison, and without considering King's letter as having been written in jail, my students have sometimes perfunctorily described its style as "sophisticated" and "well-read." With the comparison intact, students are more frequently able to explain the role King's style plays in countering the argument presented by the Alabama clergymen. Likewise, if students are to appreciate Jonathan Swift's "A Modest Proposal," they may need exposure to two or three samples of the writings of social activists from that time. When the text is considered in isolation, Swift's condemnation of the English landholding class is overwhelmingly clear. Only when seen in its literary context is it clear that Swift's clinical, detached tone is a mockery of Enlightened social activists who, in his view, had become numb to the human suffering they intended to solve. This exemplifies the sort of significant but unstated meaning Milic encourages literary scholars to discover through attentiveness to style, and it is within the reach of beginning composition students.

The use of an old document as the examined artifact offers several unique advantages. First, it reduces the cognitive dissonance students feel when reading about contemporary controversial topics. They do not have to work to clarify or re-categorize their own position about the causes of starvation in eighteenth century Ireland before examining Swift's stylistic choices. Similarly unlikely is the prospect that Wollstonecraft's and Hays' call for women's education would seem like anything other than a foregone conclusion. Comparing the styles of old documents also counteracts the myth, often fostered inadvertently through curricular omission, that style does not matter. Students will see that through style, authors have been able to demonstrate credentials or assert membership in a group to which their society denied them access. They will internalize the ancient sense of "ethos" as the confluence of one's sense of self, character on the page, and ethical standards. Finally, the use of old documents will challenge the myth that style simply happens. Even when reading authors who claim to "write the way they feel," students will be able to draw meaningful conclusions about why an author's feelings were expressed in that manner at that point in history. In the course of performing the first two steps, students will have assembled a glossary of rhetorical techniques, or at least augmented their vocabulary of style. It is advantageous for beginning students to hand-craft their own glossaries, annotating them with examples.

3. How should an author's stylistic choices be understood in today's cultural and literary context?

The third step of this heuristic is intended to help students transfer their stylistic awareness into the present day. Their glossaries become tools for examining a variety of current samples of persuasive prose including op-ed pieces, political speeches, and advertisements. It is common for courses in persuasive writing to require at least one assignment based on a rhetorical analysis of a document or artifact. Such an assignment could easily be altered to ask students to focus only on the style of the artifact and to analyze its rhetorical impact.

The sequencing of this step is also intended to help students put today's conflicts in their historical contexts since their discoveries about stylistic continuities or departures can lead to discoveries about ideological ones. It also hoped that the previous two steps will have offered students means to grapple with and more adequately express their cognitive dissonance. Well-articulated cognitive dissonance is the basis, or at least the starting point, of effective persuasive prose. This step in the heuristic can increase the chance that students will find themselves productively invested in current affairs instead of responding to cognitive dissonance with despondency and vapid writing.

4. How will my stylistic choices be understood in today's cultural and literary context?

The culminating process of transference is that students would apply their stylistic awareness to their own writing in relation to a contemporary audience. Obviously, this can be done with a completed text through a style-oriented workshop. But it can also be fruitfully applied to an essay in its early drafting stages. Writing instructors, myself included, typically prompt students to plan the main points of an essay before attempting to generate a complete text. Yet in doing so, we may be subverting deeply ingrained cognitive and creative processes; upon reflection, it seems that in many rhetorical situations, locutors crystallize their stylistic decisions before refining their content. Do we not enter most verbal arguments with a fuller sense of how we feel (and thus our tone) than of exactly what we will say? In the process of crafting written arguments, then, students should be prompted early on to inventory their feelings about their topic and to strategize about ways to channel their feelings into effective stylistic decisions.

Although this iteration of the heuristic is calibrated for first and second year students, it can be adapted for application at various levels of university writing instruction. In an intermediate class in persuasive writing, it could be used to turn a favorite paper from the semester into a capstone project by refining its sense of audience and ethos. In advanced and graduate courses, this heuristic can be introduced early in the semester as a tool to guide the drafting process. I also recommend adapting the level of transparency in one's pedagogy to the students' maturity as writers. Beginning writers may only be able to see in retrospect what they have gained through these guided reading activities, and they may be initially distrustful that discussions of historical conflicts and literary techniques will aid their present efforts. Graduate students, though, should appreciate the opportunity to refine their methodologies and increase awareness of their own metacognition. Finally, this heuristic accommodates adjustment in terms of its scope. It can be used relatively quickly to illuminate students' understanding of one document, or it could be the framework on which scholars conduct a corpus analysis that seeks to catalogue and contextualize the stylistic decisions in an entire body of literature, such as the essays and pamphlets of the American Revolution.

This project aspires to integrate formerly disparate pedagogical approaches. Whereas Milic himself postulated that a different approach to style may be needed for literary analysis and for writing instruction, a large degree of harmony and transference seems possible. The application of the combined reading and writing methodology presented here can help writers mature as they become more eclectic, interdisciplinary, and holistic in their experience of language. Integration—an indispensible step in development—can also help student writers more clearly see their agency as individuals who can contribute to the discourses that shape society.

REFERENCES

Adams, R. M. (1940). Mary Hays, disciple of William Godwin. *PMLA 55*(2), 472-483.

Bloom, B. S. (Ed.). (1956). *Taxonomy of educational objectives* (Vol. 1). New York: Longmans, Green and Co.

Brody, M. (1996). The vindication of the writes of women: Mary Wollstonecraft and enlightenment rhetoric. In M. J. Falco (Ed.), *Feminist interpretations of Mary Wolllstonecraft* (pp. 105-23). University Park, PA: The Pennsylvania State University Press.

Cixous, H. (1976). The laugh of the Medusa. *Signs 1*(4), 875-93.

Foss, S. K., & Griffin, C. L. (1995). Beyond persuasion: A proposal for an invitational rhetoric. *Communications Monographs 62*, 2-18.

Gerhart, S. M. (1979). The womanization of rhetoric. *Women's Studies International Quarterly 2*, 195-201.

Hays, M. (1974). *An appeal to the men of Great Britain in behalf of women*. New York: Garland.

Milic, L. T. (1969). Theories of style and their implications for the teaching of composition. In G. Love & M. Payne (Eds.), *Contemporary essays on style* (pp. 15-21). Glenview, IL: Scott Foresman.

Rogers, K. (1987). The contributions of Mary Hays. *Prose Studies 10*(2), 131-142.

Wollstonecraft, M. (1792/1974). *A vindication of the rights of woman: With strictures on political and moral subjects.* New York: Garland.

Zaido, V. & Leonard, M. (2008). *Laughing with the Medusa: Classical myth and feminist thought.* New York: Oxford University Press.

STYLE AND THE PROFESSIONAL WRITING CURRICULUM: TEACHING STYLISTIC FLUENCY THROUGH SCIENCE WRITING

Jonathan Buehl
Ohio State University

INTRODUCTION

Recent scholarship on style and writing pedagogy suggests that rhetoric's third canon is experiencing a renaissance in composition studies. Anchored by recent monographs (e.g., Butler's *Out of Style,* Holcomb & Killingsworth's *Performing Prose*, and Johnson's *A Rhetoric of Pleasure*), rich collections (e.g., Butler's Bedford/St. Martin's anthology and Johnson & Pace's *Refiguring Prose Style*) and numerous articles, this corpus attempts to reposition *style* as central to the writing process and to writing pedagogy. But this refiguring neglects an important site for style-centered pedagogy—professional writing curricula.[1]

Whether its operating model is the single-shot service course or elective, a minor, a major, or a concentration within a major, a professional writing program should take style seriously. Unfortunately, professional communication texts often present narrow conceptions of professional style. For example, in a study of popular textbooks, Wolfe found that most general technical communication texts prescribe universally avoiding passive voice. For Wolfe, the "injunction against the passive" is a specific disservice to engineering students who will likely write reports requiring passive constructions—traditional markers of scientific styles (2009, pp. 355-358). She concludes, "In place of prescriptive injunctions against particular styles, we need more thorough discussions of the rhetorical considerations that prompt specific language uses" (2009, p. 358).

Empirical studies confirm that responding to variable stylistic demands is an important workplace skill. For example, Angouri and Harwood's case study of style in a multinational consortium indicates that stylistic expectations (e.g., the level of formality) for seemingly standardized documents (e.g., memos and minutes) vary widely, even *within* an organization. They suggest rethinking traditional model-based pedagogy: "Although models can serve valuable awareness-raising purposes, writing teachers need to stress how and why such models may bear scant resemblance to the templates and variations students may encounter on the job" (2008, p. 58). All students must develop a stylistic sensibility if they are to navigate the stylistic variability of professional life; such a sensibility is especially important for students planning careers as communication professionals.

Students planning to compete for jobs as writers and editors must develop stylistic fluency—a meta-mastery of style—if they are to adapt successfully to the rhetorical situations they will face in ever-evolving workplaces. This chapter argues that professional writing students can develop transferable stylistic fluency by engaging style in those rhetorical spaces where science and writing interact. However, using science to teach style requires reimagining how science can fit into writing classes.

When science and writing meet in teaching spaces, the pairing tends to be stylistically monochromatic. Writing courses for future or working scientists focus on technical genres and the conventions of scientific discourse. Writing-intensive science courses also focus on formal stylistic conventions, whether of school genres (e.g., lab reports for canned experiments) or documents supporting novel research (e.g., reports and proposals). Science journalism courses focus on styles of popular accommodation—news reporting, the "gee whiz" style, etc. Finally, science-themed composition classes use science topics when teaching students about general "academic discourse," but those students rarely read or write scientific language (Moscovitz & Kellogg, 2005, p. 311). In short, approaches to science and writing tend to fall on either side of a line between "scientific writing" (or "writing science") and "science writing" (or "writing about science").[2]

I do not catalog these approaches to criticize them. Having taught science-themed sections of first-year composition as well as scientific-writing courses for both fledgling scientists at universities and scientists in industry, I can anecdotally confirm that specific stylistic foci are often required by programmatic mandates or pedagogical objectives. However, some courses and some students require polychromatic approaches to science and style.

Rhetorical situations involving scientific content demand stylistic flexibility. When writing about science, a communication professional might read and write prose in technical, explanatory, and wonder-inducing styles. As a consultant and researcher, I've designed curricula for pharmaceutical companies wanting stylistically consistent reports; I've been tasked with revising grant proposals to make them more compelling; I've created marketing materials for research institutions demanding "punchy," precise prose; and I've written histories of scientific discoveries to support my research on the rhetoric of science. Each of these situations has distinct constraints demanding an adaptable proficiency with prose style. Although most professional-writing students will not choose careers engaging science, they all can benefit from working with its demanding discourses in the context of a course. Moreover, science offers pedagogical benefits.

Science is an ideal conduit for teaching style for three reasons. First, the styles of science communication have been well documented by rhetorical theorists; this foundational work provides conceptual frameworks that support effective teaching. Second, rhetorical situations involving science are stylistically complex. Although discourses of science seem to sort into clear categories of prose style (e.g., technical, explanatory, entertaining), these categories are highly variable (e.g., the "scientific" register differs from field to field and from journal to journal). Therefore, scientific topics are ideal for teaching students how to assess and engage variation within marked styles. Third, scientific discourse is difficult and "strange" for many students—even students in scientific fields. Contrary to conventional wisdom, this strangeness is manageable and advantageous.[3] By reading, writing, and writing about scientific prose, students engage unfamiliar discourse, which encourages them to apply newly learned strategies.

The course described in this chapter capitalizes on the robust base of rhetoric-of-science scholarship, the consistency and variability of the styles of science discourses, and the beneficial difficulty of scientific prose. After explaining the rationale for the course, I summarize its projects and activities and document the merits of specific approaches with student-evaluation comments. Although this course is designed as an upper-level elective, its assignments and strategies might be productive in other contexts; course materials are reproduced in an appendix.

FROM THE RHETORIC OF SCIENCE TO A PEDAGOGY OF STYLE

Our understanding of the macro- and micro-level rhetoric performed in both the genres written for scientists and the various genres "translating" science for non-experts has grown dramatically over the past few decades. Pioneering studies by rhetoricians (e.g., Bazerman; Gross), sociologists (e.g., Latour & Woolgar; Myers), and linguists (e.g., Halliday; Swales) document the historical development, epistemological orientations, and contemporary conventions of technical scientific prose. Theorists have also explicated the rhetorical features of popularizations (e.g., Fahnestock), textbooks (e.g., Martin), and press releases (e.g., Graube et al.).

Although this corpus enhanced our understanding of the discursive activities pervading and surrounding scientific activity, some scholars argue that the relationship between this knowledge and composition curricula is vexed. According to Zerbe, subfields of rhetoric and composition engage science in partial and problematic ways:

> [E]ven when science becomes an area of interest ... rhetoric and composition does not engage science head-on: either scientific discourse itself is ignored in favor of texts that are merely about science, (as is the case with composition and technical communication), or scientific discourse is analyzed but issues of pedagogy, literacy, and culture are disregarded (as is the case with the rhetoric of science). (2007, p. 50)

My course attempts to resolve the "silo" problems Zerbe identifies. It uses the machinery of the rhetoric of science to support a sequence of activities through which students engage—at a professional level—the practical problems of reading and producing both scientific texts and accommodations of science.

Inspired by Fahnestock's observations on the rhetorical distinctions between scientific communication and accommodations of science, my course is structured by the tripartite division of Aristotelian genres (1998, pp. 332-346). It contains a module on technical prose (forensic discourse), a module on writing about science for decision makers (deliberative discourse), and a module on popularizing science (epideictic discourse).[4] In each, students apply rhetorical theory to assess stylistic variety and to produce appropriate prose for stylistically distinct situations.

MODULE 1: THE TECHNICAL PROSE MODULE

In the technical prose module, students learn to assess unfamiliar styles, they learn to recognize features and "problems" of scientific prose, and they practice editing it. The module's major project asks students to comment on research reports by graduate students studying educational psychology. A colleague in that field invites her students to provide papers they plan to revise for publication. These documents are rhetorically flawed; some contain errors associated with learning English as a second language. My students analyze the papers, edit them to conform to a specific journal's style, and compose letters to the authors that explain corrections and recommend more substantive rhetorical revisions.

Published text: "Dam Safety: Problems with Metal Materials"	Text after "plain language" revisions
Corrosion is a common problem for spillway conduits and other metal appurtenances. Corrosion is the deterioration or breakdown of metal because of a reaction with its environment. Exposure to moisture, acidic conditions, or salt will accelerate the corrosion process. Acid runoff from strip-mined areas will cause rapid corrosion of metal conduits. In these areas, conduits made of less corrodible materials such as concrete or plastic should be used. Soil types also factor into the amount of corrosion. Clayey soils can be more corrosive than sandy soils since they are poorly drained and poorly aerated. Silts are somewhere in between clays and sands. Some examples of metal conduits include ductile iron, smooth steel, and corrugated metal. Corrugated metal pipe is not recommended for use in dams since the service life for corrugated metal is only 25 to 30 years, whereas the life expectancy for dams is much longer. In areas of acidic water, the service life can be much less. Therefore, corrugated metal spillway conduits typically need to be repaired or replaced early in the dam's design life, which can be very expensive.	This document explains how to prevent and repair safety problems for dams with metal parts. **How can metal parts cause safety problems?** Metal parts create safety problems when they fail. For example, a compromised spillway conduit can lead to the complete collapse of a dam. **Which metal parts are potential safety risks?** Metal dam parts posing safety risks include spillway conduits made of iron, smooth steel, or corrugated metal. They also include other appurtenances, such as drain valves and sluice gates. All metal parts can be damaged by ***corrosion***. **What is corrosion and what causes it?** Corrosion occurs when metal deteriorates because of a reaction with the environment. Environmental factors that accelerate corrosion include exposure to moisture, salt, or acidic conditions.

Figure 1. Example of revising according to the Federal Plain Language Guidelines produced by the Plain Language Action and Information Network (PLAIN). The source text is a fact sheet authored by the Ohio State Department of Natural Resources. To save space, some topics in the "before" column are not represented in the "revised" column. Although plain-language edits emphasize concision, beneficial design changes (e.g., headings and generous spacing) often increase document length.

To prepare for this assignment, students study rhetorical features of scientific articles, including stylistic features. We discuss grammatical "problems" associated with technical scientific prose, stylistic issues related to writing about numbers, and traditional ESL "trouble spots."[5] Students also learn to assess variation in technical styles through a quantitative norming activity inspired by Leech and Short's work on stylistic norms and Corbett's style exercises from *Classical Rhetoric for the Modern Student* (1990, pp. 404-421).

In the norming activity, students determine the discursive norms of educational psychology journals by coding and counting instances of specific features of scientific prose, such as voice preferences, pronoun use, and the Swalesian structures of introductions.[6] They also identify other features, such as average sentence length, passage length, and information about citations. After accounting for these features in a small set of articles, students use their data to develop style guidelines for their editing project. For example, if quantitative analysis revealed a plethora of personal pronouns—anomalies for "traditional" scientific language—then students could confidently advise their editorial clients that personal pronouns are appropriate. Similarly, if each article contextualizes its research by articulating how it "continues a tradition," then students have data to justify revisions to their clients' introductions. Although this exercise focuses on style in the discourse communities of educational psychology, quantitative norming is a useful tool for any situation in which "outsiders" approach unfamiliar and difficult styles.

Compared to other fields, educational psychology is relatively accessible, but its discourse is initially challenging for students. Once we discuss terms for the features of scientific discourse, most students do reasonably well in diagnosing problems in drafts. For example, Halliday's list of "grammatical problems" in scientific English coupled with Gopen and Swan's discussion of cohesion helps students determine if sentences are confusing because of syntactic, semantic, or pragmatic problems.[7] Once equipped with functional terminologies, students approach this unfamiliar language with greater confidence.

Although difficult, the technical editing project is a crucial first step. Editing for scientific style makes students better readers of technical prose, and they use these reading skills when accommodating scientific texts for other audiences. Student evaluations confirm the importance of the project in the assignment sequence.

Many students mention that the first module was their least favorite, but they appreciated its role. For example, one student wrote "I liked the last [project] the best, but I learned the most from the first one." Another recognized it as a necessary challenge: "Personally, I had the most trouble with the first assignment, but I think it could be argued that it was simply a necessary struggle in learning how to write about science." Yet another student explained how the first module increased scientific literacy: "We started with the hardest assignment first, which taught me how to read science." Indeed, the ability to read difficult technical prose is essential both for other course projects and for science writing generally.

Module 2: The Deliberative Prose Module

In the second module, students learn to describe science for decision makers, and they practice writing both in the "plain language" style and in a more energetic science-marketing style. They produce two related documents: a memo for a legislative official and a marketing brochure describing the same research. In completing both projects, students translate material from a scientific style into a plain style and from a plain style into a more ornate style.

Plain styles have a long and complex history in the rhetorical tradition and in contemporary culture. (See Kurlinkus and Bacon, respectively, in this volume.) Certainly, composition teachers must be wary of venerating some version of the "plain style" as the ultimate or primary goal of writing courses. Nonetheless, plain styles offer both rhetorical and pedagogical affordances. Sometimes, a plain style is the right tool for a task; it can also help students to notice differences between styles. For example, students can easily recognize the differences between scientific prose and the "plain language" style.

What I describe as the "plain language" style is the style advocated for in the *Federal Plain Language Guidelines,* a document produced to help Federal employees produce more accessible documents. This plain style does stress writing precise and concise sentences in audience-appropriate vocabulary, but it also emphasizes the importance of rhetorical arrangement and good document design. My students apply these principles in their legislative memo assignment.

In the memo assignment (a.k.a. "Defending Your Earmark"), each student is assigned an article by an OSU professor and asked to imagine that earmarked funding for the project has been scrutinized publically. The earmark's legislative sponsors need "plain language" summaries they can use to generate talking points to support the research. To prepare the students for science in plain language, we first discuss occasions where plain language descriptions are necessary. Specifically, we read case studies describing ethical, administrative, and political issues that arise when science enters deliberative spaces.[8] The students also practice translating technical texts into "plain language" by revising overly technical fact sheets distributed by a state agency. Figure 1 presents part of one of these sheets—a document on dam safety. The published text (left column) meets one prescription of the *Federal Plain Language Guidelines*: "use short sentences." However, it also suffers many of the problems that students must learn to recognize when revising for "plain language." The revised text (right column) reflects "plain language" advice for audience (e.g., "identify and write your audience"), structure (e.g., "organize for the reader's needs," "use lots of headings"), paragraphing (e.g., "cover only one topic in each paragraph"), and grammar (e.g., "prefer the active voice," "don't turn verbs into nouns"). Typically, students do well in revising for sentence length and voice, but they struggle with revising nominalized actions and organization. The revision exercise gives me an opportunity to comment on students' facility with these skills before they develop their memos.

In the second graded assignment for Module Two (the science marketing brochure), students work in groups to create documents about interdisciplinary research areas (e.g., music cognition) that the University's Office of Research could use in its development activities. The groups write about the research described in the "Defending Your Earmark" memos, but they must transform four one-page plain-language documents into two and a half pages of exciting prose.

This assignment's rhetorical situation mimics a project I consulted on for a different institution. A program executive wanted a library of one-page "abstracts" to take to meetings with agency officials, foundation executives, legislative directors, or other decision makers needing succinct but inspiring summaries of the institution's capabilities. Each abstract was to describe an emerging area of interdisciplinary research (such as nanotechnology) and to demonstrate the institution's expertise in that area by summarizing the research agendas of several scientists. Although described as "technical abstracts," the promotional purpose of the documents demanded a promotional style. Indeed, the initial efforts of my co-consultants were sent back for revisions because they "read like boring magazine articles" and "were not 'punchy' enough."

To prepare students for the brochure assignment, we discuss strategies for describing processes (e.g., Johnson's nested "black box" technique [134-135]), tactics of definition (categorical, partition, example, etc.), and tools for controlling sentence rhythm through alliteration, parallelism, and various types of phrasal modification. Students then practice developing compressed, evocative descriptions by producing profiles of rocks displayed in the University's geology museum.

The "writing about rocks" exercise begins with physical descriptions. The class visits the museum, and each student gathers details about the appearance of a rock. After drafting a description at the site, they return to the classroom and research the chemistry, the formation, and the historical, cultural, or industrial significance of the rock. They then revise their initial descriptions into profiles appropriate for an institutional newsletter.

The process of describing the visible features of the rocks leads students to generate evocative similes quickly; for example, "Dioptase is rough-looking, like sparkly green dried-out sea coral or a mass of green candy Pop Rocks." This practice with physical comparisons ties into deeper discussions of other figures of comparison, such as analogy and metaphor.[9]

Ken Baake's *Metaphor and Knowledge: The Challenges of Writing Science* offers precise, productive descriptions of how metaphors work, how they work in science, and which other figures of comparison offer alternatives to metaphor (2003, pp. 62-78). Such theorized descriptions offer a vital grounding in the figures of comparison.

Figures of comparison are essential tools for science writers because these authors often describe unfamiliar objects. For example, in the following passage, Stacey Burling uses both simile and metaphor to describe images of a brain destroyed by Alzheimer's disease:

> What struck [the Alzheimer's researcher] right away was what was not there. Slides from a normal brain would be solid pink. Many of these were dappled with white spots that made them look like slices of baby Swiss or leaves eaten down to the veins. The white holes were the abandoned homes of dead cells. (2007, p. 118)

After discussing the uses of simple figurative comparisons, we discuss how these figures can introduce ambiguities or create inaccurate associations. For example, we discuss a press release whose metaphoric title—"A Dinosaur Dance Floor"—originated in comments by a paleontologist when she discovered a site containing hundreds of overlapping dinosaur tracks from multiple species:

> Get out there and try stepping in their footsteps, and you feel like you are playing the game 'Dance Dance Revolution' that teenagers dance on," says Marjorie Chan, professor and chair of geology and geophysics at the University of Utah. "This kind of reminded me of that—a dinosaur dance floor—because there are so many tracks and a variety of different tracks."
>
> "There must have been more than one kind of dinosaur there," she adds. "It was a place that attracted a crowd, kind of like a dance floor."

In discussing the "dinosaur dance floor," students tease out the implications of the analogy. Clearly, mappings between the domains of human and dinosaur activity were at work as Chan thought about the site, and the phrase "dinosaur dance floor" is certainly evocative. However, "dance floor" might generate images of behavior unlikely to have occurred at the site; i.e., the dinosaurs were not actually *dancing* around the watering hole that attracted them. Also, as some students have noted, dancing often has romantic implications, which may or may not pertain to this situation.

Although an imprecise figurative description of dinosaur behavior might not represent a major ethical concern, the example helps to transition the discussion to cases where imprecise metaphors could have greater consequences. Accompanying a discussion of comparative figures with Ceccarelli's study on mixed metaphors in descriptions of genomic science helps students understand the stakes of using metaphoric language that is both productive and partial. We continue to discuss the benefits and ethical implications of figural language in the third module on popularizations of science.

Student comments on open-ended prompts often focus on two aspects of the second module: writing in groups and practicing concise description. Although many students dislike writing in groups—and vent that frustration in evaluations—it is an important skill to practice. And some students found the team-developed brochure to be the most useful assignment. According to one, "The group brochure assignment was the most helpful because it got us working in an interdisciplinary fashion." Other students have appreciated the scaffolding assignments for this module. For example, one student wrote, "The [activities] that taught me the most about concision while still being descriptive were the writing about rocks and instructions assignments."

MODULE 3: EPIDEICTIC POPULARIZATIONS OF SCIENCE

In the third module, students produce popularizations of scientific topics. Each student must choose a publication venue and assess the typical stylistic features of its articles. After locating story ideas and assessing potential venues, students prepare "pitch" proposals, which I must approve before they write their stories.

To prepare for this assignment, we discuss a range of popular accommodation styles—polemical essays, "gee whiz" science writing, health writing, broadcast styles, and science on the Web. Students also practice stylistic assessment by comparing many months' worth of science features from our local paper—*The Columbus Dispatch*. When examining all of these examples, we discuss the rhetorical features of popular science, tactics for creating compelling introductions, narrative structure, aspects of explanatory and contextualizing visuals, and rhetorical figures beyond metaphors and similes. Learning about rhetorical figures is especially important because these devices help students gain control over style at the phrase and sentence level.

An upper-division science-writing course is an ideal place to teach students about figural language because of the consistency with which rhetorical figures appear in science communication. As Fahnestock has shown, rhetorical figures function as inventional resources in primary science communication (*Rhetorical Figures in Science*), and figural patterns persist when science is translated for non-experts ("Preserving the Figure"). Moreover, popular science articles provide clear and provocative examples of a host of rhetorical figures.

In my class, we spend half a session discussing the figural resources deployed in just the titles of *Dispatch* science columns. These titles serve as examples that help students learn to identify both specific figures as well as broader patterns of figuration in a specific publication. For example, our discussions have revealed that *Dispatch* authors tend to use titles with alliterative phrasing (e.g., "Aid, Abet, Achoo," "A Mollusk Mystery," "Royal Research"), rhetorical questions (e.g., "Have You Seen This Frog?"; "Can Animals Be Gay?"), and various substitutions involving movie titles and other cultural allusions (e.g., "When Silkworm Met Spider," "Magma P.I."). Less frequently deployed figures include antitheses (e.g., "Shrinking Glaciers, Rising Oceans"), analogies (e.g., "Toxic Soup"), and even rhymes forced through intentional error (e.g., "Boxes of Rockses"). (Additional examples are available online via the *Dispatch's* "Science Pages" archives.) For their final projects, some students choose to write *Dispatch*-style pieces, and they tend to appropriate the figural markings of the style effectively. For example, a student paper about the rapid shrinking and projected demise of the star Betelgeuse was punningly titled "The Life and Death of a Super Star."

Practicing with rhetorical figures gives students more than strategies for generating clever titles. For example, figures used in creating and managing lists are important sentence- and paragraph-level resources. By discussing and experimenting with asyndeton and polysyndeton along with incrementum, gradatio, and lists seeming to lack any trajectory, students learn about the conceptual and rhythmic consequences of listing. For example, in the following sentence describing an Alzheimer's patient, Stacey Burling controls sentence rhythm through nested lists, parallelism, and conjunction:

> Here was the essence of a man who had gone to Yale, loved a woman, fathered six children, loved ice cream and Mozart and e. e. cummings, favored questions over answers and change over complacency, hated camping, loathed golf, and,

over the last 20 years, had slowly lost the capacity to understand any of it. (2007, p. 106)

Similarly, Matthew Chapman's polemical account of the *Kitzmiller v. Dover Area School District* case is a rich source for rhetorical lists. In describing stakeholders in this debate over teaching Intelligent Design, the author often deploys figurally-managed series. For example, the following polysyndetonic list emphasizes why Dover's curriculum-committee chair was unqualified to make curricular decisions: "The chair of the curriculum committee was Bill Buckingham, an ex-cop and corrections officer and self-confessed OxyContin addict" (Chapman, 2007, p. 160). As the module progresses, we move from identifying such stylistic devices to imitation and production.

The popularization assignment offers productive opportunities for imitating strong styles through short exercises and more elaborate activities. In one exercise, students identify noteworthy passages from our reading and use them as structural models for their own paragraphs. Longer modeling exercises include an in-class exercise in which students draft seven different introductions in thirty-five minutes. This activity generates much useful material, and student comments suggest that the exercise is productive. For example, one student mentioned that "the multiple introduction activity was particularly effective for me; it really helped my project along." Many students recounted similar experiences. Both of these modeling exercises are reproduced in the appendix.

Overall, student comments about the third module have been extremely positive. Students appreciate getting to choose the scientific topics they write about. They also appreciate how earlier assignments build up to the popularization article. One student noted, "The third assignment was the most exciting, but all of the assignments played a role in helping prepare for the final module."

CONCLUSION

In "Science Communication in the First-Year Writing Course," Moscovitz and Kellogg argue that scientific documents—what they call "primary science communication" or PSC—can be included successfully as readings in FYC courses. After making the case for the pedagogical value of PSC in first-year curricula, they address four counterarguments: 1) Including PSC overspecializes the composition classroom and emphasizes skills that might not transfer to other contexts, such as humanities courses; 2) PSC resists standardized programmatic frameworks—the rhetorical vocabularies grounding most FYC curricula; 3)

PSC is just too difficult to read; and 4) PSC readings will not interest students as much as readings from popular culture or humanities fields (2005, pp. 311—319). Moscovitz and Kellogg convincingly refute each argument; in concluding this chapter, I repurpose their refutations to reinforce the claim that an upper-level course engaging scientific discourse is an ideal site for teaching style.

First, transfer is a problem for any course, but good teachers can use specialized content to teach transferable skills. Although Moscovitz and Kellogg are concerned with the transferability of *reading* scientific discourse, this argument is also valid for *writing* it. Writing (about) scientific discourse provides students with opportunities to practice strategies—such as quantitative norming and structural imitation—which they can use when approaching any style. Moreover, by producing prose for diverse, stylistically distinct purposes, students are better prepared for the diverse communication tasks they will tackle in future positions. Finally, students themselves recognize that the skills they learned while engaging science and style are both specific and transferable. For example, one student mentioned that "Plain language style is useful in the humanities as well as scientific disciplines." Another noted, "I never really write much about science, so [the course] helped me branch out; it also taught me valuable non-fiction [writing] skills."

Second, rhetorical theory is robust enough to handle science. Rhetoricians have spent decades analyzing scientific rhetorical situations, and their projects are easily adapted for style-centered composition courses. Aristotelian genre categories and rhetorical figures are but two of the resources from rhetorical theory that help students understand style at the macro- and micro-scale. Terms typically used in FYC—such as ethos, pathos, and logos—are easily extended to discussions of both scientific writing and popularizations of science. For example, Prelli's accessible discussion of scientific ethos demonstrates how this familiar concept works in scientific situations (1997, p. 87-104).

Once equipped with enhanced rhetorical vocabularies, students can approach scientific discourse with confidence, and they recognize the power of these conceptual systems. When asked to describe how the course made students better writers, one student wrote that his or her writing skills had been improved by "the rhetorical tools I learned, as well as learning about problems like lexical density and syntactic ambiguity." Although recalling sophisticated stylistic vocabulary in a course evaluation does not demonstrate stylistic proficiency, it does indicate that this student gained a more nuanced understanding of issues affecting prose style.

Third, the difficulty of scientific discourse is overstated; difficult texts are good for teaching. Both Moscovitz and Kellogg and Michael Zerbe note that "impossible" scientific jargon is no more difficult than other advanced vocabularies we expect students to learn and use. For Zerbe, even the "language" of statistics can be productively encountered in composition classrooms through rhetorical vocabularies: "Statistics are essentially equivalent to Toulminian warrants in a text" (2007, p. 49). Indeed, I have found that Toulmin's framework helps students approach the rhetoric of numbers. Material from number-minded style guides (e.g., Miller's *Chicago Guide to Writing about Numbers*) can also help students compose texts engaging statistical concepts.

In short, students can learn to approach and use strange styles. Scaffolding assignments provide students with the tools and the practice they need to engage difficult texts in longer assignments. Evaluation comments suggest that students appreciate such sequencing. One student noted, "The short assignments helped pave the way for the more difficult projects." Another noted that scaffolding assignments made the larger assignments "less daunting." Moreover, students see the value in working with difficult discourse. One student commented, "The course pushed me to write about the unfamiliar."

Finally, students *are* interested in science. According to Moscovitz and Kellogg, many FYC students are highly interested in scientific topics, and we should capitalize on that interest (2005, p. 319). Similarly, many students take my course because they like science and want to write about it. Even those students who only take my class to satisfy an elective in our professional-writing minor tend to find the material on style engaging. By directing either their interests in science toward style or their interests in style toward science, the course helps students develop stylistic proficiencies, making them more effective communicators and more marketable professionals.

NOTES

1. I use an expansive definition of professional writing: Any workplace writing. Professional-writing courses include courses teaching general workplace literacies (such as "service" courses called "business writing" or "technical writing") and courses for students planning careers as technical writers, communications officers, etc.

2. Although some excellent scientific writing textbooks include material on accommodating science for non-experts, typically that material plays second fiddle to technical prose. For example, Penrose and Katz significantly expanded *Writing in the Sciences* for the third edition, but they did not expand the chapter on accommodation. Moreover, a chapter on procedures in the second edition was cut for the third, reducing the number of marked styles treated in the book. Thus, the third edition is even more focused on teaching research genres to upper-level science students—a purpose announced in its preface (2004, p. xiv). Similarly, good writing-about-science guides neglect technical

prose. For example, *A Field Guide for Science Writers*—required reading in my course—offers good advice on science journalism, including advice on how to read scientific articles when reporting on them (see Siegfried, 2006, pp. 11-17). However, it does not discuss producing or revising "technical" genres.

3. One argument against teaching scientific discourse to "general" composition students is that scientific prose is notoriously difficult for non-experts (Moscovitz & Kellogg, 2005, pp. 317-318). The "science is too hard" claim is refutable. Moscovitz and Kellogg argue that the difficulty is overstated, and they point to examples of accessible technical documents that FYC students can read (2005, p. 307). They also provide criteria for selecting accessible texts (2005, p. 322). Alternatively, the "difficulty problem" can be reframed as a pedagogical virtue. For Kelley and Bazerman, the "very strangeness" of scientific discourse "makes easier the task of explicitly introducing the genre conventions, social practices, and linguistic features of scientific texts" (as quoted in Moscovitz and Kellogg, 2005, p. 317).

4. In "Accommodating Science: The Rhetorical Life of Scientific Facts," Fahnestock uses classical and contemporary rhetorics to account for the metamorphoses that occur when writers adapt scientific content for popularizations. She demonstrates that genre shifts (from forensic to epideictic), stasis shifts (from fact to value), and modality shifts (from hedged claims to assertive or highly conjectural statements) are consistent transformations with clearly identifiable markings (1998, pp. 332-346). Fahnestock does not address deliberative discourse in her article on epideictic popularizations; however, science does generate deliberative situations with specific stylistic demands.

5. Scientists whose first language is not English often hire editors; therefore, consultants should understand how to respond to ESL "errors." In my experience, however, the most significant problems of scientists who struggle with writing are rhetorical rather than grammatical—regardless of when they learned English.

6. Swales' work on research articles classifies consistent rhetorical moves used to contextualize research. In early work (1981), he marked these moves with just a numerical scheme: move 1) establish the topic and significance, move 2) review previous research, move 3) establish a gap in the research, and move 4) explain how the article fills the gap. Later (1990), Swales developed an ecological analogy for what he relabeled the Create a Research Space (CARS) model: move 1) identify the territory, move 2) identify a niche within the territory, move 3) occupy the niche. Each move is comprised of a set of variable, context-dependent steps (1990, pp. 140-143). Researchers have used both schemes when analyzing discursive norms.

7. Halliday identifies seven features contributing to the difficulty of scientific prose: interlocking definitions, technical taxonomies, special expressions, lexical density, syntactic ambiguity, grammatical metaphor, and semantic discontinuity (1993, p. 71). Gopen and Swan apply Joseph Williams's advice on style to scientific writing (1990, pp. 550-558).

8. These case studies have served as provocative readings: Schoenfeld's "The Press and NEPA," Scott's "Limiting Prevention, Limiting Topos," Wadell's "The Role of Pathos in the Decision-Making Process," and West's "How Not to Publicize Research."

9. For compelling arguments for teaching metaphor and analogy in technical communication courses, see Giles (2008) and Graves (2005).

REFERENCES

Angouri, J. and Nigel Harwood, N. (2008). This is too formal for us…: A case study of variation in the written products of a multinational consortium. *Journal of Business and Technical Communication 22*(1), 38-64.

Bazerman, C. (1988). *Shaping written knowledge.* Madison, WI: University of Wisconsin Press.

Baake, K. (2003). *Metaphor and knowledge: The challenges of writing science.* Albany, NY: SUNY Press.

Bloom, D., Mary Knudson, M., & Marantz-Henig, R. (Eds.). *A field guide for science writers.* Oxford University Press.

Butler, P. (2008). *Out of style: Reanimating stylistics in composition and rhetoric.* Logan: Utah State University Press.

Butler, P. (2010). (Ed.). *Style in rhetoric and composition: A critical sourcebook.* New York: Bedford/St. Martin's.

Burling, S. (2007). Probing the mind for a cure. In G. Kolata (Ed.), *The best American science writing of 2007* (pp. 106-120). New York: Harper Collins.

Ceccarelli, L. (2004). Neither confusing cacophony nor culinary complements. *Written Communication 21*, 92-105.

Chapman, M. (2007). God or gorilla. In G. Kolata (Ed.), *The best American science writing of 2007* (pp. 158-185). New York: Harper Collins.

Corbett, E. P. J. (1990). *Classical rhetoric for the modern student* (3rd ed.). Oxford University Press.

A dinosaur dance floor. (n.d.). Eurekalert.org.

Dostal, E. (2009, August 2). When toads collide. *The Columbus Dispatch.* Retrieved from http://www.dispatch.com/content/stories/science/2009/08/02/sci_toadtoes.ART_ART_08-02-09_G3_HDEKORN.html

Fahnestock, J. (1998). Accommodating science: The rhetorical life of scientific facts. *Written Communication 15*, 331-349.

Fahnestock, J. (1999). *Rhetorical figures in science.* New York: Oxford University Press.

Fahnestock, J. (2004). Preserving the figure: Consistency in the presentation of scientific arguments. *Written Communication 21*, 6-31.

Federal Plain Language Guidelines. (2010). Plain Language Action and Information Network. Retreived from http://plainlanguage.gov.

Ferenchik, M. (2010, January 10). New dimensions. *The Columbus Dispatch.* Retrieved from http://www.dispatch.com/content/stories/science/2010/01/10/sci_threedcam.ART_ART_01-10-10_G3_P3G7TMC.html

Giles, T. (2008). *Motives for metaphor in scientific and technical communication.* Amityville, NY: Baywood.

Gopen, G., & Swan, J. (1990). The science of scientific writing. *American Scientist 78,* 550-558. Retrieved from http://www.americanscientist.org/issues/pub/the-science-of-scientific-writing/

Graves, H. (2005). *Rhetoric in(to) style: Style as invention in inquiry.* Cresskill, NJ: Hampton Press.

Gross, A. (1990). *Rhetoric of science.* Cambridge: Harvard University Press.

Graube, M., Clark, F, & Illman, D. (2010). Coverage of team science by public information officers: Content analysis of press releases about the national science foundation science and technology centers. *Journal of Technical Writing and Communication 40*(2), 143-159.

Harris, R. A. (Ed.). (1997). *Landmark essays on the rhetoric of science.* Mahwah, NJ: Lawrence Erlbaum Associates.

Halliday, M. A. K. (1993). Some grammatical problems of scientific English. In M. A. K. Halliday, & J. R. Martin (Eds.), *Writing science: Literacy and discursive power* (pp. 69-85). Pittsburgh: University of Pittsburgh Press.

Halliday, M. A. K. & Martin, J. R. (Eds.). (1993). *Writing science: Literacy and discursive power.* Pittsburgh: University of Pittsburgh Press.

Holcomb, C., & Killingsworth, M. J. (2010). *Performing prose: The study and practice of style in composition.* Carbondale, IL: Southern Illinois University Press.

Hunt, S. (2009, September 27). A legacy preserved. *The Columbus Dispatch.* Retrieved from http://www.dispatch.com/content/stories/science/2009/09/27/sci_berra.ART_ART_09-27-09_G1_3RF66LD.html

Hunt, S. (2009, October 18). Visitors or residents? *The Columbus Dispatch.* Retrieved from http://www.dispatch.com/content/stories/science/2009/10/16/invasive_insects.html

Johnson, G. (2006). Explanatory writing. In D. Bloom, M. Knudson, & R. Marantz-Henig (Eds.), *A field guide for science writers* (pp. 132-137). New York: Oxford University Press.

Johnson, T. R. (2003). *A rhetoric of pleasure: Prose style in today's composition classroom.* Portsmouth, NH: Boynton/Cook.

Johnson, T. R., & Pace, T. (Eds.). (2005). *Refiguring prose style: Possibilities for writing studies.* Logan, UT: Utah State University Press.

Kolata, G. (Ed.). (2007). *The best American science writing of 2007*. New York: Harper Collins.

Latour, B., & Woolgar, S. (1986). *Laboratory life*. Princeton, NJ: Princeton University Press.

Leech, G., & Short, S. (1982). *Style in Fiction: A linguistic approach to english fictional prose*. New York: Longman.

Martin, J. R. (1993). Literacy in Science: Learning to handle text as a technology. In M. A. K. Halliday, & J. R. Martin (Eds.), *Writing science: Literacy and discursive power* (pp. 166-202). Pittsburgh: University of Pittsburgh Press.

Miller, J. (2004). *The Chicago guide to writing about numbers*. Chicago: University of Chicago Press.

Moskovitz, C., & Kellogg, D. (2005). Communication in the first-year writing course. *College Composition and Communication 57*(2), 307-334.

Myers, G. (1990). *Writing biology: Texts in the social construction of scientific knowledge*. Madison, WI: University of Wisconsin Press.

The Ohio Department of Natural Resource; Division of Soil and Water Resources. (2001, March 24). Dam safety: Problems with metal materials. Retrieved from http://www.dnr.state.oh.us/water/pubs/fs_div/fctsht57/tabid/4144/Default.aspx

Penrose, A., & Katz, S. (2004). *Writing in the Sciences: Exploring the conventions of scientific discourse* (2nd ed.). New York: Pearson.

Penrose, A., & Katz, S. (2010). *Writing in the sciences: Exploring the Conventions of scientific discourse* (3rd ed.). New York: Pearson.

Perry, M. (2006, March). Health secrets from the morgue. *Men's Health 13*. Retrieved from http://www.menshealth.com/health/health-secrets-morgue

Prelli, L. (1997). The rhetorical construction of scientific ethos. In R. A. Harris (Ed.), *Landmark Essays on the rhetoric of science* (pp. 87-106). Mahwah, New Jersey: Lawrence Erlbaum Associates.

Schoenfeld, A. C. (1979). The press and NEPA. The case of the missing agenda. *Journalism Quarterly 56*(3), 577-586.

Science pages from 2010. (December 2010). *The Columbus Dispatch*. Retrieved from http://www.dispatch.com

Scott, J. B. (2008). Limiting prevention, Limiting topos: Reframing arguments about science and politics in the HIV prevention policy debate. n D. IZarefsky, & E. Benacka (Eds.), *Sizing up rhetoric* (pp. 273-284). Long Grove, IL:Waveland Press.

Siegfried, T. (2006). Reporting from science journals. In D. Bloom, M. Knudson, & R. Marantz-Henig (Eds.), *A field guide for science writers* (pp. 11-17). New York: Oxford University Press.

Somerson, M. (2009, December 28). Get your 2009 Dispatch science pages here! *The Columbus Dispatch*. Retrieved from http://www.dispatch.com/content/blogs/science-environment/2009/12/get_your_2009_dispatch_science.html

Swales, J. (1990). *Genre analysis: English in academic and research settings*. Cambridge, UK: Cambridge University Press.

Swales, J. (1981). *Aspects of article introductions*. Birmingham, UK: University of Aston Press.

Wadell, C. (1997). The role of pathos in the decision-making process: A study in the rhetoric of science policy. In R. A. Harris (Ed.), *Landmark essays on the rhetoric of science* (pp. 127-150). Mahwah, NJ: Lawrence Erlbaum Associates.

West, L. J. (1986). How Not to Publicize Research: The UCLA Violence Center. In J. Goldstein (Ed.), *Reporting Science: The Case of Aggression* (pp. 33-41). Mahwah, New Jersey: Lawrence Erlbaum.

Wolfe, J. (2009). How technical communication textbooks fail engineering students. *Technical Communication Quarterly 18*(4), 351-375.

Zerbe, M. (2007). *Composition and the rhetoric of science: Engaging the dominant discourse*. Carbondale, IL: Southern Illinois University Press.

APPENDIX: COURSE MATERIALS ORGANIZED BY MODULE

This appendix contains assignment sheets and exercises. Some details, such as due dates and grading criteria, have been removed.

MODULE 1: ASSESSING AND REVISING TECHNICAL SCIENTIFIC PROSE

Science-writing professionals are often asked to revise articles, proposals, or other formal scientific documents written by and for experts even though they are not experts on the scientific content. Such tasks might seem difficult; however, research from the fields of rhetoric, writing studies, applied linguistics, and technical communication provides concepts and tools that help writers approach scientific texts successfully.

For this assignment, you will critique a draft of a research report written by an advanced graduate student in the field of educational psychology. The author plans to revise the paper for publication. Your assessment and revision of the document should guide the author in producing a more effective submission.

Objectives

In completing this assignment you will …
- Become familiar with communication practices in science
- Become familiar with conventions of scientific prose
- Practice analyzing variations in technical scientific prose
- Practice writing about technical scientific prose
- Practice revising technical scientific prose

Deliverables Description

You will (1) produce an editorial critique in the form of a letter and (2) produce an electronic revision of the author's draft.

We will discuss how to track your changes to the draft. You do not have to make the revised draft perfect, but you should demonstrate how the author could fix the most significant problems. Comments can include questions.

When planning, drafting, and revising the letter, consider the following items:

Audience
The audience is a graduate student in the field of educational psychology. This person is accustomed to reading documents in this field; however, he or she may not have any formal training in scientific writing. You may need to explain the rationale behind some of your comments and revisions.

Purpose
Your letter should provide a candid assessment of the author's draft and offer sound revision advice.

Your revision should identify problems in the text. Show how you fixed them or why you couldn't fix them.

Constraints
Your document must be at least four but no more than eight full pages, double-spaced. Maintain a courteous and professional tone; criticism should be constructive, and not nasty.

Components
Your critique should mention aspects of the text that are working well and draw attention to pressing problems. You might include comments on global rhetorical concerns (e.g., addressing the journal's audience appropriately, establishing exigence, etc.), genre concerns (e.g., using sources rhetorically, adhering to the IMRAD form, etc.), or stylistic concerns (e.g., tense, voice, hedging language, etc.).

Exercise 1: Article Analysis

For this exercise, you will analyze a research report to determine its structural and stylistic features. In the next exercise, the "journal analysis," you will work in groups to synthesize your findings. I will provide details for the "journal analysis" on another sheet.

Further Detail

Our clients for Assignment 1 are not sure which journals are right for their pieces. For example, the author of Document 1 is not sure if *The Journal of Experimental Education* or *Educational and Psychological Measurement* is the right venue.

To determine the best venue and to guide revision, we need to gather information from articles in these journals. This data will help us determine the rhetorical norms of the publication.

To distribute data collection, I've created groups based on the documents you were assigned for Assignment 1. Each group will work on a different journal; each member should analyze an article from a <u>different issue</u> of the journal. Choose issues from the last two years.

Getting Started

Follow the steps described below. Record your findings. Bring an electronic copy of your data DD/MM.

Steps

To complete the article analysis, complete the following steps:
1. Confer with your group; each person should select a different issue of the journal.
2. Select an article from your issue. The article should be an IMRAD article, NOT a literature review or letter. If you are unsure if the article is appropriate, ask me.
3. Title and abstract.
    How long is the title?
    How specific is the title?
    How many sentences are in the abstract?
    Tip: Use the "word count" tool in Word. You can copy and paste sections of text from Acrobat to Word.
4. Introduction.
    Label segments of the introduction according to the "four moves" model. What is the sequence of moves?

Label segments of the introduction according to the CARS "moves and steps" model. Which step does the author use to "establish a niche" for his or her work?

How long is the "literature review" section of the introduction? (word count)

Tip: There may not be a specific heading of "literature review," so pay close attention to where summarizing ends and "occupying the niche" begins.

How many citations are in the introduction?

Determine the tense of the main verb in each sentence. Tally each tense.

5. Methods.

    List this section's subheadings.

    Determine the voice for each main verb. How many are active? How many are passive?

6. Results.

    Are the results purely descriptive?

    Are other rhetorical activities occurring? Use Thompson's list (125) to label and count any other "moves."

    How many visuals are included?

    How many are graphs?

    How many are tables?

    How long are the table and figure captions? (word count)

7. Discussion.

    What strategies are used to qualify certainty? Keep a tally for modal auxiliaries, hedging verbs, and hedging adjectives and adverbs.

    Are limitations discussed? (Y/N)

    How many sentences are used to describe limitations?

8. Personal pronouns and self reference.

    How many times do "I" and "we" appear in the text?

    Are authors ever referred to as "the author" or "the authors?"

    Tip: Using the "find" feature in Word or Acrobat can expedite this step.

Exercise 2: Journal Analysis/Style Guide

For the previous exercise, you collected information about a journal article. In this exercise, you will synthesize your findings with those of your groupmates to create a style sheet for its journal.

You will have class time to collate/compare your data. I will provide an Excel file to organize your findings. Submit <u>one</u> document for your group.

Further Detail

Imagine you are a managing editor who assigns projects to consultants. To help your consultants "get a fix" on new projects quickly, you provide short overviews of publications. You need to create such an overview for your group's educational psychology journal.

Consider what your consultants need to know about the audience, style, and structure of research reports <u>in this particular journal</u>. For example, if your group did not find any first-person pronouns (I, we, etc.), you should create a tip about avoiding them.

MODULE 2: SUMMARIZING SCIENCE FOR DECISION MAKERS

In the first module, we examined how science is communicated to experts through the genres of research reports and proposals. In this module, you will study issues related to communicating science to non-expert decision makers by creating documents for two different audiences and two different purposes.

First, you will summarize a research project for a government official who needs to justify its funding. Second, you will work in groups to produce a brochure promoting the unique capabilities of a research group at OSU. In both documents, you will write about cognitive science.

Project Objectives

In completing this assignment you will ...
- Practice writing about science for decision-making audiences
- Practice writing about complicated topics in short documents
- Practice writing explanatory materials to support political deliberation
- Practice writing marketing materials for an organization
- Practice developing definitions and descriptions
- Practice creating analogies and metaphors

Part I: Executive or Legislative Summary (a.k.a. "Defending your Earmark")

Legislators and executives often need information about research to guide policy decisions. In other cases, they need summaries of research to support or oppose its funding.

Many scientists rely on government money. Sometimes money comes from grants, and sometimes it comes from congressional earmarks. In either case, officials are often held accountable for these expenditures.

When denouncing earmark abuse in 2008, John McCain pointed to a scientific example: "Three million to study the DNA of bears in Montana. Unbelievable." In an interview with Sarah Palin, ABC anchor Charles Gibson raised similar points about research funding in Alaska: "Governor, this year, [Alaska] requested $3.2 million for researching the genetics of harbor seals, [and] money to study the mating habits of crabs. Isn't that exactly the kind of thing that John McCain is objecting to?" In these cases, earmarks were supporting worthy research with practical benefits, but the projects were portrayed as wasteful.

In this assignment you will summarize a recent OSU research project for a public official and his or her staff. Imagine that the official supported an earmark for the project and must now justify the expenditure as valuable and necessary. This official needs information to respond to claims that the project squandered taxpayer money.

Deliverable Description
Audience
Your audience consists of elected officials and political staffers. These readers probably have limited knowledge of cognitive science.

Purpose
You need to provide a clear assessment of the project and its benefits. Your document should succinctly summarize the research project and explain why it deserved funding.

Constraints
Your readers are very busy. They need a short description, no longer than one single-spaced page. The memo should be written in "plain language" style.

Components
Include a description of the study for a non-expert audience. Then, explain how the research contributes to the advancement of science and/or how it will lead to useful applications or social improvements.

Part II: Thematic Abstract/Marketing Brochure

Because scientific research can be extremely expensive, research universities like Ohio State provide resources to help faculty secure funding. The "business" of this research support is complex. Research officials often communicate directly with funding organizations to help define RFP requirements, to develop new support lines, or to coordinate the needs of funding organizations with those of researchers. These officials often need "marketing" literature to support their efforts.

For the second Module 2 project, you will work in groups to produce marketing materials for OSU's research development office. You will condense and energize your summaries from Part I to create a two-page research brochure.

The document must demonstrate the capabilities of OSU researchers in a specific area of cognitive science, and it must communicate the significance of this work in a descriptive and engaging style.

Deliverable Description
Audience and Purpose

Your audience is comprised of <u>intelligent non-experts</u>. Although these readers are not specialists, they regularly read accounts of scientific subjects accommodated to their non-expert level.

Your document will <u>support marketing and development activities</u> by succinctly describing the University's research capabilities. For example, a program officer might take it to meetings with <u>agency officials</u>, <u>legislative directors</u>, or other <u>decision makers</u>.

The document should convey that this research is exciting and important.

Constraints

The document must fit on two and a half pages (single spaced). The prose should be accurate but written in an engaging style that emphasizes the <u>novelty</u> and <u>uniqueness</u> of the research.

Components

Introduction: The introductory paragraphs should indicate a clear exigence for the research area. Describe the problems approached and solved. Demonstrate why the work is important. Who are the stakeholders? What is at stake?

Preview sentences: After the introduction, write a one- or two-sentence preview of each profile.

Profiles: Profile titles should be descriptive, accessible, and interesting. Each research profile should be composed of two to four short paragraphs. Establish <u>exigence</u> as soon as possible. Introduce the researcher. Describe the <u>problems</u> the researcher is solving. Define significant unfamiliar terms. Explain why the research is <u>unique</u>, <u>amazing</u>, <u>a significant advancement</u>, etc. Explain important <u>applications</u>. End each profile with the names and email addresses of the researchers.

Exercise 3: Writing in Plain Language

In this exercise you will practice editing for the "plain language" style by revising a policy document communicating scientific information.
1. Skim *The Federal Plain Language Guidelines* to remind yourself of the style's features.
2. Read the document called "Dam Safety."
3. Determine its primary audience; think about the needs of that audience.
4. Arrange the information into patterns that would help readers meet their needs.
5. Create new section headings to help readers find information.
6. Revise the text to conform to "plain language" style.
7. Submit your file to the dropbox.

Exercise 4: Writing about Rocks

In this exercise, you will practice developing definitions and descriptions by writing about a rock for an audience of museum supporters.

The Orton Geology Museum wants to include a "rock-of-the-month" feature in its newsletter. Your job is to create one of these features. The newsletter is not printed in color, and the museum has many supporters with vision disabilities, so the description must work without photographic support. This exercise has four parts.

Part 1: Field trip

Meet in the Orton Geology Museum on February X at XX:XX. We will only stay for 45 minutes; please arrive promptly. When we convene, I will give you the name of a display and a rock. Find the case; find your rock.

Collect information about your rock by answering these questions. (You may not be able to answer them all.)
  a. What kind of rock is it?
  b. Where is it found?
  c. What are some of the other rocks in the same display?
  d. Which minerals are contained in it?
  e. What process formed it?
  f. What color is it?
  g. What shape is it?
  h. What does its surface look like?
  i. What does it look like?
  j. What is interesting about it?

Before we leave the museum, write a paragraph describing the rock. Focus on its appearance. Write whatever comes to mind as you look at the rock from different angles.

Part 2: Research
Once we return to the classroom, research your rock. Answer the questions you could not answer at the museum and search for interesting factoids. Although Wikipedia is a place to start, you should also explore the geology sites listed on Carmen.

Part 3: Drafting descriptions
a. Write a few categorical definitions. For each, (1) identify a category to which this rock belongs and (2) explain its place within the category.
b. Revise your description from the museum; clarify the visual details.
c. Write a short paragraph describing the rock's formation process.
d. Create two or three different similes or metaphors to describe the rock. Which is more accurate? Which is more engaging?
e. Write a few sentences identifying why this rock is interesting. Is it remarkably old? Is its formation interesting? Does it have an unusual appearance? Does it have practical applications?

Part 4: Creating an exciting profile
Use the material from Part 3 to create a coherent profile of your rock. What would interest a non-expert reader?

Assignment 3: Writing about Science for Public Audiences

For the final project, you will write about science for a public audience. You will decide the topic, the purpose of the document, the characteristics of the audience, and the best communication channel to reach that audience.

Project Objectives
In completing this assignment you will ...
- Practice writing about science for non-expert public audiences.
- Examine different styles used to accommodate science.
- Develop visual supports for textual accommodations of science.

Deliverable Description
Audience
You will choose an appropriate audience addressable through a specific

communication channel. These channels could include newspapers, magazines, websites, broadcast outlets, museums, etc.

Purpose
Your document's purpose will depend on your audience, venue, and interest.

Constraints
We will discuss the constraints of your document in an individual conference. Your document must be long enough for the job.
Possibilities include …
a. Science journalism articles.
b. Descriptive guides of new treatment options for diseases.
c. Museum displays.
d. Extended profiles of a researcher or facility.
e. Documentary scripts.

Modeling Exercise
Find an interesting passage from today's reading. Point to it in your discussion-post title. E.g., "[Title], Page 2, Paragraph 2." Use the passage's sentence structure and style to develop a paragraph for your final project.

Start by separating clauses and phrases to get a sense of their arrangement and rhythm. For example …

> Dr. Stier's assistant picks up a scalpel
> and begins the autopsy
> by drawing an incision from the pubic bone to the sternum,
> where he bifurcates the incision,
> cutting toward each shoulder to form a Y.
>
> In the wake of the blade,
> skin and fat part with a delicate hiss and crackle.
>
> The assistant rolls the flesh back from the chest,
> then snips the ribs with a tool akin to pruning shears.
>
> The bones part with a wet crunch. (Perry, 2006)

Use the same structures to create your passage. For example …

> Dr. Buehl picks up a document and begins the grading by numbering

the paragraphs, which he then evaluates, writing comments in the margins. Under the pencil, redundancy and important detail separate with muffled scratches. He circles the unnecessary passives, then underlines weak verbs. Patterns emerge in the smudged graphite.

Introduction Exercise

In this exercise you will practice writing various types of introductions. You will have <u>five</u> minutes to write each type. It is ok to think, but write while you think.

A. Write a three- or four-sentence CARS (Territory—Niche—Occupation) introduction.

> "The topic of this story is X. X is interesting because… These are the problems of X. [and/or] These are the new developments of X. These problems/developments are interesting because… In my document, I explain the significance/novelty of X by …. "

B. Write an introduction in the style of the brochures for Module 2. Imagine the research is a specialization of OSU or another institution.

C. Create a *Dispatch* introduction. First, describe the informative or context-setting graphic and choose a hook sentence that suits your topic.

Consider these examples:

> <u>Novel oddity:</u> [Toad pictures] "There are some things you don't send in the mail. That's why Terry Schwaner drove from Findlay to Phoenix to pick up a cooler filled with 400 frozen toad toes" (Dostal, 2009).

> <u>Description of application:</u> [3-D glasses picture and an info-graphic] "Battelle researchers are working with a Canadian company to create a camera that might change the way movies are made …" (Ferenchick, 2010).

> <u>Person focus:</u> [Pictures of creepy fish in jars and a picture of a scientist holding a shark.] "No roads lead to Tim Berra's favorite fishing spot on the Adelaide River. The OSU ichthyologist uses a small boat to get to the spot …." (Hunt, 2009).

> <u>Vivid scene:</u> [Bug pictures and maps] "The beetle was black with white spots and sported whip-like antennae longer than its inch-long body. It was clear to workers that the bug, found scurrying across the concrete

floor at the Downlite factory in Mason, Ohio, didn't belong there" (Hunt, 2009).

D. Describe a scene or process in vivid detail. If you described a scene in C, describe a different scene or process.

E. Tell your story as an author. Explain how you found this topic or describe events involved in writing about it. E.g., "Looking for the Lie."

F. Tell a story about a patient or other non-scientist. E.g., "Face Blind." (Fabricate a plausible story if you don't have a good example for your topic.)

G. Tell a researcher's story. E.g., "The Theory of Everything."

TOWARD A PEDAGOGY OF PSYCHIC DISTANCE

Erik Ellis
Stanford University

> Address the most complicated problems in our culture, we ask students, but do it in short, sweet prose, we demand. While there is merit in being able to cut to the rhetorical quick, sometimes a complex sentence best conveys a complex idea.
>
> —Nate Kreuter (2009, par. 3)

> A great secret of the academic humanities has been their quiet but consistent exclusion of the arts as an activity, as a practice.
>
> — Kurt Spellmeyer (2003, p. 23)

In this chapter I will explore the theoretical significance and pedagogical potential of the narrative, stylistic concept psychic distance, which is very much rooted in the craft of writing as an activity and practice. Rhetoric and composition, in its quest for disciplinary prestige, has for decades been slamming the door on such craft-based approaches to teaching writing. As Douglas Hesse has argued, "One quality occluded in composition's very important political and social turns is that of writing as craft, as the making of textual artifacts whose maker is important as maker" (2003, p. 263). Wendy Bishop noted in 2003, "It has been more than a decade since craft—a word used regularly in creative writing and rarely in composition—and style have been discussed with intense interest" (2003, p. 263). No doubt many scholars consider the very word craft embarrassingly unsophisticated and old-fashioned, like something Grandpa would reminisce about while sipping Country Time lemonade on the porch. After all, according to Robert R. Johnson, "Over the past two millennia, craft has become a notion allied with 'lower forms' of knowledge usually associated with mere practice and the making of mundane artifacts" (2010, p. 674).

Yet I find myself drawn to the term craft, even more than style, perhaps because I entered rhetoric and composition from the "unrigorous" field down the hall—creative writing. Rhetoric and composition may have thrived as a discipline by turning its back on craft and style, but the teaching of composition has suffered.

Fortunately, although the ghost of disciplinary insecurity still haunts the halls of rhetoric and composition, forever fleeing the jangly, rusty chains of current-traditionalism and flying through walls to avoid critics' humiliating mockery of "the enormous inertial mass of [practitioner] lore," renewed attention to style has begun to repair the damage (North, 1987, p. 371). By focusing on an important element of craft and style borrowed from creative writing—psychic distance—we can improve the teaching of composition, help rejuvenate the idea- and style-friendly genre of the essay in its Montaignian roots, and pry open the door to new lines of inquiry. Psychic distance is not so much one among many "matters of surface-level technique," as style is often characterized, as it is a powerful rhetorical strategy with far-reaching implications (Mayers, 2005, p. 17).

PSYCHIC DISTANCE

What is psychic distance? In <u>The Art of Fiction: Notes on Craft for Young Writers</u>, John Gardner defines it as "the distance the reader feels between himself and the events in the story" (1984, p. 111). In *Writing Fiction: A Guide to Narrative Craft*, Janet Burroway uses the equivalent term authorial distance, which she defines as "the degree to which we as readers feel on the one hand intimacy and identification with, or on the other hand detachment and alienation from, the characters in the story" (1996, p. 229). Gardner lists the following examples to illustrate how a writer can adjust language to reflect different degrees of closeness to a character's psychology or consciousness:

- It was winter of the year 1853. A large man stepped out of a doorway.
- Henry J. Warburton had never much cared for snowstorms.
- Henry hated snowstorms.
- God how he hated these damn snowstorms.
- Snow. Under your collar, down inside your shoes, freezing and plugging up your miserable soul ... (1984, p. 111)

The extremes of distance (sentence one) and closeness (sentence five) are easy to spot, but the "mid-range" (sentences two to four) represents a wealth of subtler distinctions. Gardner's sentences thus suggest the many rhetorical possibilities at the fingertips of fiction writers—and nonfiction writers, if we tweak the definition of psychic distance to mean the distance readers feel between themselves and the events and ideas in the prose rather than in the story, and if we consider the reader's identification with or detachment from the author or subject rather than the characters. Insofar as "identification between writers and readers is necessary prior to persuading people to other collective actions," psychic distance is tremendously rhetorical (Warnock, 2003, p. 208).

Making this shift from fictional to nonfictional psychic distance has the advantage of simplifying a complicated rhetorical phenomenon in fiction. As James Phelan explains in *Narrative as Rhetoric: Technique, Audiences, Ethics, Ideology*:

> First, the phrase "narrative as rhetoric" means something more than that narrative uses rhetoric or has a rhetorical dimension. It means instead that narrative is not just story but also action, the telling of a story by someone to someone on some occasion for some purpose. Furthermore, […] this basic configuration of teller-story-situation-audience-purpose is at least doubled in most narrative: there is the narrator's telling the story to his or her audience and then the author's telling of the narrator's telling to the author's audience. Consequently, the narrator's telling is part of the author's construction of the whole narrative, and in that sense, what is a matter of the telling at one level becomes a matter of the told the next. (1996, pp. 7-8)

I will touch upon ways to apply such sophisticated understandings of fiction to composition, but first I want to establish that studying and practicing psychic distance can help composition students better understand and write nonfiction.

Composition faculty often foreground the rhetorical situation and the rhetorical appeals, which are crucial and which figure prominently in authors' decisions about psychic distance, but disproportionate attention to audience and the conventions of academic discourse can prevent students from exploring alternative forms of communication that are equally rhetorical but more subtle and imaginative. I'm not talking specifically here about "personal" writing, except in the sense that all writing is personal. Jim Corder makes this point nicely in his essay "Academic Jargon and Soul-Searching Drivel." He argues that:

> an academic paper (research) is not less opinion because it is empirical, and a personal essay (opinion) is not less empirical because it is personal. A research methodology is made by humans, not given by God; it is constructed from the lumber of disciplinary metaphor and value, deriving from opinion; a personal essay may rest upon ten years of close empirical study. (1991, p. 315)

Moreover, according to Chris Anderson, "Rhetoric is by definition a form of language acknowledging feelings and values not provable or quantifiable in logical demonstration" (1989, p. xxiii). Psychic distance does not apply, then, only to personal essays, creative nonfiction, and other overtly subjective genres. Nor does it apply piecemeal to narrative beginnings of otherwise traditional academic texts. The concept applies to all writing, insofar as writers can select from many ways of articulating the same idea.

If we consider Gardner's list of five sentences, traditional academic writing tends to privilege the language of the first, with its more distant and "objective" tone. Although psychic distance might at first seem synonymous with tone, I see at least one important distinction. Namely, whereas tone usually implies straightforward attention to, if not conformity to, readers' expectations—adjust your tone to match your audience—psychic distance suggests a subtler and more introspective attention to language and audience. Its foremost allegiance is to the writer's ideas, not their reception. In an academic paper, if a student writes, "The essay is so damn preachy and pretentious it makes me sick," one could easily respond by pointing out that academic readers expect a more thoughtful and rational tone—something more on the order of, "The author espouses his political agenda so dogmatically and in such stifling, esoteric language that the essay risks alienating many readers." In this example, a relatively clear awareness of audience determines what tone is appropriate. If students key in to an instructor's emphasis on tone, they might well write such a sentence to begin with. Either way, the psychic distance in the new sentence is predictably far, downplaying if not disguising the presence of the author and the author's emotions. As a result, the sentence communicates clearly but remains essentially flat. By contrast, with fiction and the kind of craft-based nonfiction I suggest we teach composition students, writers arguably have much more freedom not only to follow their intuition but also to select from among a greater array of linguistic possibilities. These possibilities might not always meet an audience's expectations, but they often enable writers to create an effective ethos that transcends genre conventions.

A second revision of the original sentence ("The essay is so damn preachy and pretentious it makes me sick") might be: "The author is so busy deconstructing, demystifying, interrogating, interpolating, negotiating, problematizing, politicizing, and otherwise theorizing that he leaves nonspecialist readers in the dust." This revision also eliminates the hostile and naïve tone of the original sentence, and it goes a step further to capture, with its string of fifty-cent verbs, the sensation of overwhelming erudition the student finds so objectionable. In addition, the phrase "in the dust" enables the writer to maintain a compelling subjective presence, or ethos, without sounding self-absorbed. In short, the sentence allows readers to experience the writer's frustration, as opposed to reading a bland report of it. Viewed from this perspective, the original sentence suffered not so much because of its failure to attend to audience expectations but because of its failure to do justice to the student's idea.

If composition faculty would encourage this kind of reflective rhetorical creativity, through the kinds of analysis and writing exercises I will describe later, students would stand to become more confident and sophisticated writers. In addition, such encouragement would teach the value of taking risks and playing with language. If students remain unaware of this type of correlation between form and content, or if we invalidate their shaky but well-intentioned efforts to establish ethos, they will be inclined to learn a very different lesson: that taking risks with language jeopardizes their credibility and that if they try to play with language, they will pay. As a result, they will be more likely to passively internalize the conventions of academic writing, churning out cookie-cutter prose zapped of its original motivating energy and its potential power to communicate except on the most basic level.

What's so terrible about teaching students to communicate on a basic level? Wouldn't students in first-year composition courses, at least, be doing well to grasp the simpler concept of tone, complete with its focus on audience and conventions? Although psychic distance might seem like a luxurious linguistic indulgence best reserved for advanced composition courses, the concept can be taught in simple ways that composition students at all levels can grasp and apply. By examining how authors—including student authors—construct works of fiction and nonfiction from the inside out, in terms of craft, rather than from the outside in, in terms of disciplinary gestures and ideological critique, students can learn how "writer-based prose" can simultaneously act as "reader-based prose."

WRITER-BASED PROSE

Writer-based prose, which Linda Flower has called a "failure to transform private thought into a public, reader-based expression," has a bad reputation that is largely undeserved (1979, p. 19). Such prose supposedly indulges the selfish whims of the author while ignoring the practical needs of the reader. Flower concedes that a writer-based approach "may be a useful road into the creative process for some writers," but overall she dismisses it as "a dud for communicating that information to anyone else" (1979, pp. 28-29). Of course, it is possible to write in a way that is coherent only to the writer, and students who have no awareness of audience often fall prey to this rhetorical trap.

But writer-based prose need not be solipsistic and arhetorical. In "Closing My Eyes as I Speak: An Argument for Ignoring Audience," Elbow articulates a two-pronged defense of writer-based prose. First he argues, "It's not that writers should never think about their audience. It's a question of when" (1987, p. 51). He notes that writers can find it particularly helpful to ignore audience in the early stages of composition, especially when writing for an intimidating audience such as an instructor. "Students often feel they 'don't have anything to say,'" he points out, "until they finally succeed in engaging themselves in private desert island writing for themselves alone" (1987, p. 214). Eventually an audience will prove invaluable, but too much attention to audience early in the writing process will often result in "a stilted, overly careful style or voice" (Elbow, 1987, p. 52). So far so good, you might think—as long as we're talking about inexperienced writers and as long as the writer eventually caters to the audience. Then Elbow makes his more radical and controversial claim that "writer-based prose can be better than reader-based prose" even for experienced writers. He argues that writers who obsess about audience expectations "are acting too much like a salesman trained to look the customer in the eye. [...] 'Damn it, put all your attention on what you are saying,' we want to say, 'and forget about us and how we are reacting' (1987, pp. 53-54).

This idea that writer-based prose can be valuable not simply as a preliminary, confidence-boosting strategy for novice writers but as a hallmark of authorial integrity resonates well with psychic distance. When writers create more intimacy of psychic distance—whether subconsciously as they write or consciously as they revise—they are aligning their language first and foremost to their consciousness (in all its socially constructed complexity) and to their ideas, not their audience. Yet if writers are skillful enough and readers are open-minded enough, such writing has tremendous potential to engage and persuade. As Peter Vandenberg observes, "texts are often valued because they violate audience expectations" (1995, p. 80). John Schilb calls such writer-based choices rhetorical refusals—each one "an act of writing or speaking in which the rhetor pointedly refused to do what the audience considers rhetorically normal" (2007, p. 3). By helping writers to think about their stylistic choices in ways that may appease or frustrate an audience and be rhetorically appropriate either way, psychic distance thus reinforces Elbow's conclusion that

> [w]hat most readers value in really excellent writing is not prose that is right for readers but prose that is right for thinking, right for language, or right for the subject being written about. If, in addition, it is clear and well suited to readers, we appreciate that." (1987, p. 54)

This powerful concept—that language can be rhetorically fitting regardless of how well it matches audience expectations—lies at the heart of psychic distance.

I'm not suggesting that we urge students to forget about audience altogether. Rather, I'm claiming that students could benefit from thinking about audience in a subtler, more roundabout way. In "Audience Addressed/Audience Invoked: The Role of Audience in Composition Theory and Pedagogy," Lisa Ede and Andrea Lunsford examine Walter Ong's idea from "The Writer's Audience Is Always a Fiction" that a writer can invoke rather than explicitly address an audience.[1] According to this view, "The central task of the writer is not to analyze an audience and adapt discourses to meet its needs. Rather, the writer uses the semantic and syntactic resources of language to provide cues for the reader—cues which help to define the role or roles the writer wishes the reader to adopt in responding to the text" (Ede & Lunsford, 1984, p. 184). As Russell Long points out, this shift in perspective has major implications for composition pedagogy:

> Rather than beginning with the traditional question, "who is my audience?", we now begin with, "who do I want my audience to be?" Rather than encouraging a superficial, stereotyped view of reader[s], we are asking the student to begin with a statement about the audience she wants to create. What attitudes, ideas, actions are to be encouraged? This leads directly to questions of method: what distance between reader and subject should be established? What of diction and the creation of tone? What pieces of information do I want the reader to take for granted? Which do I want to detail and emphasize? Such questions shift the burden of responsibility upon the writer from that of amateur detective to that of creator, and the role of the creator is the most important and most basic the writer must play. (1980, p. 226)

Invoking an audience, then, is an alternative way for writers to generate the rhetorical power of identification. According to Gary C. Woodward in The *Idea of Identification*, "In its highest form identification offers the potent sensation of sharing another's consciousness. In the process, it diminishes the distance between the alien and the known, providing a sense of 'place' for ourselves in the external world" (2003, p. 18). Whereas conventional rhetorical approaches to identification stress the need to accommodate an audience's views, psychic distance implies the paradoxical need to reach out to readers by inviting them into one's own discourse.

As teachers of writing, we are very good at helping students understand why solipsistic writing is unpersuasive. But students should also be aware of the rhetorical pitfalls of thinking too much about audience. For example, if you write only with readers in mind, you'll be inclined to give them only what they want—or what you think they want. How many times have you read a student's essay and yawned at its amateurish attempt to please you with its politically correct analysis or interpretation? Who knows what the student actually thought of the story, film, essay, political controversy, or what have you? In an attempt to please you—the omnipotent reader—the student's own engagement and imagination spiraled down the drain. Yet because the student's ideological sweet nothings sound so good and because the essay shows evidence of the critical thinking and audience awareness you've tried so hard to encourage, you might shake off the fleeting impression that the paper was in fact not written by your student but by Eddie Haskell, the obsequious, two-faced friend on the TV show Leave It to Beaver. Gee whiz, Professor, affirmative action sure is valuable ... like my grade.

Legendary New Yorker editor Wallace Shawn once expressed a similar concern that excessive editorial devotion to audience can turn otherwise curious readers into narrow-minded consumers. "Now the whole idea is that you edit for a market and if possible design a magazine with that in mind," he said. "Now magazines aren't started with the desire for someone to express what he believes." As a result, magazines reassure rather than challenge readers, depriving them of opportunities to "learn and grow" (as quoted in Bagdikian, 1983, p. 54).

Rather than consider the negative implications of such attention to audience, writing faculty who put their faith in reader-based prose imply that the reader/professor/customer is always right. "Unfortunately," Flower writes of narrative approaches to academic writing, "most academic and professional readers seem unwilling to sit through these home movies of the writer's mind at work" (1979, p. 25). Anyone who thinks these readers' impatience is "unfortunate" should respond to it with resistance, not resignation. Just as Shawn had the courage and integrity to stand up for his dissenting opinion, I share Corder's view that "[s]ince we don't have time, we must rescue time by putting it into our discourses and holding it there" (1985, p. 31).

RESCUING TIME

Of course, "rescuing time" is easier said than done. Yet scholars in rhetoric and composition already acknowledge and accept the impossibility of keeping up with the field today. There is simply too much scholarship—too many books, too many journals, too many conferences. Rather than panic at this situation and scramble to read everything, which we must therefore hope will be presented to us as straightforwardly as possible, we should welcome a variety of discourse choices, in keeping with the richness of our field. If one is going to read a relevant journal of X number of pages anyway—or a stack of X number of essays—what difference does it make, in terms of time, if those pages consist of articles or essays? If anything, essays can be easier and therefore faster—not to mention more enjoyable—to read. "They valued convenience and upheld the status quo" would be a sad motto to inscribe on plaques and buildings honoring our professional legacy. If we wish to establish and assert meaningful disciplinary authority, we should advocate for causes in which we believe. Particularly with respect to teaching, time should be a significant consideration in our administrative deliberations. We should argue as adamantly for more time to respond to and assess more complicated student essays as we argue for smaller class sizes. If it is true that we often lose battles to reduce the size of classes, it is at least not for lack of effort. Why pride ourselves on our disciplinary integrity in one context and willingly sacrifice it in another?

As difficult as it may be to admit, our demand for textual efficiency may rest at least in part on our faulty association of "inefficient" texts with poorly edited "home movies." Too often we dismiss such texts without giving them a fair hearing. Flower's comment about home movies reminds me of a comment I once overheard after watching Citizen Kane in a movie theater. As my friend and I were leaving, basking in the film's brilliance, we overheard a teenager say to his companion, "Wow—movies sure have come a long way since then." If your standard for comparison and excellence is the fast-paced action flick, Citizen Kane doesn't stand a chance. Elbow describes a similar situation often faced by teachers. In "The Music of Form: Rethinking Organization in Writing," he notes that "when we read student papers in stacks of twenty or more, we easily slide into holding up each paper against a mental template of features that are supposed to be there—rather than genuinely *reading* it through time. We are short of time" (2006, p. 631, emphasis in original). As a result, "readers can be blind (deaf) to coherence that's actually in the text," albeit in subtler and more challenging forms than we expect (2006, p. 632). Elbow wisely concedes that writers cannot blame readers for failing to see coherence where it doesn't exist. After all, it would be arrogant to invoke Montaigne's assertion that "[i]t is the inattentive reader who loses my subject, not I" (as quoted in Klaus, 2012, p. 168). Still, this concession hardly invalidates the insight that audience expectations are themselves socially constructed, a fact we often forget. According to Pat C. Hoy II:

> Reading, we permit ourselves and our students to get waylaid

by theses and topic sentences instead of pausing to savor the twists and turns of the essayist's mind playing over rich material, entertaining doubt, wrestling with ambiguities. Tracking what we think of as the controlling idea, we tend to overlook what Stephen Jay Gould calls a hierarchy of ideas—the more elegant theory that accounts for the evidence and the complications, facts as well as uncertainties. (2001, p. 353, emphases in original)

To the extent that academic readers demand a "proper" tone—that is, the tone they have been conditioned to accept as natural in a given rhetorical situation—they blackmail writers into linguistic conformity.

Sometimes this conformity is appropriate, but at other times it might not be the most effective—or the most ethical—way to craft one's text. As Chris Holcomb points out, "Things fall apart when the players—writer and reader—fail to play their parts. Readers fail when they become too dismissive or prematurely impatient, and writers fail when they become too intent on dazzling" (Holcomb, p. 204). Just the same, I'll take a class of aspiring dazzlers over a class of obedient conformists any day. As Ian Barnard wonders in "The Ruse of Clarity," "Surely inexpert complexity is preferable to expert simplicity if it is indicative of intellectual wrestling and scholarly ambition rather than the complacency of comfort?" (2010, p. 446).

TONE IT DOWN?

Unlike tone, psychic distance privileges the writer's perspective—not as a vacuum-sealed celebration of romantic, dazzling individualism but as a way of more closely aligning words, phrases, sentences, paragraphs, and entire texts with the writer's ideas. If the writer fails at this admittedly difficult task, the audience will say so—for example, during a workshop. Then the writer must decide how much, or even whether, to revise. But if the writer succeeds, the audience will welcome even the most unconventional stylistic choices—provided readers are willing to engage the writer and look beyond the "mental template of features that are supposed to be there" (Elbow, 2006, p. 631).

As an example of writing whose power to resonate hinges on an audience's willingness to enter an unfamiliar perspective, consider Jamaica Kincaid's essay "On Seeing England for the First Time." After describing and reflecting on her colonialist upbringing in Antigua, she recounts a recent trip to England to see the places she had been indoctrinated to worship since she was a child. She ends her essay with this sentence:

> The white cliffs of Dover, when finally I saw them, were cliffs, but they were not white; you would probably only call them that if the word "white" meant something special to you; they were dirty and they were steep; they were so steep, the correct height from which all my views of England, starting with the map before me in my classroom and ending with the trip I had just taken, should jump and die and disappear forever. (2000, p. 220)

When I first assigned this essay in an upper-division composition course at the University of Colorado at Boulder, most students—no doubt many of them under the Anglophile spell of Harry Potter—were shocked and offended by the rhetorical one-two punch of Kincaid's "audacious" postcolonial perspective and her correspondingly unrelenting style. Granted, Kincaid wrote this essay for *Transition*, a publication that The Village Voice has called "the only decent forum for black intellectuals" ("Transition"). To the extent that my class had no black intellectuals, they were not the intended audience. Therefore, some would argue, it is irrelevant if a group of mostly white, relatively conservative undergraduates fails to appreciate the essay's ideas or literary merit. Fair enough—to an extent. Maybe I shouldn't have been surprised when the first comment of class discussion was, "I don't see what she's so upset about," followed shortly by, "This was the worst essay I've ever read."

But suppose Kincaid had written this essay for undergraduates. Or suppose she had been invited to revise her essay to better suit its new rhetorical situation of being published in *The Best American Essays 2000*, with its larger and more general audience. If Kincaid had had such an opportunity, should she have "toned down" her anger and resentment, repackaging it in more palatable prose? Should she have written less emotionally, changing "should jump and die and disappear forever" to "should perhaps be reconsidered"—the kind of suggestion we might make for a student? I think not. Even if maintaining an intimate level of psychic distance means that her essay enrages rather than enlightens most students or other readers, perhaps that's the price she must pay for being true to her experience and convictions. Maybe provoking readers is a realistic enough rhetorical goal, given the level of audience resistance. Such provocation could be more valuable in raising awareness of her perspective than the easy dismissal that a more conventional version would be likely to produce. The alienation many of my students felt from Kincaid's implied author was likely a result not of any rhetorical failure on her part to invite them into her consciousness via close psychic distance, but of students' inability to engage a perspective that threatens their identities. As Barry Kroll argues,

> If we focus too much attention on writing for an audience—whether conceived as a "target receiver," a "needy reader," or a "constructive participant"—we may narrow our view of composing, forgetting that writing is also an exploration of ideas, a quest for purpose, and a projection of oneself. (1984, p. 183)

In other words, identification is a two-way street.

But should we allow privileged white students to get away with creating zoomed-in psychic distance when writing about the unfairness of, say, affirmative action in higher education? Wouldn't it be a double-standard to celebrate close psychic distance in the work of progressives while prohibiting it among conservatives? I think the answer has to be yes. That doesn't mean, though, that we should stand back and applaud any claim based on personal experience, provided the author uses psychic distance skillfully. Candace Spigelman advocates "the interrogation of assumptions as a means of evaluating the arguments in personal experience stories" (2004, p. 102). Here is where an audience steps in and helps writers evaluate the validity of their ideas. In Kincaid's case, I imagine her assumptions would hold up quite well to critical scrutiny, considering the wealth of postcolonial scholarship that confirms her ideas and arguments. What about the student writer who assumes that racism ended with the Civil Rights Act, thus eliminating the very premise of affirmative action? Obviously this assumption would not withstand critical scrutiny. My point here is that there's a big difference between a writer using a close degree of psychic distance to explore a valid idea—whether invoking personal experience or not—and a writer using a close degree of psychic distance to explore an invalid idea. Insofar as the argument is sound, the skillful use of psychic distance will tend to make the writing more engaging and persuasive, at least for readers who have an open mind about the possibilities of academic discourse. Insofar as the underlying argument is questionable, an audience has the duty to point this out to the writer, usually during a workshop or instructor conference.

Unless writers have at least the initial freedom to indulge "writerly" impulses and to adapt their language not to an audience's expectations but to their own ideas, they will be more likely to produce a picture of a mind conforming rather than a mind thinking. Take insecure student writers and tell them to fixate on audience, and what do you often get? Timid prose that seldom takes risks, or if it does take risks, does so rarely and flinchingly. If we value safe, predictable texts that are basically five-paragraph themes taken to a "new level," no problem. But if we believe "college-level writing instruction should ask students to do something that is *difficult*, something that strives for more than mere competence," and if we want students to explore their own ideas and take rhetorical risks to create original, compelling essays, we should focus on psychic distance more than tone (Heilker, 2006, p. 201, emphasis in original).

Although I don't have much space to elaborate here, the (non-five-paragraph) essay is arguably the ideal genre for composition students to apply the rhetoric of style. According to Cristina Kirklighter in Traversing the Democratic Borders of the Essay, "Instead of working toward definitive conclusions, as in an article, the essay's spontaneity allows the writer to wander, to make connections in unusual places, to emphasize discoveries instead of conclusions" (2002, p. 6). Mind you, I'm as happy as anyone to teach students the conventions of writing, say, a recommendation report in a business writing course, but I don't pretend that such occasions offer writers a wealth of stylistic possibilities. On this point, I disagree with Andrew Bourelle, who argues that:

> [...] when writers make decisions within disciplinary contexts, those are stylistic decisions. A lab report that adheres to a specific sectional format, that contains passive sentence constructions, and that is written via a seemingly voiceless narrator—that, in other words, seems void of style—is still written with style. All students studying writing—not just those in first-year composition courses—could benefit from a closer look at the style in the types of writing they are supposed to emulate. (2010, p. 105)

I agree that such genres contain style, which students can analyze and emulate. And of course they offer some possibilities for stylistic choice. Yet we should keep in mind Nora Bacon's point in "Style in Academic Writing" that "different kinds of discourse permit different degrees of stylistic experimentation and play" (this volume). When you contrast the stylistic potential of, say, a lab report and an essay—a genre that Heilker has called "kineticism incarnate"—you can see that the lab report locks student writers in a stylistic prison and throws away the key (1994, p. 169). As a former composition student of mine, Jeremey Logan, wrote in his stylistically engaging end-of-semester reflective essay: "The best essays are like Bugs Bunny: They lean against a wall, cross one leg over the other, and shoot you straight, while munching on a carrot. They're casual and comfortable. They convince you by not worrying if you're convinced. The essayist ain't running for office, and he [or she] ain't selling windows."

BEYOND VOICE

I've explained how psychic distance differs from tone, but how does it differ from voice? And why would it be a more useful element of craft for reclaiming the essay? As the most craft-based pedagogy, expressivism already privileges voice—to its credit. As Christopher Burnham points out in *A Guide to Composition Pedagogies*, "Expressivist pedagogy encourages, even insists upon, a sense of writer presence even in research-based writing. This presence—'voice' or ethos—whether explicit, implicit, or absent, functions as a key evaluation criterion when expressivists examine writing" (Burnham, 2001, p. 19). Elbow has called voice "the life and rhythms of speech" (1985, p. 291). Enos has explored voice as "transforming ethos" that requires "dialogic action, where both writer and reader are aware of, and enjoy, the engagement" (2007, p. 194). Robert M. Gorrell has argued that voice "manifests itself by establishing a position in space and time and by expressing a tone, an attitude toward the audience and toward the subject matter" (1984, p. 158). Voice, ethos, tone, presence, style, psychic distance. I tend to agree with Darsie Bowden that such "distinctions are seemingly endless and often more confusing than illuminating" (1995, p. 187). Ultimately it's not the terms that matter so much as what you do with the concepts. But by exploring psychic distance alongside voice, I hope to show that there are some conceptual differences with practical implications for teaching.

Clearly psychic distance and voice share much in common. I don't mean to imply that the former should replace the latter as a key term in our professional lexicon. As a rhetorical strategy that appeals to readers obliquely, psychic distance resembles voice in Elbow's less popular sense that

> the music of prosidy enacts some of the meaning so that we "hear" it. It's as though the meaning comes to us rather than us having to go after it. So if a writer is skilled enough to write sentences that readers actually hear—hearing the accents, rhythms, and melody in the silent words on the page—readers will actually "hear" some of the meaning. (2006, p. 643)

Work in linguistics on the poetic function of language supports this "latent tendency, which may become patent in certain circumstances, for the sounds of a given word to be congruent with (similar to) their meanings" (Waugh,

1985, p. 156). Understanding how to fine-tune psychic distance or voice can help students—and scholars—pull off this rhetorical feat of enabling readers to "hear" meaning, and not just with individual words.

At the same time, psychic distance implies more of an invoked audience than voice, and thus it invites if not demands even closer attention to the relationships between language and meaning, form and content. It is certainly possible to praise a piece of writing for its "strong voice" and then go into detail about how the writer creates that voice, but it is equally possible—and perhaps more common—to praise a "strong voice" or criticize a weak one without specifying its subtle dynamics. However, when you praise or critique a piece of writing for its use of psychic distance, you have little choice but to elaborate on the details of language that create it.

Of course, close attention to the details of language isn't everything. Elbow makes this point when he explains why voice is a more useful pedagogical term than style:

> To talk about style is to focus on the actual language and syntax itself. To talk about voice, on the other hand, is to be in a way more roundabout and imprecise, that is, to talk about how the words ask to be performed or spoken. (2000, pp. 169-70)

He goes on to note that "students and untrained readers are often more sophisticated in getting at how language works when they talk in terms of voice than when they talk about textual style" (2000, p. 170).

Psychic distance offers the best of both worlds. For writers, in particular, it can create a comfortable balance between psychology and craft. It enables them to think broadly about how closely they want their writing to mirror their thinking—and therefore the degree of identification they wish to foster—yet it also demands sentence-level attention to the nuances that will create the desired distance. Another difference between voice and psychic distance returns us to the question of audience. Just as students are often asked to adjust their tone to their audience, Gorrell refers to "the importance of fitting voice to audience" (1984, p. 157). Even Elbow argues "for crafting a voice that fits the audience" ("2007, p. 179). He offers the example of a student who must write "for a reader who wants a very restricted academic voice or register—a reader who is not just uninterested in my presence but who will in fact be put off if she feels too much contact with 'me'" (2000, p. 215). Like Flower's reader who is "unwilling to sit through these home movies of the writer's mind at work," this reader in effect coerces the writer into conformity (1979, p. 25). In a characteristic attempt to embrace contraries, Elbow argues that it's possible to "let the 'wrong voice' have free reign, and then in late drafts adjust or get rid of the offending bits but keep the energy" (2000, p. 216). No doubt this strategy sometimes saves the day, but what about when a writer, such as Kincaid or an ambitious composition student, wishes to write in such a personal voice—even in a research-based essay that contains zero autobiographical references—that conservative readers would object to the whole text, not just a few "offending bits," no matter how sophisticated and talented the writer? In other words, what if the text's energy is the "offending bit," in the form of a strong voice or an intimate level of psychic distance? Must the writer conform and revise her entire work? Of course it's up to her. She can cave in completely to audience demands—and probably silence her voice the next time around. She can change nothing and admit rhetorical defeat—and, if she's a student, risk a bad grade. Or she can compromise. Compromise is often necessary and good, but only when it's reciprocal. Unfortunately, many academic readers in positions of power, including writing instructors, have no strong incentive to embrace voice-driven writing, to meet voice-driven writers halfway—except in explicitly personal essays, which are often followed by thesis-driven research papers that forbid a strong voice and a narrative structure. In "'Playing Safe': Undergraduate Essay Writing and the Presentation of the Student 'Voice,'" Barbara Read, Becky Francis, and Jocelyn Robson present research suggesting that "the unequal power relationship between student and lecturer, constructed through hegemonically dominant academic discourse, influences the way in which the student voice is presented" (2001, p. 390). This fact bothers me to a degree that it doesn't seem to bother Elbow. The main problem, as I see it, is that more academic readers need to become better listeners, not that more writers need to lower their voices or become ventriloquists. Jane E. Hindman has voiced a legitimate concern that "our [reading] practices undermine, if not censure, innovative textual production, disciplining their subversive potential" (2003, 14).

More than tone or voice, psychic distance offers readers the two attitudes that Carl Rogers claimed foster creative thinking: psychological safety and psychological freedom. According to William Zeigler, "Psychological safety means that one feels one's own worth is unconditionally assured, that one fears no judgment or criticism, and that one is understood empathetically. Psychological freedom means that one feels free to express oneself symbolically" (p. 464). Whereas freewriting provides these conditions only initially in the writing process, before writers subject their voice-driven writing to what is often a gavel-wielding, voice-stifling audience, psychic distance preserves these conditions even at the revision stage. That doesn't mean writers acquire a Get-out-of-Audience-Free card. As always, readers need to assess an argument's assumptions and evidence. In addition, audience remains crucial to the extent that readers must evaluate how compelling a text is.

The term psychic distance also has metaphorical appeal. I don't want to overstate it, lest I fall prey to Philip Eubanks's cautionary note that "[t]oo often writing scholarship alternates between assertions that a particular metaphor is pernicious and speculations that another metaphor may be the answer to all of our aspirations" (2001, p. 115). Still, just as voice has power in writing because it helps us think of texts as vocal expressions, psychic distance has its own unique power to evoke the visual/spatial metaphor of distance. In my experience, composition students often welcome the term psychic distance—in part, I think, because it helps them visualize themselves as writers in proximity to readers, or as readers in proximity to—or at a great remove from—academic writers. But again, this kind of audience awareness is a far cry from the kind of deferential audience awareness often implied by tone.

Finally, for scholars who criticize voice for its implicit association with "authentic self," psychic distance might prove a more defensible term. Elbow has made the case that:

> even if we are completely at odds about the nature of selves or identities, about whether people even have such things, and about the relation of a text to the person who wrote it, we have a good chance of reaching agreement about whether any given text has audible voice, what kind of dramatic voice it has, whether it has a recognizable or distinctive voice, and whether the writer was able to achieve authority of voice. (2000, p. 205)

As Elbow has acknowledged, "I clearly failed to get people to use those distinctions" (2007, p. 183). For scholars such as Frank Farmer, who feels that we need "to deliver voice from its long romance with the true self" (1995, p. 318), and Bowden, who argues that "[t]he assumption that language is first and foremost a social activity seems to be obscured by the use of voice […]," psychic distance could be more appealing, given its subtle but unmistakable relationship to audience (1999, p. 65). In its very name, psychic distance reinforces the need to negotiate the space between writer and audience.

Of course, faculty can decide for themselves how much leeway students should have to experiment with psychic distance in their writing. You might agree with David Bartholomae that students "have to speak in the voice and through the codes of those of us with power and wisdom" (1997, p. 610), or you might agree with Berlin that

> we are not simply offering training in a useful technical skill that
> is meant as a simple complement to the more important studies
> of other areas. We are teaching a way of experiencing the world,
> a way of ordering and making sense of it. (1996, p. 246)

Or perhaps you hold any number of other complicated, overlapping views about the nature and value of academic discourse. But regardless of whether you ask students to slavishly uphold or steadfastly subvert every convention—or perhaps more likely fall somewhere in between—you can still use psychic distance rhetorically to suit your particular purpose and pedagogy.

PSYCHIC DISTANCE IN THE CLASSROOM

How can we help composition students internalize an awareness of psychic distance? Of course one might take any number of approaches, in any number of contexts. At the risk of sounding like "someone tell[ing] about their experiences on drugs"—that is, someone who values classroom experience—let me outline a few of the techniques I've used with some success at various curricular levels, ranging from first-year composition to upper-division courses such as Topics in Writing and Writing on Science and Society (Dworkin, 2004, p. 604).

I often introduce psychic distance by giving students a handout (see Appendix A) that shows Gardner's and Burroway's definitions, Gardner's list of five sentences, and a short excerpt from Oscar Wilde's *The Picture of Dorian Gray*. (Please take a minute to read this excerpt.) Because students sometimes grasp the concept of psychic distance more easily by first considering examples from fiction—perhaps because the definition of psychic distance comes to us from creative writing—I explain the context of *The Picture of Dorian Gray* and read the excerpt aloud, asking students to focus, in small groups, on the shift in psychic distance that begins most noticeably in the third paragraph. Some groups focus so much on the action in this paragraph that they fail to see the shift in psychic distance. A student might say to me as I check in on his or her group, "The language gets more intense. There are some really strong words like groan, choking, and stabbed." I tell them that this is true, but I ask them to think more about the relationship between language and identification. "Why," I might ask, "does Oscar Wilde say 'someone choking with blood'? Why does he say 'The thing was still seated in the chair'? Those are curious word choices. Why would Wilde use this kind of language?" At this point students sometimes veer in the opposite interpretive direction, noting the vague language and concluding that Wilde is pulling back the psychic distance so that readers cannot easily identify with him. Other groups hit the nail on the head. Inevitably, though, even if it takes some encouragement, students point to more examples of the suddenly distant language—"the outstretched arms," "the man did not move"—and realize that it perfectly reflects Dorian's consciousness and guilty conscience (Wilde, 1988, p. 123). The writing reflects his attempt to distance himself mentally from his actions and from the humanity of his friend turned victim.

After making sure that students grasp the basic operation of psychic distance in this admittedly sophisticated excerpt, we look at other details of Wilde's language. As early as the first sentence of the second paragraph, in the phrase "an uncontrollable feeling of hatred for Basil Hallward came over him," we can see the relationship between Wilde's diction and Dorian's psychological withdrawal from his emotions—and their moral implications. The fact that Wilde uses Basil's full name in this sentence is significant. It mirrors Dorian's perception that Basil is suddenly more of a stranger than a friend. In addition, the phrase "came over him," with its implication that Dorian is unaccountable for his own hatred, not only reinforces the conceit that the portrait is the controlling force but also foreshadows Dorian's imagined absence from the scene of the crime. Students benefit from considering the similar second-paragraph phrases "he loathed the man" and "crushing the man's head down on the table" (Wilde, 1988, p. 123). Simply asking students why Wilde might have made these language choices can elicit good responses and focus the discussion on psychic distance.

Whether or not readers consciously recognize this shift in psychic distance as they read the novel is irrelevant, so long as they experience it. Although we often teach students the paramount importance of writing for an audience, it seems doubtful that Wilde dwelled on audience in the passage above. During John Douglas's libel trial, after all, Wilde said, in response to questions about the novel, "What concerns me in my art is my view and my feeling and why I made it; I don't care twopence what other people think about it" (as quoted in Holland, p. 80). According to Donald Lawler in *An Inquiry into Oscar Wilde's Revisions of The Picture of Dorian Gray*, "the dominant motive underlying all the important changes made by Wilde was an artistic desire to suppress an underlying moral which Wilde considered too obvious and, for that reason, distracting." Lawler notes that "such revisions were far from haphazard nor were they made, as has commonly been supposed, either in self-defense following the criticisms of the Lippincott's version or required to fill out the needed pages for a full-length novel" (1988, p. 2). Wilde's additions to the ending "help to direct our interest to the hero's mental state rather than to his moral state" (Lawler, 1988, p. 38). In other words, it seems that Wilde was not thinking much about pleasing his audience. He was too busy paying attention to Dorian and how best to craft the scene so that it would be, in Elbow's words, "right for thinking, right for language, or right for the subject being written about" (1987, p. 54). Talking with students about how published writers such as Wilde seem to have crafted their work without slavish attention to audience "demands" can help them imagine ways that they, too, might appeal to readers in a roundabout fashion by focusing more on issues of craft and less on the need to conform to their professors' expectations.

After students discuss psychic distance in *The Picture of Dorian Gray*, I read students the section of the handout about how psychic distance translates to nonfiction. Then I invite students to complete the short writing exercise on the handout (see Appendix A). Hearing volunteers read their revisions of the sentence "The weather is very cold today" helps students recognize the range of possible language available to them when they consider psychic distance. Their revisions often feature more visceral, embodied language than the original sentence.

Continuing with the handout, I briefly explain the unique advantages of the term psychic distance—why it can be better than tone, voice, or style (see Appendix A). Then I ask students to read and discuss the opening two paragraphs of an essay by my former student Jeremy Kellogg, an undergraduate at CU-Boulder. Students discuss the ways that Jeremy, in this rhetorical analysis of a local commercial space, uses psychic distance to help readers share his perspective as a man who feels uncomfortable in such a feminine environment (Victoria's Secret). For example, we analyze the ways in which his use of impersonal, "masculine" language reflects his feelings of discomfort and alienation, and we discuss the rhetorical role and stylistic dynamics of the military metaphor.

Next I like to show students the title sequence of *To Kill a Mockingbird*. Judging by the number of hands that shoot up when I ask who has read the book or seen the film, it's a good example because it's familiar and creates a kind of common ground. Before I show the title sequence, I make sure everyone realizes that the film is told from the perspective of children, and I ask them to keep an eye out for details that establish psychic distance. After showing the clip, I ask students, "What did you see? What's going on with psychic distance here?" They point out a number of ways the film invites viewers to share the perspective of children. For example, even before we see the first image of the film, we hear the slow, simple opening notes of a piano while the earth of the Universal International© logo spins. It sounds like a child practicing the piano. The crucial first image of the film shows a weathered cigar box, shot from overhead, which is presently opened by a pair of young hands. Inside we see two wooden dolls, several coins and marbles, a variety of crayons, and other objects traditionally associated with childhood. The camera slowly zooms in on the box, as if we have been invited to leave our adult concerns and join the childhood world of play. We hear a child's voice humming idly, and an extreme close-up reveals a small hand grabbing a crayon and proceeding to color over invisible words on a page that reveal the film's title. We hear the crayon slide across the paper.

Throughout the sequence, we never see what this child looks like. To have shown someone specific would have compromised the psychic distance, snapping us out of the immediacy of the moment. Tight close-ups enable us to identify far more closely. To children, of course, small objects are not so small, but even more important than this literal fact is that the close-ups reflect the intensity of children's playful imaginations—the large presence of small things. The remaining shots of the sequence consist of more extreme close-ups of childhood objects, such as crayons, marbles, and a whistle. Each shot is filmed with the unrushed fluidity of a summer afternoon, a sensation furthered by the choice of transitions—slow dissolves that give the impression of one moment melting into the next. The sequence ends when a piece of paper drawn with a bird is ripped down the middle, revealing a patch of black into which the establishing shot of the town dissolves seamlessly, tree branches sprouting over the frayed edges of the page. The title sequence lasts just three minutes, but it packs a powerful lesson in the craft of psychic distance.

The way I have analyzed this sequence might give the impression that I stand in front of the class and pontificate about psychic distance. Nothing could be further from the truth. Students are perfectly capable of analyzing many of these subtleties of craft, and I invite them to do so. Their familiarity with film and their attunement to visual rhetoric never fails to impress me. To build their critical confidence and to help them better understand psychic distance—and, more importantly, to apply their understanding of psychic distance—I show students more film clips and ask them to analyze and interpret the use of psychic distance.

Because students always comment on the correlation between the opening scene's close-ups and psychic distance, I like to follow *To Kill a Mockingbird* with a short clip from Krzysztof Kieslowski's *Bleu* that features an important close-up at a key moment in the film. Juliette Binoche's character Julie, a recent widow seeking to block out all memory of the tragic deaths of her husband and daughter, is thrown off guard momentarily by the sudden appearance of her husband's assistant, who is in love with her. In the scene, which takes place in a café, she rejects the man and he leaves. Then we see a very tight close-up of her cup of coffee as she dips a sugar cube into its surface. The sugar cube slowly sucks up the coffee, and then she lets it fall into the cup. It's a quick shot, lasting just a few seconds, but as Kieslowski explains in an interview on the film's DVD, the close-up is a significant reflection of Julie's psychology. Sitting in front of his editing machine, Kieslowski replays the clip and asks, "What does this obsession with close-ups mean?" He explains:

> Simply that we're trying to show the heroine's world from her point of view, to show that she sees these little things, things that are near to her, by focusing on them in order to demonstrate that the rest doesn't matter to her. She's trying to contain, to put a lid on her world and on her immediate environment. [...] We made a very tight shot of the sugar cube sucking up the coffee to show that nothing around her matters to her—not other people nor their business, nor the boy, the man who loves her and went through a great ordeal to find her. She just doesn't care. Only the sugar cube matters, and she intentionally focuses on it to shut out all the things she doesn't accept.

Kieslowki's comments serve both to demonstrate the value of psychic distance and to validate students' observations about film technique in *To Kill a Mockingbird*.

I sometimes ask students to analyze the relationship between film techniques and psychic distance in clips from concert videos by Coldplay and The Dave Matthews Band. The Coldplay video that I show uses chaotic camerawork and fast-paced editing to mirror the fast pace of the music and to capture the energy and immediacy of the concert experience, while the video I show by the Dave Matthews Band uses slow dissolves and lengthy shots of the performers to focus more on the musicianship. Each clip uses the language of film to create a particular degree of psychic distance.

Following up such an introduction to psychic distance with collaborative presentations that ask students to analyze effective and ineffective examples in print and multimedia can help ensure that the concept does not evaporate from the class. One group of students presented two car-chase scenes from popular films. Students argued that the first clip was much more effective in inviting viewers to identify with the protagonist driving the car. The scene's use of point of view and cinematography, such as shots of the driver shifting gears and pressing the gas pedal, created a greater degree of intimacy, students argued. By contrast, a different film that also featured a protagonist driving a car in a chase scene tended to alienate viewers by "zooming out" the degree of psychic distance. For example, the scene was filmed from many more points of view, including that of frazzled pedestrians scurrying not to be run over by the swerving vehicle.

Another way to emphasize the importance of psychic distance is to include the term as an explicit assessment criterion on writing assignments and grading rubrics. Unless you follow through on your desire to reinforce the importance of psychic distance by making it a vital part of the class vocabulary, students will forget about it—and justifiably so.

INTERNALIZING PSYCHIC DISTANCE

The goal of analyzing and experimenting with psychic distance is not to train students to consult some mental psychic-distance yardstick every time they write a sentence. Rather, the goal is to help them internalize an awareness of psychic distance. I imagine that the majority of literary novelists—as opposed to genre writers who follow clear, predictable formulas and whose works many instructors duly disparage—do not write with more than a vague consciousness of audience or psychic distance. Yet such inattention hardly diminishes these writers' accomplishments or their works' rhetorical power. What difference does it make to readers that Virginia Woolf, while writing *To the Lighthouse*, did not ponder the fact that some of her sentences "contain unanchored tenses, requiring an RT from a neighboring narrative present predicate" or that she uses the linguistic elements of "semantic connector linking, temporal linking, and the progressive aspect" (Ehrlich, 1990, pp. 97, 102)?

The same process of internalization applies to professional writers of nonfiction, including Woolf in *A Room of One's Own*, a work Pamela J. Annas cites as an "example of powerful writing that can be produced out of the very tension between writer and audience." Annas notes that "Woolf breaks all the rules about thesis statements by burying hers in the middle of a two-page paragraph and undercutting it by calling it 'an opinion upon one minor point'" (1985, p. 365). No doubt such masterful rhetorical moves did not fall into Woolf's lap from her heavenly muse, but neither did she most likely think, "Aha, I'll disguise my thesis here to throw off the reader." Of course she made rhetorical choices, but I'm suggesting that accomplished writers often make these choices subconsciously and intuitively—as well as by consciously revising, like Montaigne, to adjust psychic distance. According to Fenton Johnson, author of nonfiction, novels, a memoir, and numerous essays in publications such as Harper's, "When writing, I don't think a split second about the reader" (Johnson, Fenton. personal interview, February 3, 2004).

Good writers are often too busy paying attention to their own ideas and how best to express them to contemplate the rhetorical triangle. Subconsciously, thanks to a cultivation of craft, these writers know exactly what they're doing. Just as students can enrich their writing by internalizing linguistic structures using the techniques of sentence pedagogies, they can also study and practice shifts in psychic distance to cultivate an inner ear for what language will be most appropriate in a given situation. As Robert J. Connors argues in "The Erasure of the Sentence," when students internalize linguistic structures, they become "free to engage in the informed processes of choice, which are the wellspring of creativity" (2000, p. 102). Sharon A. Myers has refined sentence pedagogies to focus less on the grammar of phrases and clauses and more on the "grammar of words" (2003, p. 617). She argues that "words are much more real to students than abstract rules" (2003, p. 621). Even more real, perhaps, are the words and phrases and clauses that students attend to when they think about psychic distance in particular sentences and paragraphs and texts. Because psychic distance demands attention to context, it is more conducive to internalization. Therefore if we invite students to explore ideas that sincerely interest them, without shackling them to the rhetorical triangle, and if we encourage them to pay attention to psychic distance—a very different kind of audience awareness—then their writer-based prose will likely end up being reader-based as well.

Attention to craft—and psychic distance in particular—has the potential to expand students' understanding of rhetoric and to spark fresh interdisciplinary scholarship devoted to narrative. "Art is better understood as a verb rather than a noun," Spellmeyer writes in *Arts of Living: Reinventing the Humanities for the Twenty-First Century* (2003, p. 167). Instead of "methodically dismissing as irrelevant the inner experience of writing," composition instructors should be fostering an "*intensification of subjectivity*" (emphasis in original). Ironically, rather than theorize the "textual" world in a never-ending quest to zap false consciousness, we might achieve better results in the classroom by considering the perspective(s) of the artist. "The way in becomes the way out," Spellmeyer writes (2003, p. 196). To the extent that psychic distance can help us and our students find our way in—for example, into original, idea-driven essays and into meaningful scholarly conversations—it deserves an active role in our composition classrooms and scholarly journals.

NOTES

1. In "Representing Audience: 'Successful' Discourse and Disciplinary Critique," Lunsford and Ede revisit their earlier essay and acknowledge that in it they had not "consider[ed] the powerful effects of ideology working through genres, such as those

inscribed in academic essayist literacy, to call forth and thus to control and constrain writers and audiences" (1996, p. 171). In both essays they note that "students have less power than teachers and thus less freedom in some rhetorical situations than in others" (1996, p. 170). Therefore, it seems that ideology tends to "control and constrain" academic writers more than audiences.

REFERENCES

Anderson, C. (Ed.). (1989). *Literary nonfiction: Theory, criticism, pedagogy*. Carbondale, IL: Southern Illinois University Press.

Annas, P. J. (1985). Style as politics: A feminist approach to the teaching of writing. *College English 47*, 360-72.

Bacon, N. (2013). Style in academic writing. In M. Duncan & S. Vanguri (Eds.), *The centrality of style*. Anderson, SC: Parlor Press.

Bagdikian, B. H. (1983, May). "The wrong kind of readers": The rise and fall of the New Yorker. *The Progressive*, 52-54.

Barnard, I. (2010). The ruse of clarity. *College Composition and Communication 61*(3), 434-451.

Bartholomae, D. (1985). Inventing the university. In M. Rose (Ed.), *When a writer can't write: Studies in writer's block and other composing-process problems* (pp. 134-65). New York: Guilford. (Reprinted in Villanueva Jr., V. (Ed.). (1997). *Cross-talk in comp theory: A reader* (pp. 589-619). Urbana, IL.)

Berlin, J. (1996). *Rhetorics, poetics, and cultures: Refiguring college English studies*. Urbana, IL: Southern Illinois University Press.

Bishop, W. (2003). Suddenly sexy: Creative nonfiction rear-ends composition. *College English 65*(3), 257-75.

Bourelle, A. (2010). Teaching with style. *Currents in Teaching and Learning 2*(2), 104-7.

Bowden, D. (1999). *The mythology of voice*. Portsmouth, NH: Boynton/Cook.

Bowden, D. (1995). The rise of metaphor: "Voice" in composition pedagogy. *Rhetoric Review 14*(1), 173-88.

Burnham, C. (2001). Expressive pedagogy: Practice/theory, theory/practice. In G. Tate, A. Rupiper, & K. Schick (Eds.), *A guide to composition pedagogies* (pp. 19-35). New York: Oxford University Press.

Burroway, J. (1996). *Writing fiction: A guide to narrative craft*. New York: HarperCollins.

Connors, R. (2000). Erasure of the sentence. *College Composition and Communication 52*(1), 96-128.

Corder, J. W. (1991). Academic jargon and soul-searching drivel. *Rhetoric Review 9*, 314-26.

Corder, J. W. (1985). Argument as emergence, rhetoric as love. *Rhetoric Review 4*, 16-32.

Dworkin, C. (2004). opinion: Mycopedagogy. *College English 66*(6), 603-11.

Ede, L., & Lunsford, A. (1984). Audience addressed/audience invoked: The role of audience in composition theory and pedagogy. *College Composition and Communication 35*(2), 155-71.

Ehrlich, S. (1990). *Point of view: A linguistic analysis of literary style*. London: Routledge.

Elbow, P. (1985). The shifting relationships between speech and writing. *College Composition andCommunication 36*(3), 283-303.

Elbow, P. (1987). Closing my eyes as I speak: An argument for ignoring audience. *College English 49*(1), 50-69.

Elbow, P. (2000). *Everyone can write: Essays toward a hopeful theory of writing and teaching writing*. Oxford, UK:Oxford University Press.

Elbow, P. (2006). The music of form: Rethinking organization in writing. *College Composition and Communication 57*(4), 620-66.

Elbow, P. (2007). Reconsiderations: Voice in writing again: Embracing contraries. *College English 70*(2), 168-87.

Enos, T. (1997). Gender and publishing scholarship in rhetoric and composition. In G. A. Olson & T. W. Taylor (Eds.), *Publishing in rhetoric and composition* (pp. 47-56). Albany, NY: SUNY Press.

Eubanks, P. (2001). Understanding metaphors for writing: In defense of the conduit metaphor. *College Composition and Communication 53*(1), 92-118.

Farmer, F. (1995). Voice reprised: Three etudes for a dialogic understanding. *Rhetoric Review 13*(2), 304-20.

Flower, L. (1979). Writer-based prose: A cognitive basis for problems in writing. *College English,* 19-37.

Gardner, J. (1984). *The art of fiction: Notes on craft for young writers*. New York, Knopf.

Gorrell, R. M. (1984). Bottom as rhetorician: Voice and tone. *Rhetoric Review 2*(2), 157-62.

Heilker, P. (2006). *The essay: Theory and pedagogy for an active form*. Urbana, IL: NCTE.

Heilker, P. (2006). Twenty years in: An essay in two parts. *College Composition and Communication 58*(2), 182-212.

Hesse, D. (2003). Who owns creative nonfiction? In T. Enos, & K. D. Miller (Eds.), *Beyond postprocess and postmodernism: Essays on the spaciousness of rhetoric* (pp. 251-63). Mahwah, NJ: Erlbaum.

Hindman, J. E. (2003). Thoughts on reading "the personal": Toward a discursive ethics of professional critical literacy.

Holland, Merlin. *The real trial of Oscar Wilde*. New York: Fourth Estate, 2003.

Hoy, Pat C. (2001). The outreach of an idea. *Rhetoric Review 20,* 351-58.

Johnson, R. R. (2010). Craft knowledge: Of disciplinarity in composition studies. *College Composition and Communication 61*(4), 673-90.

Kieslowski, Krzysztof. (1993). Krzysztof Kieslowski's cinema lesson. *Bleu.* Dir. Krzysztof Kieslowski. Perf. Juliette Binoche, Jerzy Fedorowicz, and Roman Talarczyk. Miramax, 1993. DVD. 2003.

Kincaid, J. (2000). On seeing England for the first time. In R. Atwan, & A. Lightman (Eds.), *The best American essays 2000* (pp. 209-20). New York: Houghton Mifflin.

Kirklighter, C. (2002). *Traversing the democratic borders of the essay.* Albany, NY: SUNY Press.

Klaus, C. H. (2012). Essayists on the essay. In C. Anderson (Ed.), *Literary nonfiction: Theory, criticism, pedagogy* (pp. 253-70). Carbondale, IL: Southern Illinois University Press.

Kreuter, N. (2009, Spring). Style, student writing, and the handbooks. *Composition Forum 19.* Retrieved from http://compositionforum.com/issue/19/style-writing handbooks.php

Kroll, B. M. (1984). Writing for readers: Three perspectives on audience. *College Composition and Communication 35*(2), 172-85.

Lawler, D. (1988). *An inquiry into Oscar Wilde's revisions of the picture of dorian gray.* New York: Garland.

Long, R. C. (1980). Writer-audience relationships: Analysis or invention? *College Composition and Communication 31*(2), 221-26.

Lunsford, A. A., & Ede, L. (1996). Representing Audience: "Successful" Discourse and Disciplinary Critique. *College Composition and Communication 47*(2), 167-79.

Mayers, T. (2005). *(Re)writing craft: Composition, creative writing, and the future of English studies.* Pittsburgh: University of Pittsburgh Press.

Myers, S. A. (2003). ReMembering the sentence. *College Composition and Communication 54*(4), 610-28.

North, S. (1987). *The making of knowledge in composition: Portrait of an emerging field.* Portsmouth, NH: Boynton/Cook.

Phelan, J. (1996). *Narrative as rhetoric: Technique, audiences, ethics, ideology.* Columbus, OH: Ohio State University Press.

Read, B., B. Francis, & J. Robson. (2001). "Playing safe": Undergraduate essay writing and the presentation of the "student voice." *British Journal of Sociology of Education 22*(3), 387-99.

Schilb, J. (2007). *Rhetorical refusals: Defying audiences' expectations.* Carbondale, IL: Southern Illinois University Press.

Spellmeyer, K. (2003). *Arts of living: Reinventing the humanities for the twenty-first century.* Albany, NY: SUNY Press.

Spigelman, C. (2004). *Personally speaking: Experience as evidence in academic discourse.* Carbondale, IL: Southern Illinois University Press.

Transition: An international review. (2008). *Inscribe.* Indiana University Press/Journals. Retrieved from http://inscribe.iupress.org/loi/trs

Vandenberg, P. (1995). Coming to terms: Audience. *The English Journal 84*(4), 79-80.

Warnock, T. (2003). Bringing Over Yonder Over Here: A personal look at expressivist rhetoricas ideological action. In T. Enos, & K. D. Miller (Eds.), *Beyond postprocess and postmodernism: Essays on the spaciousness of rhetoric* (pp. 203-16). Mahwah, NJ: Erlbaum.

Waugh, L. R. (1985). The poetic function and the nature of language. In K. Pomorska, & S. Rudy (Eds.), *Roman Jakobson: Verbal art, verbal sign, verbal time.* Minneapolis: University of Minnesota Press.

Wilde, O. (1988). *The picture of Dorian Gray.* L. Lawler (Ed.), *Norton Critical Edition.* New York: Norton.

Woodward, G. C. (2003). *The idea of identification.* Albany, NY: SUNY Press.

Zeigler, W. (1985). The exploratory essay: Enfranchising the spirit of inquiry in college composition. *College English 47*(5), 454-66.

APPENDIX A: PSYCHIC DISTANCE HANDOUT

Psychic distance is a term John Gardner uses in *The Art of Fiction: Notes on Craft for Young Writers.* He defines it as "the distance the reader feels between himself and the events in the story" (111). In *Writing Fiction: A Guide to Narrative Craft,* Janet Burroway uses the equivalent term *authorial distance,* which she defines as "the degree to which we as readers feel on the one hand intimacy and identification with, or on the other hand detachment and alienation from, the characters in the story" (229). Gardner lists the following examples to illustrate how a writer can adjust language to reflect different degrees of closeness to a character's psychology or consciousness:

1. It was winter of the year 1853. A large man stepped out of a doorway.
2. Henry J. Warburton had never much cared for snowstorms.
3. Henry hated snowstorms.
4. God how he hated these damn snowstorms.
5. Snow. Under your collar, down inside your shoes, freezing and plugging up your miserable soul ... (111)

Notice how these sentences take us progressively closer into the character's perspective, into his head, so that we experience what he thinks and feels.

Now consider how psychic distance works in three paragraphs from Oscar Wilde's *The Picture of Dorian Gray*.

Context: Dorian never ages, but a portrait of him does. The portrait reflects his moral corruption. In this scene Dorian's friend Basil is trying to persuade him to repent and change his sinful lifestyle. Dorian doesn't want to hear it.

1. [Basil:] "You have done enough evil in your life. My God! Don't you see that accursed thing [the portrait] leering at us?"

2. Dorian Gray glanced at the picture, and suddenly an uncontrollable feeling of hatred for Basil Hallward came over him, as though it had been suggested to him by those grinning lips. The mad passions of a hunted animal stirred within him, and he loathed the man who was seated at the table, more than in his whole life he had ever loathed anything.... He rushed at him, and dug the knife into the great vein that is behind the ear, crushing the man's head down on the table, and stabbing him again and again.

3. There was a stifled groan, and the horrible sound of someone choking with blood. Three times the outstretched arms shot up convulsively, waving grotesque stiff-fingered hands in the air. He stabbed him twice more, but the man did not move. Something began to trickle on the floor.... The thing was still seated in the chair, straining over the table with bowed head, and humped back, and long fantastic arms. Had it not been for the red jagged tear in the neck, and the clotted black pool that was slowly widening at the table, one would have said that the man was simply asleep.

How and why does the psychic distance change, especially in the third paragraph? Point to details of language.

How Does Psychic Distance Translate to Nonfiction?

Fiction writers who think about psychic distance have many rhetorical possibilities at their fingertips. But so can nonfiction writers, if we tweak the definition of *psychic distance* to mean <u>the distance readers feel between themselves and the events *and ideas* in the *prose*</u> (rather than in the story) and if we consider the reader's identification with or detachment from the *author* or *subject* (rather than the characters). To the extent that identification between writer and reader is a prerequisite for persuasion, psychic distance is very rhetorical.

Now it's your turn to experiment with psychic distance. Revise this sentence so that it more intimately captures the experience of a cold day.

1. The weather is very cold today.
Your revision:

Why Psychic Distance?

Psychic distance can help writers identify with and persuade readers. Arguably it has some advantages over these (also useful) terms:
- *Tone*, which can imply conformity to an audience's expectations, thus sacrificing authorial integrity.
- *Voice*, which can imply a neglect of audience, thus privileging individual expression.
- *Style*, which can imply excessive attention to the details of language, thus obscuring the Big Picture.

Example of Psychic Distance in Nonfiction

From a student's rhetorical analysis of a local commercial space:

> Your mission, should you choose to accept it, is to infiltrate enemy territory and conduct a thorough and covert reconnaissance of the area. You will gather intelligence on the physical layout of the compound and find anything you can about enemy tactics, techniques, and procedures. Due to tight security of the enemy perimeter, our only option is to send you in alone. Understand that if things go sour, we won't be able to conduct an extraction to get you out. Good luck—we're all counting on you!

> It was on this fateful day that I was about to go where no man had ever gone before—the secret stronghold of women: Victoria's Secret. However, I wouldn't be going in alone after all. I'd found someone on the inside; her name was Vanessa, and she had agreed to let me in quietly and serve as my cover throughout the mission. She was going to help me explore this commercial space so that I could find out how the enemy ... I mean the customer ... is

engaged by the store's marketing and selling scheme.

How Does Psychic Distance Translate to Multimedia?

Let's look at some examples.

WHAT SCORING RUBRICS TEACH STUDENTS (AND TEACHERS) ABOUT STYLE

Star Medzerian Vanguri
Nova Southeastern University

This collection argues that style should be considered central to the enterprise of composition, from how we theorize the work we do as a discipline to how we teach students to write. While the other chapters in this section provide ways to enact such a style-centered pedagogy, this chapter investigates a place where style already exists in many composition classrooms: the scoring rubric. I submit that grading style *is* teaching style, and that part of making style central to our pedagogies is recognizing the pedagogical function of our evaluation of student writing, and how it shapes students' understanding of what effective writing is. This means not just actively and consciously bringing style into our classrooms, but also interrogating the places where it silently lurks.

By examining how style is graded, we can better understand our processes as evaluators of writing, specifically how the ways we read and comment are captured in a final score and how those scores reflect greater ideologies about what constitutes good writing. Studying the process of grading further helps us understand how students internalize their performance as writers. For students, a final grade is a synecdochal representation of their performance that defines a semester-long experience well after the course has ended. Despite its influence, however, grading has been underemphasized in assessment scholarship in favor of the processes of reading and responding to student writing. Of the scholarship that addresses grading, "almost none confronts the task of actually deciding how to assign a grade" (Speck & Jones, 1998, p. 17). Process-oriented approaches to assessment stigmatize grading as merely a chore—not a part of the writing process, and certainly not a legitimate area of scholarly inquiry. Pat Belanoff famously calls grading "the dirty thing we have to do in the dark of our own offices," a practice that takes place behind closed doors, in isolation (1991, p. 61). Even more significant than our field's general devaluing of grading, though, is our lack of agreement about which features of student writing we value. This can be seen in a long history of low inter-grader reliability and single-grader consistency (White, 1994); even as a field of writing teachers, we cannot agree on what constitutes "good" writing. While this inconsistency can be explained in part by our inclination as rhetoricians to favor appropriateness (to genre conventions, audience, purpose, etc.) over fixed "rules" about what makes writing good, the fact still stands that the process of grading writing remains grossly under theorized.

In an effort to understand just how we assign style a grade and how we convey our expectations for effective style to students, I have analyzed scoring rubrics that I collected from composition teachers of various levels of experience and within a variety of institutional contexts nationwide. Because scoring guides are an attempt at standardizing grades and thus increasing inter-grader reliability and consistency from student to student and paper to paper, they serve particularly well as a site for analysis of grading practices. Further, all the rubrics that I have collected have been used in a composition classroom, making them genuine artifacts that were created by teachers, for students, and for specific writing assignments. As such, they provide insight into actual beliefs about style and how those beliefs are communicated to students.

What happens when the values that guide our judgments about style are placed into a format that compartmentalizes them into discrete criteria and assigns grades to them? What is gained or lost when we attempt to standardize and quantify good writing? Do our values remain intact? In order to address these questions, in this chapter I provide a history that establishes an important relationship between scoring guides and the concept of style in student writing. I then offer several definitions of style that emerged from my analysis of style's place within the rubrics and argue that based on those definitions, there are four key evaluative terms used to describe effective style: appropriateness, readability, consistency, and correctness. Finally, I argue that even when we tend to see style as global, we are restricted in how pedagogical our assessment can be because of the very structure of the rubric and the type of evaluation that the rubric encourages.

HISTORY OF STYLE AND RUBRICS

Rubrics and writing style have been intimately related throughout the history of writing assessment, making rubrics a useful place to begin a study of how style is graded. According to Bob Broad, "Modern writing assessment was born in 1961," when *Factors in Judgments of Writing Ability* was published by the Educational Testing Service (ETS) (2003, p. 5). The authors of the study, Paul B. Diederich, John W. French, and Sydell T. Carlton, sought to "reveal the differences of opinion that prevail in uncontrolled grading—both in the academic community and in the educated public" (1961, "Abstract"). To do so they recruited fifty-three readers in six fields—English, social science, natural science, law, professional writing and editing, and business—to grade three hundred essays written by college freshmen. By choosing random readers and classifying their comments, Diederich, French, and Carlton developed fifty-five categories that were divided into seven main topics: ideas, style, organization, paragraphing, sentence structure, mechanics, and verbal facility (1961, p. 21). From these seven topics, the authors of the study decided on five factors that they felt best represented the readers' comments, acknowledging that the readers may or may not agree with these characterizations because they did not identify them as such:

> I. Ideas: relevance, concise-wordy, clarity of ideas, quantity of ideas, development, too brief or long, persuasiveness, ending, generality
>
> II. Form: spelling, clarity of expression, organization, coherence of ideas, reader agreement, analysis, maturity
>
> III. Flavor: quality of ideas, style (general), mechanics (general), originality, interest, beginning, sincerity, information and illustrations
>
> IV. Mechanics: punctuation, grammar, sentence structure, phrasing, idiom
>
> V. Wording: general, word choices, logic, clichés, jargon-slang (1961, p. 24)

This taxonomy initiated the birth of the "rubric" as we currently know it. Further, it established an important relationship between rubrics—as representations of value-systems—and style.

When Diederich, French, and Carlton condensed their seven topics into five "factors," style was repositioned from its own category to a component of the category "flavor." The flavor category is characterized by "a predominant emphasis on style and interest; a weaker emphasis on sincerity; and an emphasis ... on the quality of ideas—ideas that will sell an article rather than ideas that will pass an examination" (1961, p. 37). That is, this category represents writing that is enjoyable to read. Furthermore, the comments on style that make up the factor of flavor have to do primarily with the "personality expressed in writing (forceful, vigorous, outspoken, personal, inflated, pretentious, etc.) rather than with the word choices and felicities of expression associated with [the "wording" category]" (1961, p. 36). Not only did *Factors in Judgments of Writing Ability* establish a relationship between rubrics and style, then; it also instilled a notion of style as "personality" within the context of the rubric.

This study also illustrates the difficulty of assessing style in student writing: "It is likely that Factors IV and V can be measured by objective tests well enough for a practical judgment, but we see no way at present to measure Factors I, II, and III reliably, either by objective tests or by essays" (1961, p. 42). This could be the result of the conception that the "idea," "form," and "flavor" categories represent creative aspects of writing. The authors note that while the word "creative" itself did not appear enough in the readers' evaluation of the essays to be acknowledged in their study results, the description bearing the greatest similarity to creativity, "originality," was mentioned most frequently in Factor III, "Flavor." Cherryl Smith and Angus Dunstan reflect this romanticized notion of writing as a primarily creative endeavor when they argue that "[t]he writing student is not asked simply to learn about writing but to create it" (1998, p. 164). They elaborate on the idea that writing is a creative process, an art rather than a skill, and point out the subsequent problem this creates for assessment:

> Writing courses ... can be considered to be much like other courses in the creative or performing arts, music or drawing or dance, in which the student's entire assignment consists of producing original work rather than mastering a particular body of knowledge.... . Traditional grading is not appropriate for a creative activity and the result of this mismatch is that we have adopted ... evaluation tools that are ultimately in conflict with our own pedagogical goals. (1998, p. 164)

This passage is useful when combined with Diederich, French, and Carlton's problematizing of style assessment because it illustrates the conflict, or "mismatch," that can exist between our beliefs about what constitutes effective style and how we assess it. If we value style as a productive art, rather than mastery of "a particular body of knowledge," then the means by which we assess it should allow for the encouragement of that productivity; it should be pedagogical as well as evaluative.

Furthering the notion that style is creative is another finding by Diederich, French, and Carlton that "the factors do not run along occupational lines ... with one exception: the three readers with highest loadings on the factor called "Flavor" ... were all writers or editors" (1961, p. 42-43). That is, of the six fields that comprised the essay readers (one of which was college English teachers), the group "writers and editors" most noticed stylistic features of student writing. Susan Miller's oft-cited 1982 study, "How Writers Evaluate Their Own Writing," reports similar findings. Her study analyzed the ways in which three groups—professional writers, undergraduate and graduate students, and teachers and professionals in writing programs and publishing—self-evaluated their writing. Miller found that "[w]ith the exception of the English professors and graduate students attending the Big Ten writing directors' conference, none of the writers interviewed, student or professional, noted specific qualities of the sentences, form, dialogue, plot, or style of a piece" (1982, p. 180). The findings of these two studies—that those involved in commercial industry were more focused on style (i.e., effect), while those in academia were focused on ideas and precision—highlight the relativity of values related to writing and writing assessment and the contextual nature of value systems.

The historical connection between style and rubrics established by *Factors in Judgments of Writing Ability* marked style as an aspect worth considering in our evaluations of student writing, albeit one that is complex and inextricably linked to value systems guiding conceptions of good writing. Because rubrics are often created programmatically and then used in individual classrooms with little modification, they may encourage teachers who otherwise would not acknowledge or teach style to consider it in their evaluations of student writing. While this may increase style's presence in the classroom, it can also perpetuate negative and/or outdated notions of style:

> If ... checklists are included in required texts for composition classes and alluded to in teachers' injunctions and paper responses yet are not being taught in the composition class, they become a means of mystifying the act of writing ... [y]et if the items on style checklists are taught in composition classes, those classes become current-traditionalist purveyors of context-free standards for writing. (Howard, et al., 2002, p. 216)

Howard's statement illustrates the double-bind that exists if instruction and evaluation do not work together and if/when they are guided by problematic notions of style. However, while our commentary on student writing is shaped by and limited to our experiences with writing, reading, and teaching, rubrics allow us to move beyond personal experience and impressions by requiring specificity. We can see rubrics, in this sense, as not merely tools for assessment, but also for teacher education. Rubrics have the ability to guide teachers to particular qualities of writing that otherwise may have gone unnoticed, and to teach students at least one definition of good writing.

TREATMENT OF STYLE IN SCORING GUIDES

To better understand how style is defined, approached, taught, and evaluated in various classroom situations, I collected assignment sheets and scoring rubrics from composition teachers nationwide and conducted interviews to further clarify and elaborate on the teaching documents and the rationale for their use. On May 5, 2009, I made an initial request for these teaching documents via the Writing Program Administration listserv (WPA-L), which had 2,648 subscribers at the time of my query. I asked specifically for one assignment sheet for an essay of any genre (i.e., research, narrative, analysis, argument, reflection, etc.) and any level (i.e., first-year composition, advanced composition, etc.) and the corresponding grading sheet for that essay. One week later, I contacted individual composition instructors at institutions of various types, regions, and program sizes and asked them to post the same request to their Writing Program listservs.[1] On May 30, I followed up on the WPA-L to ask once more for participants.

As a result of these multiple requests, I received 120 total rubrics with corresponding assignment sheets. In a few instances, the grading criteria were embedded into the assignment sheets and therefore I received only one document from participants rather than two. Some participants sent materials for more than one assignment, as well. One hundred twenty represents the total number of rubrics I received, taking these other factors into account. After analyzing all 120 rubrics, I narrowed the documents down to the twenty-three that included the word "style." Those 23 are the subject of my analysis here.

Of these rubrics, 21 provided scores for individual subskills and are therefore considered analytic rubrics. The other two rubrics are holistic, grouping criteria together under the larger headings of letter grades ranging from A to F. While analytic rubrics are designed to provide information that holistic scoring cannot, they are often problematic in practice despite their prevalence here. As Edward White points out,

> [t]here is as yet no agreement (except among the uninformed) about what, if any, separable subskills exist in writing ... [and] [r]eliable analytic writing scores are extremely difficult to obtain, because of the lack of professional consensus about the definition and importance of subskills. (1994, p. 233)

Most often, the scores in these analytic rubrics were in the form of descriptive words or phrases, such as *excellent, good, needs improvement*, and *unacceptable*. Letter and number scores were the next most frequent, and two of the rubrics used a combination of descriptions and numbers. The number of categories in the rubrics ranged from two to 11, within which there were subcategories in several of the rubrics. Despite this range in number of categories, however, the style category was located in the bottom half of the rubric in all but one instance.[2]

ABSENCE

Of the 120 scoring guides collected, only 23 included the word *style*.[3] This means that in over eighty percent of the rubrics, features of writing that could be considered stylistic were either not assessed or were identified by synonymous terms. A reason for this absence could be the general resistance to style in our discipline in recent history. If we are not talking about style as a discipline and therefore not explicitly teaching it, style will not likely turn up in departmentally created rubrics to be used in composition classrooms or in those created by teachers to reinforce their assignments' expectations.

Table 1: Abbreviated Rubric- Style and Expression

	Competency	Fails to Meet Competency F to D	Meets Competency C	Exceeds Competency B to A
Style and Expression	Uses stylistic options such as tone, word choice, sentence patterns			
	Writing is clear and precise			
	Sentence meaning is clear			
	Sentence structures generally are correct			
	Reflects current academic practices, including non-sexist language			

However, that the word *style* is absent in the majority of the rubrics that I collected is not necessarily because it is not valued or assessed, but that it is not being *called* style. This may be less a result of a devaluing of style, and more an effect of the structure of rubrics themselves. That style is often not called style and is, instead, replaced with terms that better suit our discipline's current values is an observation that has been made by style scholar Paul Butler, and this idea is reinforced by the very nature of the rubric as an assessment method. Because it is the work of rubrics to compartmentalize features of prose into discrete categories and to assign them individual scores, concepts as broad as style may be broken down into subcriteria for the sake of the rubric. When the word *style* is not present, then, it may be because the elements that constitute effective style, according to the creator of the rubric, are replacing it. Because I am concerned here with how we define the word *style* and communicate our expectations for stylistic effectiveness to students through the use of that word, however, the remainder of this chapter will explore only those instances in which the term itself is used.

Presence

When the word *style* was present, there was little agreement on what it meant. From the 23 rubrics that used the word *style*, I identified seven main definitions for the term, determined by the placement of style in the list of criteria and within the descriptive standards for a given assignment. The most frequent characterizations of style in the rubrics I analyzed were style as eloquence and style as rhetoric, each occurring in eight of 23 rubrics. Style was also defined as tone, mechanics, sentence structure, documentation, and word

Table 2: Abbreviated Rubric- Style and Readability

Style	Readability Readability
A	Essentially error-free. Demonstrates control except when using sophisticated language.
B	Demonstrates emerging control, exhibiting frequent errors that make reading slightly difficult.
C	Demonstrates developing control, exhibiting error patterns and/or stigmatizing errors that make reading difficult.
D	Repeated weaknesses in mechanics, spelling and/or grammar, demonstrating a lack of control.
F	Mechanical and usage errors are so severe that ideas are hidden.

choice, in that order of frequency. These characterizations of style, when listed from the most to least frequent, also tended to move from global to local, with eloquence, rhetoric, and tone comprising the most popular characterizations of style, and mechanics, sentence structure, documentation, and word choice comprising the least. I will explore each of these characterizations of style with examples from the rubrics I collected, in order to highlight the implications of these definitions of style on our evaluations of student writing.

MAJOR THEMES

In eight of the 23 rubrics, style was equated with eloquence, which includes references to expression, grace, and readability. Perhaps obvious because of the longstanding association of grace with style in Joseph Williams' work, as noted by other authors in this collection, this theme was also the most prominent in the interviews I conducted with teachers, which indicates that the teachers both valued expression and were aware that they assess expression in their students' writing. In other words, this category and its prominence in the rubrics appears to reflect most closely teachers' actual values. One of the eight rubrics had a criterion explicitly titled "style and expression," while the others related effective

Table 3: Abbreviated Rubric- Style and Rhetorical Effectiveness

Rubric	Style
Beginning Competencies	The style is appropriate for the rhetorical context and the language choices suit the audience.
Developing Competencies	The writing is clear and language is appropriate to the rhetorical context and audience but may call attention to itself in minor ways (e.g., the purpose of this paper is … ; I feel that … ; etc.). The student is beginning to use language in a way that is appropriate for the particular discipline and/or genre in which the student is writing.
Practicing Competencies	The writing is clear and language use is precise. The student makes above average use of language in a way that is appropriate for the particular discipline and/or genre in which the student is writing
Accomplished Competencies	The writing is clear and language use is precise. The student makes proficient use of language in a way that is appropriate for the particular discipline and/or genre in which the student is writing.

style to readability and grace. The one rubric that contained the criterion "style and expression" included five subcriteria, or competencies, that are evaluated on a scale ranging from "fails to meet competency" to "exceeds competency" with corresponding letter-grade scores (Table 1). This rubric functions differently than the others analyzed here because it does not include descriptive standards for every score category; instead, scores for each of the subcriteria are indicated to students by check marks in the appropriate boxes. The grouping together of style and expression in this example treats them as one criterion that can be achieved by the same means. While this may not have been the intent of the creator of this rubric, the lack of definition between the two criteria makes the referent of the subcriteria unclear. It cannot be determined whether "nonsexist language," for instance, is a concern related to style or expression, or both. Further, the inclusion of "sentence patterns," "sentence meaning," and "sentence structures" in the subcriteria for "style and expression" suggest that effective expression and style are achieved at least partly by local-level writing competencies and are evaluated by their correctness and clarity. This conception of style differs dramatically from those of the other rubrics in this category, despite the fact that they all relate to expression in writing.

In the instances in which style was its own criterion or was included within a descriptive standard for another criterion, it was defined as grace and/or readability. In two rubrics, style is defined by way of grace, while in two others, grace is defined by way of style. When style is defined as graceful writing,

Table 4: Abbreviated Rubric- Style and Audience

Rubric	Assignment's Audience
Great (10-8)	The paper is written in a style and genre applicable to the assignment's audience, which are members of the scientific community.
Good (7-5) Competencies	The paper is written in a way that either the style or genre is not applicable to the assignment's audiences, which are members of the scientific community.
Fair (4-2)	The paper is written in a way that the style and genre have problems which make the paper not applicable to the assignment's audience, which are members of the scientific community.
Grim (1)	The paper is written in a genre that does not fit the purpose of the paper, nor does it meet the needs of the intended audience.
Total	

grace describes local-level writing features. For example, within a criterion titled "Prose," the descriptive standard for A-level work is that the writing "exhibit stylistic grace and flourishes (subordination, variation of sentence and paragraph lengths, interesting vocabulary)." That is, writing will be graceful when sentences and paragraph lengths are "varied" and when vocabulary is "interesting." In another example within a holistic rubric, A-level writing is described as such: "The style is energetic and precise: the sentence structure is varied and the words are carefully chosen. *How* the writer says things is as excellent as *what* the writer says." Again, varied sentence structures and word choice are the primary factors contributed to graceful, or "energetic," style. In this case, the description of words as "carefully chosen" is slightly more specific than the former description of "interesting," but both assume that there is a universal standard for graceful style.

In other instances, grace was defined by way of style. One holistic rubric includes a category titled "Grace" that includes "organization, sentences, source-use, and style" as its subcriteria. The expectations for performance for each of these qualities are not defined. But what is significant is that this particular rubric measures the degree to which several aspects of the prose ranging from global to local (organization, sentences, source-use, and style) embody grace. Grace, then, is not a quality related solely to sentences or words, but rather one that describes prose as a whole. Another rubric includes the criterion "how gracefully you present your writing (including grammar and style)." Grammar and style act as the subcriteria, or means, to creating graceful writing. That grace is defined two different ways means that how we frame the relationship

Table 5: Abbreviated Rubric- Style and Ethos

Style	Ethos
A	Sentences are clear and concise; may use advanced vocabulary; demonstrates knowledge, credibility, and trustworthiness.
B	Sentences are mostly clear and concise; diction is generally appropriate; tone is mature and appropriate to audience, subject, and purpose; demonstrates knowledge and credibility.
C	Sentences show some variety and complexity; may use words inaccurately; leaves some question about knowledge and credibility.
D	Uneven control; sentences are simplistic; diction is inaccurate; tone is inappropriate for audience, subject, and purpose; creates questions about knowledge and credibility.
F	Superficial and stereotypical language; oral rather than written language patterns, erodes confidence in knowledge and credibility.

between style and grace is meaningful. When style is graceful, it is because it is functioning at the sentence level in a way that is appealing to a reader. When style is a component of grace, however, it is but one contributing factor to an overall effect.

Categorized under the larger heading of "eloquence" is another conception of style: readability. Despite readability being an effect of writing and not a quality that can be created by a writer, in one of the examples of style as readable writing, readability is defined in terms of an author's control over his/her prose (see Table 2). What this assumes is that when a writer is in control, his/her prose will be error-free and thus easier to read. In another example, style is defined as "[h]ighly readable, engaging prose that provides evidence of the writer's ability to think critically and read/view/listen closely." In this instance, readability is not defined as control over error but rather a reflection of the writer's thinking and analytical processes.

What is significant about the category of style as eloquence is that expression, grace, and readability are all related but interact in complex ways that are based in the element of control. Expression is something a writer does, a way of describing a writer's control over his/her prose; grace is a quality a writer embodies but that serves the aesthetic desires of a reader; and readability lies solely with the reader but is expected to be somehow created by a writer. In these three conceptions, which are all related to each other by way of the rubrics, varying degrees of control are represented, as is the expectation that style is a way to relate to a reader.

Rhetoric was another characterization of style occurring eight times in the 23 rubrics. To demonstrate how I arrived at the characterization of style as rhetoric, I use segments—the heading columns and the relevant row only—of three rubrics to demonstrate the relationship between style and various rhetorical aspects of writing. In the first example, the criterion on which the student writing is evaluated is style and the descriptive standards that outline expectations for stylistic performance are rhetorically focused (see Table 3). That is, whether or not a student paper meets the "beginning competencies" or the "accomplished competencies," or any level in between, for the criterion *style*, is based on how rhetorically situated the student's style is. In this particular example, the emphasis on rhetoric can be seen in the use of the terms *audience*, *context*, and *genre*. What is of particular importance in this rubric is not only how each level of competency is defined but also how the expectations for stylistic performance change as competency levels increase. In the transition from beginning to developing competencies, the expectations become much more specific, moving from "appropriate" style to that which is clear and appropriate "but may call attention to itself." The word *audience* also becomes much more specifically defined as "the particular discipline and/or genre in which the student is writing." In the transition from developing competencies to practicing competencies, clear writing becomes clear and "precise" writing, and language use develops from "call[ing] attention to itself" to "above average." The specificity of the teacher's expectations similarly shifts just as the standards from writing that calls attention to itself to that which is above average do. Specific examples are given for writing that calls attention to itself while no examples are given for the already ambiguous description of "above-average" writing.

Finally, as the rubric progresses from practicing to accomplished competencies, there is one minor change in the descriptive standards—from "above average" to "proficient" use of language. Again, the expectations are expressed in terms of value judgments, which can already be assumed by the titles given to each category, instead of referring to textual features of the student writing. Here, the most specific descriptive standards are those in the "developing competencies" category, which appears to correlate with a C or D grade. More importantly, the categories all seem to be communicating to students the same basic standards, just with varying levels of specificity. That is, the "beginning" competencies (of style that is "appropriate for the rhetorical context" and "suit[s] the audience") are essentially the same as the "accomplished" competencies, except that the accomplished competencies are more accurately defined within the rubric.

In another rubric that equates style with rhetoric, "audience" is one of the criteria on which the writing is being evaluated while style is included in the descriptive standards (see Table 4). That is, in this rubric, *style* is a term used to define what constitutes audience awareness. Even though style is not the criterion being evaluated here, it is defined though this rubric in relation to audience and genre, two recurring rhetorical concepts. Here, style and genre are defined as ways in which a writer can and should reach an audience. As in the last example, the expectations change as competency levels change (in this case, decrease, from "great" to "grim"). "Great" consideration of audience requires that the essay "is written in a style and genre applicable to the assignment's audience;" both style and genre must be considered. Attention to audience is "good" when *either* style or genre is "not applicable to the assignment's audiences." So, style and genre are no longer joint considerations, but rather they are interchangeable and given equal value, such that a "good" paper is one that uses a style applicable to audience *or* uses a genre applicable to audience. The "fair" essay is one that has style and genre problems and therefore is "not applicable" to the intended audience. Style is dropped out of the "grim" category altogether, suggesting that either "grim" writing would not embody style anyway, or that it ceases to be an important consideration at that grade level.

In another example of style as rhetoric, "ethos" is a subcategory of the criterion "style" (see Table 5). So implicit in the structure of this rubric is that ethos is one contributing factor to style and that effective style is that which is rhetorically situated, a point Rosanne Carlo explores in the first section of this collection. Because style is defined in terms of ethos here, we can look to the descriptive standards that measure the effectiveness of the writer's ethos to see how they relate to specific stylistic features of the student prose. For instance, the descriptive standards for an A-grade include "clear and concise" sentences and "advanced vocabulary," as well as the demonstration of "knowledge, credibility, and trustworthiness." We can assume, although not stated outright, that there is a causal relationship between how students use sentences and vocabulary and how knowledgeable, credible, and trustworthy they appear to be in their writing. In the B-grade and D-grade categories, tone is also a consideration and is measured according to its maturity and appropriateness for the rhetorical situation of the writing assignment.

These examples illustrate three ways in which the theme of style as rhetoric was communicated through the rubrics I analyzed. While they all measured different criteria—style, audience, and ethos, respectively—they used the term *style* in regard to rhetorical concepts including audience, context, ethos, and genre.

In all eight of the rubrics that defined style as rhetorical, including the three discussed here, stylistic effectiveness was evaluated according to appropriateness. In the first example, effective style is that which is appropriate for context, audience, and genre. Appropriateness for audience and genre are also considerations in the second example. And in the third, diction and tone were judged on their appropriateness for the assignment's particular rhetorical situation. What these rubrics reveal is that when style is tied to rhetoric, it is also evaluated according to appropriateness. To make language choices appropriate is to understand the conventions of the genre and the needs of a particular audience. As a result, what is being evaluated in these instances is students' understanding of the *effects* of their prose, more so than individual stylistic features.

In six instances, style was defined by how it is "heard." In five of the six rubrics, the word *tone* was used to describe style while in the other instance, effective style was defined more broadly as that which "pleases the eye and ear." Despite the fact that sound metaphors such as tone describe the reaction of a reader, rather than the actions of a writer, tone was described twice as a tool, something to be "used" by the writer. In one instance, good writing is that which "uses stylistic options such as tone, word choice, sentence patterns,"

While tone is certainly achieved by the relationship between a subject and writer and is accomplished by word choice and sentence patterns, the listing of tone, word choice, and sentence patterns together as "stylistic options" treats them all as tools a writer can control and "use" to create a particular style. All three "stylistic options" are given equal weight, instead of word choice and sentence patterns being "stylistic options" that *contribute* to tone. Another rubric defines good writing as that which "uses a formal, academic tone, devoid of the words "you," "thing," and other informal styles." Again, tone is "used," but in this case, it is defined in terms of formality, which itself is even further defined by specific words (*you* and *thing*) that should be avoided. Using tone as a tool, then, requires avoidance of "informal styles" created by specific word choices.

If tone is a tool to be "used" by a writer, other rubrics offer insight into the ways it should be used. Two rubrics contained categories that pair style with tone and describe effective use of style and tone as consistent ("style and tone consistent" and "consistent style and tone"). In another example, writing should "maintain an articulate tone." The word *maintain*, like *consistent*, assumes a degree of control and regularity. Perhaps the most relevant premise apparent in this grouping of rubrics, then, is that when style is defined as tone, it becomes a tool a writer can use and that must be used consistently. Consistency as a measure of tone is a carry-over from the sound metaphor itself; it is the conceptualization of tone as a tool that one uses that disturbs the metaphor. Evaluating a criterion that resides solely with the evaluator on the basis of the writer's control over it, however, presents conflicting expectations to students and a challenging assessment task to teachers. It is not the conceptualization of style as tone that is problematic here; when style is tone, it is inherently audience-based and therefore rhetorical. Rather, the concern is the placement of an audience-based criterion into a structure that purports to evaluate a student writer's use of particular "tools." The major themes analyzed here begin to illuminate the ways in which our values (specifically, a rhetorical notion of style) are communicated to students when placed into the scoring guides that are supposed to accurately represent and quantify them.

MINOR THEMES

The other conceptions of style present in the rubrics were much more local, defining style as synonymous with, or the result of, mechanics, sentence structure, documentation, and word choice. While these themes emerged in the other categories already discussed, they were all framed as means to a more global conception of writing. For example, style, when equated with tone (a global feature), is created by word choice (a local feature). In the rubrics I discuss in this section, however, style was equated directly with local features of writing. This suggests that unlike the more global conceptions of style as rhetoric, expression, and tone, these local conceptions define stylistic effectiveness by adherence to rules. Style is not evaluated by appropriateness, readability, or consistency, but rather by correctness.

Style was defined as mechanics six times in the rubrics. In four of these instances, style was grouped with a term that suggests this relationship: two rubrics included categories titled "style and mechanics," another included a "style/grammar/format" category, and yet another had a "style/conventions" category under which the descriptive standard of "mechanical precision" was listed. It can be assumed that when qualities of writing are lumped into one category together, the creator of the rubric sees them as parallel, if not synonymous. In another example, the criterion style fell under a larger category titled "language use and mechanics," signifying that style and mechanics were not synonymous but that "appropriate style" is one element that contributes to effective language use and mechanics. The opposite was also present, a category called style under which "correct use: sentence fragments, run-on sentences, misspelling, usage, punctuation" were listed. While all of the rubrics that conceive of style as mechanics also impart a rules-based notion of style, this last example does so more obviously through the phrase "correct use." Also relevant is that many of the features listed after "correct use"—"sentence fragments, run-on sentences, misspelling, usage, punctuation"—are negative and therefore cannot be used correctly.

Style was defined in terms of sentence structure in five instances. In one rubric it was simply listed as "sentence structure" within the criterion heading "style." In the others more specificity was given as to what qualifies as effective sentence structure: maturity ("mature style"), variety ("varied sentence patterns"), clarity ("sentence meaning is clear"), and correctness ("sentence structures generally are correct"). Despite these qualitative terms, there is still little indication of what constitutes maturity and clarity. Variety and correctness are slightly more specific but still depend on a knowledge of how to vary sentence patterns and compose a structurally "correct" sentence. One rubric that lists "sentence-level issues" as a subcriterion under the heading "Style and Language" provides more insight, as it offers a list of descriptive standards on which the prose will be evaluated:

- Varies sentence length (avoids short, single sentences in favor of stylistic variation that includes compound-complex sentences)
- Uses effective parallel structure

- Does not overuse "to be" verbs (is/are/was/were, etc.)
- Remains consistent in point of view, without switching between 1st, 2nd, ("you"), and 3rd person

When style is defined at the sentence-level, as these examples and others show, it is equated with correctness and, therefore, with a student's ability to follow specific rules in his/her writing.

Four times, style was defined in terms of documentation style, or proper use of MLA or APA formatting. This use of the word *style* is perhaps the broadest, though, because it refers not to the concept of *style,* but to the concept of *a style,* or a way of doing something. Twice in categories titled "style," the descriptive standards for the category involved documentation. In one rubric "MLA format in heading, paging, Works Cited" were listed as stylistic concerns. In another, "Uses MLA citation conventions without error (at least eight sources are cited in the Works Cited page)" was a descriptive standard within a style category. Style also appeared as a descriptive standard for the criterion of documentation, as well. In one category explicitly called "documentation," effective documentation was defined by "appropriate style accurately used in documenting sources." In an "incorporation of research" category, style was also listed as a standard. This use of the term *style,* because it relates to a method versus traditional rhetorical style, is conceptually very different from the others this chapter explores. However, its prominence in the rubrics is an argument in itself for its inclusion in this chapter. Its presence in these rubrics also further illustrates the ambiguity of the word *style* and the consequences of basing our evaluations of writing on a term with so many meanings.

The phrase "word choice" was actually present in more rubrics than any other language feature analyzed here, but it was the least popular characterization of style. That is because although word choice was mentioned in ten of the 23 rubrics, it was grouped with other writing features. Word choice was the primary descriptor of style in only three instances. In only one of these instances, descriptions were provided for what constitutes effective or ineffective word choice once. In this example, "word-level issues" included writing that is "correct in terms of diction and usage, avoids wordiness, avoids cliché, shows sensitivity to gender, ethnicity, religion, class, nationality, and disability, [and] offers effective sensory detail and figurative language." The other two times, the criteria were simply listed as "diction" and "word choice," with no indication as to what makes its use effective or ineffective. Word choice, when considered an element of style, was never described with specificity and never held a prominent place in the rubrics. It was listed, in every instance, as a single item in a list of equally vague criteria.

CONCLUSIONS

From the definitions of style conveyed by the rubrics emerge four evaluative criteria for style: readability, appropriateness, consistency, and correctness. When style was equated with eloquence, its effectiveness was judged by the readability of the prose, including the reader's enjoyment of it. In the rubrics where style is seen as inherently related to rhetoric, appropriateness is the primary criterion for effectiveness. Style is not developed by adherence to rules but rather by an awareness of genre and audience expectations. Tone was another term linked to style, suggesting that style is not only created, but also heard. This conception of style is tied to audience perception and thus creates a reciprocal relationship between writer and reader, or listener. Finally, in the more local conceptions of style, stylistic effectiveness is determined by correctness, or how well the student writer follows a particular and universal formula. What all of these conceptions and their related evaluative criteria reveal is that there is little agreement on what we mean by style, at least within these rubrics, and that each definition we attribute to style results in its own expectations for effectiveness.

Despite the prioritization of global conceptions of style in the rubrics, the form of the rubrics themselves matters: When global conceptions of style are placed into an assessment method that serves to compartmentalize and quantify aspects of writing that are conceptually bigger than the rubric allows for, they are reduced to the same quantification as local writing concerns. That is, the rubric in itself restricts how we can evaluate style, regardless of how we conceptualize its value. What this means is that we are more specific about those aspects we value least (according to their frequency in these rubrics) while we are less specific about the qualities we value most. Qualities like eloquence, rhetorical appropriateness, and tone are less quantifiable when placed into the context of a rubric than are the qualities we value less about style—mechanics, sentence structure, documentation, and word choice.

While this critique can be made about rubrics in general, it is especially relevant to style, as rubrics that are created programmatically often supply the word *style* for teachers who otherwise would not consciously assess it. Consequently, teachers are forced to acknowledge style's presence in student writing and to assess it, perhaps without even knowing how to define it or what it constitutes in student writing. This means that a rubric's confining structure has the potential to impede how teachers and students alike understand style.

Further, the rubric, restricted by its form, may not serve a pedagogical function beyond designating right and wrong, despite its users' intentions. Building on the premise of this chapter, that assessment is a form of style instruction (and often the most explicit form students ever receive), the fact that rubrics do not teach students how to *reproduce* the style we value means that they may serve more as judgmental measures than instructional ones. This is a limitation of rubrics in general, one that is further enhanced by a term whose ambiguity already poses problems for assessment. Assessing style in a way that is productive for students, then, requires much more than conceptualizing style in ways that move beyond mere form. It requires assessment practices that allow us to express our values and to teach students how to achieve them.

NOTES

1. Institutions include University of Maine, Duke University, University of Alabama, Highline Community College, University of Hawaii, Mount Union College, Fort Lewis College, Columbia University, Madisonville Community College, and Denver University.

2. In seven of the 23, it was the bottom category, in nine the second-to-last, in six the third-to-last, and in one it was in the second of four categories.

3. In fourteen of these 23 rubrics, style was a criterion, and in nine, it was a descriptive standard. I use the term criteria to refer to the features of writing assessed by the rubrics (typically falling in the left-most column) and descriptive standards to refer to the statements that describe expectations for performance for each criterion.

REFERENCES

Belanoff, P. (1991). The myths of assessment. *Journal of Basic Writing 10*(1), 54-66.
Broad, B. (2003). *What we really value: Beyond rubrics in teaching and assessing writing*. Logan, UT: Utah State University Press.
Butler, P. (2007). Style in the diaspora of composition studies. *Rhetoric Review 26*(1), 5-24.
Carlo, R. (2013). Jim Corder's reflective ethos as alternative to traditional argument: Style's revivification of the writer-reader relationship. In M. Duncan & S. Vanguri (Eds.), *The centrality of style*. Fort Collins, CO/Anderson, SC: The WAC Clearinghouse/Parlor Press.
Diederich, P. B., John W. French, J. W., & Carlton, S. T. (1961). *Factors in judgments of writing ability* (ETS Research Bulletin 61-15). Princeton: Educational Testing Service.
Howard, R. M, Beierle, H., Tallakson, P., Taggart, A., Fredrick, D., Noe, M., & Peterson, M. (2002). What are styles and why are we saying such terrific

things about them? In C. R. McDonald, & R. L. McDonald (Eds.), *Teaching writing: Landmarks and horizons* (pp. 214-27). Carbondale: Southern Illinois University Press.

Miller, S. (1982). How writers evaluate their own writing. *College Composition and Communication 33*, 176-83.

Smith, C, & Dunstan, A. (1998). Grade the learning, not the writing. In F. Zak & C. C. Weaver (Eds.), *The theory and practice of grading writing: Problems and possibilities* (pp. 163-70). Albany, NY: SUNY Press.

Speck, B, & Jones, T. (1998). Direction in the grading of writing? What the literature on the grading of writing does and doesn't tell us. In F. Zak & C. C. Weaver (Eds.), *The theory and practice of grading writing: Problems and possibilities* (pp. 17-29). Albany, NY: SUNY Press.

White, E M. (1994). *Teaching and assessing writing* (2nd ed.). Portland, ME: Calendar Islands.

www.ingramcontent.com/pod-product-compliance
Lightning Source LLC
Chambersburg PA
CBHW022008300426
44117CB00005B/83